FEARLESS

FEARLESS

A Memoir

MOHINDER AMARNATH

WITH

RAJENDER AMARNATH

Harper
Sport

An Imprint of HarperCollins Publishers

First published in India by Harper Sport 2024
An imprint of HarperCollins *Publishers* India
4th Floor, Tower A, Building No. 10, DLF Cyber City,
DLF Phase II, Gurugram, Haryana – 122002
www.harpercollins.co.in

2 4 6 8 10 9 7 5 3 1

Copyright © Mohinder Amarnath, Rajender Amarnath 2024

P-ISBN: 978-93-6213-031-0
E-ISBN: 978-93-6213-090-7

The views and opinions expressed in this book are the authors' own and the facts are as reported by them, and the publishers are not in any way liable for the same.

Mohinder Amarnath and Rajender Amarnath assert the moral right to be identified as the authors of this work.

All rights reserved. No part of this publication may be reproduced, stored in a retrieval system, or transmitted, in any form or by any means, electronic, mechanical, photocopying, recording or otherwise, without the prior permission of the publishers.

Typeset in 12/16 Sabon Lt Std at
HarperCollins *Publishers* India

Printed and bound at
Replika Press Pvt. Ltd.

This book is produced from independently certified FSC® paper to ensure responsible forest management.

Dedicated to
Papaji, Mummyji, Bickoo and Nikki

CONTENTS

	Prologue	ix
1.	Childhood	1
2.	First Step towards the Goal	18
3.	Test Debut and Wilderness	45
4.	New Zealand 1975: Comeback 1	67
5.	West Indies 1976	87
6.	Australia 1977–78	121
7.	Pakistan 1978	152
8.	Left in the Lurch: 1979–82	169
9.	Pakistan Tour 1982–83: Comeback 2	189
10.	Calypso Music and Fast Bowling: West Indies 1983	216
11.	World Cup 1983	255

12.	The Lucky Break: Comeback 3	285
13.	England in India: 1984–85	301
14.	Australia, Sharjah and Sri Lanka: 1985	311
15.	England 1986	360
16.	Tied Test Match: Madras 1986	374
17.	Pakistan in India 1987	382
18.	Taken for a Ride	397
19.	Bunch of Jokers	403
20.	Controversy and Comeback 4	417
	Acknowledgements	429
	Special Portrait	431
	Index	437

PROLOGUE

THE STORY OF MY CRICKETING LIFE FLOWS LIKE A Hitchcock thriller: a little twist here, another there to create suspense. I was simply an actor going through the scenes as best as I could, unaware what the scriptwriter had in store for me. After more than fifty years since my international debut in 1969, the time has come to lift the veil and reveal to the world some things that only a few people close to me have known so far. I have endured several exclusions, many machinations in the cricket board, stepmotherly treatment and back-stabbing. My story is also about aspiration, rollercoaster rides, happy moments, depression and triumph. My comebacks would not have been possible without the support of my family. My parents and my wife, Bickoo, stood by me like the Rock of Gibraltar!

My mother played a prominent role in streamlining my life and moulding my character. I was a short-tempered child, ready to grab someone else's share; if denied, I created a ruckus. Not only was my mother a very beautiful woman, but she also carried a heart of gold. Her influence rubbed off on me and my evolving character. Under her influence, I gradually acquired calm, composure and balance. However, on the field, I inherited my father, Lala Amarnath's, spirit. Although I did not exhibit his aggressive posture, I had the same sort of willpower. I spoke little but carefully observed every person around me. At times, I realized the advantage of being an extrovert to tackle complex situations. Otherwise, I kept quiet—and suffered!

Being relegated to the wilderness after my debut in 1969 was frustrating. However, the tours of New Zealand and the West Indies in 1976 brought me great happiness. But my joy lasted for only a while, and I was discarded again till destiny smiled on me in 1982. I was part of most international tours till 1986.

In 1987, I was dropped yet again for the Sharjah Cup. Still, I did watch the proceedings from the gallery. During the match, I was invited to the commentators' box; a Pakistani commentator enquired about my plans for the future. I remember telling him that I had enough fire in my belly to play for India for at least a couple of years more; I would take the final call once events unfolded. Since the Indian team did not fare well at Sharjah, the press lambasted them for the slipshod performance. After the match, I happened to chat with Mudassar Nazar. He summarized the Indian players' approach by comparing it with the Pakistan team of the early seventies, a very talented side but weakened by factionalism.

While taking the flight back to India, it was a coincidence that the former president of the Board of Control for Cricket in India (BCCI), P.M. Rungta, occupied the seat beside me. He was quite upset with the performance and wanted the Indian team to be revamped. He asked for my opinion. I stated categorically that it would be unfair to put the onus of failure on the players and let the selection committee go scot-free. They should also be held accountable. Then came a bombshell from Rungta. He enquired if I would be interested in taking charge of the Indian team and guiding them through the upcoming

Reliance World Cup in India. This statement not only perplexed me but it also made me uncomfortable! What was going on in his mind, I wondered. I politely declined the offer and told him I would rather play for India. He was not amused with my response. His next statement was even more shocking. He said, 'You may not be picked for the Reliance Cup!' Why? He didn't answer! Rungta was no selector; how could he predict the composition of the team? In the past, too, the supposedly 'five wise men's' decisions had come under scrutiny.

That a mere suggestion from me would bring about such a drastic change took me by surprise. A few months later, the entire selection committee was sacked and new faces emerged. However, I spent the summer with my family in England. When the list of probable players was announced for the Reliance Cup, my name was missing; Rungta's prophecy had come true! I was disappointed because I had played all the World Cups since its inception, and this would have been the fourth and, in all likelihood, my last. It would have given me great joy to perform on home turf and bid goodbye to Indian cricket!

I returned to India in September, determined to prove my adversaries wrong by performing in the domestic season. However, another shock awaited me; both Madan Lal and I were not even part of the North Zone side for the Deodhar Trophy. The North Zone selector, my former colleague from Delhi, expressed reservation in selecting players above thirty years of age. I was quite sure that it had nothing to do with my age; on the contrary, it was more about fear than anything else. What if I performed well and proved him wrong? The best possible way to avoid embarrassment was to deny me any opportunity.

Despite these drawbacks, I remained focused on my goal, following strict regimens. I chose Nehru Stadium in New Delhi for my training; during one such session, I met two young journalists, Mudar Patherya and Andy O'Brien. After exchanging greetings, they asked me about India's prospects in the World Cup and my plans. I said, 'I'll be back in the squad for the series against the West Indies.' This response stumped the journalists because they had also written me off!

With destiny smiling on me in another comeback, I not only performed well in the Test series but also in the ODIs. I was the leading batsman of the Indian team in the limited overs format. My greatest satisfaction was when I scored a century in the ODI against the West Indies at Faridabad. This performance proved two things: my credentials were intact, but the selectors were assessing me by age and not ability! Though elated by another comeback, I was aware that the wheel of fortune was not stationary. It continued to churn, and one bad performance would find me standing in front of the firing squad.

With Sunil Gavaskar not donning the whites, he was content with producing a television cricket programme: *Sunil Gavaskar Presents*, where he chatted with cricketers about their experiences. During the interview, I remember sharing my apprehension with him; a failure would, in all probability, put my head on the chopping board. He laughed at this preposterous idea, but I had experienced it.

In the absence of an injured Dilip Vengsarkar, Ravi Shastri led the Indian team against the West Indies and proved successful. Having tasted victory at Chennai, he wanted to carry forward this record. The rumours of fresh blood being incorporated in the team for the Sharjah tournament were nipped in the bud; Shastri insisted on taking the best available players. This decision confirmed my belief that the captain could withstand the pressure of selectors if he was sincere, though not many did. I regained my place in the team and scored a century, followed by a half-century. I did well in the Asia Cup in Bangladesh too but was dropped from the team for reasons best known to the selectors. Frustrated and angry, I provided the wise men with a new identity: a 'bunch of jokers'. To be honest, it was directed against one person in the selection committee, who unfortunately embarrassed all the other members.

However, the worst was still to come. There is an old phrase 'never trust your enemy', which kept me vigilant. But what do you do with friends who promise to stand by your side but invariably lead you up the garden path to the altar of sacrifice? I learned a bitter lesson (though thankfully late in my career). Should I call it destiny or an act of betrayal? In my nineteen years of international career, I lost nine productive years and forty Test matches because of lopsided judgements, or, one could say, partiality.

After retirement, I looked forward to streamlining my life. By then, the BCCI had formulated a policy to give a portion of the proceeds of an ODI match to former cricketers, provided they had played the equivalent of a hundred or more Test matches. I was short by a few when ODI and Test matches were combined. However, for a change, the BCCI had two cricketer-friendly officials in I.S. Bindra and Jagmohan Dalmia; they came to my rescue. I picked the ODI between India and South Africa at Mumbai as my testimonial match because my father also had his benefit game in this city in 1961. However, the Mumbai Cricket Association (MCA) was reluctant.

Balasaheb Thackeray was a cricket enthusiast and he had watched me play before. He was also a great fan of Papaji. I had met him on many occasions and enjoyed his company. The doors of Matoshree were always open for me; I decided to approach him. He listened to me patiently, then spoke to the chief minister of Maharashtra, Manohar Joshi, who also happened to be the president of the MCA. The rest is history!

Life is full of surprises and it could not have found someone better than me. In November 2017, the management committee of Delhi Cricket Association (DDCA) honoured me by naming the eastern stand of the Feroz Shah Kotla ground as the Mohinder Amarnath Stand.

Mohinder Amarnath
Mumbai

1

CHILDHOOD

MY INTRODUCTION TO THIS WORLD WAS CLASSIC. MY maternal grandfather, Nanaji, wanted to announce my birth with the firing of guns. While my mother held me, guns were fired to draw the attention of everyone around. However, the celebration turned into a nightmare when my mom and grandfather realized I had fainted, probably because of the high decibel levels. While my panic-stricken Nanaji fumbled for words, my mother shook me violently; it worked, and I opened my eyes! The gunmen were also relieved. After everything was calm again, the gunmen were paid handsomely; they thanked Nanaji and asked for their leave. However, my mother was not pleased with the ceremony, and asked the gunmen to reload the guns and fire ten rounds. The shocked relatives, Nanaji and gunmen pleaded otherwise. It had no effect on my mother; she was adamant and kept repeating, 'My son cannot be a coward!' Finally, guns were fired one after another. This time, I heard each shot calmly!

This was a period of large families in India and ours was no different. It was made up of four sisters and three brothers. Though my father (Papaji) didn't come from a sporting family, he was fascinated with cricket. He spent his early childhood in Kapurthala, Punjab, where the Royalty and British were the privileged class who could enjoy cricket at their leisure. My grandfather, Nanak Chand, rose from a humble background to become a successful sahukar (money lender), a profitable business. This enabled him to buy large tracts of farmland and commercial properties. With his business growing, he wanted his son to join him.

However, my father had a different dream. Determined as he was, he desired to be a member of the elite society associated with cricket. The presence of elegant European women dressed in flowing outfits and sun hats was an irresistible sight; even the royalty fussed over them. He also noticed the respect and encouragement for the established Indian cricketers; the regimental band entertaining the guests during these matches left a permanent impression on him. This was a regular scene during the British Raj in the 1920s; the Empire was at its zenith. However, common Indians were not allowed to enter the exclusive European clubs or step on cricket grounds without strings attached.

Eager to play cricket, my father requested his mother for a cricket bat; he knew she would search heaven and earth to procure one. Unfortunately, there was no shop in the town selling this product. Finally, she approached a local carpenter to get a bat made. The crafty carpenter chiselled a cricket bat costing one paisa. With the prize possession in his hands, he began pursuing his dream. However, my grandfather was not amused and he discouraged him. Many times, he burned the cricket bat and reprimanded him for wasting time. Undeterred, however, Papaji continued playing cricket, thanks to the full support of his mother. After his mother's untimely demise, he was sent to his grandfather's place in Lahore. Nanak Chand thought this move would solve two problems: keep his son away from mischief and, more importantly, keep him away from cricket! However, little did he realize that this would become a turning point in his son's life.

I remember hearing another interesting story about an astrologer and his prediction. He prophesied that my father would become a celebrity. This story was confirmed by Dadaji (paternal grandfather) as well. He said, 'When the astrologer prepared Amar's [my father] horoscope, he was startled. He predicted that one day this boy would become a household name in India. However, at that time, I did not believe a word of any of it. How was I to know it would become a reality!' Lala Amarnath became the first Indian cricketer to score a century on debut against Douglas Jardine's England in 1933. Jardine was the proponent of bodyline tactics against Australia in the Ashes, which had shocked the cricket world. Papaji remained a prominent figure in Indian cricket; he was the first captain of independent India, chairman of selectors, manager, journalist and an expert commentator. He knew the game better than anyone in India.

Despite playing international cricket for almost two decades (twelve years of international cricket were lost on account of the Second World War), he was dissatisfied and wanted to achieve more. The route lay with his sons to keep the tradition alive and fulfil his dream. Much against his plans, the first three children were daughters named Bimla, Kamla and Promila/Alka. However, the news of the birth of his first son was conveyed to him while leading the Indian team on a tour of Australia in 1947-48. When I was born, he was again away playing the Lancashire league in England. After a gap of a few years, Rajender and then our youngest sister, Dolly, joined me.

Free from international cricket, Papaji meticulously planned our future in the field he knew best. He gave each of us a pet name like the princes of Patiala. Surinder was named Tom, Rajender was John and I was Jim. From an early age, one could see tremendous batting talent in Tom. He was a gifted cricketer. He could bat comfortably and competently both as a left and a right-hander, till Papaji made him train seriously as a left-hander. He did not wish to see his two sons competing against each other. When Tom was very young, Papaji tied his left hand behind his back with a small rope and forced him to hold the top of the handle of the bat with his right hand; he practised the swing for hours till he cried in pain. Gradually, his right forearm and wrist became strong and his bat-lift perfect. Thereafter, he was allowed to hold the handle with both hands.

I was initiated into cricket the moment my father held me in his hands. Once I walked and talked, I accompanied my elder brother to the Baradari Gardens cricket ground and watched him play. The cricket coaching commenced the moment we understood the difference between bat and ball. Papaji showed us the grip to hold the bat; he demonstrated shots and strokes, and instructed us to repeat his motions. We were given an hour each day to shadow-practice defence and attacking shots. It was both fun and a pain playing each shot with the outsize bat of Papaji. The only consolation was that I could lift it a bit due to its light weight, only 2.2 pounds. After the session, he never forgot to pat our backs. However, the feel of his strong iron hands was never comfortable. He knew how to encourage us from a tender age.

At the age of four, life changed. Evenings were reserved to play cricket at the beautiful Baradari cricket ground across our bungalow. Tom and I dressed up like boys from Eton or Harrow, carrying a full-size Gunn & Moore Autograph bat of Papaji. Being the sons of the Indian captain, we received attention and privileges. We batted for as long as we wanted with ball boys, bowling and fielding. Papaji also kept a constant watch on our progress. His only love in life was cricket. This passion preceded his wife and children!

Life in Patiala was still fixated on a bygone era. The roadshows of monkeys and bears dancing to the tune of madari (street performer) attracted lots of people, including us. However, we couldn't be seen amongst them because of our status. My mother was also fond of wild animals and asked Bir Singh to arrange an exclusive show for us at home. This was only possible when Papaji was on tour and it happened in short order. Mummyji remembered this show vividly and teased me all my life. She recalled, 'The madari asked the bear to do several tricks and all of us clapped at the end of the performance. However, you went behind the bear and jumped on his back to shock everyone, including the animal. All hell broke loose. The bear stood up in panic and growled; my sisters ran helter-skelter and the servants scrambled for safety while you clung precariously to the long strands of hair around its neck. Finally, the old Madari calmed the agitated bear and Somiji lifted you to safety with a few strands of hair in your hands.' Henceforth, she called me 'Jamvant', a character from the Indian epic, the Ramayana.

Come March, Bir Singh, Somi and Hardam got busy packing the paraphernalia for the cooler climate of Chail. We spent the entire summer here. The drive from Patiala through present-day Chandigarh to Kandaghat and further gave us a first glimpse of snow-capped mountains and the tall deodar forests of the Himalayan foothills; the scene fascinated us. The summer palace of Maharaja Rajindra Singh and the famous cricket ground established in the late nineteenth century was still used by Maharaja Yadvindra Singh. It was a beautiful ground atop a mountain with an all-weather wicket to play matches. Once upon a time, there was a huge oak tree with a machan on the far edge of the boundary, enabling the royal ladies to watch cricket matches in a serene environment.

The Sid Cottage where we lived was just a few yards from the ground. I got my first cricket lesson at Chail; I batted and bowled. The honeymoon with the mountains continued till 1958. We bid goodbye to the mountains then, leaving behind wonderful memories. I am sure it must have been a difficult decision for Papaji to leave Patiala and join Rajkumari Amrit Kaur Sports Foundation in Delhi. After a year or so, the future chairman of the Railways, Sardar Karnail Singh, approached him to establish proper sporting facilities in Delhi and to help the Railways get an affiliation with the BCCI. My father's reputation and links within the BCCI secured membership for the Railways.

Right from our childhood, we (three brothers) were encouraged to play only cricket. There was a valid reason; my father had closely watched the princes of Patiala playing all sports. He did not wish us to be jacks of all trades and masters of none! Tom and I were given full freedom to play cricket round the clock, even at the cost of our studies—which suited us just fine since we were never studious in the first place. But Papaji eventually realized schooling was equally important and soon encouraged us to get back to our books.

My father was chairman of the Indian selection committee; he travelled across the country to watch matches and scout for talent. Simultaneously, his heart and soul were stuck on the development of railways cricket, which gave him little time to take us around for possible school admissions. Hence, he put the onus on a junior officer to get us admitted in any good school. Being Lala Amarnath's sons, any school would have enrolled us. However, we were taken to a school a little distance from our flat, at Ram Nagar near the New Delhi Railway station. To reach it, we had to walk through a narrow lane.

On reaching a small patch of land, we got a shock. There was no building, only tents.

We also observed that there were no tables, benches or chairs for the students. Furthermore, no one carried any books or copies, except a takhti (a wooden plank), a kalam (a bamboo stick pen) and dawaat, or an ink pot, in their cotton jholas, or bags. Each teacher read the syllabus from a book he carried or did arithmetic on a small portable blackboard for the class to understand. This was another world we had never seen. We failed to understand why Papaji admitted us in this school. Worst of all, there was no cricket ground or any space to play either! In fact, there was hardly any space to even *sit*. Although we were aghast by the facilities, we were too shy to protest!

Every afternoon, we returned home for lunch; we cleaned the takhti with a special soap called gatchi to erase ink; we coated the surface with a special white clay pack to use it again for writing. These planks were specially made for underprivileged children and their schools. After lunch and a brief siesta, we would return for the second session. One afternoon, we returned home early from school and found Papaji at home. He had returned after a two-week tour and enquired about the reason for returning early. We stated there was a flood-like situation in the school because of the previous night's heavy downpour. He refused to believe a word; thinking his little boys were fooling him, he lost his temper and control. Each slap seemed like a boxer's punch till Mummyji intervened and saved our skin.

The next day, he decided to meet the principal and asked us to lead the way to school. We were petrified of our reports not being encouraging. The moment we entered the narrow lane, he asked us if we were going in the right direction. We both nodded and led the way. He was shocked to see the place and the school. He could not believe what he saw; without a word, we returned home. Our father immediately had us enrolled at MB High School, near the famous Birla Mandir; we studied there for a year and then moved to an even better institution called Harcourt Butler School. They had a cricket team as well and Tom was an instant hit. He excelled in all the matches and became the principal's favourite. I was too young for the school team, so I played cricket with my classmates during the recess.

The Butler School was about four or five kilometres from our house. Tom and I preferred to walk all the way. For some strange reason, school books never gave us joy and studying just seemed like an enormous burden. We simply wanted to play cricket in our bungalow or secretly indulge in other games in the vicinity. We were fortunate to have parents with extreme temperaments. If Papaji was a short-tempered disciplinarian, Mummyji was cool, lenient and flexible. She allowed us to do anything under the sun—as long as we did not cross the line.

I recall a certain incident. We had returned from Chail and our residence at Baradari Gardens in Patiala was still under renovation. We temporarily moved to the first floor of Rajindra Gymkhana Club, overlooking the cricket ground. One morning, I asked Mummyji for extra candies, which she refused. As a kid, I was ill-tempered and demanding. I regularly threw tantrums to achieve my objectives. This time, however, I went too far. I climbed the railing of the balcony on the first floor and threatened to jump down if my demand was not met. Mummy ji refused to budge, while my other siblings and the servants begged her to give in to my demand, fearing a fatal injury if I fell. What I witnessed next permanently changed my attitude towards life and my mother. She calmly said, 'Jump, but remember, you will not die, only break your leg and remain crippled for life!'

I never expected this response. With one leg dangling over the railing, I stood frozen. Next came another shock to me. She said, 'If you don't jump, I will throw you down!' I got down rather sheepishly from the railing and never challenged her again!

When my father was away on tours, we enjoyed unrestricted freedom. Unlike Punjab, Delhi encouraged kite flying in the hot summer months. It tested our skills and endurance on the terrace or garden for hours, in the blistering heat of over forty-degrees Celsius. This hobby trained us to deal with heat and to concentrate. There were two famous markets to purchase kites in Delhi: Paharganj and Lal Kuan. I walked a good six kilometres from our residence at Panchkuian Road to an area called Lal Kuan, beyond Ajmeri Gate. Here, one could buy razor-sharp glass-coated threads called maanjha, and different colours, sizes and shapes of kites. Lal Kuan is situated in the walled city, or Old Delhi, once called Shahjahanabad. This was the new capital of the Mughal Empire established in the early seventeenth century by Emperor Shah Jahan. Now, it had become overcrowded and congested. However, this area maintained a certain old-world charm and nostalgia. A little distance from it is the famous Chandni Chowk, or moonlight market, with Kinaari (embroidery) bazaar, Sarafa bazaar, or jewellers market, and Kapara or cloth, merchants' stores attracting hordes of customers. The alleys around it led to the palatial mansions once occupied by Seths, the rich Marwari businessmen or the powerful nobility in the court of the emperor.

Jama Masjid and the area around it continue to serve famous Mughlai food, and traditional snacks like chaat and sweet delicacies. Each lane had its own history and folklore; the same could be said for Lal Kuan. During the construction of Shahjahanabad in the seventeenth century, this 'sweet water well' quenched the thirst of the labourers. Though this well is untraceable, the area around it retained its name for reference.

Walking back alone with kites and maanjha was never safe as street urchins lay waiting to rob me. However, all their attempts failed. I had good stamina and sharp eyes, so I managed to spot these little thugs from a distance, enabling me to either change the route or sprint past them at high speed. The challenge to catch me left them exhausted and frustrated. They always shouted, 'Next time!'

Both Tom and I were experts in other outdoor rural games: gilli danda played with a small stick and a bail; marbles and cigarette packets. Like ragpickers, we searched for empty cigarette packets in the streets and parks: Four Square, Charminar and Red Lamp were favourites and always in high demand. These packets were stacked on top of each other like a minaret, and we placed them in the centre of a circle two metres in diameter; all the participants targeted the minaret with a small stone to get at least one packet out of the circle. We played the same game with Coca Cola caps as well. Pitthu (seven tiles) was also very popular with the boys, using a rubber or tennis ball.

There was immense competition to rule the sky; the losers' kites floated cordlessly and were available for free to the swiftest pursuer. The poor boys who could not afford to buy such expensive kites scrambled to lay hands on the stringless kites. At times, I also joined the bandwagon, running fast and furiously in pursuit of floating kites, till it fell on the ground for a pick. The 'prize' brought tremendous satisfaction and fear too. What if Papaji saw me indulging in this activity and behaving like the street urchins. However, chasing kites had its advantages, and we gradually built stamina and determination.

Playing with my sisters was also quite enjoyable. They loved playing chokri square, multicoloured stones or marbles. It was played with five to six stones in a circle using only one hand. The player had to toss a stone in the air and immediately pick another stone from the circle, and then catch the stone in the air. However, the task became difficult with excessive stones in hand and catching another in mid-air became challenging. There are references to this ancient game in the Indian scriptures.

Running long distances brought a feel of freedom and delight. I won my first cup in a three-legged race in the inter-Railways family sports day. When I received the winner's cup, the feeling of elation was nothing short of lifting a World Cup!

Another habit I developed was going for a morning walk to India Gate. I enjoyed the challenge of the blistering sun in the summer heat and the long distance. Despite the rigor of such a walk, it failed to dampen my spirits and resolve. I also played with my friends pakram pakrai, chasing each other until we were overtaken by exhaustion. The morning excursion terminated with a dip in the boating pond or the splashing water of the large fountain and subsequently lying on the lawns under a large jamun tree to enjoy the cool breeze and regain strength.

The entire family, apart from Papaji, were music lovers. It was a period of radio and films, and each provided sufficient entertainment. Evenings were reserved for listening to Hindi songs and later humming a few lines. However, Wednesday evening was special for the entire country, including us. At eight in the evening, we tuned to Radio Ceylon (relayed from Bombay) to hear the enchanting voice of Ameen Sayani and *Binaca Geet Mala*. The popularity of this programme was also reflected in cinema. The best song of the week enhanced the reputation of the leading actor and box-office performance of the film. Each song and commercial was important to us, almost as if our lives depended on them. This passion for music continued during my playing days. I carried a two-in-one music system as a convenient way to unwind.

In 1960, Papaji organized a private cricket tour to Pakistan. He selected young and talented players from across the country.

It was indeed a novel idea to give exposure to the players on either side of the border. He formed a club by the name of Indian Starlets and selected some of the future stars of Indian cricket: M.L. Jaisimha, Farokh Engineer, Milkha Singh and a few others got a big break. Although the tour lasted six weeks, it revived fond memories of my father, especially childhood. The absence of the patriarch made us bold, and at times even a bit careless. Tom and I were like free birds, exploring new frontiers and taking chances without a care in the world. John was still very young, thus conveniently ignored. We did not include him in our daily activities, except for cricket. Mummy ji gave us liberties to do anything—but if she didn't, we used emotional tactics to receive favours.

The New Delhi railway station was in the vicinity; locomotives and the sound of trains fascinated us. Whenever Papaji was on tour, Tom and I joined the locality boys on weekends at New Delhi railway station and travelled without tickets to Nizamuddin. It gave us tremendous thrill. The half-hour journey and peeping out of the windows to feel the breeze was exhilarating; the sound of the engine whistle thrilled us but the smoke of the locomotive turned our faces black. If I hummed a song, I equated myself with Mohammed Rafi; if I looked at the mirror and smiled, I felt like Dilip Kumar or Dev Anand; when I thought of cricket, I wanted to be an icon like my father. This adventurous journey was only known to us and the children of the compounder or first-aid assistants working in the Northern Railways medical clinic. This adventure continued without any mishap; we returned home before sunset, pretending that we had been playing in the neighbourhood.

If I thought these escapades would never end, we were in for a rude shock. As usual, we (two friends and John) took the train without realizing it was an express train and not the usual passenger train halting at every station. Like experienced travellers, we occupied the wooden seats of the third-class compartment. The train set off from New Delhi Station towards Nizamuddin. Instead of slowing down at Nizamuddin Station, it gathered speed, causing panic and confusion amongst us. We had no idea where this train was heading. After a roughly ninety-minute journey, the train stopped at a small station called Kosi Kalan. We were stiff and tired after an unusually long journey, which no one had anticipated. With the sun setting, our secrets lay exposed. We wondered about the reactions at home. It was beyond the curfew time.

Hungry and helpless, we looked at the snack stalls but dared not approach it because none of us was carrying any money. We sat on the benches, thirsty and starving, awaiting the next train to take us back to New Delhi Station. Then came the best news; Johnny took out two annas from his pocket. I don't know how many times we thanked him. I purchased roasted grams for two annas and it tasted like almonds. By now, the sky had turned grey and we had been waiting for an hour or more for the next train to ferry us back. Our faces were covered with dust and our hair was a mess; we looked like ghosts. We knew our absence would have drawn a reaction—what kind, we had no idea.

Our friends were petrified at the prospect of facing their father late in the evening, while we were comparatively safer. With evening sinking into night, Mummyji asked our elder sisters to search the neighbourhood. They spoke to children of our age, checked different houses—but without success. By then, we had managed to reach the vicinity of our house and were in the process of sneaking into the compound when we were spotted by our sisters. Thank God Papaji was not around. However, my mother was not happy to see our miserable state and she scolded us, though mildly. Before she let us go, a stern warning shook us that she may tell Papaji about it. We begged her to spare us and also promised never to repeat it again.

I wondered what the scale of punishment would have been if Papaji had been at home. The thought made us tremble with fear! The passionate and exciting trips to Nizamuddin concluded prematurely. After this episode, I never saw or met my friends from the compounder's family again. I was informed that they were hung upside down from the ceiling fan and thrashed. Later, the father issued a warning to them to keep away from the Amarnath boys. The concerned father thought we were a bad influence and that we might ruin their future prospects.

Unlike our classmates, books failed to bring a smile to our faces. Yet, we left home as usual with a daily allowance tucked neatly in our pockets. The morning rituals of hugs and kisses planted on Mummyji's cheeks continued unabated before heading for school. However, our goal was Birla Mandir, listed as a tourist destination, adjoining the school. We spent valuable time in the prayer hall, listening to the sermons; we participated in the aartis like sincere devotees; we received prashad and dispersed. This devotion had a deep impact on everyone around. Even pundits were impressed with our dedication. Soon, our share of the prashad doubled.

Outside the Birla Mandir was an old-fashioned portable studio known as jhat-pat (instant), which enticed tourists for a pose and memories. The unique studio consisted of a bench with large portraits of Red Fort, Qutub Minar or Taj Mahal hanging in the background. The customers had the option to choose a monument. Interestingly, the cameraman ducked under the black cotton sheet covering the camera. However, he kept one hand held high outside and said, 'Ready!' and clicked; immediately, the glass plate was removed, then submerged in a small tray of a pink solution and, within a few minutes, a black-and-white print emerged from the tray. Like an expert hand, it was hung with small clips on a string attached to small bushes outside to dry. Wow! It was ready in no time!

Spending six hours of school time in a temple was a difficult proposition. Therefore, we devised another plan. We followed a group of tourists and listened to the guide narrating stories about this temple. Still, we had sufficient time at our disposal. We had to do something different to use our time—but what could we do? That was the million-dollar question. We were given eight annas each to enjoy snacks; this amount could easily let us buy tickets for the front-row seats in any theatre. Unfortunately, kids our age were not allowed to watch morning or afternoon shows except when accompanied by parents. However, this yardstick did not apply to mythological films. We were thrilled!

Khanna Talkies in Paharganj was a ten minutes' walk from our house. The morning show coincided with school timings. The movie was *Sampoorna Ramayana*. The show started at around ten in the morning and finished at one in the afternoon, which allowed us to reach home in time for lunch. The stunts and camera tricks in the movie fascinated us. Without giving it a second thought, we lined up for the movie instead of school each day. We memorized every dialogue. Ram, Sita, Lakshman, Hanuman were our favourites, while Raavan of course remained a villain.

Soon, the gatekeepers at the cinema hall recognized our faces; the love affair with *Sampoorna Ramayana* continued for quite a long time. We reached home tired, and received plenty of attention and affection from our mother. For a month, we kept going to the same cinema hall to watch *Sampoorna Ramayana* not because of curiosity, but to be inspired by the feats of Lord Ram and the flights of Hanuman!

The adventure and thrill were difficult to digest. As luck would have it, one day we decided to impress Johnny. We divulged the minutest details of our activities but he refused to believe a word, which frustrated us even more. Then, we told him how we bunked school and watched *Sampoorna Ramayana* at Khanna talkies. He still did not believe a word we spoke. After a pause, he requested us to include him in the scheme of things. We declined because he was too young. It was a grave mistake! Hardly had Papaji stepped into the house from an arduous tour of Pakistan (followed by a long train journey from Lahore to Amritsar and finally to Delhi) when all hell broke loose. Our mischievous little brother told Papaji about our adventures—bunking school and watching movies. Papaji simply hated films and had given us strict instructions not to watch movies, because he felt that it affected one's eyesight. On the contrary, my mother loved films and watched at least one movie a week, if not more.

Being in a foul mood, Papaji called us at the top of his voice, setting off alarm bells. Tom and I were confused; we were expecting a big hug from him. On the contrary, the atmosphere had become alarmingly charged. Each of his explicit Punjabi adverbs were like bouncers hurled our way. Mummyji tried to calm him but it was of no use. He asked everyone to leave the drawing room, except for Tom and me and the little chatterbox! There was no place to run or hide as he had locked all the doors. He removed the thick rubber-sole shoe from his foot and spanked us liberally on our butts, followed by a few quick slaps. All the while, Johnny sat in the corner, holding his chin and enjoying the dressing-down with a mischievous smile. How we regretted divulging our secrets to him! The harsh treatment we received was not for missing school, but for watching a movie!

Realizing his kids were on the wrong path, Papaji pondered over our bleak future. His plans to provide us a good education along with cricket seemed to have hit rough weather and it needed an immediate resolution. It was a tough call for him to choose between education and cricket. Using his wisdom, he decided to follow his instinct and opted for cricket. I am sure he must have weighed the pros and cons before arriving at a conclusion.

He decided to carve out our future in cricket and Punjab was the most suitable place for Lala Amarnath's kids. He knew we would not get fair opportunities from Delhi and the District Cricket Association. The stories of the Lahore rivalry with its president and how Papaji frequently captured his wicket became a sour point in their relationship. When my father became a celebrity, a few cricketers from Lahore were consumed by jealousy. However, he had a large following in erstwhile undivided Punjab (Lahore, Amritsar and Patiala) and the rest of the country. When Papaji conveyed his desire to send his sons to Jalandhar, the response was instant and encouraging. Thus commenced our journey in cricket!

2

FIRST STEP TOWARDS THE GOAL

Whenever international cricketers visited our residence, we were presented to them as if we were precious commodities. We would troop into the drawing room with a cricket bat and a ball. Papaji would clap and say, 'Jimmy, play forward defence! Tommy, play the cover drive! And tell Johnny to show his leg spin grip.' We followed all his instructions quite seriously. After the demonstration, all the guests would smile and applaud our efforts. Papaji would also give us a big smile, then nod his head and give us a marching order; like disciplined soldiers, we held our chin high and obeyed his command!

Papaji was a genius; he rectified all our mistakes sitting either in the drawing room amongst trophies or in the garden, surrounded by flowers, with minimum effort and fuss. I remember listening to him about his regimental training schedule and how it had helped him in cricket. The atmosphere in the drawing room created the magic of a bygone era and it was mesmerizing to listen to his experiences. We simply nodded our heads and dared not question or interrupt him as he held court. Time flew by in his company; he transported us to the world of the maharajas or the cricket grounds in England or Australia.

Then, out of the blue, Papaji would order me to fetch talcum powder, and he would line up all three of his sons and sprinkle it on our palms. Holding each one's palm, he predicted several visits to England to play cricket. The thought excited us and the night was blissfully sweet. I dreamt of London and walking around Piccadilly Circus, as an after-effect of Papaji's personal album. It was indeed a novel way to encourage us and set a goal. I remember reading an article in an Australian newspaper from 1947. The article said, 'The captain of the Indian cricket team can not only play good cricket, but he can also read palms and make predictions.' Papaji had impressed the captain and chief airhostess of Australia Airlines and caught the attention of the Australian public!

We had not yet played any grade cricket. However, Papaji was far-sighted and knew what was best for us. He did not wish to feel sorry in case something was left unattended. He wanted us to be perfect and consistent. He created a virtual world of cricket during his conversations and in the nets. While kids pursued hobbies, we had our daily routine worked out for the holidays. Stories of his punishing training were narrated to us by Mummyji, as well as Bir Singh, Somi and Hardam, who were employed for daily chores. Papaji shared all his experiences and made us aware of the benefits of a fit body. He stressed on the importance of long-distance running, daily exercise and skipping. He was an early riser, getting up at half-past four in the morning to train. He never missed a day of his schedule.

When we moved to Delhi from Patiala, we set ourselves up temporarily in a flat at Basant Lane and then to a bungalow at Panchkuian Road. It was an old-fashioned red-brick colonial-style house accommodating a large family of nine. A little distance from home was the posh Connaught Place shopping centre. There was sufficient space at home; three manicured gardens, along with space for a special kitchen garden and a ladies' courtyard. We brothers used the gardens, courtyard and driveway to play cricket.

Papaji was a self-made cricketer, therefore a hard taskmaster. Tom and I were both woken up by him at five-thirty in the morning and he took us to the cricket ground for physical exercises, followed by net practice. Later, we shadow-practised our strokes, and, if we failed in our endeavour, he demonstrated each stroke to perfection. Surinder (Tom) and I practised at the Railways' stadium at Paharganj, Delhi, with all the first-class players of the Indian Railways' team. It helped me to bowl long spells at the nets under his watchful eyes, and whenever I erred in line and length, I received additional tips from Tom. Thus, bowling to a left-hander eventually became quite easy. If there was any match at the Railways' stadium, we moved to the National Stadium near India Gate for our practice. Papaji shaped us into aggressive batsmen against spin and pace, a style for which he was famous.

Apart from that, we were grilled at home under severe winter and summer conditions. I remember walking barefoot on dew in the months of December and January to please my father. He professed that it was good for eyesight—so be it! We obeyed him till our toes grew numb in the freezing cold, yet we never complained; his word was final and it was in our interest. We practiced on wet grass without shoes and pads. We soon learned the value of using our bats against the skidding ball on wet grass; any miss led to excruciating pain, especially around the shins. Afternoons were booked for target practice against the brick wall. We made use of every corner of the house to master new conditions and improve our strokes.

Papaji was a passionate gardener; he planted over a hundred pots of pansies, roses, carnations, lilies and other flowers. These were placed around the lawns to decorate the house and make it look more beautiful. The lush green lawns were decorated with beds of colourful flowers, which gave one the impression of a nursery. He must have developed this passion in Patiala or when visiting the beautiful gardens in England where he spent many summers. All of us were given the task of watering plants with a twenty-litre sprinkler, which proved to be a boon. It strengthened our arms and shoulders without any weight training. As a matter of fact, he never encouraged weight training, favouring freehand exercises instead. He made us shift the heavy 'gamlas', or clay flowerpots, from one area to another to help develop our back, wrist, arm and shoulder muscles. Every time we bent our knees to lift these valuable pots, it made our calves and thighs stronger. He loved his flowerpots, like they were precious commodities, and, in case of any mishap, told us to plant a fresh pot.

He created a match-like situation in the garden for us. We placed flowerpots at different positions as if they were fielders and, according to his instructions, played strokes between the pots on the front and backfoot. He remained seated on his cane chair, sipping tea and watching us till he was convinced that we had mastered the art. Playing on the uneven grass surface helped us to tighten our defence as well as play different strokes. He wanted us to handle different surfaces and adapt to inconsistencies at an early age. He guided us with the minutest details and shared his vast experience to our advantage. Whenever we faced any difficulty, he demonstrated each stroke and guided us with encouraging words.

Tom and I played cricket on the lawn or the tar path with cricket or tennis balls. To play fast rising balls and face constant bouncers, Papaji felt it was important to remove fear. In 1960, he developed a unique method. He kept a bucket full of water and a few tennis balls soaked in it. The length of the pitch was reduced to fifteen yards and we were asked to bowl short-pitch deliveries. At first, we failed to play hook or cut shots; we even found ourselves in the firing line and received stinging blows on the cheek or chin from a wet tennis ball, attended by serious pain!

However, Papaji discouraged us from showing pain and this mantra became an integral part of my cricket! The wet ball came at a lightning speed. We were not allowed to duck, but told to take the blow on our body. To boost our confidence, he would laugh and say in Punjabi, 'Sher de puttar parwa nai kardey (Lion's cubs fear none).' Gradually, we mastered the hook shot, though at times the wet ball managed to leave a big pink mark on our cheek or chin. However, we started enjoying this contest. I remember us counting the dirty marks on each other's shirts or the pink marks on our knuckles, chin or cheeks. We were always greatly satisfied by these sessions.

Till now, we had not played any level of cricket, but Papaji was confident and far-sighted enough to not bother about it. He was also aware of petty jealousies harboured by certain officials in the cricket board. Fortunately, in him, we found not only an excellent father but a true friend, a perfect guide and a fine philosopher to carve our path and lead us to the destination. He was our Dronacharya! He knew the challenges awaiting us and prepared us accordingly.

We were given full freedom to play cricket anytime, anywhere and on any surface. Papaji chalked out our daily programme for the holidays. Early in life, we were taught different exercises to tone up various muscles. He laid specific emphasis on skipping, and encouraged us to increase the speed and duration every day. He felt that skipping improved footwork and made batting easy. During his playing days, he maintained a 3000 mark of non-stop skipping. To help our concentration and footwork, a badminton court was set up in one of the gardens.

Another area to play was against the ten-foot-high wall. We practised different strokes, consuming hours without anyone stopping us. We often missed lunch but never complained because the task given mattered more to us than our bellies. We wrapped up the session after middling the ball consistently, gorging our ears on the sweet sound of the willow. Interestingly, we made use of every corner of the house to master strokes following the direction of the sun. Later, these practice sessions took the shape of a tough competition. We three brothers tried to outperform each other by batting for a maximum period in the sweltering heat of the afternoon sun. Tom was a natural cricketer, and he made us toil for hours and coolly played every shot in the book.

Papaji was an early riser who pulled us out from the comfort of our beds. We were not the only ones—even the groundsmen suffered, rolling the centre pitch and erecting temporary nets for us. He always demonstrated every stroke with fluency and perfection, and put the appropriate fear in us. What if we failed to rise to his expectations? However, he never shouted if we failed in our endeavour but rather encouraged us. He ensured Tom and I received uninterrupted net practice, whether in Punjab or in Delhi. Despite our tender age, Surinder and I were at the nets at the Railways' stadium at Paharganj, rubbing shoulders with the first-class players of the Indian Railways' team.

Whenever Test cricketers visited Delhi, they made a beeline to pay their respects to my father. The evenings invariably graduated into late nights because of the anecdotes he related. The guests were glued to every word he spoke and burst into laughter at his moments of humour. I remember, on one such occasion, Papaji called for me. I thought he wanted me to demonstrate cricket shots; instead, he asked me to get a matchbox. I had no clue what the word matchbox meant because at home we spoke in Punjabi and my knowledge of foreign languages was limited! I left the room unsure and confused.

However, using my limited comprehension of English, I assumed it had something to do with cricket. I concluded, 'match = cricket; box = kit bag'; therefore 'match box.' I barged into the store, where I spotted my father's old leather kitbag. I tried to lift it but found it to be a bit heavy with his old pads, shoes, bats, et cetera. High in spirits, I lifted the kitbag and placed it on my head, resembling a coolie, or a porter, and I proudly walked into the drawing room where Papaji was regaling the guests. All heads turned towards me in astonishment. Papaji was also baffled, but he smiled, and said in Punjabi, 'Oye, eh kee layanda hai (Hey, what have you brought)?'

I proudly said, 'Matchbox!' While the confused guests kept quiet, Papaji shook his head in disbelief and said, 'Oye, bevakoofa, machis mangi see (You fool, I asked for a matchbox)!' I replied, 'Ji.' Holding the heavy kitbag on my head, I marched out sheepishly to fetch a machis!

My father was known for his immaculate sense of fashion. Even the maharaja of Patiala complimented him. Before attending any function, he checked his appearance in front of a six-foot mirror. This came in handy for us, not for dressing up but to rectify our cricket flaws. Unlike modern facilities available to cricketers today, especially video recording, we had none at our disposal. Papaji was innovative; he made us stand in front of a huge mirror placed in a big verandah and encouraged us to practise various shots or to refine our bowling action. We checked the front shoulder and followed through while bowling. He showed me various grips with the new and old ball, and its use in different conditions. I watched myself in the mirror playing shots with precision and bowling leg cutters or outswing with different grips.

Like most kids, we also formed a cricket team with the help of the locality boys. We organized Sunday matches at a park right opposite Lady Hardinge Medical College, near Connaught Place. Across the road was another landmark, Madras Hotel, famous for south Indian meals (the hotel does not exist anymore; the park has been replaced by Shivaji Hockey Stadium). We carried our kit and measured the length of the pitch with long strides before placing three stumps at the batting crease and one stump at the bowler's end. Matches were invariably played on an uneven surface where the ball flew past our nose. However, we faced few problems tackling them. Tom was the star batsman of the team, fluently playing every shot. This exhibition attracted many passers-by; they stood or sat on the bench or grass to watch him bat in disbelief! After every match, we provided all the information about the contest and performances to our father.

Papaji always professed that if net practice helped to improve skills and rectified mistakes, friendly matches and local competitions tested capabilities and concentration. These parameters, he felt, allowed the player to mature and gain confidence. This theory was permanently embedded in our minds. He spoke to various people and clubs to ensure that Tom and I played as many matches as possible, irrespective of the surface and the opponents. All the matches drew good crowds, whether it was at Salwan School or President's Estate opposite Talkatora Gardens. Soon, Tom and I were making headlines in the daily newspapers. Like obedient sons, we kept Papaji informed and received a pat on our backs!

Finally, the time had come to move to the next level. One evening, Papaji said to Tom and me that we were going to a boarding school. The next few nights kept me awake with excitement. I thought of Doon School and Lawrence School, and their beautiful buildings; the dress code and green cricket fields thrilled me. It was the opportunity of a lifetime to improve my English because at home we conversed in Punjabi or Hindi. We could have joined any English-medium school in Delhi, including Modern, St. Columba's or Delhi Public School. Unfortunately, none of them had much of a sports culture in general, and they were particularly lacking in cricket.

We packed our suitcases, kitbags and bedrolls, consisting of a handmade cotton quilt, mattress, pillow and towels for Punjab winters, and we accompanied Papaji to the station. A special saloon—consisting of a lounge and a bedroom accommodating four people, a pantry, shower, toilet and a staff room—was exclusively attached to the Frontier Mail train for us. During the British Raj, Frontier Mail covered the entire length and breadth of Punjab and terminated at Rawalpindi in the North-West Frontier Region, now in Pakistan. After the partition of India, this train terminated at Amritsar, some thirty kilometres short of Lahore. The night journey in the saloon to Jalandhar city was as comfortable as our bed at home; I slept like a log, till shaken out of my slumber.

When I checked my watch, it was five in the morning and still dark; Papaji told us to get ready and pack. Mr. A.B. Bhasin, an admirer of my father, was supposed to receive us at the station, but he was untraceable. Until he arrived, we had a few cups of tea, followed by breakfast at the railway platform canteen. The Jalandhar city station in the sixties lacked transport facilities; taxis and autorickshaws were a rare sight. The only available means of transport were tongas and cycle-rickshaws. We hired two tongas to accommodate the baggage and us.

We travelled through the city to the highway, without a trace of any human being or boarding school. The pin-drop silence was occasionally broken by the clip-clop beat of the horse's hooves! The first rays of the sun were both welcoming and depressing; there were fields on both sides of the road but still no sign of life. We crossed the railway track to reach a beautiful red-brick building with a huge iron gate; the sight made my heart skip a beat. However, much to my dismay, it was not our destination. After a good forty-five minutes into our tonga ride, we halted at an L-shaped building. It was old and unpainted; I assumed we had stopped to enquire about the route to the boarding school. When I was asked to get down and remove my baggage, I was shocked. All my dreams of Doon and Lawrence Schools lay shattered!

We were welcomed by the superintendent of the school hostel, Mr Sharma, with tea and snacks. He was overwhelmed at the sight of Lala Amarnath and his two sons. He asked Tom and me if we would like to see our room. The moment we entered, I was horrified! It was a small dark room with a tiny window for sunlight, a bulb, but no ceiling fan. No chair or closet, just two cots to sleep on. Tom and I couldn't believe what we saw. It was worse than a jail cell.

We enquired about toilets; we were told that tube-well water facilitated bathing and that there was an area behind the bushes for nature's call. The Brahmacharya Ashram hostel rules and regulations further dampened our spirits. The kitchen and mess were about a hundred-metre walk from the main building with minimal seating facilities. I was convinced that it was a nightmare; I pinched myself. Alas, it was real. I assumed Papaji also had no idea of the place and I looked at him for an escape!

The Sai Dass Anglo-Sanskrit Higher Secondary School was four kilometres from the hostel and most students travelled by bicycle. Principal Arora was waiting to receive us; he was equally thrilled and took us on a tour. The day passed quickly but that night was sleepless. The next day, when Papaji was about to board the train for Delhi, I became rather emotional. When my father hugged us, I started crying. To my surprise, his eyes were also moist! I couldn't believe that someone as aggressive and strong as him carried a soft heart. I had never seen tears in his eyes, no matter how tough the situation was. I knew he was going to miss his sons.

Once the sun set, I missed my mother, sisters and, of course, Papaji, as well. How I cursed myself for watching *Sampoorna Ramayana* thirty times! The miseries continued, till I realized there was no going back. We brothers had been sent here for a purpose and we decided to concentrate on cricket. Once the inter-school tournament commenced, there was no looking back. We hogged the limelight—scoring runs, taking wickets and winning one tournament after another for school. Suddenly, Sai Dass became the talk of the town and we the favourites of the principal. The move to transfer us to Punjab had proved correct.

While Tom made a few friends and attended classes, I remained a recluse. I started missing classes; yet, the principal never pulled me up. Encouraged, I started spending the morning hours on the railway track leading to the station some six kilometres away; I watched people boarding the train for Delhi. This routine continued for a month and still no one in the school noticed my absence. It did not take long for me to note the departure time of the Flying Mail to Delhi. The thought of boarding it was tempting but my father's temper held me back.

Unable to restrain my own instincts any longer, I bickered with Tom on purpose and walked out of the hostel. Determined to go back to Delhi, I walked along the railway track and reached the station to board the next train to Delhi. Everything had gone according to plan, except one thing. I had no money in my pocket to buy a ticket, let alone eating aloo puris or samosa. My best option to travel without a ticket and not get detained was in the third-class unreserved compartment. However, the passengers were packed inside like sardines. With little choice, I plunged into the crowd and occupied a vacant seat. With no ceiling fans functioning, it was like a furnace inside the compartment and the wooden planks did not provide any comfort either. As the train picked up speed, I heard people saying it would reach Delhi very late at night, which worried me.

I wondered about the excuse I would give and, if I was not going home, where would I spend the night? Hungry and covered in dust, I reached the main gate of the residence. The lights were switched off and I waited outside the gate, but didn't have the courage to open it. After a while, I realized no one would come to my rescue. With no money in my pocket and dying of hunger, my last hope was a tuck shop across the street. Unfortunately, the shutters were down even here.

Reluctantly, I walked to the park near Ramble Restaurant, opposite Regal Cinema. I sat on the bench, hungry and clueless, afflicted with stomach cramps. For the first time, I experienced the hard life of a street urchin and I sympathized with them. The value of my loving parents and the good life provided to me made me emotional. Tired and helpless, I dozed off on the bench. I opened my eyes with the first rays of light and the chirping of the birds. I didn't remember when I'd dozed off. I was covered in dust and my clothes were reeking of sweat.

The prospect of going home and facing Papaji sent shivers down my spine. Instead, I decided to meet my friends. I was welcomed with affection, tea and biscuits. While I was contemplating my next move, one of my friends informed Johnny about my arrival and, of course, he was sceptical. To prove his point, my friend asked him to come along. My little brother could not believe what he saw. Without wasting any time, he ran back to inform the family. Soon, I saw my elder sister Kamla arriving at the scene. I had to do something to prove my innocence and so I started crying loudly.

My sister felt sorry and consoled me, before walking me back home. When I entered the main gate, the sight of angry Papaji standing on the lawn made me freeze. I started crying even louder at the prospect of punishment. My mother and sisters came to my rescue, and I was saved. Looking back, I can imagine the plight of my elder brother and the trauma he must have undergone. He had to search the entire city and even visit the police station to know if there was any accident case registered. Feeling guilty about the altercation and my ensuing absence, he dispatched a telegram home. Even the school staff and the principal were traumatized by my absence. Papaji immediately asked Johnny to run to the Eastern Court at Janpath and dispatch a telegram about my presence at home. I spent the next few days without anyone mentioning the name 'Jalandhar'. However, my worst fears rose to the surface again when Papaji informed me to get ready to join Tom in Jalandhar; he also issued a strict warning: 'Do not repeat this mistake again!'

Little did I realize that a scene in the principal's office would prove to be a turning point and change my life forever. Papaji's first sentence on meeting the principal, Mr Arora, was an apology and a request for forgiveness. The principal was embarrassed by my father's humility and reminded me of my duties towards him. Here was a legend apologizing for a mistake committed by his son. I felt ashamed! Instantly, I took an oath: 'I will never ever let him down; I will do anything in my power to make him proud and prove his decision was correct!' Papaji was returning to Delhi the same night and I insisted on seeing him off at the station.

Before he boarded the train, he hugged Tom and me tightly. I was not crying anymore but rather, had a smile on my face. I took one last glance at his glowing face and bent down to touch his feet for blessings. His firm hands lifted me and he said, 'I am proud to be your father, God bless you!'

My attitude towards life changed; the room that was once worse than a cell brought me a real sense of tranquillity. I did not miss home anymore, and stopped venturing to the railway tracks once and for all. I played cricket with enthusiasm. The harder we played, the better we performed, and local newspapers predicted a bright future for us brothers. Since most of the matches were played on coir matting, pull and hook shots came handy. At times, I did take a few blows to my body. We travelled with the school team across Punjab and played various tournaments. The school team was like a platoon, disciplined and dedicated.

Since the school team travelled in an unreserved third-class compartment, securing vacant seats remained a huge challenge. While passengers disembarked, our boys squeezed through the windows and placed suitcases or bags on vacant wooden seats. During outstation matches, we stayed in classrooms converted into dormitories. Each member spread his holdall on the floor and slept. We ate whatever food was offered by the hosts and travelled with other boys by tongas or pedal rickshaws. How Tom and I laughed remembering our journeys by railway saloon or first class; eating in the best restaurants and sleeping on spring beds, the dining table laid in advance with various dishes and set by the servants at home! We were simply following Papaji's instructions to be part of the team and not behave as the sons of Lala Amarnath!

In the 1960s, meals in Punjab were cheap yet flavourful. Food was prepared using desi ghee and served piping hot. The dhabas', or restaurants of Punjab, had a peculiar ambience. The sight of manjis, or cots, wooden tables and cane chairs provided comfort to enjoy meals under the sun or stars. I remember an Amritsar Dhaba owned by a Sardarji. He welcomed us with a broad smile, twirling his moustache. The order for the meal was with mutual consent. Since tandoori rotis came free with the dishes, the Sardarji asked how many rotis each player would need. Gleefully, each member placed his thumb on the table and stretched his little finger towards the sky and, in chorus, everyone said, 'Ghit vargi!' meaning as many as the tray could hold. On hearing our response, the Sardarji burst into laughter and soon there were minarets of rotis being served straight from the tandoor. The hungry bellies consumed all the dishes and rotis in no time. If anyone still remained hungry, the Sardarji provided him with extra vegetables and dal, free of charge!

In 1965, my next target was to represent the Northern Punjab State U-19 team for the Cooch Behar Trophy. By now, Tom had already established himself as a premier batsman. He had successfully toured Ceylon (Sri Lanka) with the Indian school's team in 1964, played the Moin-ud-Dowlah Gold Cup and represented Northern Punjab in the Ranji Trophy. While he was named captain, I was selected as an all-rounder for interstate matches at Patiala. Whether coincidence or destiny, my career commenced from Patiala.

Childhood memories came rushing back to me. I was thrilled at the prospect of meeting Somi, Hardam and Bir Singh. They had worked for our family for almost two decades, and had brought me up with the utmost care and affection; so I had a soft spot for them in my heart. Lalaji (an assistant to Papaji) dressed like a Pathan, took care of Patiala cricket and also attended to my needs. Throughout the journey from Jalandhar bus stand to Patiala, riding a rickshaw through Mall Road, passing the lake or the Chandi Mandir made me nostalgic. I yearned to meet everyone. The moment I entered Baradari Gardens, I had goosebumps. I observed old trees that were still lush, lining both sides of the road; the trimmed hedges, beautiful gardens and bungalows, all looked as fresh as they had been eight years ago. It seemed as if the clock had been turned back to another era!

When I was told that the Northern Punjab U-19 team was staying at Rajindra Gymkhana Club, I could not control my instinct and rushed upstairs to the bedroom where I had stayed with my parents. I opened the door leading to the balcony and had a glimpse of the beautiful Baradari cricket ground. I noticed the majestic clock tower, the big black scoreboard, and the tall jamun trees by it and the railway track behind the trees; nothing had changed. (I have played all over the world but Baradari Gardens remained my absolute favourite). It was a good omen to start my long cricket journey from the same ground that had shaped my father's international career.

We played our first match against Delhi, the champion team of the north zone. Many friends of Papaji's came to watch us play and returned home satisfied. Tom sent the strong Delhi attack on a leather hunt and Northern Punjab cruised to the finals to face the host: the boys of Southern Punjab. Although I had impressed everyone with my bowling, I was disappointed with my batting. I rectified my earlier mistakes and scored a double hundred to receive accolades from many admirers of my father. They said that Tom's and my style reminded them of Lalaji—a priceless compliment!

The president of the Delhi and District Cricket Association was the chief guest. When my name was announced as the best batsman of the tournament, his face went pale and his smile vanished. He seemed very uncomfortable shaking my hand and presenting the cup. Instead of saying a few words of encouragement, he discouraged me from playing too many shots, especially my favourite, which was the hook shot. It didn't take long for a fifteen-year-old boy to understand what lay ahead for him. However, Mr Bange, a cricket lover in Patiala, lifted my spirits with additional gifts and words of encouragement.

Both Tom and I were selected to represent the North Zone at Bombay (Mumbai). I was fortunate to have Tom around; he was more like a friend than a big brother. However, at that age, he seemed like a father figure; I could count on him for advice and direction! This was my second trip to Bombay, the previous one having been in 1963 when we three brothers accompanied Papaji for the National Relief Fund match at Poona (Pune). He was the captain of Governor's XI. Vinoo Mankad was leading the Chief Minister's XI. Before travelling to Poona by the Deccan Queen, we stayed at CCI at Brabourne Stadium. The moment we entered the clubhouse, all the members and the officials scurried to meet the legend. It was then that I realized my father's status, reputation and popularity.

The next day, we accompanied Papaji to P.J. Hindu Gymkhana, where he was playing a match; the present and former Indian international cricketers were present there as well. Our visit caught the attention of a teenaged Sunil Gavaskar. He wrote, 'I can never forget the first time I saw Lalaji. He had come to play a charity game at the P.J. Hindu Gymkhana at the old building, not the current building. I was a 15-year-old fielder for one of the teams and enjoying the heady feeling of being in the same changing room with Mumbai stalwarts like Umrigar, Vinoo Mankad, Bapu Nadkarni, Ramakant Desai and others. Vijay Manjrekar was also there, and as Lalaji entered the change room regally, he stood up in respect along with all the others. A few seconds later, Surinder walked in with Jimmy and Rajender. As they went to where Lalaji was sitting, Manjrekar produced a classic in Marathi: 'Look, he has got all Dandekars, and look at me—I have only Holekars!' He had two daughters; Sanjay was not born then. The room collapsed in laughter, and when Lalaji asked what it was about, Manjrekar explained. Lalaji laughed heartily and said, 'Tu kabhi sudhrega nahi!' Meaning, you will never change.

This trip was different; we arrived in Bombay as players, yet our father's reputation preceded us. The media and former cricketers were keen to see Lala Amarnath's sons in action. I was impressed with the facilities in Bombay. Each gymkhana had its own ground and turf wicket, while Jalandhar possessed the only turf wicket at Burton Park. We played the first match against South Zone at Wilson College Gymkhana, established in 1832. I think I got seven wickets and Surinder once again amassed runs.

The final match was scheduled at the Bombay Gymkhana, the venue that had transformed my father's status forever. He became the first Indian cricketer to score a century (on debut) for India. When we reached the ground, many elderly people met us and also spoke of his innings. The big names of the Bombay press, Dicky Rutnagur, K.N. Prabhu, Berry Sarbadhakari, et cetera, also landed at the venue for their reporting and commentary. All India Radio covered the match live, which spoke volumes about the importance of school cricket. Although we did not win the final, Surinder was once again the most successful player of the tournament. We were selected to represent the Indian Schoolboys' team against MCC Schoolboys for the home series.

The first schoolboys' test match was played at the famous Brabourne Stadium in Bombay. This stadium was the brainchild of Maharaja Bhupindra Singh of Patiala and he inaugurated it in 1937. Ever since then, all international matches were played at this venue. About 25,000 spectators turned up to watch the schoolboys' test match. Although I failed to make it to the final XI, watching the contest was in itself a thrilling experience. Furthermore, when teenaged boys and girls sought our autographs, it gave one a feeling of celebrity.

After the match, a teammate from Bombay introduced me to a young girl. We shook hands and she started talking in English while I looked around for cover; my response to her came through a smile or simple yes or no! This player continued to be my roommate for other test matches across India. Every time he received a letter from his girlfriend, there was a small note for me as well.

I played the last Test match as an opening batsman in Bengaluru. We finished the series and returned to Jalandhar, where the principal organized a big function to honour us. Tom and I had made history for Punjab by representing India at this level. Suddenly our status rose sky-high and we added flavour to it by wearing the Indian Schoolboys' blazer to school. The proud principal gave us blanket permission to go to Delhi and pursue cricket. This gesture gave us an opportunity to spend precious time with Papaji and to hone the finer points of the game.

At home, our day commenced with exercises in the garden under the watchful eyes of Papaji. While we sweated it out, he enjoyed himself, smoking his pipe with a cup of tea. One day, however, this session was interrupted by two gentlemen who sought permission to enter the premises. Papaji chose to meet them briefly at the gate and then he returned to his chair. He resumed puffing his pipe and kept his gaze on us. After a while, he called out to Tom and reprimanded him for spoiling his reputation. We were stunned; we just stood silently. He continued, 'Those people came from the Crime Branch and were enquiring about a missing girl from Bombay. She had left a note that she was going to Jalandhar to meet Surinder.'

Tom, utterly in shock, denied knowing her. Of course, Papaji didn't believe a word we said. His temper was rising; he switched from English to Punjabi and, in a raised voice, demanded to know the truth. We knew the worst could come at any moment.

While Tom kept his eyes glued to the ground, I wondered why these policemen came here. They should have gone to Jalandhar. 'Yes,' Papaji said suddenly, 'they had gone to Jalandhar and met the school officials; they informed the police that both brothers were in Delhi.' I almost fell down on the lawn; how could my father read my mind? Later, I came to know this information had been divulged to him by the visiting policemen. I knew my brother was innocent because I had received a letter from the missing girl's boyfriend, enquiring if she had come to meet us. I did not take the incident seriously. But why write Tom's name? That remained a mystery.

Nonetheless, the riddle was solved on reaching Jalandhar. The moment we entered school, all eyes turned towards us and jaws dropped in disbelief. The principal and staff were agape; boys spoke in whispers and pointed fingers at us. We could not understand this behaviour till one of my classmates pulled me aside and said, 'A young girl in tight jeans had visited the school, and enquired about Surinder.' Punjab in the 1960s was quite conservative and girls never wore Western attire, let alone venturing into a boys' school! Because she spoke English, the excited boys found her too hot to handle; they simply directed her to the principal's office. She told the principal that she was from Bombay and expressed her desire to meet Surinder. However, she was disappointed to know we were in Delhi and decided to return home. The news of a chirpy girl from Bombay visiting the institution spread like wildfire.

Then I remembered S.P. Singh; he was part of the team in Bombay and his full name was Surinder Pratap Singh. I frequently discussed with him about exchanging letters with a girl from Bombay. One day, he had asked me to share her address and I obliged. Tom and I decided to meet him to shed some light and help us solve this riddle. The moment he saw us, he blurted out the truth. He had started corresponding with her using the name 'Surinder'. Since his English was atrocious, he took the help of a university student doing his Masters in English to write letters to the girl and impress her. The contents of his letters probably made the girl infatuated and she decided to take this unfortunate step. I asked him, 'Why didn't you meet her?' He confessed, 'I cannot speak a word of English and I am not what she thought: Surinder Amarnath.'

Now I understood why the girl's parents thought of my elder brother. We kept this secret to ourselves to enjoy the uninterrupted attention and adulation, which made us the talk of the town; people referred to us as 'Cat'.

After a few weeks came the exciting news of Australian school teams visiting India. Tom was already an established player but I had to work hard to retain my place. Papaji organized net practice sessions for us at the Railways' ground and even pressed the seasoned Railways' first-class bowlers into action. I remember facing Hyder Ali and William Ghosh with the new ball, and Ghulam Murtaza, Mushtaq Ali and Madan Mehra with the old ball. Before we reached Jalandhar, Papaji had already spoken to the secretary of Northern Punjab Association, H.R. Mohla, for special nets at Burton Park. Here too, Punjab Ranji bowlers were pressed into service.

The Australians brought a reasonably strong team, including the future Test star in the making, leg spinner Kerry O'Keeffe. Surinder was nominated captain of the Indian team and I also made it on merit. The hard work and planning had paid dividends. I contributed with the ball and bat in the entire series. However, the star performer of the series was my elder brother. He was in a great form and played a wonderful innings of 201 not out, and 190 and 50 in the Test matches to stake his claim for a higher grade. India was leading the series when the selectors decided to replace him with another captain in the last test match (I think it was in Calcutta). We were shocked by the news; normally the losing captain is changed, but here the winning captain in full form had been replaced! With the England tour already announced for the summer of 1967, Papaji asked us to play. For once, Tom failed and India lost the match. How the Bombay press blamed him for letting down the new captain from their state! It was certainly a wake-up call for us. Then came encouraging words from the Australian leg spinner to Tom: 'See you in Australia.' The Indian team was due to play the Test series in Australia and New Zealand in 1967-68.

The selectors announced the team for the England tour based on the last series' performance and both of us made it. However, Tom was denied the honour of leading the team. My father's prediction that we would play in England had now come true. The itinerary included matches at Lord's, Trent Bridge and other famous county grounds. I remember listening to the deep, husky voice of the famous BBC commentator John Arlott during the BCCI camp in 1966 at Fateh Maidan (Lal Bahadur Stadium) in Hyderabad. His poetic description not only left a deep impression but also transported me to the match between England and the West Indies. Both sides possessed famous players: Gary Sobers, Rohan Kanhai, Wesley Hall, Charlie Griffith, Tom Graveney, Colin Cowdrey, Geoffrey Boycott, John Snow.

Before leaving for England, the BCCI organized a cricket camp in Delhi under former Test player and now team manager

Col. Hemu Adhikari. We were put up at Air Force Station near Safdarjung Tomb and used the Army grounds for net practice. It was a very hot summer, so cricket training was split into two sessions. More than cricket, I recall this training particularly for table manners and other etiquette classes that took the steam out of everyone. The evening dress code was a white shirt with long sleeves, a tie, a woollen blazer and grey trousers with polished black shoes, all of which made us sweat in the blistering heat. We struggled to eat continental meals with a fork and knife, and to socialize with the air force officers in broken English; the effort left us exhausted.

However, before the end of the camp, we managed to impress everyone with our grasp over a few English sentences, as well as our table manners and social etiquette. The team departed from Palam Airport, adjacent to present-day Indira Gandhi Terminal 3 in Delhi. It was a small single-storey airport with basic facilities. No frisking, no metal detectors or X-ray machines to check passengers and bags; only a handful of policemen guarded the entrance of the airport. Our entire family accompanied us to the airport to see us off. My sisters applied a 'tilak' on our foreheads to wish us a safe journey and success.

We boarded an Ashok Leyland bus for a short ferry to the stationed Air India 707 aircraft. It was a transitional period for the aviation industry; Air India had replaced Dakotas with jet-engine aircraft. The first halt was Beirut for refuelling, followed by Rome, Paris and then London. I had earlier only travelled by bus or train, but sitting high in the sky over the clouds was most exhilarating. Passing through immigration counters in the modern Heathrow building reminded us of five-star hotels in India. The city of London looked exactly as my father had described, beautiful and organized. The next day, we drove to Lord's to meet the senior Indian team led by Mansoor Ali Khan

Pataudi and we subsequently commenced our tour across the British Isles.

In the sixties, England was reasonably priced. We received five pounds per week as pocket money, primarily for laundry. All meals were free and in case we wished to eat in some restaurant, it was enough to have a decent meal and do a little shopping. We travelled by the Tube to Oxford Street; we shopped at Marks & Spencer, C&A or Littlewoods. I purchased Stuart Surridge bats at the factory for five pounds each.

Travelling by luxury coach and staying in hotels was like living a fairytale for me; the ambiance of these hotels was intensified by the soft music in the lobby and the young women who served the guests. Quite a few of our boys had never seen a tub bath before; they filled it with bubble soap, and jumped in and out to create a ruckus. However, one excited player left the tap open and flooded the entire corridor, and he of course received a thorough dressing-down from the strict manager. Once, J.K. Mahendra, Jitendra Bhutta and I were late by two minutes, and we were left stranded in the hotel's parking lot. To avoid similar censure from the manager, we hired a local taxi to the cricket ground, which took up most of our weekly allowance!

We played aggressive cricket, far better than the senior team, and we defeated almost all of the competition. Apart from cricket, the tour was crammed with official functions in the evenings. One thing was common: a toast to the Queen, continental food and being surrounded by English guests who tested our vocabulary in English. Despite our handicap, we did fairly well. When the toast was raised to the Queen, everyone, including us, stood up, raised our glass and said, 'To the Queen!' However, on one occasion, we were caught on the wrong foot. The host raised a toast to us; everyone stood up and we also followed suit. The amused host understood the confusion and said that the toast was in fact in our honour, so we need not stand for it!

The trip gave us the opportunity to meet the last English Governor General of India, Lord Mountbatten, the Prime Minister of Britain Harold Wilson and many other important dignitaries.

By the time we returned to London, Pakistan was playing against England at Lord's. The Marylebone Cricket Club (MCC) invited us to watch this match. The atmosphere at Lord's excited me and I yearned to be out on the field, bowling or batting. We occupied seats in the West Stand and witnessed Hanif Mohammad's fabulous innings. Even the fiery John Snow was unable to keep the 'little master' quiet; Mohammad raced to a century. We also had a one-day fixture against MCC Schools after the Pakistan Test match. I was desperate to sit in the same dressing room my father had used in 1936 and 1946.

A day before this match, we had a practice session at the 'Nursery'. After the session, we proceeded towards the pavilion when our manager, Hemu Adhikari, spotted the former Australian all-rounder Keith Miller. The excited manager almost sprinted to meet the Australian great, closely followed by us. He introduced himself and simultaneously reminded him that he had been part of the Indian team to Australia in 1947. 'Oh! You mean Lala's team!' replied the Aussie. It was refreshing to hear him talk so highly of my father even after twenty years. Later, Keith not only spoke about English conditions but gave us valuable tips.

The match against the MCC schoolboys' team shall remain etched in my memory forever because of Surinder's outstanding performance. As for me, I failed with the bat but took four wickets. The Indian schoolboys needed 11 runs in the last over and Surinder was at the non-striker's end batting in his nineties. The first three deliveries fetched no run, but on the fourth, Inder

Raj managed to rotate the strike. It was a hopeless situation for us: we needed 10 runs from two deliveries. Surinder pulled the first one over midwicket for a six. Everyone in the dressing room jumped in joy. There was, at that time, no rule about having a certain number of fielders in the thirty-yard circle; hence, the MCC captain placed all his fielders on the boundary line. The pressure was immense on the hosts, particularly the bowler. Surinder's biggest asset in batting was that he never shuffled, but rather stood calmly, and judged the line and the length of the ball. While we held our breath, Surinder repeated the stroke with elegance and the ball travelled to a greater distance for another six, thereby winning a wonderfully exciting match.

The famous commentator and *The Times* correspondence John Arlott who watched this game compared the last two hits by Surinder with the fireworks of the legendary Sir Garfield Sobers. This was a big compliment for a schoolboy. Later, he came to our dressing room and congratulated Surinder for his outstanding performance. He also told us that he was a great admirer of Papaji's and it was such a pleasure to watch us in action.

After the successful tour of England, most of the players represented states and played first-class cricket. While Surinder performed exceedingly well in the first-class matches, I prepared myself for another test on Australian soil with the Indian schoolboys' team in 1968-69. The culture and attitude of the Australian people made an instant impact. However, unlike England, the members of the Indian schoolboys' team stayed with the families, which was a marvellous experience for me. Hans Raj Mahajan, Jalandhar, had crafted cricket bats with my autograph (thanks to Papaji's initiative); this was a morale booster for me and it also impressed the Australian schoolboys. At the end of the tour, they requested me to give them my bat as a parting gift. The most memorable part of the tour was meeting cricket's greatest figure, Sir Don Bradman. He too spoke fondly of the India tour of 1947 and about Papaji. I presented to him a silver salver with Papaji's message, which made the function more personal and enjoyable. My dreams were turning into reality and I looked forward to representing India in Test matches.

3

TEST DEBUT AND WILDERNESS

THE SWITCH FROM THE SCHOOL CRICKET TEAM TO THE junior state team had been quite smooth. With every success came recognition and, also, a reward in the form of a sports scholarship. The Punjab government had always encouraged sports, which facilitated sportspersons in achieving greater goals. My next goal was to play first-class cricket and finally represent the country like my father. I attended selection trials for the Northern Punjab team to play the Ranji Trophy at the tender age of fourteen and I impressed the selectors with my performance. However, they felt I was too young to play first-class cricket. But they could not hold me back for long. On turning seventeen, I got an opportunity to represent Northern Punjab, under the leadership of the old war horse Chaman Lal Malhotra, against the strongest team in the North Zone, Delhi.

This transition undoubtedly came with a lot of pressure. Like any other youngster of my age, I also had butterflies in my stomach. Was it the excitement of playing first-class cricket or the desire to do well and make my father proud? Probably both. Surprisingly, the tension vanished the moment I stepped on to the field to bat. I remained undefeated on 49, ultimately running out of partners. When I held the red cherry, I was confident of excelling in this department as well. I bowled a long spell and took four wickets. This performance gave me enormous pleasure and boosted my confidence. I may have been the baby of the team but, by performing better than many senior players, I managed to fit quite well in the company of the Big Boys!

This performance allowed me to find a regular place alongside my elder brother Surinder in the Northern Punjab team. Having crossed the first barrier, Papaji started spending more time with us. He spoke at length about the wickets around the country: how to tackle different bowlers and be effective against the leading batsmen, as well as the mindset of the opponents and how to overcome different challenges. During off-season, we practised hard under his watchful eyes at Karnail Singh Stadium, National Stadium, President's Estate or at Central Secretariat Grounds. Furthermore, he arranged powerful opponents and encouraged us to play matches. This prepared us better than most players for first-class matches.

In 1968, the Australians arrived for a five-match Test series. They were a group of positive, aggressive and athletic cricketers. The Aussies were led by an experienced opening batsman, Bill Lawry, followed by talented players like Ian Chappell, Ian Redpath, Keith Stackpole, Graham McKenzie and several other luminaries.

The Australian itinerary consisted of side matches against various zonal teams. The North Zone match against them was scheduled at Jalandhar before the third Test match in Delhi. Ever since my first-class debut in 1967, I was performing consistently in the Ranji Trophy; I had also impressed the zonal selectors to play the Duleep Trophy for the North Zone team. Although the team for the third Test was already announced and Surinder was part of the Indian squad, I also craved the same. Both Surinder and I were picked for the North Zone team to face the Aussies.

Since foreign teams visited India after long intervals, there was no real exposure for Punjab players or the spectators to enjoy international flavour. Earlier, it was Lahore, Amritsar or Patiala, but after the partition of India, Lahore was of course no longer part of the country, and therefore Amritsar remained the only venue in Indian Punjab to host such prestigious matches. Now, Burton Park at Jalandhar emerged as an alternative venue. Although it lacked facilities of the other venues in Lahore, Amritsar and Patiala, it still worked well for the locals to witness international teams in action. People from different faiths and parts of Punjab scrambled to the venue to enjoy cricket whenever they had the chance.

Before this important engagement, I spoke at length with Papaji, and accordingly conceived a strategy for my batting and bowling. I knew that as an all-rounder I had to perform well in both departments of the game. A little chat with Surinder released whatever little pressure remained within me. The three-day cricket carnival created a wonderful atmosphere. I took two wickets with my medium-pace bowling and scored an unbeaten half-century. I was satisfied with my performance and equally impressed with the approach of the Australians.

If the Aussies enjoyed the flat pitch at Burton Park, they were thoroughly exposed on the turning track at Delhi and India won the match easily. The selectors decided to retain the same squad for the next test match at Calcutta. In the five-match series, both teams had tasted victory each with two matches remaining. Although I had watched the Delhi Test, Papaji, for some strange reason, wanted me to accompany him to Calcutta and watch the fourth test match too. He was a strong believer that one could learn important lessons of cricket not just by playing but also by watching.

Eden Gardens in Calcutta remained the best venue to play and watch the game. I was amazed by the passion and knowledge of the cricket followers in this city. If at all it could be matched elsewhere, it was at Brabourne Stadium in Bombay and Chepauk in Madras. I tagged along with Papaji to Eden Gardens, where I was introduced to the Indian captain, Pataudi, and other members of the team. Without asking anyone, Papaji told me to sit with the Indian team and watch the match. Due to his aura and personality, neither the captain nor the players, nor even the officials, objected. I seemed to be part of the team, not because I was allowed to sit with them but because I also had access to the dressing room. The feel of the change room and atmosphere at the ground for a boy of eighteen felt like a dream. Regrettably, however, India could not match the strong performance of the Australian team and lost the Test match within four days.

With India down by two Tests to one, I wondered whether there would be any change in the Indian team. If there was, would I be picked? I couldn't be sure. So far, the Indian medium-pacers hadn't captured the headlines. Then came the biggest surprise for me; Papaji enquired if I was carrying my whites. I was amazed because I had come to watch the Test match and not practice. I had no idea what was going on in his mind; I replied with a simple no.

However, he organized shoes and whites, and asked me to bowl to a few Indian batsmen in the nets. This unscheduled net practice was organized after India's dismal performance.

Test Debut and Wilderness

The selectors wished to boost the confidence of certain batsmen who were worthy for the next Test match and to test the skills of those who did not rise to their expectations.

Having seen the surface for practice, Papaji acted like Chanakya and whispered secret mantras in my ears. No one in the cricketing world had better knowledge of the pitches than him. Due to the short notice to prepare a practice pitch, he knew that watering and the use of a half-ton roller would retain moisture and naturally assist pace bowlers. He simply asked me to use the shoulder and bowl a little short in length. 'Hit the deck hard' was his parting advice. I followed his instructions and, as expected, the ball flew in all directions, as if it had grown wings! The movement and bounce were a nightmare for the batsman who faced me. The ball consistently beat the outside edge of the bat and hit the top half of the net; I was encouraged to no end. All the selectors watching the practice session were impressed with my bowling. I bowled for a while, till Papaji gestured for me to take a break. I changed into my casuals and left for Binod Shroff's place.

In the evening, I was having a cup of tea, lost in my thoughts whether I would have any opportunity to represent India anytime soon. The team for the next Test match was to be announced in the evening and I didn't consider myself a serious candidate.

Papaji was covering the Test series for one of the leading English newspapers; after filing the match report, he arrived late in the evening. He entered the room with a big smile, as if he had conquered the world. He opened his arms and hugged me tightly with all his affection, and said, 'You've been selected for the final Test match in Madras!' His heart was still pounding with excitement. I could not believe these words and I really didn't know how to react to this news. However, Papaji's reaction revealed another feature of his persona; I had always thought he was a tough nut to crack but within him was the soft heart of a father. He was thrilled to see both his sons in the fifteen-member squad for the final Test in Madras. I was thrilled to see him so happy and I forgot about my selection. I kept looking at his radiant face with sparkling eyes and his pipe. He was clearly delighted to have both his sons in the Indian team. There could not have been a better occasion to make him feel proud and carry his legacy forward.

Chepauk Stadium was quite different from the present-day concrete structure. It had an old wooden pavilion built by the British. The dining room was filled with plaques, naming Indian and foreign players, and, of course, team photographs from a bygone era. Each picture made me feel nostalgic and reminded me of my father's playing days. I was proud to see his name decorating the wall. After all, he had played with distinction at this venue against the touring sides. If fortune favoured me, I also expected my name to decorate the wall for future generations to remember me. For the comfort of spectators, temporary wooden stands, covered with thin sheets of dried coconut leaves acted as a roof, were placed around the ground. The gaps between these stands allowed the cool sea breeze to maintain a comfortable temperature.

I knew in advance that I would be part of the playing eleven in this Test match. The announcement of the playing XI was made over a cup of tea and a few snacks. Since I was making my debut, all the players wished me luck. Captain Pataudi was a man of few words and the team meeting was merely a formality, concluded with minimal discussion. What surprised me was the lack of planning or strategy around this match.

However, Surinder missed another opportunity. My heartbeat remained faster than normal for the next two days, no doubt owing to my pre-match excitement. Srinivasaraghavan Venkataraghavan was the only player to understand my condition. To relax my nerves before the contest, he arranged two tickets for the evening show of an English movie; however, it proved counterproductive and, in fact, aggravated my tension. English was my handicap; what if he discussed the movie during the interval break? I prayed for relief!

The night before the Test match was probably the longest I had ever endured. Like any youngster, I was also restless, indeed anxious, at the prospect of playing before a large crowd. I tried my best to sleep, but my eyes wouldn't shut due to excitement. I kept tossing and turning in bed the entire night. On the contrary, my roommate, Michael Dalvi (from Delhi), who was in the reserves, was snoring away happily. After a sleepless night, I was relieved to hear a knock on the door; the waiter had brought my morning tea with biscuits and a newspaper. The fear of missing the team bus to the grounds was not an issue, so I quietly sipped on my tea. The trip from Connemara Hotel to Chepauk was supposedly twenty minutes, but to me it seemed like an eternity!

In the sixties, all the members of the team wore blazers and dressed in whites with formal shoes. There was no concept of physical training. Before the start of the match, Indian players were scattered near the pavilion, busy with their training. Batsmen did some knocking, while bowlers sent down a few deliveries. The Madras humidity, lack of interest in hard work and fear of dirtying the whites played on the minds of many players. India, at this stage, did not possess a strong fielding side, though there were exceptions. In the outfield, Pataudi, Rusi Surti and Abid Ali were outstanding fielders; Eknath Solkar was remarkable at forward short leg, while Ajit Wadekar and Venkataraghavan were reliable slip fielders. The rest could be categorized as average.

As a young boy, I had watched many Test matches from the gallery but now the time had come to feel the pulse of a Test match. The packed house and the noise made me restless and excited. It was like a dream coming true. Before the match, I expected captain Mansoor Ali Khan Pataudi to say a few encouraging words and guide me. Surprisingly, not a single word came from him. Maybe, coming from a royal background, he avoided interacting with new players, but his indifference nevertheless disappointed me. At this stage, I realized that everyone here was for himself. However, Papaji spoke a few encouraging words and offered tips for this match. His presence as an expert commentator for the All India Radio was a big bonus for me. Since there wasn't enough time to stitch a new blazer for me, I carried my Indian Schoolboys' blazer. However, they presented me with the 'crest of the Indian team' during the lunch break.

Australia won the toss and elected to bat. The stadium was filled to the brim and everyone was expecting India to square the series. After bowling a couple of overs, Pataudi came to me and said, 'Just this over.' The way he said it was incredibly discouraging. Before I could commence the over, I received another instruction from the mid-off fielder 'not to shine the ball'. If this was not enough, the next action shocked me. After the first delivery, the slip fielder rolled the new ball on the ground to the point fielder, who then rolled it to the mid-off fielder before tossing it to me. It was evident that selecting me to open the attack was a mere formality; other pace bowlers had met a similar fate in this series.

The Australian innings revolved around Doug Walters. He tackled the Indian spinners on a turning track with aggression, while the rest looked like novices. His positive attitude and nimble footwork forced the Indian spinners to search for comfort; he scored a fine century. In return, the Indian innings faltered against the pace and spin bowling of the Kangaroos. The highlight of the Indian first innings was a half-century by

Pataudi. I batted at number eight, which felt quite low since there were only tailenders to follow. When Venkataraghavan joined me at the crease, however, he offered some encouraging words. I thought it was decent of him to help ease the tension.

But our partnership did not last long; he was run out taking a quick single. I was a bit concerned because Venkataraghavan was known for his quick temper. Right through my innings, I kept wondering how to handle him in the dressing room. I remained 16 not out on my debut. As expected, he was waiting for me in the dressing room. Instead of criticizing, shouting or swearing at me, he offered encouragement and wished me luck for future Test matches.

The Australians had about half an hour to bat before the close of the day's play. When Bill Lawry and Keith Stackpole opened the second innings, I had no idea how many overs would be offered to me. I expected at the most two or three overs to remove the shine off the new ball because the Indian captain had no faith in pace bowlers. I knew it was my last chance to impress the large crowd at Chepauk. I took a deep breath to give my best shot. My first over was tight but did it impress the captain? When I walked towards my bowling end for the next over, Pataudi was holding the ball. He said, 'One more over and do not shine the ball.' With fielders already rolling the new ball, I could feel the beginning and the end of my Test career.

I trudged towards the Balaji Rao End bowling mark with a heavy heart. There was little faith left in the leadership and I prayed for a miracle. I knew that once the spinners got into the action, I would have no role in the second innings. If I had to survive the agony, I had to do something special in these six deliveries. Was it providential? My first delivery squeezed through the narrow gap between Stackpole's bat and pad, and uprooted the middle stump! If the sound of timber made me ecstatic, it shocked the rest of the team! They could not believe that a pace bowler had provided them with a much-needed breakthrough.

While the large crowd roared in appreciation, I thanked the Almighty for his generosity. I looked around the stadium, feeling as if I had conquered the world. I didn't know how to react, how to celebrate. I just stood looking in the direction of the commentator's box where Papaji was seated with the rest of the commentary team. I folded my hands and took a bow to seek his blessing; surely millions must have come from his heart. It gave me immense pleasure to hear my teammates say 'well done' and 'well bowled'. Music to my ears! Now I was confident of bowling a few more overs.

With excitement building in the stands and homes across India, everyone listening to the commentary on the radio, Ian Chappell walked briskly and took guard. He was the portrait of a true professional cricketer. One success changed the attitude of my captain; he allowed me to shine the ball and also instructed the fielders to throw the ball in the air directly to me. The following over also brought me and the team great joy; I dismissed Ian Chappell! The entire Chepauk stadium erupted like a volcano. The crowd was astounded by what they were witnessing. Equally excited were my teammates; they could not imagine that a lanky boy of nineteen could produce such a magical spell.

While I gathered momentum to bowl, each step made me feel taller, stronger and more confident. There was support in the gallery and on the ground. For a change, Pataudi smiled and encouraged me to go in for another kill. The two wickets that fell in the Australian second innings helped me leave my mark. The commentators' box also witnessed an extraordinary scene. Overwhelmed by my success, Papaji could not control his emotions. Like a proud father, he distributed sweets amongst the journalists and friends gathered there. It was hard to believe a tough man like him giving in to his emotions. I knew he must be desperate to congratulate me, but as usual he honoured his commitments and filed the match report first.

The hotel lobby and the corridor leading to my room were packed with enthusiastic supporters. The moment Papaji entered the lobby, he was mobbed. The next moment, the door opened and I saw the glowing face of my father. He gave me his patent bear hug, which almost broke my ribs, and he laughed loudly. This was an expression of a proud father! Then, holding my shoulders with his strong hands, he said, 'I'm proud of you, son.' At that moment, I noticed my younger brother, Johnny, whom Papaji had flown to Madras just to watch me play in this Test match. He still carried that unforgettable grin, which actually changed Surinder's and my destiny. All three sons hugged Papaji to celebrate the occasion, probably the happiest for us!

That night I slept like a log. No sound, not even the beat of drums, could invade my thoughts. I was at peace with myself. I don't think I could have asked God for a better gift. Papaji's hard work had finally paid dividends.

The following day, I bowled a long spell to restrict the flow of runs while an incredible drama unfolded from the other end. In the first hour of play, Erapalli Prasanna bowled one of the best spells of his career. Every Australian batsman floundered against him. At one stage, they were struggling at 24 runs with six wickets down. Prasanna was a man on a mission, but a lack of concentration from the others changed the complexion of the game. First, an easy stumping chance of Ian Redpath, stranded halfway down the wicket, and later, an easy skier of McKenzie (to Prasanna's bowling) cost us dearly. The two batsmen stitched a crucial partnership to take the Aussies to safety. Though India managed to skittle Australia for a mere

153, the first innings lead of 95 runs made our task difficult on a decaying pitch.

The tourists believed in the pace battery of McKenzie, Mayne and Connolly to use the uneven bounce, while off spinner Ashley Mallett found the crumbling pitch an ideal surface to exploit. He captured five wickets and the rest were split amongst the pace bowlers. For India, Ajit Wadekar and G.R. Vishwanath showed some resistance, scoring half-centuries each; they added 102 runs to raise our hopes. However, once they departed, the rest of the line-up could not match the Aussies. The visitors won the Test match by a comfortable margin of 77 runs, and the series as well.

I had a reasonable debut taking two wickets in the second innings and bowling 24 overs. It was the longest spell by any Indian medium-pacer, especially in a team armed with three spinners. Although I didn't get many runs as a batsman, I still fancied myself more as a batsman than a bowler. I knew I had made an impact on the selectors, the media and the people. I wore an Indian blazer on all occasions with great pride. For a change, I had developed my own identity and was not referred to as Lala Amarnath's son. The following year's domestic season was important and both of us brothers performed well. However, we were overlooked for the West Indies tour in 1971. This exclusion led to an identity crisis; I was once again referred to as Lala Amarnath's son.

Since there was no serious cricket played during the summer months in north India, I decided to take a break with my elder sister Kamla and brother-in-law (late) Suresh Sharma, who was posted in Jaipur. He was a senior geologist with the government of India and much respected at home. Speculations were rife in all the newspapers about my inclusion for the England tour. However, on the day of selection, time ticked with an excruciating slowness. I paced up and down the house, and sitting in one place became horribly difficult. It was the longest day to watch the sunset.

This was a period without internet or mobile phones to receive important messages or news. The quickest mode of transmitting the news was through radio or telegrams, while telefax was available to high-ranking officials only. Keeping our fingers crossed, all three of us sat next to the radio awaiting the mystery to unfold. One name after another spelled doom for me till my name was announced. Excitement overwhelmed us and, without bothering to hear the full news, we switched off the radio set. I quickly packed my belongings, and took leave from Kamla and Suresh to reach Delhi.

With no seats available in the first-class compartment on the last train leaving for Delhi, I decided to take a chance in the unreserved third-class compartment. Luckily, a young porter recognized me and, with his help, I occupied the top berth. It was made of solid wooden planks and I had no mattress to give me comfort. For a change, the hard surface did not bother me. I took a deep breath and smiled. Even a great man like Mahatma Gandhi had travelled in the same class! I was visibly happy and I dreamed of cricket grounds in England. It was hard to close my eyes and sleep. The entire journey went by consuming freshly brewed hot tea served in a clay pot (called kullar) at various stations. Each kullar of tea cost two annas. Finally, the train arrived in the early hours of the morning at Old Delhi Railway Station. The platform bore a deserted look, but my eyes searched for a book stall.

The moment I saw one, I rushed towards it and grabbed the *Indian Express*, the *Times of India*, the *Statesman*, and other available newspapers to read the headlines and see my photo. The old man at the stall was quite amused by my actions and presumed I was either an eccentric or a professor, but I was obviously neither! I hurriedly skipped past the undesired pages to reach the sports page of *Times of India* to read my name—but I saw neither my name nor my photo. I cursed the misprint and picked up another newspaper, and here too there was no mention of me. Even the third attempt was equally disheartening; I was bewildered. Eventually, I read the list of players and my name appeared with the caption 'subject to the absence of Farokh Engineer'. It made no sense to me; Farokh Engineer was a wicketkeeper and I was an all-rounder.

Finally, my focus stopped at the statement of the BCCI about Engineer. He was playing for Lancashire Cricket Club and they were not prepared to release him for the length of the entire tour. Eventually, an understanding was reached for the Test matches. I still stood a fair chance, as another wicketkeeper, Krishnamurthy, was selected, and two keepers were enough for a three-match Test series and a few side games. How wrong I was in my presumption! Through a reliable source I had come to know that my name had come up for earlier discussions too but was never supported by certain members of the selection committee; I happened to be Lala Amarnath's son. Unfortunately, petty politics and machinations at the zonal level ensured my exclusion. The third wicketkeeper in the form of Syed Kirmani was added to the team. Within a year, I missed two opportunities to represent India.

Possessing 'Amarnath genes', however, I was not the kind of man to give up the game, despite several rejections. Burgeoning maturity strengthened my resolve to play for the country even more. I had full faith in my abilities and talent, and so I feared no competition or deception. Every new season started with a ray of hope, but ultimately brought me disillusionment. I took the first two lines of The Moody Blues' song and rephrased them for myself: 'Knight in white satin, never reaching the end.'

Dejected, I took refuge in my father for a solution. A little chat and encouragement from him invariably revived my determination. He spoke of his career and struggle, beginning with his exclusion for the England tour in 1932 when he was a young man of only twenty-one; he made his debut against England in 1933 to become a celebrity; he was sent back home from England in 1936 but played against the unofficial English team led by Lord Tennyson in India in 1937; because of the Second World War, he had to wait for twelve long years to play the second official series against England in 1946. After leading India against Australia in 1947-48 and the West Indies in 1948-49, deprived of Indian captaincy and ignored for the England tour in 1951, he made a final comeback at the age of forty to lead India successfully against Pakistan in 1952 and retire on a high note. Each word and event had its impact. Dejection was replaced by determination. I took a silent oath to fight injustice with performance. My goal was, quite simply, to make my father proud of me.

THE CITY OF THE GOLDEN TEMPLE: AMRITSAR

I had compromised my studies by playing constant cricket. Now the time had come to complete my matric or the tenth standard; it was more difficult than playing a defensive shot. Having crossed this hurdle, I realized nothing was impossible; it just required 'focus'. This was to become my mantra in life. Surinder was already studying at DAV College, Amritsar, and a decision had to be made whether I should join him, or proceed to Aligarh Muslim University (AMU) or Delhi University.

My father had been a student at Aligarh University in the early 1930s; he took me to watch an inter-university match at Aligarh for two reasons: one, Surinder was representing Guru Nanak Dev University, and two, he wanted me to get a sense of the atmosphere at AMU. The rousing reception he received at the campus after four decades was astonishing. The young and old staff members, officials and elite citizens competed to shake hands with him. The crowd forgot the match and waved at him. Within no time, he was heavily garlanded. However, the thought of two brothers competing against each other dissuaded him from choosing AMU for me.

The holy city of Amritsar remained synonymous with the Golden Temple, the epicentre of Sikh religion. Situated in the middle of a sacred pond, the beautiful Harmandir Sahib is covered with tons of gold; visited by hundreds of thousands of Sikhs and Hindus each day, the constant recitation from the Guru Granth Sahib, the Sikh holy scriptures, offers great solace. After the partition of India, Amritsar became the cricket nursery for Indian Punjab, while Lahore was the counterpart in Pakistani Punjab. For centuries, both cities remained centres of culture and education. The language, temperament and habits continued to remain the same till 1947, when culture and traditions took a beating on both sides of the new border. The vibrant cosmopolitan fabric of the society was replaced by fundamentalist beliefs, leading to the cross-border exodus of millions from other faiths.

DAV College had a great cricket culture and tradition, and the institute accepted me with open arms. Tom and I were provided all the facilities to focus on cricket. In addition, we were promised free education and accommodation; a monthly scholarship of 150 rupees for maintenance was the icing on the cake. Breakfast cost one rupee, which included one litre of sweet lassi—made from fresh curd, milk and paerras (an Indian sweet), topped with a thick layer of cream—and chana bhaturas; lunch and dinner made using desi ghee cost one rupee and eight annas each at Kesar da Dhaba near the Golden Temple.

However, little did we realize that there was a hidden agenda behind the magnanimity. The final against arch-rival Hindu

College was nothing short of war; the honour and prestige of DAV College depended on its outcome. The principal desired a return gift from us; help lift the inter-college trophy. Bir Singh Bange, Surinder Mohan and Dogra, along with a 'team of professors', were entrusted with the responsibility to work out a plan and achieve this goal.

Alexandra Cricket Ground, today called the Gandhi Ground, was the venue of the tour match between Southern Punjab, led by Maharaja Bhupindra Singh Patiala, and Douglas Jardine's MCC in 1933. This venue had seen the emergence of Lala Amarnath as a future star of India when he scored a brilliant century and repeated the feat in the Bombay Test match. When I arrived at this ground for practice, I saw Bhupindra Pavilion, and the history of the bygone era flashed before my eyes. The local clubs and other colleges practised on matting pitches outside the boundaries of the cricket ground. We also had a designated area for nets but no change room or showers. Nevertheless, after nets, we washed our faces or sponged our bodies down using the nearby tap water; we changed and headed to Lawrence Road to enjoy the lively atmosphere and a cup of tea.

Unlike many of the relatively progressive cities in India, Amritsar provided few opportunities for girls to pursue higher education. My college was primarily a boys' institution but with an exception. There were four girls pursuing their Masters of Arts in English and they were naturally major attractions for the undergraduate BA (Bachelor of Arts) students. These young boys never missed college; they were punctual yet failed to attend lectures that happened to coincide with the girls' time of entry into the campus! I was amazed at their infatuation. Seasons changed from blistering summers to monsoon rains and shivering winters to vibrant springs—they never missed a glimpse of these girls. However, none dared approach them for fear of an English conversation, a major handicap for Punjabi-speaking boys! Yet, quite a few boys staked their claim on unaware girls. This factor even led to numerous skirmishes amongst die-hard suitors.

So, incapable of talking to the girls, most of these admirers devised plans to draw their attention, either by watching them from a distance or accidentally wandering into their path. These girls travelled to college by bicycle and were invariably followed by some exuberant boys from a distance; others stood waiting at the entrance, tying their shoelaces, some kicking the dust, others pretending to look at the sky. Yet, none had the guts to approach them. I remember two incidents that kept me amused for the entire year.

There happened to be a young, sturdy Sardar. He was boastful and aggressive. One day, he stood by the gate, rolling his moustache, making inappropriate remarks and laughing at the approaching girls. The girls' response shocked everyone, including the teaser. The moment they confronted him with a few English sentences, he folded his hands and apologized like a timid lamb. Another spectacle was that of the cricket team members trailing a few girls on their bicycles till their residences. On returning, each of the boys pumped the air with his fist, claiming victory. Everyone exclaimed, 'Oof! Bara mazaa aa gaya, ghar chadh aye (We thoroughly enjoyed dropping them home)!' Despite these adventures and tall claims, the girls kept serious faces to keep all these roadside Romeos at bay.

The finale of the inter-college contest was a much-awaited event in the city. Both DAV and Hindu Colleges declared holidays, which allowed the students to watch the showdown; students from other institutions also assembled at the ground to support either team. Principals R.N. Mehta and C.L. Arora along with the staff watched the finals at Gandhi Stadium. It was a festive atmosphere: some people played the dholak or the drums, while others performed bhangra—a Punjabi folk dance. When the situation became tense, tempers ran high on the pitch and in the gallery. Whenever I bowled a bouncer, the supporters of Hindu College cursed and abused me, though with little effect. With the support of the team members, both Tom and I kept our promise. DAV College lifted the prestigious trophy.

The distance from Gandhi Stadium to DAV was approximately three kilometres, which took an hour to traverse that day. The victory parade of more than a thousand die-hard supporters commenced with the beating of drums, Bhangra and an uninterrupted commentary of DAV College's achievement. The traffic moved at a snail's pace but people never complained because sweets were being offered to them. The procession culminated at the college campus where the principal and staff garlanded each player, followed by high tea and gifts.

After the cricket season, I faced another major challenge: grasping the knowledge of my books and clearing the exams. The pressure made me more nervous than conversing with girls in English. To bail us from a tight situation, Surinder and I sought help from a few bright students and accordingly purchased specific books. One day, Surinder was studying when the sports professors entered our room and asked for a cup of tea. While I ordered tea from the adjoining canteen, Surinder glanced through the book in front of him. 'What are you reading?' one of the professors asked. Surinder said we were preparing for exams. The professor asked him to hand over the book; he opened the window and immediately tossed the book out onto the street below! Surinder was aghast and didn't know how to react. According to Hindu philosophy, books were a storehouse of knowledge and indeed equated with Saraswati, the Goddess of knowledge. Before he could run down and retrieve the book, the professor smiled and held him back. When he said, 'Asi mar gaye han (Are we of no use)?' we were even more baffled!

With the paucity of time staring us in the face and no books available for preparation, we surrendered to fate and prepared to repeat the class. A few days before the exams, a sports professor visited us again with our roll numbers and an examination schedule. Looking at our bewildered expressions, he said, 'Do not worry', and left us on the verge of crying. Later, one of the cricketers appearing for the MA exams also gave us a similar assurance, which sent us into a tizzy. We were mystified to learn that we had ultimately passed our exams; it could best be described as divine intervention!

While we prepared for a fresh cricket season, the radio and newspapers brought to us disturbing political news. The atrocities committed by the Pakistan Army on its citizens in East Pakistan (Bangladesh) brought back memories of the holocaust and the sufferings of the Jews. The pictures and the news of arson, loot and rape shook every sane soul, yet the West kept quiet. To save their lives, thousands of Bengali refugees crossed the international border and sought refuge in India. The influx of over 1 million people combined with India's poor economic condition aggravated the situation. A possibility of war between the two neighbours loomed large on the western front, and Attari border was barely twenty-odd kilometres from Amritsar.

Despite the tense situation, Guru Nanak Dev University organized a cricket camp. However, it barely lasted a few days. During this period, I often visited Jasbir Singh's home to partake in vegetarian dishes and parathas cooked by his mother and sisters. The city of Amritsar had a unique topography. All buildings extended on either side with no gaps; one could jump from one terrace to another and cover miles this way. One day, we were excited to see several fighter jets flying very low over the city towards the airport. The next moment, we heard loud explosions. Not sure of what was happening, everyone switched on their radio sets for information; the news of Pakistan bombing the airport and declaring war on India was conveyed to the nation by Prime Minister Indira Gandhi. We could repeatedly hear the horrible noise of shelling from the border. In the night, air-raid sirens plunged the entire city into darkness and people took refuge in the newly dug trenches in parks or basements.

To keep the morale of the citizens of Amritsar up, all shops, offices and educational institutes functioned as usual. Nevertheless, the deafening sounds of fighter aircraft compelled everyone to drop their work. The shopkeepers rushed to the streets; officers and clerks scrambled to the terrace; women peeped out of the windows and students left the classrooms to witness what was going on. There were no more surprise attacks on Indian airports as the Russian MiG-21s of the Indian air force knocked down the American F-104 jets of the Pakistan air force in dog fights to rule the sky; the rest of the Pakistani jets scrambled for safety beyond Lahore. It brought back the sweet memories of the 1965 war when tiny Gnats shot down the much superior American Sabre Jets. No doubt, technology had changed, but for the simple folks of Amritsar, the contest remained between Gnat and Sabre. They pointed to the sky and said in typical Punjabi, 'Dekho, G-NAT Sabre jet nu maar raheya weh (Look "G-nat" is shooting down the Sabre jet).'

One evening, I wore Papaji's army jacket, with three stars on its epaulet (Papaji was an honorary captain with the Maharaja of Patiala) and visited a dhaba for a meal. The owner mistook me for a serving officer, and refused to charge me for the meal and tea. There was genuine respect for the Indian armed forces and people went out of the way to make their lives more comfortable whenever they could. The hot topic amongst the Amritsar business community was restarting business in

Lahore, while others contemplated regaining their ancestral properties. My parents in Delhi were worried but I felt quite safe experiencing the conflict in the war zone!

While the entire world hoped for an early solution, Pakistan sang a different tune. The frequency from the Lahore radio station was easily accessible on this side of the border in Amritsar. The President of Pakistan, Gen. Yahya Khan, went live on Pakistan radio; his fumbling for words amused me. To raise the sagging spirits of Pakistani forces in Dacca (Dhaka), he boasted about apparent successes on the western front; in his narrative, the brave Pakistani soldiers had entered the Hall Gate area of Amritsar and captured the entire city. My college was in the proximity of Hall Bazar and I didn't see a single Pakistani soldier. It did not take much time to realize that the Pakistani government lived on lies; they soon lost East Pakistan.

The authorities took a call to discontinue the camp because of the prevailing situation. I booked my seat to Delhi by Flying Mail. Since I was wearing Papaji's Patiala army jacket and the feeling of patriotism was flying high, I received special treatment. At every station, tea, snacks and sweets were offered to me, free of cost. If I refused, it was packed and handed to me. They also assumed I was one of the Indian army officers.

India recognized Bangladesh as a sovereign nation and Russia followed suit; courtesy of India, a new nation had come into the world to occupy a seat in the United Nations, headquarters at New York.

4

NEW ZEALAND 1975
COMEBACK 1

SIX PRODUCTIVE YEARS OF MY CRICKET CAREER WERE LOST. However, the desire to play for India kept my fire burning. Papaji's early warning and his assessment of such an eventuality had been proved correct. Our exclusion was not because of performance but because of the name 'Amarnath'. In fact, some disgruntled board officials were trying to hit my father below the belt and I was hell-bent on shielding him from such assaults. The best possible way was to gatecrash into the team, but as to how I would do that, I had no answer. Papaji was not only my idol, guide, mentor and guru, but indeed the most admired and precious person in my life.

With the passage of time, my volatile emotions were overcome by maturity. But, deep down within me, my greatest desire remained unfulfilled. I wanted to secure my rightful place in the team and so I was perennially motivated. I kept scoring runs and taking wickets in the domestic matches. It brought me immense satisfaction to see Surinder responding positively as well. Together, we brought great joy to Papaji and he kept encouraging us to compete harder not against new opponents but with our earlier performances. All of us knew it was just a matter of time before the reluctance of the selectors would be conquered by our willpower and consistent performance. I feared no test or opponent. 'Pure gold fears no flames' became my motto.

The setbacks made my resolve even stronger. I was not the kind to sit back and be spanked; I let my talent give a fitting reply. Although our performance strengthened strong public opinion in our favour, it got little response from the selectors; they simply ignored us. When the West Indies toured India under Clive Lloyd in 1974 and left, we were still in the wilderness. Surinder had missed a precious seven years of international cricket; I had missed five. Many a time, I wondered if we had not been the sons of Lala Amarnath and had instead belonged to some unknown family, we would have quit cricket a long time ago. Fortunately, we had the full and strong support of Papaji and Mummyji to guide us. My father kept giving us examples of his struggles and simultaneously pushed us harder towards the goal!

Since the late nineteenth century, Bombay had been the nerve centre of Indian cricket. This factor enabled local cricketers to come into the limelight faster than equally talented players from other zones. The local media also played a prominent role in pushing new faces and the coverage of Times Shield influenced the selectors. Unlike today, there was little money in cricket; Tata, ACC, Mafatlal, Nirlon, SBI and so forth came to the rescue of international and first-class cricketers with a steady job. Shrewd as all corporates were, they realized the potential of cricket and an easy route to advertise their company's products.

The popularity of Times Shield attracted another Bombay corporate giant, JK Industries. Its chairman, Vijaypat Singhania, decided to form a cricket team along the lines of Tatas, ACC and others. The forefathers of this industry had links with Kanpur, and Kamlapat Singhania knew my maternal grandfather, Charan Das, quite well. His son, Padampat Singhania, was also a good friend of my father.

Vijaypat Singhania approached Papaji to allow us to play for his team, led by Pataudi. The list of players included Karsan Ghavri, Laxman Singh, Hrishikesh Kanitkar and a few local boys. However, the inclusion of Salim Durani made the JK team popular with the masses. Singhania's wish was instantly granted and we moved to Bombay. The conditions in Bombay were loaded in favour of batsmen and Surinder smashed each bowler in the town to his heart's content. I also contributed handsomely with the bat and ball to occupy the limelight. These performances made former Test players from Bombay take notice of us and the media started questioning our exclusion from the Indian team.

Another pleasant surprise for me was Tiger Pataudi's attitude. It was so different from the Madras Test match in 1969. He was approachable and communicative, which put me at ease. Maybe the pressure of international cricket was gone and he could simply enjoy the game. He was humorous, yes, but his tongue-in-cheek remarks were often difficult to grasp; so British!

At this stage, Bishan Singh Bedi was leading the Delhi team and yearned to win the premier competition of India, the Ranji Trophy. It was a difficult proposition considering Delhi's batting strength. His plan got a boost, however, when Surinder scored a double century and I a century against them. Bishan understood our importance and decided to include both of us in his team to fulfil the dream project. Still, there remained one major hurdle—the president of the Delhi Cricket Association. Once bygones were forgotten, Papaji took another major decision and shifted us from Punjab to Delhi. This became a turning point in our careers.

Papaji was far-sighted; he knew we stood a better chance to play for India under Bedi, the future captain of the Indian team. He also happened to be a product of Punjab before shifting to Delhi for greener pastures. We could gel easily in the new environment.

When the decks were cleared, we brothers shifted to Delhi for a better future. West Zone and Bombay had been calling the shots in Indian cricket for a long time, but things were going to change. No doubt, Bombay had produced great players, but average players also received preference over cricketers with greater potential from across the country, thanks to the influence of the BCCI. However, fortunes changed in favour of the North Zone players and the 1974 domestic season gave us the first glimpse of a new era. The contest between North and West Zone (or Delhi versus Bombay) was emotionally charged. It was nothing short of a War of the Roses between Lancashire and Yorkshire. Bedi took these contests seriously. The spark in his eyes ran parallel with his emotional speeches, leaving many faces crimson.

The genes of mistrust amongst players from West and North Zones had its misgivings from the Pentangular Tournament. In addition, the BCCI headquarters at Brabourne Stadium enabled Bombay to control the administration and make policies to suit itself. They had two votes in CCI & BCA, while Gujarat's three (Baroda, Gujarat and Saurashtra) and one vote of Maharashtra allowed them to rule the roost. To accommodate players from this region, players from the North Zone suffered the most. This became a rallying point. Bedi's burning desire was to inflict humiliating blows on the opponents and remind everyone of the injustice committed against North Zone players. On the eve of our matches against Bombay or West Zone, Bedi's fiery speech motivated every member of the team. He reminded us of our sufferings; it was now time to prove our worth. I am sure it was no different in the Bombay or West Zone camp. No wonder players from both teams were mentally and physically exhausted after each contest. Victory brought satisfaction to the winning team and the vanquished started planning their future action to redeem their lost prestige.

The collective efforts of Punjabi cricketers secured the Duleep Trophy in 1974, and sent a strong signal of change to West and South Zone teams. It was a major achievement for the team and captain Bishan Bedi. This effort took him closer to the coveted post of captain of India. Bishan's greatest quality was that he was a team man first and leader second. Taking up the cause of his players, he found himself on the wrong side of the fence with the BCCI. Still, his desire for the betterment of players was appreciated by all the cricketers. As a captain, he appreciated hard practice sessions and was not amused with players preferring shortcuts. After each net session or match day, a glass of beer was invariably offered to those eligible; jokes refreshed exhaustion, and fear was conquered by the jovial and healthy atmosphere.

The only big match I got to play in 1974 was against the West Indies at Jalandhar. Their team consisted of Viv Richards, Gordon Greenidge, Alvin Kallicharran, Andy Roberts and, of course, Clive Lloyd at the helm of affairs. The first Test match was in Bangalore and Pataudi was recalled to captain India after a gap of three years. Bishan Bedi had some issues with the BCCI; he was replaced by another left-arm slow bowler, Rajinder Goel. The veteran bowler had bowled his heart out in the nets and impressed all, except the captain. It may sound a little odd that Pataudi did not turn up at the nets. The poor chap came so close to playing for India. The second Test match in Delhi did not begin well for India. Pataudi failed the fitness test and was ruled out. Since no vice-captain was announced, confusion prevailed till the toss.

Finally, the crown was placed on Venkataraghavan, but the subsequent defeat left him bleeding. My father was covering the match as an expert for Doordarshan, the national TV channel. After India's poor performance, the television producer desperately wanted Venkat's reaction. Knowing the acting Indian captain's temperament, no commentator was willing to interview him. As a last resort, the producer approached Lala Amarnath to do the necessary. Although he had never interviewed any cricketer, he accepted this challenge as well.

My father was known to be a blunt and straightforward person. He never believed in beating around the bush, a quality that had made him popular with the masses. Immense self-confidence was the hallmark of his personality. The interview was short and crisp. He asked the acting Indian captain just one question: 'I am sure you must be a disappointed person after India's poor show and defeat; tell me, who along with you should be dropped from the team?' The selection committee kept faith in Venkat but reduced his status to twelfth man in the next Test match.

The West Indies batsmen made an instant impact on the Indian bowlers and vice versa with their battery of pace bowlers on Indian batsmen. This approach made me realize that if I had to survive at the international level, my medium-pace bowling alone was not sufficient. I had to be a good batsman against formidable pace attacks and I, of course, had to be aggressive in my shot selection to relieve pressure. Though I did not play this series, I developed respect for another little master from South India, Gundappa Vishwanath. He was a cut above the rest, and played all the West Indian fast bowlers with ease and elegance.

If I am not wrong, he won more matches for India with his batting skills than any other batsman in the side. It was strange that the media still rated him below Sunil Gavaskar.

The success of the Gillette Cup and John Player league matches in England attracted larger crowds to the venues than county cricket or Test cricket. This concept got approval from the ICC to make international matches more interesting and results-oriented. The inaugural Cricket World Cup was held in England in 1975. English conditions suited swing bowlers, I was selected as an all-rounder to bowl a quota of twelve overs. It was a long journey after my debut in 1969. If I had not been sidelined, I would have been an established player and not fighting to regain my place in the team.

On the eve of the first match of the World Cup against England, a team meeting was held in the captain's room. Many combinations were discussed; when my name came for discussion, surprisingly, a senior Bombay player tried to dissuade the captain from including me. The reason offered was that the England opener, John Alexander Jameson, would make mincemeat of my bowling. Though his choice was overruled, I realized there was no support for me. If I had to survive, I had to perform with faith in my own instincts. The challenge to prove this player wrong added to my resolve. There was joy when I took Jameson's wicket early in the innings. The celebration amongst the team members resembled the Madras Test match of 1969, but my feelings were not the same.

India lost one match after another in this competition, except against East Africa. The dismal performance in the World Cup left a lone contender, Sunil Gavaskar, to assume the responsibility. But an innings of 36 not out from 174 balls in the 60-over match against England exposed his attitude. Watching a truly unusual batting display, the other batsmen banged the dressing room wall with their fists and muttered a few objectionable words. At this stage, a couple of MCC members came to the Indian dressing room and pleaded with the manager to recall the slow batsman. A moment later, the manager instructed Abid Ali, Farokh Engineer, Madan Lal and me to get padded. There was great confusion as to who would go next if a wicket fell. When Gavaskar returned to the dressing room undefeated, however, there was no remorse. It sealed his fate to become the next captain of India.

The Indian cricket calendar of 1975-76 was full of activities, beginning with Sri Lanka's tour of India and, subsequently, twin tours of New Zealand and the West Indies. The selectors had seen enough of Pataudi, Wadekar and Venkataraghavan; they were on the lookout for fresh a face. This left three spinners, Prasanna, Chandrashekhar and Bedi as the senior-most players with the responsibility. Bedi's aggressive leadership qualities stood taller and he won the race. For a change, the Bombay press supported the man in a colourful patka. The direction of the wind indicated better times for North Zone players. Having known the selectors' mindset, it augured a better future for us. How correct was Papaji's observation!

Ceylon, as Sri Lanka was known till then, had surprised the best of teams with their attitude and performances. However, they were still not recognized as a Test-playing nation by the ICC. In 1975, Ceylon toured India for an unofficial Test series under the captaincy of Anura Tennekoon. The mild-mannered Ceylon captain was an attractive batsman, but unfortunately lost his best years playing unofficial international matches.

Keeping in mind immediate tours, the selectors used the Ceylon series as a base for selection. Many new faces were put on trial to build a strong combination for the forthcoming tours of New Zealand and the West Indies. Sunil Gavaskar scored a double century in Hyderabad, while my elder brother, Surinder, scored a brilliant century on debut in Ahmedabad.

He emulated my father to create history, but the media raised the status of the unofficial Test match to deny him this honour. Surinder's batting was a treat to watch; his bat flashed like a magic wand and tore up the Ceylon attack. He was a class apart from the rest of us; he hated the feel or impact of the ball on his pad; he played all the shots in the book with ease and power to command respect from the opponents. His brisk walk and body language portrayed confidence. While many cricketers were deterred by difficult situations or conditions, his skills countered with ease to baffle the critics and bowlers.

When Bedi was announced captain for the twin tours, I knew destiny would smile on both of us too. It was a fair conclusion and it did not disappoint me. After the selection committee meeting, Bishan Bedi returned to the hotel with a broad smile on his face. Without wasting any time, he said, 'Jim, you and Tom are part of the touring side.'

I was thrilled by the news of Tom's return to the squad after being sidetracked for a long period. What a pity that he was not part of the Indian team for the 1975 World Cup! It raised the question of fair selection; despite scoring two half-centuries in the two trial matches conducted by the BCCI, he was not selected. The reason for his exclusion was mind-boggling; he played too many aggressive strokes to give confidence to the selectors, so instead they picked plodders. Strange was the thinking of the five wise men. Tom, with his swashbuckling approach, would have been a great asset to the team.

My return to Test cricket after a gap of six long years was equally exhilarating! Finding both of us in the team reminded me of the childhood and Schoolboys' tours that we had variously undertaken. Those tours had bonded us forever. The only difference at this moment was our age and the status of the tour; it was a national team. I guess more than us, Papaji was the happiest person on earth. His decision to shift us to Delhi yielded the ripest fruit.

Bedi's experience of several tours had taught him the value of team spirit and unity. In the past, he had noticed the Indian team divided into small camps and how it harmed the overall performance. He knew no captain could win a match without the full support of the team. He was enthusiastic and vocal—two qualities needed for leadership to win support. The composition of the team reflected a mix of experience and youth. Barring a few married players, the rest were single.

Since conditions in New Zealand suited pace bowlers, green-top wickets were on expected lines. To counter this threat, Indian batting depended on the success of Gavaskar and Vishwanath, while bowling remained in the safe hands of spinners. Thank God the selectors did not repeat the same mistake of the 1967 England tour. This time, Madan Lal, Eknath Solkar and I could operate with the new ball—by no means a threatening pace attack, yet capable of picking up wickets at key moments.

This tour was important for me; I was yet to cement my place in the team. It was a God-given opportunity; even if someone happened to get injured, no replacement was likely to come for the next several months. The reason: paucity of funds in the BCCI coffers. On our arrival, the New Zealand media gave us little chance of winning any Test match against the pace attack led by Richard Hadlee and supported by a strong batting line-up. To demoralize us, they dubbed India as an ordinary side, incapable of beating local teams. Overconfidence and underestimating the opposition can be absolutely destructive; it became evident after the statements by certain players and critics in newspapers.

On the contrary, we were more circumspect and cautious in our approach. We assessed the strengths and weaknesses of the opposition. No doubt, the Kiwis were a better fielding side and quite lethal with the new ball, compared to us. On the green-top surface, spinners were unlikely to get assistance; this made the home team overconfident. However, every Indian player knew his job and most of us were itching to prove the local media wrong.

Despite the curator's desire to give the home team an advantage with a green-top pitch in the first Test match, luck tilted in our favour. Auckland received unusually heavy showers for days together, which left the ground staff twiddling their thumbs. It forced the curators to cover the pitch. However, we were amazed to see the drainage system on the ground and how well it worked. Despite the heavy downpour, the water was drained out. I was sure, under similar conditions in India, the match would have been abandoned. The main square in the middle was protected by a hut-shaped cover and what lay under it was anyone's guess.

Eventually, when the rain stopped and the sun shone brightly on the horizon, the much-awaited moment came: the covers were finally removed. The moment the strip was exposed, the smiles on the faces of the New Zealand players, officials and ground staff froze. The continuous rain and lack of sunlight changed its colour to brown, quite like that of our skin. We were gladdened by the sight; it was likely to prove a paradise for the Indian spinners. Bishan, Prasanna and Chandra could not hold back and they laughed loudly. It seemed like we were playing in our backyard at home.

However, destiny set its own course for Bishan Bedi. Exuberant as he was with the prevailing conditions, a day before the match, he stretched and pulled his calf muscle. He could barely walk. The pain was both mental and physical, and disappointment was writ large on his face. He knew there would not be another spinner paradise on this tour.

The concept of a physiotherapist accompanying the team had not been considered yet and most cricketers used experience to tackle such problems themselves. Bishan was desperate to play, and even approached a local clinic to repair the torn muscle and reduce the pain. Unfortunately, it was too little and too late. The day of the Test match, Bishan undertook the fitness test wearing a combination of rubber and spike shoes to reduce the pressure, but failed to find any comfort. The suspense continued, till he accepted his fate and handed over the responsibility to his deputy, Sunil Gavaskar.

If Sunil was making his debut as captain of India, so were Surinder Amarnath, Dilip Vengsarkar and Syed Kirmani as players. I was pleased for Surinder because he had missed many opportunities in the past. Nine years' wait is a pretty long period for any cricketer to make his debut. Ironically, he should have been an automatic choice for the New Zealand and Australia tour in 1967 after a deplorable batting performance by India in England the same year.

To select a fresh team, the five wise men made the Irani Trophy contest equivalent to a trial match. The best Indian cricketers were included for the 'Rest of India' team, including Surinder, merely nineteen, vying for a place in the Indian team for the twin tour. His dynamic approach and scintillating batting display in the recent series against the Australian youth team had brought him a double hundred and 190 to refresh his father's exploits.

However, petty politics and selfish interests remained the hallmark of the selectors. A few feared losing their position if no player from his zone was selected, and what if Surinder produced another impressive performance? To deny the young Amarnath a chance to prove his worth, he was handed the responsibility of twelfth man for the Rest of India. The talented youngster was made to serve drinks and watch the proceedings from the dressing room!

However, where there's a will there's a way. After a long, excruciating delay, Surinder got his due. Despite scoring a century against Ceylon a few months back, he had to prove his ability once again. I knew from experience that the night before a debut was always restless; I pitied my brother. To be honest, I was also sailing in the same boat, but for a different reason: I was on a comeback trail. We brothers shared every conceivable plan and we felt it would be better not to share the room. This decision gave us space with other players and to absorb quite a few things on the tour.

Although the Indian team was in high spirits, the standard of umpiring through the series raised concerns. It was a period when quite a few venues around the world lacked facilities to telecast Test matches and the print media was quick to ignore poor decisions against the touring teams. The venues had limited cameras to spot dubious decisions. Overstepping by home fast bowlers was a common phenomenon and leg-before-wicket decisions in favour of the home team also tested the patience of the touring team's bowlers. Some umpires were already known to be biased, but they continued to officiate. I knew it was a thankless job and human beings made mistakes, but repeated blunders certainly aroused our suspicions.

To maintain uniformity on and off the field, the BCCI provided each member a set of flannels (shirts and pants), and cardigans, a lounge suit and a blue blazer. The BCCI had a shoestring budget. Because of the paucity of funds, dry-cleaning cricket whites was out of the question; the cheapest option was to locate a washing machine in every city. If one problem saved money, another made a mockery of the quality of the flannels. The perfect-fitting trousers shrunk after every wash to steadily rise above the ankle. This sight was not frowned upon but rather became a butt of jokes and reminded us of a famous Indian film star.

Bright sunshine and a brown strip in the middle of the green outfield made our eyes light up. On the contrary, it became an eyesore for the pace attack led by Richard Hadlee. New Zealand won the toss and elected to bat on a dry pitch. Seeing the conditions, the team needed no scientific knowledge about Indian pace bowlers' role with the new ball. The local media had been rather quick to judge our capabilities and gave us little chance of winning. Even our fielding was not spared—they placed us below local clubs. However, they did not realize that, except the spinners, the rest were agile fielders.

Finding conditions ripe and ready for exploitation, the three spinners, Prasanna, Venkat and Chandrasekhar, came into their element. Together, with brilliant support from close in and outfield fielders, wickets tumbled. It left the scornful press dumbfounded. Our hearts were filled with joy to see the ball turning in the pre-lunch session itself. Bishan Bedi must have truly missed this golden opportunity and I felt sorry for him. As the match progressed, every member of the team enjoyed proving the critics wrong. The deadly trinity of Prasanna, Venkat and Chandrasekhar made the New Zealand batsmen struggle. If any batsman survived the two off spinners, the freakish leg spinner made their life miserable. Not only did he bowl well with his polio-afflicted right arm, but he also surprised batsmen with nasty bouncers. If a batsman survived the shock, he invariably deceived him with a googly.

Wicketkeeping to Bhagwat Chandrashekhar was not an easy task, rather a nightmare. Farokh Engineer and Syed Kirmani testified in this regard. They hopped on their toes to collect deliveries and, at times, took an evasive action against those bouncing awkwardly towards their throat. Chandra was the only spinner to terrorize the batsman facing him and the wicketkeeper collecting the ball behind the stumps. He had many fine performances to his credit, but none could beat the match-winning effort at the Oval against England in 1971.

A man of few words, Chandra was jovial by nature. He was the only bowler in the international circuit to bowl with his right hand and throw with his left from the outfield into the gloves of the keeper. Once, in an interview, a foreign journalist asked him the reason for using his left arm for throwing and right for bowling. The response was simple but convincing. 'I use my right arm exclusively for bowling and the other for throwing. Any problem?' Chandra enjoyed listening to Hindi music, especially the melodious songs of the famous singer Mukesh. One could hear Mukesh's songs in the hotel room or Chandra happily humming in the hotel corridor or by the poolside. It did not surprise many to hear his soft voice singing songs during the water break on the cricket ground. He was one of Mukesh's greatest fans. When the famous singer passed way, Chandra flew to Bombay to attend his funeral.

The Kiwis danced to the tune of the Indian spinners, particularly Chandra and Prasanna, picking six and three wickets respectively. India took the honours of the day. Sunil Gavaskar opened the innings with Dilip Vengsarkar, but the partnership lasted only 16 runs. Surinder, being an aggressive and stylish left-hander, retained his favourite one drop slot. Unlike many nervous debutants, he was the very picture of confidence and showed no sign of apprehension. Even in the first unofficial Test match against Ceylon, I had watched him play pace and spinners with such authority that they squirmed while bowling to him. His early coaching by Papaji ensured that aggression remained the best mode of defence. It was highlighted during his innings at Auckland as well.

Surinder matched every stroke of Gavaskar's with such impunity that he looked like a Test match veteran. He was in a belligerent mood and punished all the bowlers, be it spin or pace. Batting bareheaded and with rolled-up sleeves, the top three shirt buttons open to expose his chest, he reminded me of my father. He made batting look so easy and all of us in the dressing room watched his performance in disbelief. He was severe on Richard Hadlee, especially his short-pitched deliveries. Time and again, he cut, pulled or hooked him to the fence. When fast bowlers pitched the ball up to him, he drove them elegantly through the covers. When Kiwi spinners operated, he danced down the track and punished them. He was like an expert conductor of an opera, revelling in the music of his bat.

The majority of batsmen playing their first Test or otherwise tend to get bogged down in the nineties as they near the hallowed milestone of a century—but not Surinder. He was so absorbed in his stroke play that he forgot he was batting on ninety-three. He ran down the wicket to left-arm spinner David O'Sullivan and lofted him with barely any effort over mid-on. The moment the ball rose high in the sky, all the players in the dressing room stood up in anxiety—but when it landed outside the boundary for a six, there was relief and jubilation in the dressing room. I was watching the proceedings through a pair of binoculars and saw Tom smiling. The next ball, he pushed for a single to complete a well-deserved hundred. My heart was filled with joy and I felt immensely proud to be an 'Amarnath'. This performance of father and son both scoring a Test century on debut set a world record!

The partnership between Surinder Amarnath (124) and Sunil Gavaskar was worth 204 runs. Surinder outscored his senior partner before he was dismissed, leaving Gavaskar to complete his well-deserved century too. This strong platform gave advantage to the lower-order batsmen, and I did exactly what was expected from me. I scored my first half-century in a Test match; it brought immense satisfaction. With a healthy lead under our belt, we knew this match was in our grasp. If Chandra tormented the Kiwis in the first innings, Prasanna spun a web around them in the second. His control on the flight and the vicious turn demoralized the home team. He captured one scalp after another to finish with a tally of eight wickets in the second innings and the match overall with eleven wickets.

Chandra's magic spell in the first innings (six wickets) was marred by debatable decisions by the umpires in the second innings; he managed only two victims. Normally a cool character on the field, he never argued with the batsmen or the umpires. However, these close calls frustrated him. The Indian fielders and bowlers had a hard time controlling their tempera. Chandra was also enraged at the denial and was left with his only alternative, which was to hit the stumps. Finally, after dismissing a batsman bowled out, Chandra turned and appealed to the umpire. The appeal caught the man in the white coat off guard. The baffled umpire replied, 'He's been bowled!'

'Yes, I know,' Chandra replied, 'but tell me whether he is out or not!'

India won the match by eight wickets to lead the three-match Test series.

While champagne flowed in the Indian dressing room, the New Zealanders plotted their revenge. We knew the following match would be on the green pitch, unless and until Indra devta, or the rain God, played His part again. Bedi's recovery and return to the team was a welcome sign. Our prayers were partially accepted and the match at Christchurch was frequently interrupted by rain. Although conditions favoured the New Zealand pace bowlers, our boys rose to the occasion. Collectively, we put up a decent score. When we took to the field, the pitch still retained its bounce and pace. It suited my kind of bowling and I bowled long spells with Madan Lal, taking four wickets while he got one more than me. The second Test match ended in a draw.

With India maintaining the lead in the series, we expected the hosts to go hammer and tongs against us. We arrived at Wellington for the final battle. The Basin Reserve was undoubtedly picturesque, surrounded by high hills and a lush green outfield. However, when we reached the venue for practice and peeped out from the dressing room window, we could not locate the central pitch. It merged with the outfield. It was only after the practice session that we saw the curator marking the crease to give us an indication. It was tailor-made to suit Hadlee, Cairns and Collinge.

The last match commenced under harsh conditions. We batted first and immediately ran into trouble. Our modest score of 220 disappointed us but we never lost hope. The next day, the city was hit by a severe cold wave and strong winds. When we ventured out to the field, we were frozen down to the bone. Adding to our woes were the woollens provided by the BCCI; the cardigans were made from cotton thread and the open field gave us little respite from the sharp, icy wind. Finding the Indian team in such a sorry condition, the team manager, Polly Umrigar, introduced a novel method to keep his boys warm. He offered the entire playing XI brandy with warm water. I was thoroughly amused to find the dressing room resembling a bar and the mood no less than that of a cocktail party.

The moment we gulped down the brandy, we immediately felt warmer. The mood became buoyant and spirits soared high. After a while, I felt a little tipsy. My confidence was nothing short of a lion's but with a slight difference—I could not roar! The New Zealand batsmen made good use of the conditions and made us toil. The longer we stayed on the field, the less effective we proved to be. I remember joking with another player, 'We may need a shot during the drinks break to keep us warm.' No matter how hard we tried to raise our morale, the conditions failed to improve and bring joy.

Bowling with the wind was comfortable but bowling against it was painful. The Indian pace bowlers hardly shined the ball on their way to the mark; both the ball and the hands remained in the pocket. I remember bowling against the wind and it was quite challenging. While running to deliver the ball, the velocity of the winds threw me back and, at times, my vision was blurred because my eyes were stinging. During one over, the wind froze my forehead and I had to leave the field.

For the first time, the Kiwis belted the spinners all over the park. Sunil Gavaskar, fielding at short leg, received a terrible blow; a full-blooded sweep shot crushed his cheekbone. He was rushed to the hospital for treatment and later shifted to America for further investigation. This was a period of no protective gear (a grilled helmet or shin guard) for close-in fielders, except an abdominal guard. He never fielded in the same position again.

In the earlier Test matches, we had overcome critics, opponents and umpires, but in the middle of this Test match another element was discovered—tampering with the conditions. According to ICC regulations, it was mandatory to mow the grass on the strip. However, on the third day, the curator ingeniously adjusted the blades of the grass-cutting machine a little too high. This factor became evident when the machine moved up and down the strip but hardly any grass was collected in the container. Dismayed and shocked, we simply threw our hands in the air. With our main opener, Gavaskar, ruled out due to injury, Surinder was pushed up the ladder to take his place. The juicy green-top pitch added to Richard Hadlee's advantage; he bowled a devastating spell, taking 7/23, and bundled us out for 81 runs to win the last Test match.

Only Surinder counter-attacked the fast bowlers to become the top scorer with 27 runs.

I had a reasonable series with the bat and the ball. Still, I was not satisfied with my performance. With the series over, my thoughts shifted to the Caribbean islands. I was told it had beautiful beaches, carefree people and a fine cricket culture. My biggest concern was how we would manage the battery of fast bowlers on the West Indies tour, when only one genuine pace bowler, Richard Hadlee, had made life so miserable for frontline batsmen.

5

WEST INDIES 1976

ALL THE EARLIER TOURS OF THE WEST INDIES WERE routed through Europe to the USA, before culminating in one of the island nations. Accordingly, we prepared ourselves. Travelling from Wellington to Barbados was like flying from one corner of the earth to another; no one had any clue about the route. Polly Umrigar (now manager) was a member of the Indian team that had travelled to the West Indies and England in the 1950s, but he was also clueless about the itinerary and the different time zones. Fortunately, we had a seasoned leader in Bishan; he took charge of the situation. The entire team followed him like meek schoolboys. It must have been some sight to see the sleep-deprived Indian team slumping on airport chairs. We travelled economy class; we ran to transfer desks at various airports to inquire about what we should do and where we should go next; we stood in the queues at check-in counters with a bundle of tickets to board different flights. We had no idea about the time or date. We were lost in the maelstrom of varying time zones.

The flights were exhausting. Most of us barely slept in the cramped economy class cabins. However, there were exceptions; some of the shorter players could stretch out more easily. On several occasions, the air hostesses gave us a polite nudge to serve breakfast, lunch or dinner, disrupting our sleep. At times, we were served similar meals twice on the same flight because of different time zones.

It took us a long time to reach Barbados—and what a relief it was when we finally arrived! We were dead tired and looked forward to stretching out on a comfortable hotel bed. While the fun-loving people waited to welcome us, the West Indies were making plans to salvage their pride; on their recently concluded tour of Australia, fast bowlers Dennis Lillee and Jeff Thomson had mauled their batsmen into submission, winning the series 5-1.

The next couple of days were spent catching up on sleep. However, I was still in flight mode in my dreams. Finally, when I ventured out, I was welcomed by a beautiful blue sky. The pleasant breeze, bright sunshine and blue seawater were indeed refreshing, compared to freezing Wellington. Barbados had a rich cricket history and the world of course knew of the exploits of the Three Ws (Weekes, Walcott and Worrell). How I looked forward to meeting Everton Weekes and Clyde Walcott! The third great, Frank Worrell, was no more, but I'd had the good fortune of spending time with him in New Delhi in 1966. I remember Papaji telling the family, especially us three sons, about a special guest coming for dinner. Meeting the legend was the experience of a lifetime and I recall how wonderfully he encouraged us to follow in our father's footsteps.

Another player on my list was cricket's greatest all-rounder, Sir Garfield Sobers. His domination of world cricket seemed like folklore. No doubt, his name, along with the Three Ws, was uttered with respect and admiration.

The exploits of fast bowlers Gilchrist, Hall and Griffith in the 1950s and early sixties were narrated to me by several Indian Test batsmen. Bouncers had been part and parcel of cricket, but Gilchrist unleashed a new weapon, the beamer, against Pankaj Roy in Bombay to send ripples through the Indian dressing room. While avoiding the red missile going past his head, Roy lost his balance; his cap and spectacles flew in different directions. The seasoned opening batsman was shaken beyond belief. With trembling hands, he adjusted both his cap and spectacles, but did not last long. However, the brave batsman scored 90 in the second innings. In Delhi, Chandu Borde scored a fine century; he survived a nasty bouncer from Griffith to tell the tale. He said the visibly shaken Rohan Kanhai, fielding at slip, came up to him and said, 'Maan, you owe me a drink tonight. I thought you were gone!'

We knew this series would be tougher than 1971. The obvious reason was that the West Indies had been humbled by Australia and they were desperate to salvage their reputation. Apart from that, memories of the series loss to India in 1971 had troubled them for years. The West Indies' cricket had found itself at a critical juncture; the captain along with several players were under the microscope. We were conscious that they would unleash their battery of fast bowlers against us.

The West Indian cricketers came from a group of independent island countries playing cricket as one unit, otherwise participating in the Olympics as individual nations. The combination of Holding, Roberts, Julien, Vanburn Holder and Daniel formed a potent attack, each trying to outclass the other in a healthy competition. Their batting was settled, more or less, beginning with Fredericks, Greenidge, Kallicharran, Richards, Lawrence Rowe and captain Clive Lloyd. However, the pressure on the home players was evident: perform or perish.

Our link with the people of Guyana and Trinidad dated back to the nineteenth century when the British Empire was at its zenith, and thousands of Indian labourers from Uttar Pradesh and Bihar were transported to work in the sugarcane plantations here, never to return home. They were offered little money and, later, forced to work beyond their contracts; so they, reluctantly settled down on foreign soil. To keep Indian traditions intact, temples were built at various locations and all the Hindu festivals were celebrated with gusto. No wonder, ethnic Indians outnumber the local population during the Test matches! Interestingly, ever since India first toured the West Indies in 1952-53, someone or the other from the touring party fell for a local maiden and settled down permanently, beginning with Subhash Gupte, Dicky Rutnagur (a journalist) and later Govind Raj from Hyderabad.

Would this tradition continue after this tour? This remained a hot topic amongst eligible bachelors. If so, who would be smitten remained a mystery. The Indian team boasted of seasoned performers in Bedi, Prasanna, Chandrashekhar and Viswanath, but none could match Sunil Gavaskar in the West Indies. He'd amassed a massive fan following since his memorable debut in 1971.

The opening match of the tour was against the strongest team of the Caribbean islands. There were hot discussions in the bars, restaurants and streets as to whether Gavaskar could contain the ferocity of the Windies' bowling attack and repeat his 1971 performance. The rest of the team members were equally eager to perform well and carry that confidence into this series.

We got a taste of the happy-go-lucky attitude of the people watching cricket. Rum and Coke flowed like water to enhance the effect of the steel band playing. Caribbean music was everywhere, on the ground and on the beaches; the atmosphere brought smiles to our faces too. However, our joy came to an abrupt end when we saw the wicket; it was solid, like a rock, with cracks, and it looked very, very good for pace bowling. Our fears turned into reality when the four-day match finished in less than three days, obviously not in our favour. The Barbados fast bowlers, especially Wayne Daniel conveyed what lay ahead for the Indian batsmen; their warning to us was crystal clear.

The outcome shocked our team management. They decided to seek the services of local fast bowlers in the nets. This move was nullified when several batsmen declined to face rookie bowlers. The reason: they not only bowled fast, but they also overstepped and tested some of the batsmen with bouncers! To avoid injury, Indian batsmen preferred the friendly medium-pace bowling of Madan, Solkar and me.

Since we stayed at one destination for a long time, the locals became our friends. We followed a simple philosophy: when in Rome, do as the Romans do. As soon as the sun set, we could hear Bob Marley's music playing in dozens of parties all over the beautiful island. The parties were, of course, full of music and drinks. This deadly combination led youths to the dancing floor, and we were no different, except we avoided hard drinks and sticked to beer. Bob Marley's music had its effect on us too, though in a different way. While the locals danced in rhythm, quite a few of us did not know how to dance. Unmindful, we developed our own style to send those around us hopping or scurrying for cover; the rest sought refuge in the comfort of the bar chairs!

The biggest handicap for some players was the English language, hence, maintaining long conversations was a difficult proposition. Bishan was aware of this. He encouraged each of us to go and practice the language. If Bishan found us seated, while ladies stood and spoke, he would yell at us in Punjabi to get up immediately and offer them a seat. Or if he found us simply listening and nodding our heads, he would sidle up to us and whisper, 'Badshao, bollo!' meaning: gentlemen, speak! These valuable tips taught us good manners and reduced our inhibitions; soon, we appeared to be rather seasoned campaigners. With a few mugs of beer down the throat, Bishan became Bish; it did not matter whether we spoke English, Pinglish or Hinglish! No wonder we entertained everyone around us! The young crowds flocked to us, listening to us intently, trying to understand the meaning of what we were saying, which we did not know either. When we laughed, they too joined the revelry in the same spirits; the fun stopped when we exhausted our limited vocabulary! With every passing moment, the drinks took their toll and words became inaudible; high-spirited laughter rapidly replaced coherent speech.

The three-star 'Britto Hotel', overlooking the beach, was comfortable as well as enjoyable. The facilities were marvellous and the staff courteous. This became evident when the manager of the hotel took extra care of Madan Lal. The rustic Amritsar boy presumed it to was a privilege to be served by the manager of the hotel early in the morning with tea, cookies and pastries. The service continued after the practice session and late into the evening. Madan Lal was enjoying exclusive service till this gentleman started touching his fingers while serving tea. Initially, Madan ignored it but the manager's infatuation for the muscular, good-looking Punjabi did not stop there. One fine morning, Madan was rudely woken from his sleep; a soft hand was on his cheeks. That was it; Madan Lal told him in Punjabi English: 'You will not get what you are looking for!' The way he narrated the incident in the dressing room had us doubled over with laughter!

The concept of television in the hotel room had not yet hit the deck. The latest news reached us through newspapers or the radio. We avoided reading the local newspapers or listening to sports bulletins for obvious reasons. Still, we came to know of an elegant athlete named Michael Holding and his fiery bowling. I remember seeing him for the first time from my hotel room; a tall, lean yet athletically built young man walking on the beach. It made me wonder: how could he bowl fast? Was the media trying to terrify us?

With a couple of days still to go for the first Test, our morale was boosted by the local radio station playing 'Sunil Gavaskar', a song. It was a fine tribute. However, the West Indian players were not amused and were still hell-bent on salvaging their pride after Lillee and Thomson had mauled them during the tour of Australia. They were like wounded tigers waiting to pounce on us.

The stadium was packed on the first day of the Test match; people in the general stands wore colourful outfits, while those in the pavilion enclosure seemed fashion-conscious. Barbados did not have a big stadium; it had a capacity of 12,000–15,000, and each stand was different in shade and style. What really caught my eye was a certain gentleman in a white outfit, dressed like some sort of king. He wore a big black hat, a white suit, white gloves and a flowing purple robe over it with medals pinned to it. He held a wooden stick in his right hand and swung it around, addressing the crowd. His theatrically regal gestures and speech entertained the crowd, and they couldn't help laughing.

The West Indies script was already written; it was a matter of time before we faced lethal fast bowling. Live telecasts of matches was not in vogue in this part of the world, but radio commentary gave a description of the proceedings and the latest score. The calypso batting depended on Clive Lloyd, Viv Richards, Lawrence Rowe, Kallicharran and the fearless opening batsman Roy Fredericks; the fast bowling was in the hands of Holding, Roberts and the seasoned Julien.

I distinctly remember when Sunil Gavaskar and Parthasarathy Sharma went to bat in the first innings—the entire Indian team came out of the dressing room to the sitting area. It was normal practice to enjoy Sunil Gavaskar dictating terms to the bowlers, but this time it was different. We wanted to see Michael Holding operating from the far end of the pavilion and quite a few members of the team started measuring his run-up from the dressing room. Our focus was his run-up and bowling action; nobody moved from their respective places till Holding finished his first over.

I had heard about the long run-up of fast bowlers in the 1960s, especially Wesley Hall's, almost touching the boundary rope near the sight screen and running in like a steam locomotive. Michael Holding also adopted a long run-up to the wicket; unlike Hall or Griffith, he was rhythmic and silky-smooth. Admirers gave him different names; the one that stuck was 'Rolls-Royce' and that ultimately became his nickname. His long strides were delightful to watch. I was told by one of the local journalists that if Holding had not chosen cricket, he would have qualified for Jamaica as an Olympic-level sprinter. Spellbound, the entire Indian dressing room admired him.

Earlier West Indies tours had left a permanent impression on the Indian players. The stories of the 1962 tour were conveyed to us by one of the members of that team. 'The Indian team had a wonderful time in the evenings, drinking and dancing. However, when Nari Contractor was hit on the head and lay bleeding on the pitch, select few batsmen were left shaking in the dressing room. They seemed reluctant to play; they were petrified of facing the fast bowling of Hall and Stayers. On the eve of the Test match, they reported sick or feigned injury. Nevertheless, there were a few brave hearts in the team. Polly Umrigar and Salim Durrani took on the challenge, and scored centuries in the fourth Test match. On the funny side, some batsmen responded positively to a half-hearted appeal; they preferred to walk off the pitch, which left the umpire confused and the fielders amused!

India's overseas team had three categories of players. On the top of the list were established players, followed by those vying for a place in the final eleven in the Test matches. The last category consisted of those who were content with playing side games, going sightseeing or collecting souvenirs as fond memories. Sunil Gavaskar's earlier performances had raised the bar quite high. He could not cope with the fast bowlers on Barbados's hard, bouncy pitch. Like all mortals, he failed in both the innings. He was dejected and his fans were crestfallen.

While the Indian batsmen failed, the hosts, of course, relished the conditions. I remember a mid-pitch conversation, though brief, between Clive Lloyd and Viv Richards; Lloyd had just hit Chandrashekar for a six but was not happy with the stroke. In a typical Calypso accent, he said, 'Maan, the ball hit the toe of my bat,' gesturing to the area where the ball had made contact. I was aghast; the ball had travelled a long distance and, in fact, had bounced on the roof of one of the general stands. I wondered: if Lloyd had middled the ball, it would have vanished in the ocean! I shook my head in disbelief.

While the ball was being retrieved, another incident came flashing to my mind. Clive Lloyd, on his last tour to India in 1974, was batting against North Zone at Jalandhar. Rajinder Goel was a successful left-arm spinner in domestic cricket. His ability to stop the flow of runs was known to all; he was introduced by Bishan Bedi for the same purpose. However, the powerful straight drives of the tall, lanky, bespectacled batsman hurt his hands and punctured his confidence. The fear of injury got the better of him and he started moving back after delivering the ball, instead of moving forward in the follow-through.

This confusion put him in the firing line many times; the powerful straight drives came back at lightning speed and hit his ankle. While Goel jumped in agony, a bemused Bishan laughed, then later consoled him and kept him from one end. He hoped Goel would provide a breakthrough. Soon, as expected by Bishan, Lloyd jumped out of the crease to a tossed-up delivery, only to find it short in length. But he still went through with the shot; the ball flew straight towards Goel for a return catch! The wicketkeeper, slip fielder and Bishan jumped in excitement, anticipating a wicket. But, much to everyone's dismay, the bowler moved his hands away and the ball hit the sight screen after one bounce. At the end of the over, I asked Goel why he did not take the catch. He replied, 'Jimmy, the ball came with such force that if I had attempted a catch, it would have taken both my hands to the fence. I want to play cricket for a few more years.' Clive Lloyd was one of the hardest hitting batsmen in the world.

India lost the Barbados Test not because of destructive pace bowling but because of our poor handling of the spinners, Holford and Jumadeen. The pressure to take advantage of slow bowlers after facing express deliveries led to the downfall of many of our batsmen. The bounce and speed of the fast bowlers were phenomena we had never previously encountered in our career; at times, the ball hit the bat before we even realized it, while others sailed over our heads like missiles. With no modern-day protective equipment like helmets, arm or chest guards available, and no rules of one bouncer per over, we were forced to face a series of short-pitch deliveries. Under these circumstances, it was natural to target the spinners to amass some runs. However, the strategy proved counterproductive.

I also remember facing Michael Holding at his best; he was quick in the air and off the wicket. While facing him, my footwork could not match the express deliveries. Before I could react, the ball contacted the bat. At times, I wanted to play on the off side, but the impact of the ball turned the blade inward, enabling me to pick a single on the leg side. Honestly, I did not know how to hold the bat more firmly or cope with such blistering pace.

In the second innings, I tried to hoist the left-arm spinner Jumadeen out of the ground, but I lost my wicket. The moment I walked into the changing room, Bishan Bedi blasted me for giving it away. This dressing-down made me understand my mistake. I was made to realize that nothing comes easy at the international level; one had to fight for every run or wicket. If I had to survive on the international circuit, I had to occupy the crease no matter how torrid it got against the fast bowlers. I promised myself not to gift my wicket away so cheaply.

Our next destination was Trinidad and many senior players were excited. It was considered a sort of home away from home. The place was cosmopolitan, with Indian culture in evidence practically everywhere we went. What amazed me most was how well Trinidad jelled with the calypsos. The famous Trinidad carnival reminded us of a certain Brazilian festival. The colourful costumes and samba dancers' moves were titillating. The music greatly enlivened the atmosphere, and people drank and made merry from dusk till dawn. I was told that even cricket took a back seat during these festivities. The touring teams were fascinated; everyone wanted to participate in the proceedings and enjoy the atmosphere. A long break from cricket became a trend during Caribbean tours.

Away from the razzmatazz, I was told that centuries-old beliefs continued on and remained an integral part of the culture of Indian settlers. For generations, marriages were solemnized after the approval of the parents and divine intervention. If a boy liked a girl and wanted to marry her, he had to take the girl to the highest point of a hill and look for a sign of divine approval. If her hair flew, it was a signal of acceptance, otherwise not. Although they were dedicated to their country, allegiances changed on the cricket ground. Indian blood was thicker than national loyalty.

The wicket at Trinidad was known to make batsmen comfortable; as the match progressed, it assisted the spinners. These factors boosted the confidence of the two little masters, the spinners and, ultimately, the rest of the team. Past experience was likely to come in handy. Despite losing the first Test match, our morale was high because of the conditions at Trinidad. There was one player in particular who was eager to restore his reputation.

We were put up at a three-star motel with basic facilities. On this tour, first-class matches preceded Test matches at the same venue. This gave us some idea of the wicket and the atmosphere. Queen's Park Oval had been a happy hunting ground for Indians both on and off the field. Fine performances in the last three Test matches by the touring Indian team left an indelible mark on the Indian diaspora. The vociferous support of the local Indians at the ground invariably elevated the spirits of the team.

Queen's Park Oval was the biggest venue as far as capacity was concerned, accommodating around 30,000 people. The picturesque hills and palm trees added a touch of romance to the setting; each stand was decorated with colourful crowds; rum, beer, whisky, loud music and rhythmic bodies captivated the crowd. Each sip of rum, whisky or beer made them louder, but they remained courteous and friendly. Just outside the boundary rope was the familiar face of Ram Bhaiya, ever ready to give our bowlers a piece of advice.

The first day of the match was washed out. The West Indies won the toss and elected to bat. For a change, Madan Lal and I gave India an early breakthrough. Madan removed Roy Fredericks and I bagged the wicket of Lawrence Rowe to provide the Indian spinners a platform to spin a web around the West Indian batsmen. Viv Richards, also known as Smokey Joe, replaced Lawrence Rowe. Despite his stature, I knew every batsman is vulnerable in the early stages of the innings. I asked Bishan to strengthen the slip cordon and place a fielder at silly point. The last request startled the captain; he threw his hands up and said, 'Jimmy, are you serious?' It was simply a ploy to put pressure on Richards; he survived the over, smiling and appreciating my effort.

Once Bishan had the ball in his hand, he crafted a web so strong and effective that one batsman after another fell into his trap. The Indian captain took five wickets and Chandra took two; the West Indians were ultimately dismissed for 241. Viv Richards stood tall amongst the ruins with a century but not before getting a reprieve from the local umpire (a man of Chinese descent). Richards had gone past the half-century mark and his team was still in deep trouble. At this stage, Bishan enticed him with a flighted delivery, beating Richards with a vicious turn. Before he could regain his footing in the crease, the wicketkeeper had removed the bails.

It was a big wicket for us. However, our jubilation was ruined by the leg umpire, Sang Hue, wearing dark glasses; he rejected the appeal. The close-in fielders were bewildered with the decision; they demonstrated their anger using unparliamentary language. Others threw their floppies on the ground in frustration, while the fine leg fielder ran towards the umpire for clarification. Bishan stood in disbelief, scratching his beard and watching the drama unfold. Later, he pacified the boys with a snide remark in Punjabi, 'Koi gal nahi, agli wari sahee,' meaning, 'Don't worry; next time, we will get him.'

After Bishan completed the over, he too could not hold back his disappointment; he went to the umpire in question and asked him about the decision. The umpire was frank and brief.

He said, 'Bishan, you are here for a short time, but I have to live here!' Richards scored 130 before Bishan could get his revenge.

When we batted, the low bounce and easy pitch gave little assistance to the fast bowlers to trouble Indian batsmen. They were rendered useless by Gavaskar, scoring a fine century to restore his reputation after the double failure in Barbados. Brijesh Patel also scored an elegant century and the rest of the batting clicked to put up 402 for the loss of five wickets, at which point Bishan declared and put our opponents in the ring. With a large lead and time in our favour, we had a solid grip on this match. Since the ball was turning, the spinners became unplayable. In the second innings, we took wickets at frequent intervals and we looked set to win this match. However, the tailenders survived several confident appeals and they ended up saving the match for their team.

We returned to the pavilion frustrated and angry. I was told that during one of the Test matches in Australia, Michael Holding was so upset with a decision of an umpire that he sat down on the pitch and refused to go back to his run-up. Finally, Clive Lloyd consoled him with a few encouraging words. We faced a similar situation here. The West Indies batsmen got the benefit of doubt more often than us. It shocked me, but a senior member of the team told me that this was nothing new; this remark only baffled me further.

Our batsmen returning to form, however, gave us hope and confidence to counter the pace in the remaining Test matches and repeat the result of 1971. Our performance brought optimism and a smile to the faces of our supporters. We had a few days' rest before flying to our next destination. By now, the fan following of the Indian team had touched new heights. They came in large numbers to pack our suitcases, offered us home-made food and gifts, and they also drove us around town for shopping. It was genuine love for the Indian team. Many of these diehard fans were aware they would not get another opportunity to see us and so they wanted to really maximize their time with us.

We flew to another British colony, Guyana, where Indians had been settled for generations. They too had come looking for greener pastures but failed to return home, and so ended up living here. Beautiful and green, it was near the Dutch colony Suriname, which had little cricket history. The moment we landed, we were greeted by rain. It reminded everyone of the Bombay monsoon. The ground was flooded and we were confined to our hotel rooms. When the day was finally called off after much delay, the possibility of the entire Test match meeting the same fate became evident.

At this stage, the two cricket boards held a backdoor parley. To bail out the West Indies' cricket board from their financial crisis, shifting the match to India's hunting ground remained a strong possibility. When this news was conveyed to us by the manager and the captain, we were delighted but waited patiently for the confirmation. The good news arrived during the team meeting; it brought back smiles to everyone's faces (the broadest on Gavaskar's). It seemed as if destiny was giving us another opportunity to counter the West Indian pace attack on a batsman-friendly wicket; we were thrilled.

The result of the contest against the West Indies was linked to the pride of ethnic Indians in Trinidad. They prayed for our success because the Indian team's defeat meant a torturous future; the locals would taunt them with pinching remarks. The news of the third Test match relocating to Queen's Park Oval was celebrated by the Indian community. They had fond memories of the last Test, and looked forward to supporting the Indian team with greater vigour and numbers.

When we landed in Trinidad, a large Indian diaspora welcomed us; handshakes, broad smiles and a few pictures with the fans made the atmosphere congenial. We boarded the coach, and looked forward to taking the old route to the motel we had stayed in; instead, the team coach drove us to the five-star Holiday Inn. Baffled, we looked at each other, till Bishan's broad grin spilled the beans; he said, 'Boys, this is our new destination.' Later, we came to know that the manager, Polly Umrigar, and Bishan had applied immense pressure on BCCI officials to upgrade the team's hotel for a more comfortable stay. Normally, such demands would have fallen on deaf ears. However, our extraordinary performance in the second Test match convinced the BCCI.

Due to torrential rains in Guyana and the late decision to shift the match, the groundmen had little time to prepare a fresh track for this match. Under these circumstances, we knew they would simply sprinkle water and roll the pitch to make it fit for the match. Dry conditions and bright sunshine were unlikely to bind the surface for long; it was likely to favour our spinners and batsmen.

The West Indies won the toss and batted first on what looked like an ideal track for batting. Madan and I had a small role to play with the new ball; if we picked a wicket or two, it was a bonus. We had been selected for our batting. Since the New Zealand tour, I had batted lower in the order, but the exclusion of Surinder for this match prompted the team management to promote me. They felt I had the ability to play the hook and pull shot better than other batsmen. Later in my life, I occupied this slot and faced many hostile bowlers around the world.

It was a new experience, facing Holding with a hard new ball. The memories of the previous Test were like a bad dream; he had single-handedly destroyed the Indian batting. The low bounce and slow pace of the wicket caused no hindrance to Michael Holding. Later in my career, I faced the best fast bowlers (except Dennis Lillee), but Michael Holding was a class above Jeff Thomson, Richard Hadlee, Andy Roberts, Malcolm Marshall, Bob Willis, Ian Botham, Wasim Akram and Imran Khan. He reminded me of Cassius Clay, better known as Muhammad Ali, and the famous song, 'Float like a butterfly and sting like a bee!' He picked six wickets to overshadow a Viv Richards century in the first innings.

Sensing another victory, the West Indies went for quick runs. Kallicharran redeemed his reputation with a delightful century and Lloyd declared, giving his bowlers plenty of time to dismiss India. Keeping in mind the nature of the pitch, the West Indies had played only two fast bowlers (Andy Roberts missed this match due to an ankle injury) and three spinners, an unusual combination. Padmore, Jumadeen and Imtiaz Ali had a long spell in the first innings, but made little impact on the Indian batsmen. In fact, it was Holding who caused the maximum damage. With enough time at their disposal, the West Indies looked forward to wrapping up the series.

When Clive Lloyd declared and set India a stiff target of 406 runs to win this Test in almost two days, we had a task on our hands. While walking to the pavilion, I met an elderly gentleman. He smiled and said, 'Maybe history will repeat itself.' I had no idea about the reference. Later, I learned it was about the Test match against England in 1968. Garry Sobers was captain and Clive Lloyd a team member. Fifteen minutes before declaration, Sobers asked his players if three hours was sufficient to bundle out England. Most responded that another half an hour would have been better. Interestingly, England's run rate was 40 runs per hour and a target of 215 seemed an uphill task to win the match. However, England romped home with seven wickets to spare.

Clive Lloyd was confident that Michael Holding would repeat the first innings performance. Only Don Bradman's invincible Australians had achieved a similar target (404) against England at Leeds in 1948. Since then, no team had emulated the feat. Considering our dismal performances in Barbados and in the first innings here, Lloyd did not place us Indians in the same category. He was overconfident of victory and wanted to wrap up the series in front of this huge crowd of Indian supporters. Memories of David Holford's five wickets in Barbados, Holding's destructive spell and reminiscences of West Indian spinners bowling well in the second Test match set complacency in the rank and file.

Undoubtedly, time, conditions and a big lead favoured the bowlers on a decaying surface. However, the difference between the Indian spinners and Caribbean spin bowlers was vast and visible. While Clive Lloyd depended heavily on Michael Holding to provide an early breakthrough, we were equally determined to wear him down. In the earlier Test matches, rest day was marked after the third day's play, but, for some strange reason, it was taken after the fourth day in this one. By then, India was placed comfortably, losing just one wicket, with Gavaskar unbeaten on a century.

Clive Lloyd was now a worried man. He was expecting a few more wickets from his spinners but clearly his planning had gone astray. He knew Gavaskar had immense concentration and the capacity to play incredibly long innings. I was happy to occupy the crease and frustrate the bowlers. To be honest, we were not chasing the target, but rather trying to save the Test match. My job at number three was to seal one end, no matter if runs merely trickled from my bat. Though it may sound strange, I smelled the leather more often than hitting the ball. Normally in a big partnership, batsmen exchanged a few words or encouraged each other, but Gavaskar and I hardly spoke a word, except for maybe a brief smile every now and then. The only time we heard each other was when either of us called for a run or more.

On the eve of rest day, I decided to skip the usual parties; I felt a little odd, for some reason. The next day too I stayed in my room or by the poolside, all by myself. I loved calypso music, more for its beat than its lyrics. Despite music humming in my ears and India sitting pretty, there remained a strange feeling of uneasiness in me. I felt something sensational was due to happen—but what that would be, I had not the slightest clue.

Crowds came in large numbers on the last day to witness the tussle. India got the first shock; Gavaskar was dismissed early in the morning. Was it the first sign of a possible repetition of our first innings? Many of our fans in the crowd started abandoning the stadium to avoid any taunts from the locals. If one little master was dismissed, another replaced him. Gundappa Viswanath was as good a batsman as Gavaskar. He was a good timer of the ball and left many bowlers flabbergasted with his wristy strokes. Very rarely had these two batsmen scored centuries in the same innings. The good news for me in the middle was that I had a partner who was jovial and spoke regularly to me after each over. I certainly felt less alone!

Lloyd operated spinners most of the time to give some rest to Michael Holding. He used him as a shock bowler in spells of four to five overs at the most. Bernard Julien was no threat to the Indian batsmen, with a friendly pace and bounce. At lunchtime, a happy Bishan put his arm around my neck and asked me to carry on with the good work, giving the impression that he was content with a draw. On the contrary, Clive Lloyd was still keen to win. After each over, however, one could see the frustration and body language becoming more explicit with mounting rage. The laughter was replaced by snide remarks and smirks. The best remark came after lunch during the drinks break. Visibly frustrated, Holding came up to me and said, 'Why are you hanging around and playing slow? If you are unable to play strokes, you should go back to the dressing room.' It was the first sign of West Indian nerves cracking.

The soft, worn-out ball, slow pitch and defensive field made scoring difficult for us. I was simply carrying out the skipper's instructions and was in no hurry to accelerate the run rate. Vishwanath and I were quite content and happy to collect runs without any undue risk. We did not realize the healthy partnership we had stitched until teatime because we never looked at the scoreboard; we simply enjoyed batting and complimenting each other. When both of us walked into the dressing room, the mood was buoyant and the atmosphere lively. Bishan was happy and kept repeating the same sentence, 'Just stay there.'

Cricketers by nature are superstitious and I was no different; I kept my pads on during the tea break. The Gray-Nicolls bat that Bishan had given me was turning out to be a lucky charm, tucked between my pads. This gift was highly appreciated because only a handful of cricketers had contracts with the English manufacturers and Indian bats lacked a similar punch. Even cricket shoes of quality were hard to find till a manufacturer in Jalandhar copied the design of the boots worn by Garry Sobers. I had bought a pair of those spikes in Australia while playing for Indian Schoolboys in 1968-69. However, these boots withered away on rough Indian surfaces. I approached a local manufacturer in Jalandhar, and he promised to make it on order and later gave it the name 'Firefly'.

Firefly was ankle-high and made from soft leather with a seasoned leather sole. To give a firm grip, half-inch 'blackhead' nails were fixed to the sole. Interestingly, if any nail came off, only a cobbler could fix it, using a small iron cap and a hammer. The batting boots were also ankle-high, made from soft leather, but had crepe soles; three small round nails fixed on a small piece of leather was under the toe area. These nails came handy to mark the guard. Unfortunately, leather-based bowling boots became too heavy on rain-affected grounds. Fortunately, manufacturers in England replaced them with synthetic soles. Soon, the concept of ankle-high boots changed to comfortable shoes. Still, most Indian cricketers preferred rubber or crepe soles to field on hard and dusty grounds.

After the tea interval, Clive Lloyd opted for a second new ball to break the partnership, which was growing at an alarming rate. I knew, if we survived the new ball for half an hour, that there was an outside chance to actually reach the target. The West Indies missed the presence of the injured Andy Roberts and we knew Michael Holding could not bowl a long spell. The sight of a new ball lit up Vishwanath's eyes and he smiled at this mistake. Hitting the old ball hard presented a risk while trying for boundaries.

Clive Lloyd wanted both of us to dance to the tune of a new red cherry; instead, he faced the heat from the flashing blade of the little master from Mysore (Mysuru). He was very severe on short-pitched deliveries, cutting or flicking off his hips with minimum effort but maximum result. The ball raced to the fence at lightning speed. Holding's first over produced three boundaries, which gave Lloyd a real shock. Suddenly, the floodgates opened and the scoreboard ticked with a speed that baffled the home crowd; their eyes nearly popped out in disbelief. The tide had changed course.

The rapid ticking of the scoreboard was of course appreciated by the vociferous local Indians; drums beat harder and the fans cheered even louder. I simply admired the little master's class and confidence from the non-striker's end. After each productive stroke, he would gleefully walk a few steps on the pitch, tap the imaginary spot softly, look into the eyes of the slip fielders and wait for the next delivery. While I was content with singles or the odd boundary, Vishwanath played his strokes with utter abandon. The writing was on the wall; India was galloping towards the target. The prospect of us winning the match excited the gathering. The Indian dressing room was hyper, almost hysterical, with each stroke; they clapped, jumped and roared as we inched closer to the target to rewrite cricket history.

The shock was visible on the opposing team and the expression of each West Indian player spoke louder than words; drooped shoulders reflected sagging spirits. They feared a harsh reaction from local supporters; so much so that they refused to retrieve the stationary ball beyond the boundary rope. It was happily tossed back to the fielder by Indian supporters. The scenario had clearly changed.

In the morning, after Gavaskar's dismissal, quite a few Indian supporters had vacated the stadium; a similar exodus was visible now—but, this time, it was by the local West Indians, making a beeline for the exit gate.

The possibility of a historical victory spread like wildfire through radio commentary and all the vacant seats were immediately occupied by proud ethnic Indians. They cheered and danced, proud of their heritage. The sudden change in the atmosphere made it look as if we were playing in our backyard. I gave Vishwanath as much strike as possible to dominate the proceedings. He scored a brilliant century, but a misunderstanding cost him his wicket and he was run out. By then, a comfortable platform had been laid for the incoming batsman.

Brijesh Patel walked briskly to the crease to give an indication of a man in form. He did not take time to make his intentions clear; he bludgeoned the spinners with scant respect for their name or record. The stunned bowlers and fielders simply had no answer to his attack. It seemed as if he was the senior partner and I had just joined him, collecting singles to rotate the strike. With the scoreboard reading 392 and India needing 14 runs for a victory, we decided to enjoy the proceedings taking singles; how I looked forward to walking to the dressing room, undefeated after a marathon innings! At that stage, I underestimated Lloyd's agility in the covers and called for a quick single, only to be run out by a direct throw. I almost collapsed seeing my dream shattered.

Grudgingly, I walked back to the pavilion; Bishan stood at the entrance and hugged me tightly to express his gratitude. The entire team surrounded me, each thumping my back or shoulders in appreciation. Silently, I waited for the golden moment to arrive. When India achieved the milestone, celebrations commenced from the stands. Acknowledging the support of the ethnic Indians, I moved inside and removed my pads. Swelling with emotion, I covered my face with a towel and tears instantly rolled down my cheeks!

For the first time, I realized the importance of representing my country and tasting victory against all odds. I had done my job to perfection but I missed those golden moments in the middle. Nevertheless, history had been created; celebrations began with loud cheers and hugs all around. One heard the sweet sound of corks popping from the champagne bottles; champagne flowed like water and a few exuberant players sprayed it on Bishan and Polly Umrigar to bring big broader smiles on their faces. At that moment, two different worlds remained separated by a thin wall; one dressing room was buoyant with victory and the other stunned by defeat. Later, I was told by a local journalist that Lloyd was so livid with the spinners that he asked, 'How many runs do you need to dismiss a team?'

Packing the kit bag that day was not easy; everything was strewn around. It was the messiest dressing room. Happy and content, we reached the hotel, but there was no place to park the coach. The parking lot was full of Indian fans and the lobby was also jammed. With no other option, we walked towards the entrance of the lobby to be encircled by the crazy fans, each jostling for a photo. Soon, half an hour passed, but no player objected. I had never before seen so many young and beautiful girls in one place. After obliging as many as I could with autographs and photographs, I took the elevator to my room for some much-needed rest. The moment the elevator door opened, I was mobbed by another set of maidens; the entire corridor was packed with girls and boys. Each scrambled for autographs and photos. Some overenthusiastic girls planted kisses all over my cheeks, shirt and hands. The scene was no different outside my room and it was impolite to shut the door.

Polly Umrigar was a seasoned cricketer and had played in this country too, and he simply could not believe his eyes. He had never seen such adulation in his playing days. The celebration did not end here; these youngsters insisted on parading us through the city centre in open Chevrolet cars. Happily, we obliged; the town centre wore a festive look, with ethnic Indians waving and running after our cars. Time flew and our fatigue evaporated in thin air.

The defeat of the West Indian team did not go down well with their critics. They blamed Lloyd's tactics for the defeat; they wanted his head on a platter. He may have been deposed if he had not already been appointed captain for the entire series. Word spread that if the home team did not win the following Test, Lloyd would face the music. The warning was amply clear: win or leave! Henceforth, the policy of three spinners became history and they went back to pace as their main weapon.

Our last destination was Jamaica, the birthplace of Bob Marley. He gave music a new direction. His long hair and calm expression became his trademark, though understanding the lyrics was difficult for me; yet, I found his tunes and beats quite soothing. Kingston was the hotbed of music lovers, and one could see tall and well-built Jamaicans carrying equally big two-in-one music systems on their shoulders. Their colourful headgear and mystical appearance, and their rhythmic walk, in conjunction with the beat of the music, could mesmerize anyone.

The match against Jamaica was our last first-class match before the final showdown. Since the series stood even, the West Indies' selectors decided to rest Michael Holding, though he represented Jamaica in the domestic first-class matches. It was a clever ploy not to expose their trump card on the fast wicket against the Indian line-up again. I was also rested for this game to give one last opportunity to the bench players to perform and be considered for the final Test match. I had observed on this tour that some players were happy to play side games but dreaded facing the actual litmus tests. One particular batsman had played the home series reasonably well; he also batted well in the first innings of this match and continued his fine form in the second innings as well. During drinks, I was sent with a message from the captain that he must get his hundred, as he stood a good chance to make it to the playing XI for the final Test match.

I did as I was told and returned. The moment I stepped into the pavilion, a big roar forced me to turn around. I saw the same batsman walking towards the pavilion and Bishan furious at his poor shot selection. By the time he reached, I was sitting in the dressing room to hear his version. The first sentence he spoke was not of remorse but of relief. He said, 'Who wants to face Holding and company on this fast, bouncy wicket?' I was aghast at such a statement; I thought every player on this tour was itching to secure a berth in the team, but here we had a feeble heart in our ranks.

During this match, we watched the curator consistently rolling the adjoining pitch. On close inspection, I noticed a peculiar phenomenon at short of a length, in line with the stumps. Upon close examination, it seemed like a ridge. It remained intact on the day of the Test match too. The wicket felt rock-hard with patches of green grass. The spikes left no mark on the surface, proving that it had been especially prepared under the instruction of the home captain for Michael Holding, Vanburn Holder, Bernard Julien and Wayne Daniel. Lloyd was on trial and it was his last chance to redeem his sinking popularity as captain. This match was also special for the local boy, Holding, playing for the first time at home. There was no reminder needed for how charged up he would be to perform in front of a home crowd!

Before the Jamaica Test match, players would mingle and chat over a glass of beer. The defeat in Trinidad, however, had changed that concept. Camaraderie was replaced with hostility. The home team looked belligerent and gave us cold glares as if we had committed a crime by defeating them. This strange behaviour forced us to conclude that they had been instructed to act in such an obnoxious manner. Were we at war or were we playing cricket? No one had a clue. It was certainly not the gentleman's game we were taught. When Bedi went for the toss for the last time in the series, there were no handshakes or any words exchanged. The change in attitude showed another side of their character. They refused to smile back or respond to our greetings. Was it amateurish or professional? Hard to say. But it was fairly obvious now that the friendly remarks and jokes were history.

Clive Lloyd won the toss and asked India to bat first on the freshly prepared track. This ground was smaller in size and capacity, compared to Queen's Park Oval in Trinidad. It had temporary stands and a small wooden pavilion reminiscent of the colonial era. The wall on one side of the ground was painted white, acting as a sight screen, while the other side had a fixed white canvas sheet supported by poles, tied using jute ropes.

The commentators' box was not enclosed; a table and a few chairs were placed above the sight screen for a clear view. Behind them were rows of chairs to accommodate spectators, regretfully moving any time between the overs. The height of the sight screen was not good enough to keep the tall, lanky figures of Holding and company within the white screen. The distraction due to movement behind the sight screen forced the Indian batsmen to back away many times. This action received an adverse reaction from the crowd, booing and blaming us for wasting time. But we did not wish to sail in the same boat as Nari Contractor. Little did they understand, when a five-and three-quarter ounce (163 grams) hard leather ball is hurled at over 90 miles an hour on a bouncy, fast track, the weight of the ball multiplies greatly. With no protective gear like helmets, chest or arm guards available, any blow could prove fatal.

The Indian openers surprised the pundits, the large crowd, the fast bowlers, Clive Lloyd and the rest of the West Indies team with their resolve. Although Michael Holding got a nasty kick from the ridge, forcing the opening batsmen to rise on their toes to defend or avoid the ball going past the nose, they performed their job reasonably well. When the ball went past the Indian batsmen's face at lightning speed, many people threw their hands in the air in awe. The proceedings were not meant for weak hearts. The way the ball was collected by the wicketkeeper at head height gave an indication of the kind of bounce and pace in the pitch. Yet, the Indian opening pair stood their ground and showed great courage in the face of a lethal attack. Gavaskar continued his good form and scored a fine half-century before Holding uprooted his stumps.

I joined Anshuman Gaekwad and held the fort, despite receiving several blows around the ribcage. India finished the day with the loss of one wicket: Gaekwad remained undefeated at 58 and I on 25. The press and commentators left no opportunity to criticize Lloyd's decision to put India to bat.

The next morning, we noticed that the cracks on the pitch had opened wider to allow the index finger to slip in easily. It looked like a parched base of a dried lake, cracks all over the pitch. It was certainly a new experience for me; I had never come across such a surface in my career. Although Bishan decided to go for the mandatory rolling, I doubt it had any effect on the surface. The first ball of the day by Michael Holding flew at a lightning pace to the wicketkeeper, Murray, standing thirty meters behind the stumps. He had to jump high in the air to gather it above his head. This was the first indication that all the moisture in the pitch had evaporated.

The previous day, moisture on the pitch had not allowed the ball to skid and gather speed, but the conditions had changed. Seeing this, Clive Lloyd instructed the slip cordon to move a few yards back and he signalled the bowler to come round the wicket. It shocked everyone, including Gaekwad and me. We knew sighting the ball from this angle would be challenging. The sight screen could not be adjusted to spot the ball. Added to this were the hanging branches of a tree above the sight screen, occupied by enthusiastic spectators in multicoloured shirts, constantly shifting to get a better view, which drew our attention.

The strategy of bowling round the wicket was nothing new in cricket. In the Ashes series of 1932, it was effectively used by the English captain Douglas Jardine, adopting the infamous bodyline tactics in Australia. It did not take long for us to realize the intention of the home team. A series of short-pitched deliveries were directed at the body to make us fear injury. Lloyd thought the 'fear factor' would work and the Indians would retreat to expose the stumps; but he was disappointed. Holding had an exceptionally long run-up; each time he reached his mark, the crowd sitting on the branches incited him to bowl with hostility. I was taken by surprise by a snooter of a delivery; I tried my best, but the ball touched the shoulder of the bat and fell safely into the hands of Julien at backward short leg. I was angry at having become complacent and losing my wicket at 39.

The chanting from the crowd released more adrenaline in the fast bowlers, who bowled aggressively. Every time the ball hit the batsman, the fielders and insensitive supporters applauded the bowler. Vishwanath was also tested with a series of short-pitch deliveries, till one crushed his index finger and flew to backward short leg for an easy catch. He threw down his bat, removed his glove to check the damage and found it fractured beyond repair; he was retired to the hospital. The chants of 'get him!' by drunken spectators in the cricket stadium immediately made one think of the Colosseum in ancient Rome, when gladiators were encouraged by the bloodthirsty crowd to finish off their battered opponents.

Here, the contest was one-sided. Missiles were fired from both ends, giving little relief to the Indian batsmen. There seemed to be a competition amongst the West Indian fast bowlers, each trying to hit the batsman hard. Surprisingly, the two umpires stood like mute spectators; they never cautioned the fast bowlers of their dangerous ploys, they never checked the bowlers overstepping the crease. Another centurion of the second Test match, Brijesh Patel, was subjected to similar punishment. Taking his cue from fellow fast bowlers, Vanburn Holder hit Patel on his mouth. While the batsman held his mouth in agony, blood oozed out and drenched his shirt. The two main batsmen had been left incapacitated for the remaining part of the match.

The first session of the second day proved we were not playing cricket; we were at war. Despite these setbacks, Gaekwad kept one end secure. His determination and bravery were, at times, painful to watch. He endured several blows to his body but did not flinch. This frustrated the West Indian fast bowlers and the inebriated supporters even more. The Indian dressing room was seething with anger but there was nothing we could do. Unchecked, the fast bowlers sprayed each batsman with a series of bouncers, some hitting them, others going past the nose or sailing over the head of the batsmen and the wicketkeeper.

The Indian dressing room was already short by three players, all being attended to by the doctors. The previous night, Surinder underwent an emergency surgery for appendicitis; he found the company of Patel and Vishwanath. Then came another shock for us: Gaekwad was caught in no man's land defending a rising delivery from Michael Holding. It squeezed past his defence to crush his left ear. The nasty blow forced Gaekwad to clinch his left ear in pain. The frame of his spectacles lay shattered on the pitch and he was writhing in pain. The close-in West Indian fielders refused to comfort him. They stood around chewing gum with hands on their hips. It reflected poor sportsmanship and indeed poor character.

Polly Umrigar was concerned at the unfortunate scene unfolding before him. He did not want the Nari Contractor episode to be repeated, so he advised the retired hurt Gaekwad to undergo a check-up; now, we had a fourth player admitted in the same hospital. India managed to get 306 runs for the loss of six wickets, when Bishan decided enough was enough; he declared the innings at that score. He was aware that even the tailenders would not be spared by the hostile fast bowlers, so he played it safe with his timely declaration. Twenty-one no balls and twelve wides were registered in the total, indicating how far the bowlers had overstretched to target the Indian batsmen. What about those deliveries that were overlooked by the umpires? It could have doubled the recorded number of illegal deliveries.

We wanted to pay them back in the same coin but did not have any fast bowler to match their arsenal. Madan Lal and I hardly sat in that category; we failed to trouble any of the West Indian batsmen. However, the Indian spinners came back with a vengeance to restrict the strong batting line-up till Michael Holding used a long handle and scored a half-century in front of the home crowd. Every unorthodox shot received a positive response from the excited crowd, leaping and boxing the thin air. Restricting the West Indies to 391 brought us back into the contest but another injury left us in a hopeless position. Chandra bowled a magnificent spell on the hard, bouncy pitch, taking five wickets. Unfortunately, he injured his left hand taking a return catch off Clive Lloyd. The brave bowler continued bowling with a bandaged hand, but was ruled out for the rest of the match.

Throughout the twin tours, the Indian dressing room wore a festive look in terms of noise and antics. However, the bloodbath we were witnessing had changed the atmosphere. Before each innings, Bishan spoke a few words of encouragement to bolster the confidence of the batsmen, but now he remained silent. The opening batsmen were quiet too, busy buckling their pads. The poor lighting of the dressing room made the mood even more depressing; silence was omnipresent. The sound of the bell indicated the start of the second innings; no one was in good spirits. The strength of the team had been cut to half; how many more would occupy the hospital bed remained unknown.

The reserve players had the duty to inform the opening batsmen that the umpires and fielders were in the middle; they were equally affected and they forgot their responsibility. Despair had overtaken hope, and we were merely completing the formalities, going through the motions. India had only three recognized batsmen to rely on; whether the same tactics would be used in the second innings remained to be seen. The field placement indicated war was still in progress, though the angle had changed. Everyone in the Indian dressing room stood on the bench to watch the proceedings through a green-painted shutter window; not a word was spoken while Holding remained in operation. I was padded to go next; I would get down from the bench after every over, take a stroll in the room and then join the others on the bench to watch the proceedings.

At that moment, I spotted the familiar figure of an Indian batsman talking to a policeman wearing a 'bobby helmet', rather like a policeman in London. This player wore it, adjusted the strap and, holding a cricket ball in his hand, hit the helmet to feel its impact; he took his stance and shadow-practiced avoiding bouncers. The injuries had shaken quite a few players and he wanted to play it safe. After a while, he came back to the dressing room with a piece of sponge-like material, tied it around his head and wore a white floppy hat to secure his skull. Subsequently, he cushioned his pads with the rest of the sponge. This brought a question to my mind: why was he protecting his legs when a cricket ball was flying by the batsman's head?

Before India commenced its second innings, I had decided to adopt Papaji's advice that the best way to defend oneself was to attack. I had decided to follow my instinct and counterattack. The attacking field left many areas vacant to be exploited. I slashed hard at short-pitch deliveries to fetch a few boundaries. These airy shots irritated the bowlers and they dug in a few bouncers. Since I played hook shots quite well, hitting Daniel and Holder to the fence was not difficult. However, one bouncer from Holding flew past me at a fiery pace, leaving no chance for me to react. Before I could get into position, the ball went past my head and the outstretched hands of wicketkeeper Deryck Murray for four byes. It hit the white wall acting as a sight screen behind him after one bounce and left a big red mark on it. At that moment, I changed my mind and ducked under all the bouncers from Michael Holding. It was pointless taking risks against him; runs came easily from the other end.

There were no speed guns to track Holding's pace. It could best be measured by the position of the slips and the wicketkeeper standing at least thirty meters behind the stumps; Murray regularly collected his deliveries chest-high. Prasanna had toured the West Indies in 1962 and described Holding's spell at Kingston, Jamaica, as the fastest he had ever witnessed. Some deliveries must have crossed the hundred-mile barrier, but, of course, there were no speed guns to confirm this. It was probably the fastest Michael Holding had ever bowled. I had the satisfaction of scoring a breezy half-century with the help of three sixes and seven boundaries; I regretted losing my wicket to Jumadeen after scoring 60 runs.

The next batsman crossing me in the mid-field looked terrified. As luck would have it, he had to face the fury of Michael Holding. He was a good batsman and played the pull shot quite well on slow Indian pitches. He was greeted with a series of bouncers. He allowed them to sail over his head till he decided to fight fire with fire. The next delivery, he tried to play his favourite pull shot but was left thoroughly exposed. Before he could react, the ball hit his forehead, which was thankfully protected by layers of sponge and so the impact did not cause any damage. But he lost his bearings, wobbled towards square leg and then started running fast to steal a run in the wrong direction. Regaining his composure, he rubbed his forehead to check if there was any blood. There was fortunately none. However, he was badly shaken by the impact.

It was clear that he was not going to survive for long. The comical scene somehow changed the mood on the field and in the dressing room. A roar of laughter engulfed the team and we forgot the gory scenes we had witnessed. When he was dismissed, his pride was badly mauled. A fall of another wicket at 97, and Bishan declared the innings at a loss of five wickets; four batsmen unable to bat because of injuries. It remained the only instance in the history of Test cricket that a team declared both the innings closed due to injuries and lost the match. A laughable target of thirteen runs was set for the opponents. Fredericks and Lawrence Rowe came to the crease whistling and smiling at Madan Lal holding the new ball. This attitude made him livid. He tried to bowl quick and short, but he had little impact on Fredericks. The match was done and dusted in a few overs.

The Indian team was already booked to fly home two days after the match; we got additional time to do some shopping and unwind after the rather stressful series. I was not accompanying the team back to India because I had signed to play for the Durham League in England. I went to Bishan's room to seek his advice. The moment he saw me, he put his glass of beer down on the table, got up and hugged me. We chatted for a while and, at the end of it, his parting words were soothing: 'Well done, my boy! I'm proud of you!'

6

AUSTRALIA 1977-78

I FLEW TO ENGLAND FOR MY FIRST PROFESSIONAL STINT IN the Durham League. I was keen to perform well and return to India with loads of experience against swing bowling. I was excited by the announcement of the New Zealand tour to India for a three-match Test series followed by England for a five-match series. However, playing in the English league on the weekends made life boring and lonely. I was too shy to take the initiative and failed to make new friends, which added to my boredom. I missed the banter and camaraderie of my Indian teammates.

The two home series were important for me to consolidate my place in the side. I had a reasonable series against Glenn Turner's New Zealand side with a couple of half-centuries. However, an incident in Kanpur made me realize that my position was still not secure. I attempted a hook shot against Richard Hadlee and top-edged. One of the selectors saw the ball rising in the air and yelled, 'He is going to be out', as it sailed for a six. Little did this selector realize that my father was sitting behind him; he was furious, and reminded him of his playing days and technique. This attitude made me conscious that I was not in the safe zone.

I was tormented by the mental trauma of losing my place in the side. In addition, my shin developed a hairline fracture, which made running an uphill task. I needed rest but the fear of the wilderness kept pressuring me. England arrived immediately after New Zealand and played against the North Zone before the Delhi Test.

Therefore, the first Test match against England in Delhi was crucial for me. Down in confidence and a pair staring at me, I danced to the tune of swing bowling. Debutant John Lever, in particular, swung the ball quite a bit. None of us had seen the ball swing in a manner like that in Delhi and we were convinced there was something beyond his skill. The cat was soon out of the bag; it was found that he had put a Vaseline strip over his eyebrow and consistently used it to polish the ball and swing it on the dry Kotla wicket and prevailing conditions. The Indian captain became vocal about this and offended the bosses in the MCC; he lost his contract with Northamptonshire in England. The Vaseline affair generated a great deal of controversy and John Lever failed to swing the ball in a similar way in the subsequent Test matches, which gave wings to the idea of ball tampering.

I failed to trouble the scorer in the first innings and Bishan sensed my apprehension; he offered a few encouraging words. I was going through a confidence crisis and was sent to bat lower in the order. English players were professional; they knew how to apply pressure and Tony Greig was an expert. When I was marking my guard in the second innings, he was fielding at silly point; noticing my nerves, he smiled and said, 'Good luck, but I hope you don't score.' However, I scored 20-odd runs before an innocuous full toss led to my dismissal. Although I retained my place in the team for the second Test in Calcutta, I was replaced by Eknath Solkar in the playing XI. I just could not understand how failing in just two innings in a Test match made me a bad player overnight and my performance in three previous series was conveniently forgotten.

India lost the next two matches and therefore the series. Solkar's failure in Calcutta prompted the selectors to recall my elder brother, Surinder, after the West Indies tour. He was not considered for the New Zealand series and the first three Test matches against England; so he went for a holiday in the mountains near Haridwar. It was with great difficulty that Papaji located him and put him on the flight to Bangalore. He had not played cricket for some time; he took to the nets for a couple of hours, and soon regained his flair and confidence.

It was a difficult pitch to bat on at the Chinnaswamy Stadium in Bangalore. The ball was turning and bouncing; at first, Surinder also struggled against the spin attack of Underwood and Tony Greig. My father was covering this match for All India Radio and *Amrita Bazar Patrika*. Surinder remembered seeking his advice during the lunch break and asked him how to tackle the 6'6 Tony Greig. He said, 'You're moving forward before the ball is released. Wait for the bowler to release it and then decide.' Surinder did what was conveyed. After lunch, he hit the first three deliveries of Tony Greig for boundaries. Life became easy after that and runs flowed. Surinder's flawless half-century helped India to post a good total and win the match. He continued his good form in Bombay with 40 and 63 to secure his usual slot at number three. I did not perform well but looked forward to the domestic season in September to establish myself once again.

The news of the Australia tour was music to our ears. However, the frequency of series following the success of the inaugural Test series in 1947-48 led by two icons, Lala Amarnath and Don Bradman, was very low. Inexplicably, it took another eight years to resume contact and play a three-match series in India in 1956, followed by two more series, also in India, in 1959-60 (five matches) and in 1964-65 of three matches.

It may sound strange, considering the situation today, because now every cricket-playing nation aspires to host India. However, it took twenty years for the second Indian team to touch Australian shores (1967-68) and another decade for the present series to unfold in Australia. Having made my debut against them in Madras, I was longing to play Test matches in Australia. My memories of the Indian Schoolboys' tour of Australia in 1968-69, though pleasant, could not match anything remotely close to the stories constantly drummed into my ears by Papaji.

I returned to India fresh from my English league exploits to establish my place in the Indian team for Australia. The Duleep Trophy served as selection matches for this tour. I performed well with the bat and ball to secure a berth for Australia. Surinder had already booked his seat by performing well against England, which meant I would bat in the middle order.

Our selection for the Australia tour made Papaji immensely proud. However, a threat from a sect called 'Anand Margi', based in Australia, announced that they would disrupt the tour and this caught both the cricket boards on the wrong foot. As a player, I didn't know about them and why they didn't want this tour to go ahead. Even the Australian Cricket Board (ACB) was clueless. The ACB wanted this tour to go ahead because its survival was at stake. Even the International Cricket Council (ICC), based in London, was keen to see this series conducted successfully. The reason behind this support was not affection for India but to counter a 'private cricket tournament' organized by an Australian business tycoon, Kerry Packer. He had fallen out with the ACB over their refusal to extend (his) Channel 9's contract to telecast Test cricket in Australia. Annoyed, he challenged not only the local cricket authorities, but even other cricket boards around the world. He signed top international cricketers with lucrative contracts and left the ICC bankrupt in terms of talent.

The threat of Anand Margi to disrupt the Indian tour was an added headache for the host country. It was a huge challenge to guarantee the safety of the touring team. Simultaneously, the challenge of a new concept to the traditional format had to be dealt with professionally. It was a clash between the establishment and a private enterprise. When state associations refused to lease any cricket grounds to Kerry Packer, the business tycoon decided to create his own infrastructure. He conceived a novel idea that sent shockwaves through the corridors of cricket establishments. Kerry Packer ventured into the forbidden areas and turned the concept of cricket upside down. Instead of day cricket, night cricket was introduced under the stars with artificial lights around the stadium; the concept of constantly watering and rolling a pitch was replaced by ready-made baked blocks put together, which served as pitches; floodlight towers were installed to spot the ball; coloured clothing replaced white and the sight screens were changed to black; two white balls instead of one red ball added another dimension to cricket. Finally, the marketing team developed eye-catching logos and captions. The most famous were, 'BIG BOYS PLAY AT NIGHT' and 'BIG BOYS PLAY WITH TWO WHITE BALLS'!

The idea was nothing short of sacrilege to the traditional bosses, but nevertheless it appealed to the public. They latched on to this brilliant idea. The entertainment did not end here;

beautiful models were selected and introduced as cheerleaders. For the first time, summer in Australia boasted of two different versions of cricket: the official remained sober, while the private had all the brilliance of showmanship. This unprecedented opportunity gave spectators a choice to watch traditional cricket under the sun or enjoy the cool night breeze under floodlights. The second option had the attraction of top cricket stars from around the world. The concept of colourful apparel, gaudy cricket gear and the introduction of cricket helmets brought freshness to the sport and the creation of a new avatar on the cricket field.

When the Indian team landed in Australia, a tight security cover was thrown around us. Five tall and well-built muscular men from the Australian elite force gave us company 24×7. They accompanied us throughout the tour and later became an integral part of the team. Their presence in the dressing room and the hotel functions made the team's complexion more vibrant. Except for the team meetings, they shadowed us everywhere. As the tour progressed, formality replaced friendliness; they became one of us. Since most senior players preferred Indian meals in the evenings, these burly boys accompanied young players from the team in their cars and picked up food from different Indian restaurants or takeaways.

The tour commenced with an exhibition match near Perth. To practice our technique and get a feel for the bounce of the wicket, we hit the nets. The Australian pitches had been so different in nature that most players from around the world found batting difficult here and had to work hard to adjust. We also sailed in a similar boat.

News of the Australian cricket in the doldrums was flashed by the electronic and print media. All the established players, except Jeff Thomson, had signed for the World Series, introduced by Kerry Packer. This action created a vacuum in

Australian cricket. With little or no choice, they approached former Australian captain Bobby Simpson for help, and asked him to assume the role of a mentor and leader. Once Simpson came out of retirement to help the cause of Australian cricket, scouting for fresh talent fell into place. With abundant experience behind him, Simpson helped the selectors pick the right combination.

The first Test match was held in Brisbane. I was curious to know why this ground was referred to as the 'Gabba', but I found no answer till one of the groundsmen enlightened me with the history of the area. He said that the full form of this ground was 'Woolloongabba', meaning whirling waters or wallaby in the native Australian language, which was then shortened to 'Gabba'. Hearing the rich history of the indigenous Australians was fascinating, but I knew it would not be possible to venture into the remote parts of this gigantic continent.

One of my memories of the Australia tour with the Indian Schoolboys' team in 1968-69 was watching a Sheffield Shield match. We were invited to watch Western Australia play Queensland; what an experience it was to be amongst the local crowd! I still carry vivid memories of this game because of the English batsman Colin Milburn, who played for Western Australia. Looking at his frame, I wondered if he would have been allowed to set foot on any Indian cricket ground. His build was no less than that of a Sumo wrestler. However, his batting was something I had never experienced before at that tender age. His reputation as one of the finest batsmen of fast bowling was displayed with little effort.

Bare-headed, he scored 243 runs, hitting all the fast bowlers as if he was practising in his backyard with a tennis ball. The manner and ease with which he hit them off the back foot into the stands left me speechless. It was a revelation to tackle fast bowling. He was far ahead of his time, adopting an aggressive approach much like modern cricketers in the T-20 format—but in the 1960s. He entertained the large crowds in Australia, or wherever he played. The impact of his batting display convinced me that if I had to dominate fast bowlers, I had to fight fire with fire. Milburn was an extremely popular professional in Australia. Unfortunately, he lost an eye in a car accident in England and his Test career was cut short at a young age. Though he tried to emulate Pataudi, who had also suffered a similar fate, he, unfortunately, proved to be no more than a faded version of himself.

The hype created by the World Series was a big challenge for Cricket Australia. They too promoted this series in the best possible manner to counter Kerry Packer. To support the cause of Test cricket, players from both teams looked forward to making the whole event as entertaining as possible. Australia picked new faces and there were eight debutants for the first Test match, which included David Ogilvie, Paul Hibbert, Steve Rixon, Tony Mann, Peter Toohey, Wayne Clark, Max O' Connell and Tom Brooks.

The first two days of the match fluctuated on a wicket that offered plenty of help to pace and spin bowlers. Unlike most Indian pitches, I experienced movement and bounce, and so I rather enjoyed bowling 'eight-ball' overs. Even Kirmani, standing some distance from the stumps, enjoyed gathering the ball at waist height or above. Madan Lal and I provided an early breakthrough, and then Bishan Bedi bowled a magical spell to take five wickets and restrict Australia to a meagre total of 166.

Batting on the fast and bouncy pitch was not easy for us either. The Aussie fast bowlers used the conditions well. If Thomson used his pace to take three wickets, debutant Wayne Clark was equally effective with four scalps to bowl us out for an even lower score, restricting us to just 153. With the sun beating down on the surface, conditions improved slightly for batting. But there was help available for the bowlers. Madan and I ran through the inexperienced Australian top order to give us the upper hand. When the spinners came into operation, we expected them to wrap up the innings. Alas! Peter Toohey and Bobby Simpson managed to put together a fruitful partnership, rendering the Indian spinners ineffective. Once a new ball was available, Bishan opted for it, producing the desired result. The Australian captain was immediately dismissed, caught in the slip by Vishwanath off my bowling. Madan Lal was equally effective from the other end.

I was expecting both of us to continue for a longer period to polish off the tail. To my shock, however, Bishan replaced me despite the fact that I'd taken a wicket and bowled well. The successful Madan Lal was also replaced by another spinner, in the hope of finishing off the tail. Unfortunately, that proved to be a grave mistake. Finding spinners an easy target, Jeff Thomson used his long handle to maximum advantage. Madan Lal (five wickets) and I (two wickets) watched the proceedings in disbelief. To our dismay, the plan failed miserably. Out of ninety-two overs bowled by India, Madan and I had bowled just twenty-seven and taken seven wickets between us. The last wicket added an invaluable 50 runs for Australia; this certainly set the tone for an interesting match.

India was given a target of 341 to win in two days. By the end of day three, the match was evenly poised. We batted with authority, losing the solitary wicket of Vengsarkar. My confidence was high with four wickets, and I could assess the pace and bounce of this pitch. Unlike the first innings, when I was dismissed without scoring, this time I was more comfortable against the short stuff of Jeff Thomson, Wayne Clark and Alan Hurst. I did not hesitate to pull or hook any short delivery.

With the pitch improving for batting, we had a reasonably good chance of achieving the target. I had batted well the previous evening but was dismissed early in the morning at 47 by Thomson. Subsequently, Vishwanath (35) and later Kirmani (55) added valuable runs with Sunil Gavaskar. By teatime, we were on course to victory. Cricket had always been an unpredictable game; the loss of a crucial wicket changed the course of the match. Despite their lack of international experience, the Aussie pace bowlers were focused and determined. They took a cue from Jeff Thomson's never say die approach, and they put their heart and soul into every delivery to reap rich dividends.

Once the centurion Gavaskar was dismissed, our hopes diminished. It was an uphill task for the tailenders to achieve the target. Both Clark and Thomson were richly rewarded. Wayne Clark looked to be a manageable bowler till he surprised us with a bouncer. The ball came a yard or more quicker than his normal deliveries. Even from the dressing room, we were convinced he had bent his elbow to bowl the bouncer, but the umpires failed to judge it from a mere twenty-two yards.

Australia won the match by a narrow margin of 16 runs. The last-wicket partnership of 50 runs made all the difference. Cricket Australia wanted to start the series on a high note and show that Test cricket was a more thrilling experience than Kerry Packer's star-studded pajama day-and-night cricket! It was undoubtedly an absorbing match for both the teams and the spectators. I also remember Bishan Bedi introducing the concept of 'Sunday club' to relax everyone's nerves.

SECOND TEST MATCH: PERTH

Despite losing a close encounter at Brisbane, the morale of the team was high. Cricket Australia officials were overwhelmed with the response at the Gabba and also the viewership on television. The WACA pitch at Perth was known for its bounce and pace. Memories of childhood sessions at home in Delhi came flashing back to me. We played with a wet tennis ball on the concrete driveway near the kitchen and enjoyed that contest for hours.

To get a feel the environment and nature of the pitch at the WACA, India played a four-day game against Western Australia. I was given a break for this match, allowing the team management to judge other members of the team. Batsmen struggling with their form used this opportunity to their advantage and had a good outing to stake their claim for a spot in the next match. This created a healthy competition amongst us. Although I did not play the match against Western Australia, I had a fairly good idea of how to handle bouncers. I followed Papaji's simple advice and watched the game sitting not in the dressing room but above the sight screen at the south stand of the WACA.

We had a couple of days' rest before the Test match. Nevertheless, we practised hard in the pre-afternoon session at the nets and adjusted our technique for the WACA pitch. These sessions were serious but enjoyable, always concluding with jokes and laughter to let off some pressure. On the eve of the match, the team meeting concluded on a high note, bringing smiles to the faces of those who'd been selected.

We completed the formality of pre-match training and waited for Bishan Bedi to go for the toss. The moment he stepped out of the dressing room, a member of the playing XI chased after him and had a quick word. We had no idea what transpired between them but we could tell it was serious. Bishan returned to the dressing room in a huff. He picked up a pen and deleted this player's name from the playing XI. Later, I came to know the batsman in question had developed a stiff neck. It puzzled me because he had batted freely in the nets and without any discomfort.

Bishan quickly looked around the dressing room for a replacement. This unexpected development had a direct impact on the reserve players. However, instead of vying for a spot, they refused to meet the captain's eye and chose to focus on the floor instead. Bishan focused his attention on a reputed batsman in the reserve sitting next to me and put his left hand on his head, ruffled his hair and said, 'Son, you're going to be playing.' This was Bishan's typical way of cheering a player up before entering the arena; not bothering to wait for the player's reply, he scribbled down the lad's name and headed out for the toss.

I looked at the player and thought he would be over the moon at this opportunity. However, I was aghast to hear him mutter, 'Why me?' As the tour progressed, I noticed that a few players were interested in playing only in friendly conditions and subsequently to enjoy the tour as a sort of holiday. These batsmen were masters on low and slow tracks in India, amassing tons of runs season after season. Unfortunately, here, they did not want to face Jeff Thomson and the rest of the Aussie pace attack on a hard and fast Perth wicket.

Looking at the nature of the pitch, I expected the team management to rectify its earlier mistake of playing three spinners in a pace bowlers' paradise; I was wrong. India opted to play three spinners, with Venkat replacing Prasanna. Left-arm bowler Karsan Ghavri, the third seamer in the team, was once again left cooling his heels in the pavilion. The Indian think tank forgot an age-old policy: Horses for courses!

We won the toss and decided to bat. The red shining ball consistently bounced around the faces of the two opening batsmen, Sunil Gavaskar and Chetan Chauhan. The centurion of the last Test match was consumed early in the innings by Clark. When I went to bat at number three, I saw a ring of slip fielders standing quite deep from the stumps, giving a clear indication of what the bounce and pace were like on this pitch. Peter Toohey, no less than a court jester, humoured the spectators. He was stationed at forward short leg and gleefully kept up his antics. While the slip cordon remained vocal, Toohey grinned constantly to distract the batsman.

When I took my guard, the slip cordon continued to make noise. Was it to distract me or to encourage Jeff Thomson waiting at his long run-up far away? Jeff was a big man with broad shoulders and a strong muscular body. He had a rather long rhythmic run-up with a beautiful sling arm action that generated extraordinary pace and bounce. The sight of his delivery, of course, delighted his teammates and unnerved the batsman at the receiving end. I had already made up my mind to go for pull and hook shots early in the innings to counter the fast bowlers' ultimate weapon, the bouncer. This policy was drilled into my mind by my legendary father at an incredibly young age. Another piece of advice was to move forward even to short-of-a-length deliveries and counter the pace with aggressive strokes. The attacking field of five slips, the wicketkeeper, a short leg and a bowler left vacant areas on the large ground.

Conditions at the WACA tested our abilities and presented great challenges. Under the scorching heat of the bright sun, I used sunscreen for the first time to protect my facial skin. It was an experience I can never forget. How I laughed looking at my image in the mirror, resembling a tribal warrior! Then came the battle with the flies that were constantly, hovering around my face. They were a nuisance; at times, causing me to lose concentration. Fortunately, a special spray came in handy to give me a temporary respite. Once it lost its effect, I had a tough time keeping the flies at bay. At times, I used my left or right hand to push them away. The fast bowlers many a time thought I was waving at someone above the sight screen in the stand to settle down. Once I swallowed a fly and kept coughing for a while to get it out. That was some experience, to say the least!

Chetan Chauhan and I developed a good partnership before Sam Gannon, the left-arm fast bowler, tested me with a short-pitched delivery. I went for a hook but missed it due to the angle; the ball hit me on my forehead at a fiery speed and I collapsed on the turf, clutching my forehead in agony. The Aussies rushed to check if I was okay. They were genuinely concerned about my injury. This was my first experience of feeling the impact of a hard cricket ball, and certainly not the last. I checked my forehead to see if there was any blood on my glove; none. I was obviously a hard nut to crack!

Feeling a little dizzy, I was taken on a stretcher to the Indian dressing room. It was a small, simple dressing room with basic comforts. My teammates seemed more concerned with my injury than me. I applied a pack of ice on the swollen area and had some ice cream to cool myself in extremely hot conditions. Simultaneously, I was lost in my thoughts about the mistake I had committed when Bishan asked me if I was okay and fit enough to bat after tea.

If I wanted to take a break, no one would have raised an eyebrow, but the Amarnath reputation was at stake. We were taught to face challenges like brave men and not shy away. Papaji had been hit on his left eyebrow only once in his long career; he understood the psyche of an injured batsman and the bowler. To overcome the dread, he always said, 'Nothing worse can happen with the cricket ball.' This statement had forever removed the fear of injury from my heart. He encouraged us to look into the eyes of the same bowler and face him with determination. This 'mantra' was permanently etched in my memory.

Once Bishan asked if I was alright, I did not think twice I picked up my bat and walked out of the dressing room to the ground. Surprisingly, the pain was gone. There was no hesitation in my mind because I had put this incident behind me. My eyes were focused on the scoreboard to get my first hundred in Australia. I knew what was in store for me; the bowler would come hard at me and bowl with more hostility to test my nerves. I knew nothing worse could happen to me, so I decided to simply face the storm. I was peppered with short-pitch deliveries from both ends. I continued with my aggressive approach, till one grave mistake: I picked the wrong line against Jeff Thomson to play a pull shot. The ball took the top edge of the bat and landed safely in the fielder's hands at mid-on.

I was angry at having missed an excellent opportunity to score a century in Australia; dismissed at 90! India scored 402 runs, thanks to some solid teamwork. In return, we managed to restrict Australia to 394. Bobby Simpson scored a century despite a couple of close calls against Chandra. Sushil Doshi was covering the Test match as Hindi commentator for All India Radio and he was not pleased with the umpires' decisions. When a disappointed Chandra walked to his position deep in the outfield, the crowd booed him. The Indian leg spinner reacted angrily, showing them two fingers, which provoked a greater reaction. Sushil Doshi, new to international cricket, could not understand, and he said, 'Chandra is telling the crowd that it was not once but twice that Simpson was LBW but not given out!'

Although we batted well in the first innings, one batsman developed Thomson phobia. The fear factor took such a toll that he started moving away to the leg side, exposing all his stumps. Yet, he managed to pick the line of short-pitched deliveries quite well. He slashed hard and often fetched boundaries. It entertained many people in the gallery but not the Indian captain and the fast bowlers. We cheered him from the dressing room, encouraging him to adopt bolder tactics.

As the innings went on, Bishan Bedi became livid and vocal with this exhibition. Unable to control his emotions, he rankled at the uncanny display. 'This is not the way to play Test cricket! Be a man, face it or get out.' The contest continued for an hour or so. The large gallery roared with excitement at this unusual display. This frustrated the Australian captain and the fast bowlers even more. Finally, Thomson decided to change his tactics and bowled a full-length delivery to hit the base of the stumps. The batsman swung the bat harder and the red cherry flew a long distance, all the way to the sight screen. All hell broke loose and the bowler couldn't restrain himself from letting out the choicest expressions.

With crucial runs leaking, Bobby Simpson fielding at slips asked Thomson to come round the wicket and gestured to bowl short. Simultaneously, he asked Peter Toohey fielding at midwicket to come and stand at forward short leg. To make this batsman aware of what was coming at him, Simpson shouted loudly, 'Catch it, Peter!' Naughty as Peter Toohey was, he smiled at this comment and responded, 'Skipper, catch what, the ball or the batsman?'

When India batted in the second innings, the conditions had not changed. The pitch was even harder and our spikes failed to dig into the surface. While walking to the crease to replace Chauhan, I was under no illusion as to what awaited me. I had been hit on my forehead in the first innings and knew the length Australian fast bowlers would prefer to bowl against me. Sunil Gavaskar and I stitched a healthy partnership of 193. I was pleased with how I handled all the fast bowlers. Gavaskar scored a fine century.

Finally, I also scored my first century of the series. It was the 101st century for India in Test matches; the first Test century came from the bat of my father on his debut in 1933. I had narrowly missed scoring the 100th century when I was dismissed at 90 in the first innings. Personally, it was quite satisfying to amass runs, but deep down it hurt to be on the losing side. What could have been two victories for us left us frustrated with the results. Australia scrambled home with two wickets in hand to extend the lead in the five-match series.

THIRD TEST MATCH: MELBOURNE

Although 2-0 down in the series, we were still confident of making a comeback. We had come so close to winning the first two matches, but the overconfidence of the spinners to polish off the tail and several dubious decisions cost us dearly. Despite these setbacks, the Indian team looked to be a complete side. Before the series, India lacked the reputation of a good pace attack compared to the Aussie pace battery. However, our two opening bowlers proved effective and gave a much-needed breakthrough.

Unlike the 1947 Indian cricket team, which travelled by train across Australia, our domestic arrangements were made by the airline Ansett Australia. These flights were quite long, keeping in mind the immensity of the Australian continent and the fact that the venues scattered all over. The close contests in the first two matches made us popular with the pilots, cabin crew and the passengers onboard. Special attention and service in the sky made these long flights not only comfortable but enjoyable too.

The Kerry Packer World Series undoubtedly revolutionized cricket and attracted large crowds to the floodlit matches. Another novelty was the timing of the matches. They started late in the afternoon or early evening and carried on into the night to give the spectators comfort from heat. The cool seaside breeze, fun and frolic in the stands, cheerleaders dancing to loud music, fireworks and top international cricketers in action made this venture popular with every generation, especially the young. However, it could not take away the sheen and popularity of the Test matches.

The Melbourne Cricket Ground (MCG) remained one of the biggest cricketing venues in the world in terms of audience capacity. It provided every comfort to let the spectators enjoy themselves. I had seen pictures of my father at the toss with Bradman and leading the Indian team to the field with the MCG pavilion in the background. How I longed to set foot on this ground! When we reached the majestic MCG pavilion and walked through the gallery, I saw the portrait of the 1947 Indian team led by my father, which made me nostalgic. Later, I was introduced to MCC life members who had watched my father's memorable undefeated double century at this ground. There was a happy feeling, rather like homecoming for Surinder and me. Everything looked familiar, thanks to Papaji's descriptions.

Cricket grounds in Australia, like in England, had retained their historical structures, especially the pavilion. The dressing room and showers at the MCG were at ground level; the spiral staircase took players to the sitting area above, from where we could watch the match through large glass windows. The distance from the players' box to the edge of the cricket field was a walk of approximately twenty-five meters and ninety meters to the wicket. Unlike the present day, there was no rope spread on the outfield at the MCG. The ball had to touch the concrete wall of the iron railing around the ground to fetch a boundary.

From the players' box, I could see the neatly painted rows of benches reserved for guests and special invitees. Most of them had picnic baskets filled with cakes, cookies, sandwiches, all served in quarter plates, along with a thermos full of hot tea or coffee. They even carried wine glasses and enjoyed white or red wine with cricket. However, I missed the scenes I had seen in my father's 1947 tour album, especially ladies in long floral frocks or skirts, knitting cardigans and gossiping. Even the dress code of gentlemen in suits and hats, smoking pipes or cigarettes, was hard to spot; casual clothing was now the order of the day. The younger generation was happier and more comfortable in shorts and T-shirts, or even less.

A brief look at the wicket brought a smile to my face. It looked different as compared to what we'd dealt with in the two prior matches: slightly brownish in colour. We were convinced that it would help our spinners. However, the feel of hardness on the surface indicated the potential for considerable bounce and pace.

Bishan won the toss and elected to bat. India needed a sound start, but we received one shock after another. First Chauhan and then Gavaskar returned to the pavilion without a run on the board. The confidence of the previous Test match helped me to overcome Thomson and Clark's swift bowling. They tested me with short-pitch stuff. Defending one such nasty delivery from Thomson, I was hit on the index finger of my right hand. There was instant pain; blood trickled out from the pores of my glove. I knew my finger was split; what was the damage, I was not sure. I did not remove my glove, fearing I may not be able to put it back on due to the swelling and the cut. I carried on batting regardless, often wiping off blood stains with my other hand. With the little master Vishwanath at the other end, batting was enjoyable. His smiling face and delightfully wristy shots pepped me up. We stitched together a century partnership till I played into the hands of Bobby Simpson at leg slip. I saw him occupy this position but could not resist gliding a full-length delivery from Clark and falling into a trap. I was cross with myself for a soft dismissal, scoring 72. Vishwanath continued in good form, scoring another half-century. India managed to put up a healthy, decent total of 256.

When I removed the glove from my right hand, my finger was swollen, with a big gash, and it was covered in blood. Since first aid was unable to give me relief, I was advised to get it treated at the local hospital. I needed eight stitches to sew my wound. The doctor ordered complete rest. This meant the end of the Test match for me. India played with two seamers, Karsan Ghavri and me. I wondered who would open the bowling attack. The mystery was revealed after Ghavri completed a successful over, capturing a wicket: it was Sunil Gavaskar who would fulfil the formality! Once Chandrasekhar was introduced, he mesmerized all the Aussie batsmen. They had no clue in which direction the ball was turning; the bounce and pace of the wicket made him more lethal, taking 6/52 to bowl Australia out for 213.

While the two opening batsmen got ready to bat in the second innings, I tried to grip my bat and see if I could hold and swing it. It was painful and futile. The wound was raw and the swelling had not yet subsided; there was no chance of me going onto the pitch and I was devastated. The second innings of this match was crucial for India to remain relevant in this series. We needed a good start from our opening batsmen—and Sunil Gavaskar did not disappoint us. He scored his third century of the series, all coming in the second innings of every Test match. If Gavaskar was a picture of confidence and stability, the other little master, Viswanath, was a class apart—the epitome of brilliance. He scored another fluent half-century in the second innings. When India lost the fifth wicket (Gavaskar) at 265, the game stood open. Bishan casually asked me if I could bat.

I decided to take on the challenge; I gave Bishan a big 'Yes!' Tying the buckles of the pads and slipping on the abdominal guard was easy, but wearing the glove over my right hand was tough. I removed the bandage, tied a plaster around my injured index finger, held my breath and closed my eyes, pushing my hand hard into the glove; the excruciating pain made me bite my lip. It was the beginning of a battle within me to deal with the pain and understand how the brain plays a crucial role in countering it. At the fall of the sixth wicket, I occupied the crease. My focus was now solely on the main objective: make some runs. I managed to contribute 41 to the total.

Cricket was played hard on the field but there was camaraderie after the end of the day. Performances were appreciated and concern shown towards injured players from both sides. Both captains took the initiative to invite the opponents after the day's play to their dressing room for drinks. I thought it was a fantastic gesture but obviously the commitment towards their team on the following day did not change the attitude of the fast bowlers; they targeted our batsmen with vicious bouncers.

I remember an interesting episode in the North Zone vs MCC match played in Amritsar in 1972. The Nort Zone team comprised players from Delhi, Punjab, Haryana, Railways, Services, and Jammu and Kashmir. While Surinder and I represented Punjab, Bishan played for Delhi and led the team. We had an interesting character in Gokul Inder Dev. He came from an army background and played first-class cricket for the combined armed forces team called 'Services'. He kept the dressing room atmosphere alive with his sense of humour. Amritsar in the month of December was very cold and, as a host, the district commissioner invited both teams for cocktails. There was a large gathering but Gokul found the company of the English fast bowler Bob Cottam interesting. Both enjoyed their drinks and discussions till they parted ways that night. Since this match was affected by rain, nothing exceptional happened on the field apart from a solitary episode.

Gokul Inder Dev batted in the middle order; he faced his drinking partner Bob Cottam operating under heavily overcast conditions. The first delivery went past the batsman's nose to shake him. Gokul smiled and took his stance again in the hope of facing a friendlier delivery. Alas! It was practically a repeat of the previous ball. Gokul was horrified; he walked up to

Bob, standing within hand-shaking distance after the follow-through, staring at him. Gokul pleaded, 'Why are you bowling bouncers at me? Don't you remember me? We were friends at the cocktail party!' The English fast bowler looked sternly at him and replied with a profanity. There was certainly not going to be any friendship on the field!

We won the third Test match to close the gap. Chandrashekar was the chief destroyer, taking twelve wickets, and he was ably supported by Bishan with six wickets in this match. Their bowling style was a combination of hot curry and cream pudding. They cut through the Australian batting quite easily. Since the next match was on a spinner-friendly surface at the Sydney Cricket Ground, our confidence knew no bounds. We knew the result in advance.

Intense contests attract more people to the venues and television sets. Captain Bishan Singh Bedi was the centre of attraction because of his headgear, called a patka. Instead of the traditional Sikh turban, he preferred a cotton patka in different colours. He changed it at the start of each session to give the commentators something different to discuss. Chandrashekhar was another cricketer who came for attention and appreciation. He surprised everyone by fielding near the boundary and throwing the ball with his left arm to the keeper. He was exceptionally safe with return catches, rarely missing an opportunity.

Fourth Test Match: Sydney

Unlike earlier tours, the BCCI provided the Indian team with two different shades of blazers. The sky-blue blazer was used for travelling, while the traditional navy blue was used for the Test matches. With confidence running high, we arrived in Sydney. It was the most happening place in Australia, much like Bombay in India. We found the dry and warm weather most pleasing, and the spinners were excited at their prospects for the match ahead.

The sight of the Sydney Cricket Ground, where Sir Donald Bradman had scored his hundredth century against India in 1947-48, flashed back with the famous picture we had seen in Papaji's personal album. Bradman wrote in his memoirs how Papaji had surprised him with a bowling change when he was on 99. He faced an unknown bowler, Gogumal Kishenchand. 'I had no clue what he bowled and later I was told by the Indian skipper that he too did not know what Kishenchand had bowled.'

Another familiar sight was a beautiful hill under the huge scoreboard with the names of the players and, in the opposite direction, the ladies' green stand. In the late nineteenth and early twentieth century it was exclusively reserved for ladies. The green wooden pavilion had not lost its character; players from around the world had used this dressing room, including my father.

Even though I had done well in Melbourne, I had not recovered from my injury. The stiffness in my index finger became a handicap but I did not want to miss the Sydney match. Even the captain and team management were in my favour. Bishan was unlucky with the toss and Australia chose to bat. The dry nature of the pitch meant a short spell for me. However, I gave India an early breakthrough to allow the spinners to apply pressure. Once Chandra and Bishan came together in action, wickets fell like autumn leaves. Australia was bowled out for a modest total of 131.

In response, the Gavaskar—Chauhan duo provided a good opening partnership. Both batsmen had different approaches and expressions. While Sunny rarely showed his emotions, Chetan Chauhan had the habit of grinding his teeth, looking as if he was grinning. Combined with this unique habit, he looked straight into the eyes of the fast bowlers, especially after fetching a boundary. His patent square cut or slash ranged from point all the way to third man. This habit irked Jeff Thomson and the other Aussie fast bowlers. In one over, he hit Thomson over the slip cordon for a boundary and laughed; this did not sit well with Thomson. In typical fast bowler style, Thommo let out a few invectives to show his annoyance. To the Aussie's amazement, Chetan Chauhan did not hold back, responding with the choicest of Indian and harshest of English invectives. The crowd loved the tussle; they booed and clapped. Even the commentators took notice of it and replayed it in good humour to show how gruelling Test cricket could be. Sensing the gravity of the situation, Gavaskar tried to defuse the situation but Chetan Chauhan was uncontrollable; Gavaskar eventually managed to calm him down.

This unusual scene reminded me of a match between Australia and Northamptonshire in England involving a Pakistani pace bowler and Thomson. Sarfraz Nawaz tested Thomson with nasty bouncers. This had little effect on the batsman but the fielding side was badly shaken. They ran to control Sarfraz, fearing retaliation from Thomson and Dennis Lillee. It was a classic example of opponents coming to the rescue of a batsman fearing similar treatment from tearaway fast bowlers.

However, the battle today did not stop. Whenever Chauhan scored runs off Thomson, he let out a volley of abuse. And when he defended, he kept annoying the fast bowler with his trademark grin. These actions lit Thomson's fuse; he bowled one of the quickest deliveries of the spell to hit Chauhan on the thumb of his right hand. The batsman groaned in pain but refused to leave the field. At this stage, Gavaskar had a rare lapse in concentration and he fell victim to Thomson, missing a half-century by only a run.

After Gavaskar's departure, I took time to settle in at the crease. Chauhan continued to bat in pain for a while, but could not prolong his innings; he fell to Wayne Clark. When the doctor checked his thumb, the injury was worse than imagined. Chauhan was ruled out for the remainder of the Test match. The arrival of Vishwanath to the crease meant brisk business, and runs came at a rapid pace. I played a perfect hook shot to a bouncer delivered by Clark. The timing was perfect but the ball went in the direction of a solitary fielder, Gannon, at fine leg. He did not move an inch; he leaped straight up in the air and took a magnificent catch. The Indian batting continued to flourish around Vishwanath, who played another gem of an innings of 79. Bishan declared the innings closed at 8/398.

With a large lead, a spinner-friendly pitch and enough time at our disposal, India was slated to win this match. The Indian spinners, particularly Erapalli Prasanna, bowled a fine spell to pick four out of eight wickets, while the rest were equally distributed between Bishan and Chandra. By the end of the fourth day, we were in the driver's seat and Australia was relying heavily on Peter Toohey in the company of Thomson to ward off an innings defeat.

On the fifth day, Karsan Ghavri took the last two wickets to win the match by an innings and two runs. However, the talk of the day was a brilliant catch by Madan Lal substituting for the injured Chetan Chauhan. He ran almost thirty meters to his left, made a full-length dive and took an amazing catch inches from the ground to dismiss Peter Toohey.

Fifth Test Match: Adelaide

By the time we landed in Adelaide for the final match of the Test series, we had conquered many hearts. Even the jittery Australian Cricket Board placed us firmly on a higher pedestal.

The initial lack of attendance had multiplied after each contest. Our performance engendered admiration and respect. When I looked back, it seemed like a long journey, but time had flown. The threat of the Anand Margi group stood diluted; the frustration of losing the first two Test matches was replaced by two convincing victories; injuries, instead of demoralizing us, made us more determined and team spirit became the name of the game.

With the series tied at two all, this match was extended to six days to decide the fate of the series. Thank God! It was not a match like the 1939 South Africa versus England contest, which took ten days (including two rest days and a day washed out) and still ended without a result because the English team was already booked on a ship the following day to travel to England; the next ship sailed for London after weeks, which forced them to abandon the match and opt for a long journey home. Anyhow, England won the series 1-0. Interestingly, the series then and our series now had one thing in common: the eight-balls over.

Our visit to Adelaide brought back happy memories of childhood and some of the cricket stories Papaji had told us back in Delhi. He spoke about the English batsmen, namely Hammond, Hardstaff, Hutton and Crompton, but Bradman was special for his batting abilities. I never forgot when he told me about how hard he hit the ball square off the pitch. The square cut was packed with ferocious power, and the ball travelled at a lightning speed until it hit the signboard on the railing and rolled back three to four metres on the field.

Barossa Valley wineries were quite famous and we had a good experience seeing the vineyards spread over hundreds of acres. All Australian cities and cricket stadiums had different characters. The Adelaide Oval was the most picturesque, with

Two-year-old Jimmy batting with his father's bat; 1952

Early lessons in bowling for Jimmy at Railway stadium, New Delhi

Three brothers: Tom, John and Jim, 1959

Bowling practice at home, 1962

Three brothers; from left to right: Mohinder Amarnath, Surinder Amarnath and Rajender Amarnath at the Brabourne Stadium, Bombay, in 1963

Papaji with Tom and Mummyji with Jim

Mohinder Amarnath and Lala Amarnath watching Rajender Amarnath practice bowling at home, 1970

Lala Amarnath giving tips to his son Mohinder after a match. A rare occasion to catch them together on the field.

U-19 North Zone team in Bombay, 1966
Sitting left to right: S.P. Singh, S. Amarnath (Captain), D.P. Bhasin (Manager), V. Lamba, M. Amarnath

Mohinder Amarnath snapped during a cricket match in the year 1966
Photo: The Hindu Archives

Three W's: Sir Frank Worrell, West Indies captain visits the Amarnaths in 1966
From left to right: Alka, Kamla, Dolly, Sir Frank Worrell, Rajender, Mohinder, Kailash Kumari (mother), Surinder and Lala Amarnath

M. Amarnath, A.A. Asif, Harold Wilson (Prime Minister of Britain), S. Kirmani and Manager Hemu Adhikari

Indian schools' team tour to England, 1967
Sitting left to right: M. Amarnath, A. Kumar, S. Kirmani, A. Naik, S. Amarnath, A.A. Asif, Jasbir Singh

Indian schools' team in Australia, 1968
Mohinder Amarnath sitting third from left

Group picture of Indian schools' team and Australian schools' team at Melbourne Cricket Ground, 1968;
M. Amarnath sitting second from right to left

Don Bradman with Indian schools' team, Adelaide, 1968
M. Amarnath standing third from right

Leading North Zone U-19 team vs Central Zone team led by Laxman Singh, Nagpur, 1968

MCG (Melbourne Cricket Ground), playing against the Australian schools' team in 1968

Australian batsman I.M. Chappell is bowled by M. Amarnath during the fifth cricket Test match against India played from December 24 to 28, 1969 at Chepauk in Madras.
Photo: The Hindu Archives

Indian cricket all-rounder Mohinder Amarnath seen in bowling action during a cricket match on April 20, 1975.
Photo: The Hindu Archives

World Cup 1975; participating teams at Buckingham Place, 1975; with Queen Elizabeth, Prince Philip, Prince Charles

The Indian cricket team snapped before its departure to New Zealand, the first-leg of its four-month twin tour which included seven Tests and other first class fixtures in New Zealand and the West Indies.
Photo: The Hindu Archives

Mohinder Amarnath hooking R.J. Hadlee for a six on the first day of the second cricket Test match between India and New Zealand at Green Park in Kanpur on November 18, 1976.
Photo: The Hindu Archives

Photo shows Indian cricketers Parthasarathy Sharma (left), Madan Lal (centre) and Mohinder Amarnath (right) into the champagne drinks after the Indians had won the first cricket Test match against New Zealand; Auckland, 1976.
Photo: The Hindu Archives

S. Gavaskar sitting on a helmet, with M. Amarnath, S. Kirmani and A. Gaekwad

A. Gaekwad, Vishwanath, Venkataraghavan, M. Amarnath, Australia, 1977

Mohinder Amarnath, Ashok Mankad and Surinder Amarnath, Australia tour 1977/78

Indian team in Australia 1977/78

Lowerhouse Cricket Club, Lancashire, 1977

Mohinder Amarnath in a solar hat; hit wicket vs Australia at Wankhede Stadium, Bombay 1979/80 series

Photo: The Hindu Archives

Lahore, 1978: With Muhammad Zia-ul-Haq. India versus Pakistan at Gaddafi Stadium; picture signed by Zia-ul-Haq

Mohinder Amarnath of Delhi steps out and forces a ball to the on-side during his unbeaten innings of 165 during the Ranji trophy cricket championship between Delhi and Karnataka at Bangalore on March 28, 1979.
Photo: The Hindu Archives

Mohinder Amarnath of Delhi pulls B.S. Chandrasekhar of Karnataka (not in picture) being watched by Syed Kirmani, wicket-keeper in the finals of the Ranji Trophy Cricket Tournament between Delhi and Karnataka at Chinnaswamy Cricket Stadium, Bangalore on March 28, 1979. Amarnath scored 178 runs in the second innings.
Photo: The Hindu Archives

Mohinder Amarnath hooks Thomson of Australia (not in picture) to the boundary being watched by Sunil Gavaskar at the other end in the second innings during the second cricket test match between India and Australia at W.A.C.A. Ground, Perth on December 20, 1977. Amaranth (100) and Gavaskar (127) scored centuries in the second innings.
Photo: The Hindu Archives

Mohinder Amarnath of Delhi, who scored a career best of 191 runs in the Ranji Tournament steps out and lifts Ravi Shastri of Bombay (bowler) for a six being watched by Parker, wicket-keeper in the finals of the Ranji Trophy Cricket Tournament between Bombay and Delhi at Feroz Shah Kotla Ground, New Delhi on April 12, 1980.
Photo: The Hindu Archives

Mohinder Amarnath batting during the Fifth Test match between India v Pakistan at Gadaffi Stadium in Lahore on January 25, 1983.
Photo: The Hindu Archives

Captain of the Delhi Team, Mohinder Amarnath lifting the Ranji Trophy; Delhi, 1982

Indian cricket team: Tour to Pakistan; at Wankhede stadium, 1982

Indian cricket team: Tour to West Indies; at the Cricket Club of India, Bombay

India vs West Indies, Antigua, 1983

Kapil Dev, Mohinder Amarnath, Madan Lal in Karachi, Pakistan, 1982/83

At the Oval, World Cup 1983
Standing left to right: Kapil Dev, Manager P.R. Man Singh, Sunil Gavaskar and Mohinder Amarnath
Courtesy: Srenik Sett

A rare sight: Chilling with Michael Holding during the West Indies tour, 1983

'Man of the Match' vs West Indies, Barbados, 1983

Losing a front tooth to fast bowler Malcolm Marshall, Barbados, West Indies, 1983

Courtesy: Late Amiya Tarafdar, News Photo Agency, Calcutta

World Cup, England, 1983

Hooking Andy Roberts at Antigua, West Indies, 1983

M. Amarnath acting as a trainer of the Indian cricket team during World Cup 1983; at the Lord's practice ground
Courtesy: Srenik Sett

World Cup teams at Lord's, 1983

Raja Bhalindra Singh of Patiala, Jimmy and Lala Amarnath at Rashtrapati Bhawan 1983

'Man of the Match' in the semifinals vs England at Old Trafford; 1983 World Cup

Receiving the World Cup winners' medal
Courtesy: Srenik Sett

World champions with Prime Minister Indira Gandhi at Hyderabad House, New Delhi, 1983

World Cup 1983

Mohinder Amarnath's lucky charm, his red handkerchief, signed by 1983 World Cup-winning Indian Cricket Team

The fearless champion: Mohinder Amarnath with the 1983 World Cup
Courtesy: Srenik Sett

the longest straight boundary in the world. To give a clearer view of the ball to batsmen, the sight screen was placed inside the boundary. One of the senior members of the Indian team on the 1967-68 tour of Australia was a frequent visitor at home. He told me an interesting story about the Adelaide Test match and an Indian fielder. Ian Chappell played a straight drive and sprinted for runs, while the fielder at mid-off ran in pursuit of the ball, but at a rather gingerly pace. By the time he managed to reach the ball, the batsmen had already completed four runs and were turning for more when another fielder standing midway for the relay throw shouted in Hindi, 'Paanch run ho gaye,' meaning five runs have been completed. Aware of the implications of that warning, the pursuing fielder kicked the ball towards the boundary fence to register a boundary and deny any extra runs. Due to the Oval's long, straight boundary, most teams generally preferred a relay throw of the ball to the bowler's end.

Another feature of this ground was a huge scoreboard projecting the names of the players from both teams. The green area around the scoreboard was occupied for sunbathing, barbeque and beer. Straw hats were very popular with the younger generation. Girls were clad in beachwear and boys were often bare-chested, dressed in colourful shorts. Families with picnic baskets enjoyed the day out, with toddlers running around. The venue wore a festive look.

To reach the dressing room in the pavilion, one had to climb around two dozen steps. There was an exclusive sitting area with comfortable reclining chairs outside the dressing room to watch the proceedings. The change room was huge and comfortable. The wooden benches placed near the walls had a closet with space to hang a blazer and store cricketing gear. This facility left the room less congested. Unlike modern kitbags with wheels, we had big duffel bags for our kits with small handles to carry them. Carrying a load of ten kilos from the coach and climbing the steps to reach the dressing room made our arms stronger. Since most of us had never managed money at home, it was a great learning experience to handle our allowances. We had limited resources to take care of two meals and laundry.

Most evenings in the motel were quiet. However, one night, the serenity of our environment was wrecked by a commotion, right on our floor. On enquiry, it was revealed that the security boys were playing some kind of cops-and-robbers game with the Indian players. Thankfully, they had removed the bullets from their revolvers before handing them to our boys to play the role of a cop or robber!

The motel's wooden stairs were constantly used by the ascending or descending players. At times, they sprinted across the corridors; the 'police' chasing and screaming to arrest the rogues. After a little lull, one could hear a loud sound of firing mimicked by both parties hiding behind walls or furniture or under the bed. They ran from one room to another, hotly chased by the policemen firing bullets from the empty revolvers but emitting sounds from their mouths. The action and dialogue delivery reminded me of Clint Eastwood. Despite the chaos, the motel management was quite cooperative. At times, they joined in the fun, clapping at every hit.

With the series locked at 2-2, the morale of the team was high. At this stage Bedi assumed the chairmanship of the Sunday club and introduced probably the funniest and most embarrassing dress code. Each player had to wear only a jockstrap, a tie on a bare chest, lipstick and travel from different floors to the captain's room with this outfit on full display, which left the hotel guests guffawing.

Australia won and made full use of the conditions. Bobby Simpson scored another century and so did Yallop. Ghavri bowled his heart out on a docile pitch to be among the wicket-takers. Chandrashekhar continued to torment the Australians, taking another five-wicket haul. Australia was 9/458, and we looked forward to putting our feet up and relaxing in the dressing room. A pity that we had not learned any lessons from the first Test match; our bowlers failed to get rid of the tailenders before the last pair put together a crucial 47 run partnership.

Throughout the series, Gavaskar did not blossom in the first innings of any Test match, but we hoped he would rectify that. Conditions remained good for batting but Thomson got tremendous pace with the new ball. At 23, India lost Gavaskar and I too returned to the pavilion after a dubious umpiring decision. I defended a short rising delivery from Jeff Thomson and Tony Cozier fielding at forward short leg took a catch off one bounce and appealed. The umpire raised his finger to leave me bitterly disappointed with the decision; I was in good form and the conditions were perfect for batting. When I reached the dressing room, the entire team was sympathetic and Bishan patted my shoulder and said, 'Bad luck, son.'

Having bowled us out for 269, Australia could have enforced the follow-on (they were leading by 236), but they decided to bat again. They wanted to add more runs to the lead in the six-day Test match and set us a stiff target in the fourth innings. However, Karsan and Bishan bowled superbly, capturing four wickets each to restrict them to 256. We were set a target of 493 to win the series. We had achieved a target of 404 against the West Indies a few years ago; could we do it again? That was the million-dollar question. Our best bet in the chase was Gavaskar. He had scored three centuries in the second innings through this series; Chetan Chauhan was gusty and looked in fine form; Vishwanath had batted brilliantly, only if he could convert half-centuries into his first three-figure score; Vengsarkar had talent and was capable of putting up a big score; Kirmani had been getting crucial runs and I was also going through a purple patch. We knew it had to be a collective effort, like in Trinidad.

Another factor that tilted the balance a bit in our favour was an injury to the Australian premier fast bowler, Thomson, in the first innings. He had left the field after taking two wickets with a side strain and was ruled out of the Test match. However, it was still a daunting task for the Indian batsmen to achieve. Unfortunately, Gavaskar could not replicate his earlier performances and Chauhan did not last long either. Vishwanath and I added 131 runs in our partnership. We both looked set for a three-figure mark but were dismissed before either of us could make it to a century. I played a bad shot to off spinner Yardley at 86 and Vishwanath fell to Clark at 73; Vengsarkar kept up the pressure on the Aussies, but he also fell to Yardley at 78. The Indian innings folded on the sixth day at 445 and we lost the match by 47 runs. If one had to look back and search for the answer for our defeat, it was most likely the crucial forty-seven run partnership by the Aussie tailenders in the first innings.

In terms of gate collection and viewership on television, Cricket Australia was over the moon. The success of this series eventually sustained Test cricket in Australia. Personally, for me, it was a satisfying series; I wish I could have converted those near-miss opportunities into centuries. The Indian team, despite losing the series 2-3, held its head high. Indian batting flourished and so did the bowling. If Gavaskar managed three centuries, Vishwanath managed more half-centuries from either side. Chandrashekhar was outstanding, Bishan consistent and Prasanna effective as well. Ghavri grabbed the opportunity with both hands, relishing the conditions. Kirmani was terrific behind the wicket and with the bat. The only person I felt bad for was my elder brother, Tom. He looked in such terrific form in the early part of the tour but met with injuries one after another and was forced to return to India.

7

PAKISTAN 1978

BEFORE THIS HURRIEDLY ARRANGED TOUR, INDIA AND Pakistan had played only three series against each other. It began with the Pakistan tour of India in 1952 under Abdul Hafeez Kardar. India won the series 2-1 under the captaincy of my father, Lala Amarnath. India reciprocated with its first tour of Pakistan in 1954 and drew all the matches. The last series between the two neighbours was held in 1960 in India and that had also met with the same fate—all the matches were drawn. Thereafter, strained political relations put a lid on the bilateral cricket series. It remained frozen for eighteen long years. However, both nations continued to compete against each other for hockey supremacy in the Asian Games, World Cup and Olympics, while cricket found no such platform.

After the conclusion of the third series, a lot changed on both sides of the border. The two wars of 1965 and 1971 practically ended any bilateral competition. However, cricketers from both countries played together in third countries without any malice. They represented 'Rest of the World' against Australia; Sunil Gavaskar, Bishan Bedi and Farokh Engineer from India, Intikhab Alam, Zaheer Abbas and Asif Masood from Pakistan carried home happy memories of bonhomie.

A change of regime in New Delhi under the Janata Party in 1977 ushered in a new policy to engage with the neighbour. Since cricket attracted a large following in both countries, the new government of India perceived it to be a perfect tool for back-door diplomacy. India, by now, had an established spin quartet, probably the finest in the world, along with a reliable batting line-up, while Pakistan relied upon its pace attack and strong batting to test the skills of its opponents. The build-up for the 1978 series drew a positive response from across the border. My generation hadn't played against Pakistan yet and the resumption of cricket between the two nations was something we had eagerly awaited for years. Would this goodwill tour help normalize relations?

For me, this tour was special—emotionally and historically. Our family roots were in Lahore in modern-day Pakistan, and there was no better raconteur than Papaji to describe the Lahore of his childhood and youth. After all, he had chased his friends through the narrow lanes of the Old City, and had grown up to play early cricket at Minto Park and Lawrence Gardens. His love for Lahore was deeply ingrained and many of our childhood evenings were spent listening to his tales, each capturing the flavour of the city. He would invariably get sentimental when he talked about the city. One could see a glint in his eyes but with a touch of sadness because it was no longer his home. He always professed that 'of all the places in the world, Lahore was the most beautiful city'. Although we had never set foot on its soil, his descriptions gave us a virtual tour; I wanted not merely to see Lahore but to feel it.

There were celebrations at home when the Indian team was announced. Surinder had made a comeback after returning midway from the Australia tour and I was also part of the squad. To find his sons on a Pakistan tour presented Papaji with an opportunity to introduce us to his friends of yore, especially in Lahore, and that made him ecstatic. Despite little correspondence with his Lahore friends, a long list of names was drawn. Two friends came for special attention, Murawwat Hussain and Amir Elahi. They had spent considerable time with Papaji in Patiala and Lahore. If he talked about the handsomest and finest cricketer from Pakistan, it had to be Fazal Mahmood. The list was never-ending; we wondered how he would find time to meet all his friends between matches, official engagements and travel. For the first time, I saw a twinkle in his eyes; he was excited to meet everyone after twenty-four years.

While we looked forward to this tour, I was under no illusions; cricket in Pakistan would be anything but easy. It was based on two reasons: umpiring and strong opposition. We had heard a lot about the former and understood the role they played in the outcome of the previous series. The latter needed no introduction. While different cricket boards across the world had banned players who took part in the Kerry Packer World Series, the Pakistan Cricket Board lifted the ban on Kerry Packer players and raised a strong team. Pakistan was a quality side with the likes of Majid Khan, Zaheer Abbas, Javed Miandad, Asif Iqbal, Mushtaq Mohammad, Imran Khan and Sarfraz Nawaz in the playing XI! Almost all of them regularly played county cricket in England and had built reputations. When we boarded the flight for Karachi, we knew this was more of a political tour than a cricket engagement.

Before the departure, Fateh Singh Rao Gaekwad, the erstwhile maharaja of Baroda and our current team manager, invited the Indian team to his residence in Bombay. The maharaja charmed us with his hospitality and gave us valuable tips for this tour. Although we shared a common past, relations between India and Pakistan had been far from cordial. On a lighter note, the manager asked the players 'fond of drinks' to carry their quota. Many were taken aback by the suggestion, knowing the restrictions on alcohol in Pakistan. The next morning, crates of two-litre Johnnie Walker Red Label whisky arrived and was distributed among the players.

The reception at Karachi airport was unbelievable. Our flight was delayed by a few hours due to bad weather and there were still about 40,000–50,000 people at the airport to welcome us. I was told that at one point the crowd had swelled to over one lakh-strong. However, many left, rather reluctantly, because there was no place to stand while they waited for us. As we emerged from the plane and walked towards the lounge, there were garlands and flashlights all the way. This welcome made me wonder if we were dreaming. Were these the same people who had waged wars against us or had we landed in a different nation? Everyone thrust their hands forward to touch us or possibly shake hands with the nearest Indian player. In addition, many were curious to see what Indians looked like. It touched an emotional cord because, until about three decades ago, we had been part of one country.

The distance from the airport to the hotel normally took twenty minutes, but for us, it took four hours; people had occupied every inch of space on the pavement and the road, and they refused to leave unless and until they caught a glimpse of the Indian cricketers or shaken hands with us. They were warm and hospitable. We had so much in common. There was no difference in our languages. Hindustani was and is, of course, quite like Urdu—most of the time, identical. This common factor not only made communication easier, but also helped me make new friends.

However, this artificial bubble burst quicker than anticipated and hostility emerged from an unexpected quarter. Apparently, certain Pakistani players acted on the advice of seniors and kept their distance. If we spoke to them, their tone and tenor was aggressive. At least two of them, Javed Miandad and Sarfraz Nawaz, and to a lesser degree Mudassar Nazar, took the advice a little too seriously! I don't think either Javed or Sarfraz ever kept quiet on the field. This attitude extended beyond the match at Rawalpindi. An unnecessary remark by a Cambridge-educated cricketer gave us a bit of a shock. After the match, we were a bit casual boarding the bus. Gratuitously, this cricketer said, 'Bithao, bithao, in kafiron ko jaldi bithao (Board these non-believers quickly).' Would it stop here? Or was this part of the social fabric of Pakistan? I wondered. What was the use of a good education if it could not change their negative attitude towards others. Even a player of Mushtaq Mohammad's calibre was found most wanting in his attitude towards the Indian captain, once his colleague in the Northamptonshire County team in England. On the contrary, we followed protocol and the norms of decency, and we avoided making remarks.

Pakistan adopted safety-first tactics against Indian spinners. This became evident in the first Test at Faisalabad. It was the baldest batting wicket I had ever seen. Pakistan made full use of it; Zaheer Abbas and Javed Miandad gave early indications of the shape of things we would encounter. Both scored centuries. Nothing seemed to trouble them; Zaheer Abbas, in particular, was quite impressive in his approach.

We also had our first confrontation with the umpire, Shakoor Rana. I bowled my first delivery and Shakoor Rana gave me an official warning for running on the danger area of the pitch. Sunil Gavaskar fielding at first slip sprinted over, and checked the area and questioned the wisdom of the umpire. This led to a heated argument between them. An unpleasant situation was the last thing we wanted at the beginning of a goodwill tour, so Bishan Bedi changed my end. To everyone's relief, the other umpire, Khalid Aziz, found nothing wrong with my follow through!

We returned to the pavilion after the first session for a much-needed break. Little did we realize that another drama was about to unfold. The two umpires refused to take the field after lunch. They wanted Gavaskar to apologize, which the Indian vice-captain rejected outright. Perhaps this was Shakoor Rana's way of conducting a theatrical drama; it almost jeopardized the tour. The second session was delayed for quite a while, leaving the large crowd baffled. Fortunately, a compromise was reached to commence the match. If Pakistan posted a big total, so did India, thanks to a brilliant century by a little genius called Gundappa Vishwanath. India drew the match with an equally dominant batting display by Gavaskar and Vengsarkar. However, both missed the three-figure mark. It was an honourable draw for India.

A decade later, England captain Mike Gatting had an altercation with Shakoor Rana. A report filed at MCC demanded neutral umpires. Subsequently, it changed the course of international cricket and neutral umpires became the norm!

Finding Indian batsmen hard customers to pin down, Asif Iqbal produced a brilliant plan to distract us. During the match at Rawalpindi (ahead of the Lahore Test), Asif Iqbal came over and spoke about Kerry Packer's World Series and future plans. The razzmatazz and interest it generated in Australia had already been experienced by us during the Test series in Australia in 1977-78. We had also watched some matches on Channel 9. Everything seemed like a big circus under a dark sky studded with twinkling stars and a bright moon. The floodlights created a magical, theatrical atmosphere. The white cricket ball acted like a ballet dancer; loud music after big hits or fall of wickets brought cheerleaders on the stage especially built to charm the audiences. The show was no different from what we see today in the modern-day Indian Premier League (IPL) matches conducted by the BCCI.

Creating an atmosphere of excitement, Asif dropped a bombshell: inviting the Indian players to join the best cricket platform, which not only played aggressive cricket but also guaranteed a handsome purse. When he disclosed that each player would be signed for three years and paid $25,000 or more per season (exchange rate 1$ = 8.19 Rupees), every jaw in the room dropped! We were paid only Rs 20,000 for the Pakistan tour and there was no guarantee about the future. To drive home the point, Asif Iqbal promised to arrange a meeting with Lynton Taylor, a representative of Kerry Packer.

Much to our surprise, Taylor arrived by the first available flight to Lahore. In my recollection, there were quite a few players interested in meeting him, the most prominent being Gavaskar, Vishwanath, Bishan Bedi, Chandrashekhar, Kirmani and myself. There was excitement at the prospect of playing World Series cricket. It was a once-in-a-lifetime opportunity for everyone to play against the world's best players, to make good money in a glamorous contest! We met Lynton Taylor at his hotel. Though all of us were present, only Bishan and Gavaskar sought clarification and the terms of the contract. The rest of us acted like yes-men! We could not finalize the terms on such short notice. It was left to the seniors to pursue the matter and reach an understanding. Many of us started converting dollars into Indian rupees and felt thrilled. A few of us could not hold back the excitement and started counting our chickens before they hatched. Some even contacted their families in India to give the good news! In retrospect, I think it was a shrewd move by Asif to distract us with an offer and hold the meeting before a crucial Test match of the series.

Later, we met Maharaja Fateh Singh Rao Gaekwad, and told him about the meeting and the plan. He advised us not to make any hasty decision and suggested that we have a dialogue with the board. The matter rested for a while. Whether there was any meeting with the BCCI after the tour or not remains a mystery to me till date.

Despite the distraction, Pakistan could not find a way to dislodge Sunil Gavaskar; runs leaked at the top of the order and the Pakistani bowlers were frustrated. The body language of the Pakistan team reflected utter exasperation, which was a testimony to Gavaskar's class. To get an early breakthrough and strike hard at the middle order with the new ball became important for the home side to register a victory. Gavaskar's scalp was equivalent to a bag full of gold. Since Gavaskar was strong on the on-side, I wondered why Imran or Sarfraz, two of the finest new-ball bowlers in Pakistan, could not trap him with a perfect outswing. Pakistan had prepared a wicket with a distinct greenish touch. The toss became a crucial factor due to the moisture in the pitch. Unfortunately, India lost the toss and was put into bat. The ploy to include Saleem Altaf to bowl a perfect outswing delivery clicked almost immediately; Gavaskar was consumed by him early in the innings. The top order collapsed while I tried to hold the innings together, batting on 15. I adopted a safety-first attitude in my innings and was forced to discard my favourite hook shot.

While I ducked under several bouncers, a short delivery from Imran did not rise as high as I expected. I vaguely remember the stretcher being brought out to take me to the hospital. This was the second time I was knocked down, but my skull remained intact. Much to my relief, the doctor told me that the blow wasn't serious, and I could forget it and move on. However, memories of similar mishaps had left a permanent scar in the memory of several players and I was, of course, no different in that regard. I knew it would prove detrimental to my confidence if I failed to face the many challenges on the field. Normally, most batsmen forget the countless deliveries going over the head or how many were hooked for fours and sixes, but one mistake continues to haunt them and give them sleepless nights. To remove any negative thoughts, I decided to face the music the following day in the arena. I took the stance a little deep in the crease. As anticipated, I received a bouncer from Sarfraz; I connected the ball with the meat of my bat. This was the good part—but, in the process, I lost my balance and my bat hit the stumps. I was out hit wicket; I returned to the pavilion, disappointed.

When the moisture evaporated, the pitch behaved like a sleeping beauty. It favoured the batsmen and Pakistan put up a huge total again, thanks to a flawless innings from Zaheer Abbas. He was simply impossible to restrict. Pakistan declared the innings closed on the fourth day, with Zaheer having played a great knock, not out at 235.

Sunil Gavaskar and Chetan Chauhan took up the challenge. Altaf's first-innings success against Gavaskar did not bear a similar result. The memories turned into a nightmare; Gavaskar tore him to pieces in the second innings. The two Indian openers put up 192 on the board when the 'sins' of previous Tests caught up with both of them. One after another, they returned to the pavilion because of dubious decisions. Pakistan's 'trump card' had worked wonders once more. Gavaskar departed at 97; he was furious at having missed another century. It was much worse for Chetan Chauhan; he had not scored a Test hundred till then and, in fact, came closest to achieving the milestone that day. The temperature in the Indian dressing room rose to an unexpectedly high level, with both Gavaskar and Chauhan absolutely livid with themselves for having got out.

All was still not lost as Surinder and Gundappa Vishwanath tore into the Pakistan attack, both scoring rapid half-centuries. However, there was a little hiccup between lunch and tea. Mudassar Nazar produced a magic spell and took two crucial wickets, Vishwanath and Vengsarkar. After tea, when I went to bat with Kirmani for the final session, the match could still be saved. I told Kirmani that I would hook anything that came my way. This was because my ego was badly bruised by Imran's bouncer. Those days, bouncers did not take long to arrive. I hooked the bouncer from Sarfraz straight to the fine-leg fielder. It was quite stupid on my part because, had I played another half an hour, the Test match would have been saved. Pakistan scored the required runs to get their second victory after the Lucknow Test match in 1952. The celebration continued unabated and even President Zia-ul-Haq joined the team to revel in it. Clearly, Pakistan had proved a superior side. They had tasted blood and we knew they would go all-out in the final Test at Karachi.

The match in Karachi was important for me because, so far, I had not set the series alight. When Bishan gave me another chance to prove my prowess, I knew I had to pull something out of the proverbial hat. It did not happen in the first innings, where I fell to Sarfraz once more. The knock on the head from the first match was messing with my concentration and I kept thinking about how to tackle short-pitch deliveries. Pakistan got a lead of 137, which meant we had to fight to save the match again. The news of Surinder's poor health added to our problems. To fill this slot, Bishan promoted me to take my brother's position at number three. Chetan Chauhan did not last long and I walked out to the middle to replace him. Though I was concerned about my brother's condition, I took a leaf out of the book of my earlier performances at this number in Australia. I knew this was my last chance to keep my place in the team for the home series against the West Indies, due immediately afterwards.

One did not need to be a rocket scientist to know the mindset of Imran and Sarfraz. I changed my grip and held it closer to the shoulder for better control. When I walked towards the crease, Sarfraz was operating. He had a 100 per cent record against me in this series, taking my wicket every time I was at the crease. Before I could take my guard, he remarked, 'Dekho, mera murgha aa gaya (Look, my rooster has arrived).' Sarfraz was known to chide his opponents into submission. Nonetheless, I was determined not to let his tactics destabilize me and compromise my wicket.

I had made up my mind to counter-attack any short delivery; this almost worked in Sarfraz's favour. I slashed hard at the first ball and the outside edge flew straight to Zaheer Abbas at first slip—but he spilled it. In frustration, Miandad picked up the ball and tried to knock down the stumps at my end. He missed the target, the ball was overthrown and I opened my account with a boundary. Everyone saw Sarfraz's expression, except me. He was frustrated and angry, and the next two deliveries were bouncers. The first was dispatched for four and the other for six to give me momentum early in the innings. I just knew it was going to be my day. I ended up getting a quickfire half-century under an hour before Imran dismissed me.

That evening, we were invited for a party and we saw the host team huddled together like schoolboys, maintaining a distance from us. However, Imran came up and congratulated me for my aggressive approach. In the years to come, I noticed this trait in him. Even if you were from the opponent's camp, he always made it a point to compliment the good performance of his opponents after the day's play. That is how cricket was played earlier: hard on the field, but dignified and friendly off it.

Unfortunately, none of us occupied the crease long enough to take us to safety. This gave Pakistan an outside chance to get 164 from 22 overs. We understood their tactics when Asif Iqbal replaced the left-hander Sadiq Mohammad and joined Majid Khan at the top of the order. After Majid's dismissal, Miandad occupied the crease. With boundaries hard to come by, these two exhibited a good understanding to steal singles and even tested our arms to run doubles. The real drama unfolded when Imran was promoted to go hammer and tongs. He too found it difficult to hit boundaries. With the fear of LBWs ruled out, they covered the stumps and ran many leg byes. On numerous occasions, Asif, Majid and later Imran were found short of the crease; they received the benefit of the doubt and made a mockery of the rules of cricket. While we walked and changed positions after every over, we found both the umpires already stationed at their positions. They, in fact, sprinted more often in the last hour of the match than any of the fielders in either team in the last five days.

Then came the turning point of the match. Bishan decided to test Imran with his guile, only to receive a shock treatment. Imran hit him for 26 runs in one over and tilted the scale in Pakistan's favour. One apparent mistake cost India dearly and Bishan his captaincy. Despite our loss, this Test could best be remembered as Sunil Gavaskar's finest hours on Pakistan soil. He played splendidly in Karachi, scoring centuries in each innings. During the second innings, I remember an incident involving Sarfraz Nawaz. Whenever he bowled a bouncer, Gavaskar allowed it to sail over his head. When the same bowler pitched the ball up to him, it was dispatched to the fence. This annoyed Sarfraz and he vented his frustration in crass Punjabi words, which Gavaskar couldn't understand. After the over, he came to me and asked, 'Why is Sarfraz calling me pant coat?' I laughed at his ignorance and whispered, 'He meant p***c***!'

After the series, several memories accompanied me to India. Zaheer's majestic batting seemed reserved for us and we could do little to control the proceedings. All the Pakistanis were good players against spin bowling, but he was outstanding. His footwork was brilliant and, given the pace of the pitch, he played smoothly.

Syed Kirmani's performance was under scrutiny from supporters of both sides for obvious reasons. Contrary to this belief, the entire Indian team had full faith in his abilities and character. There had never been any doubt, not one iota, that Kiri would give less than 100 per cent to the national team. He was a complete team-man, both on and off the field, and his patriotism could not be questioned. He silenced those who doubted his loyalties with some fine work behind the stumps.

The most painful memory of the tour, however, was watching the decline of great Indian spinners. I must admit that this quartet was a class apart and most probably the last such collective talent ever to set foot on a cricket field. While the Indian spinners were placed in the pages of history books, a young pace bowler emerged on the horizon. He was raw and unaware of the reputations of the Pakistani cricketers. Playing his second Test match, Imran tested him with a short delivery, which he promptly dispatched it into the stands. Later, Sarfaraz too tested him with bouncers.

When Sarfraz came to bat, this young boy retaliated in a similar fashion. This unexpected retribution forced Sarfraz to seek refuge in his quick wit. He pleaded, 'Mere se kya naraazgi hai, mujhe kyun bouncer karte ho (Why are you angry with me and bowling bouncers)?' This brought a smile to the face of the youngster. It felt good to see a Pakistani pace bowler running for cover when given a taste of his own medicine. Soon, Karsan Ghavri partnered up with the young lad, though a little late on this tour. The boy was Kapil Dev. India's last quality new-ball attack was of Mohammad Nisar and L. Amar Singh in the 1930s.

The result of the Test series brought a change at the helm of affairs in the home series against the West Indies. Sometimes, I wondered whether it happened after the final Test match or the incident during the one-day international in Sahiwal. After India shocked Pakistan in Quetta in the first limited-overs international match, the home side responded well to square the series. All eyes were focused on the last encounter in Sahiwal. Batting first, Pakistan posted 205 in the allotted 40 overs. India was in a commanding position after Surinder sent the Pakistani bowlers on a leather hunt, scoring 62 off 75 deliveries; Anshuman Gaekwad (78 off 115 balls) added 119 to set alarm bells ringing in the Pakistan camp. It was unthinkable and inconceivable for Pakistan to lose a cricket series in any format at a home venue.

When Vishwanath occupied the crease at 2/183, replacing Surinder Amarnath, Sarfraz started bowling a series of bouncers that Vishwanath was unable to reach even if he went up on his toes, and the umpires refused to declare them as wide balls. Bishan was furious; the laws of one-day cricket were being blatantly ignored by the men in white coats. When the pace bowlers continued the unfair practice and umpires connived with them, Bishan became very upset. In disgust, he recalled both the batsmen to the pavilion. No amount of cajoling by the Pakistan Cricket Board officials could change his mind till one of the officials produced a classic solution. He advised the skipper to send someone taller to reach the ball! Nothing more hilarious could have come at this tense moment! It was an extraordinary cricketing phenomenon, both on the field and in the pavilion. It was the first and last time a side in a winning position walked out due to shabby umpiring and lost a match by default. India lost the series, 2-1.

My father was also covering the series for Press Trust of India (PTI) and Pakistan TV. I had never seen him happier than in Lahore. He felt as if he had returned home and wasted no time in contacting and meeting his contemporaries. Papaji was extremely popular and his cricketing exploits were still cherished. Meeting Fazal Mahmood was like a dream come true for us brothers. Fazal wrote in his autobiography, *From Dusk to Dawn*, 'When he [Lala Amarnath] came to Pakistan in 1978, he introduced his two sons, Surinder and Mohinder, to me and told them in his typical Punjabi, "Papay deh go-day naun hath lagao (Seek Fazal's blessings)." Like obedient sons, they both touched my knees as a token of respect.'

We could not meet Murawwat Hussain, because he was no more, but we met his wife. Papaji addressed her as Parjai, meaning 'brother's wife', which showed how close he was to Murawwat. For the first time, I saw emotions taking control of my father; tears rolled down his cheeks. This bond of friendship proved that religion was secondary; friendship was all that mattered. Later, Papaji took us around the narrow bazaars of Lahore—it reminded me of old Delhi, congested and polluted. However, my father's memories were frozen in time when Lahore was a city of gardens. After all, he had spent his early life here; he had a house in Shah Alami Gate Mohalla and another, much larger one was under construction in a new township near Ravi River. All his plans to settle in Lahore were marred by Partition. Another cricketer we wanted to meet was Amir Elahi in Karachi. It was fun watching them pull each other's legs and laugh like little boys!

Apart from Papaji and his old friends' company, it was fun to be with our jovial manager, Maharaja Fateh Singh Rao Gaekwad, affectionately called Maharaja Saheb, who was a great personality. I had first met him as a boy at home during my sister's wedding in 1964. He was an efficient public relations man. He spoke beautifully in Urdu, and that alone made him a popular figure in Pakistan. He too had his contacts in Pakistan and, in fact, two of the earlier Pakistani players, Gul Mohammed and Amir Elahi, had served his father in British India. He was dignified and quite a shrewd politician; he knew how to handle sensitive situations. He tackled everything with a cool mind, an important factor while touring Pakistan. The bigger cities had good hotels but facilities in the smaller cities were not up to the mark. Still, it failed to affect him—though the players, courteously silent, were disappointed with the lack of amenities. Though he was friendly and jovial, one could not take him for granted. Bishan Bedi, himself a tough taskmaster, discovered this in Karachi.

There was a team meeting but the maharaja was not present. We waited for some time and later tried to contact him by phone in his room, but he was not reachable. Agitated by his absence, Bishan grew furious with his lackadaisical attitude. It was typical of Bishan to become vocal; he kept repeating, 'So what if he is a maharaja? He is here as a manager and his job is to be with the team.' The meeting could not start without the maharaja's presence and this was agitating the captain further. After another forty-five minutes, the maharaja walked into the room and a visibly agitated Bishan confronted him. 'Manager,' he said curtly, trying to convey his disapproval. That was all he could manage; the maharaja looked him straight in the eye and said, 'Any problem, Bish?' It was the end of the conversation and the meeting commenced. Despite this incident, I think he was a great choice as manager. He happened to be a combination of many qualities: he played first-class cricket for Baroda; he was a former president of the BCCI; he was a Member of Parliament and manager of the

Indian team to England in 1959. And above all that, he came from a royal background. On the diplomatic front, he was outstanding. As a manager, he was non-interfering. He shared his observations, encouraged players and then took a backseat. At no point did he ever impose himself.

8

LEFT IN THE LURCH
1979–82

I HAVE OFTEN SAID THAT MY LIFE HAS BEEN NOTHING BUT A long and vast assembly line of fluctuating fortunes. There had been several 'highs' throughout my journey and I remembered each of those moments with great fondness. However, those highs vanished much sooner than I'd anticipated, thereby denying me the satisfaction of savouring them. However, alas, 'the lows' stayed in my memory much longer; yet, they failed to bog me down. After all, I was a chip off the old block; I had my father's more desirable qualities. And, this is of course a cliché, but, as we all know, success tastes considerably sweeter after having tasted the bitterness of struggle and defeat!

I must admit that this period of my life was particularly nerve-wracking. I had to search the innermost depths of my soul and question whether my love for cricket, my devotion to this great sport, was worth all the agony. Had I wasted my best years wooing the game that did not respond? I couldn't be sure, and I was stricken with doubt about what I'd done so far and what I was going to do in this game in the future.

I returned to India from the Pakistan tour of 1978 with mixed feelings. I had batted irresponsibly once, but, overall, the tour hadn't been disappointing. Therefore, I was looking forward to the series against Kallicharran's West Indies—hopeful and steadfast.

Bishan Bedi was replaced by Sunil Gavaskar as captain. India played the first Test match at Wankhede Stadium in Bombay: it was a high-scoring game. Amongst the delightful batsmen stood one silent figure—me. Though disappointed, I assumed more opportunities would come my way in the six-match series. Unfortunately, that occasion (almost) became my last appearance; the news of my omission shook me thoroughly. I thought deeply about my future. There was now only one chance available for me to prove my credentials, the North Zone match against the tourists before the last Test. I was convinced that someone was not comfortable with the presence of the Amarnath brothers in the team. My elder brother was discarded, despite his reasonably good performance in Pakistan. As the West Indies series unfolded, I was quite convinced it was the end of the road for me. I would never play for India again; hence, there was no point in continuing with cricket in India.

I fished out the World Series Cricket contract Lynton Taylor had offered me in Pakistan. Since no decision could be reached in Pakistan and no one had tried to contact me after that, I took a call. With a bleak future ahead, I signed the contract, sent it by post and waited patiently for the response. But it turned out to be too late; Kerry Packer was interested in the full-strength Indian XI, or a sizable contingent, to be part of the World XI, and not just an individual. Did Asif Iqbal take us for a sweet ride? I thought so.

With Australia being rather tight-lipped and my prospects of playing for India shrouded in mystery, my interest in the game gradually began to wane. Before the West Indies vs North Zone match in Jalandhar, I contemplated quitting the game forever. Although I was part of the North Zone team, I had little or no interest in this contest. Papaji was by my side; he tried to comfort me with more of his sane advice; the England tour was due to be held in the summer of 1979. This was an indirect way for me to continue playing cricket, to continue engaging with the sport I'd always loved. However, Papaji did not press his views on me; on the contrary, he gave me full freedom to take the final call! I could not break his heart by quitting the game so hastily, so I simply said, 'Ji', meaning that I would do as he desired without any further debate or discussion.

When my wife, Bickoo, agreed with Papaji, I had no option but to board the train with her for Jalandhar. She happened to be in an advanced stage of pregnancy and she wished to visit her maternal grandparents in Qadian, in Punjab. With the series almost over, I had nothing to lose. I played this match with no practice at all. For the first time in my career, there was no pressure; I was playing purely for fun. I found the atmosphere congenial and batting even easier than before. I stroked the ball without any fear of dismissal. For once, there was no tension in the nineties and I ended up reaching the three-figure mark easily.

The only vivid memory I had of this match was of facing a slim and young fast bowler, relatively unknown, named Malcolm Marshall. He was quite short compared with the other fast bowlers on his side, yet he generated immense pace and bounce from a wicket that was otherwise placid. With a century tucked under my belt, I enjoyed my spell of bowling and I even took a few wickets at crucial moments.

After the match, we took the Punjab Roadways bus to a small town called Batala. It was a fascinating journey through the heart of Punjab, which revealed a different world and way of life. The green fields, the chugging of tube well pumps and fresh water flowing from them; farmers happily tilling the field with newly acquired tractors; elders sitting under a tree chatting and laughing. All these sights were alien to urbanites.

As there was no train connection to Qadian via Batala, we boarded another local bus. On reaching the destination, we hired a horse-driven carriage, a tonga, which reminded me of those old days in boarding school. It was enjoyable and quite an adventure for us. We landed at Bickoo's nana's place late at night. We were warmly received by all the members of the family. It seemed like a happy reunion. Although it was late, they welcomed us with true Punjabi hospitality. A bottle of liquor and a few glasses were placed on the table. They were a little surprised when I declined the offer and instead requested a glass of hot milk. Instantly, I was handed a jug full of milk and everyone looked at me while I waited for a glass; apparently, I was supposed to gulp it all down! Bickoo, sitting beside me, nudged me with her elbow and whispered, 'The son-in-law is special here; satiate your desire directly from the jug!' After about an hour, we went to bed for some much-needed rest; it was maybe the best sleep I'd had in a long time.

The next morning, I was amazed to see the outlay of this huge mansion. I was told it was the haveli of Tahir Ahmad Mirza, built of red brick and surrounded by an orchard of seasonal fruit trees. The compound had a tennis court, stables and several servant quarters. The Mirza family had been greatly revered and exerted tremendous influence over the people of the

Ahmadiyya sect of Islam, till they chose to migrate to Pakistan in 1947. The story was much like what had happened with many influential Hindu and Sikh families. Sardar Harcharan Singh Bajwa was well settled in Multan, but the partition of India forced the family to flee to India for safety. In lieu of their ancestral property in Multan, the Government of India gave them this property as compensation for their loss.

There is a certain tradition in Punjab, a custom, where the ladies always ask the son-in-law about the choice of food. Because I was a non-vegetarian, I expressed a desire for a chicken dish. Little did I realize it would be one of their own home-bred chickens on the platter! Though curry looked tempting, my conscience revolted. I felt sorry for the poor bird for losing its life so I could have a full stomach! This was rural Punjab, ready to make a sacrifice for the happiness of a guest; but it must be said that, on this occasion, I was not exactly the happiest guest they could hope for!

Later, we went across town to the cultural centre of the Ahmadiyya community. However, most of the inhabitants had migrated to Pakistan, leaving behind some beautiful monuments and memories. The dress code of this town was much like that of the inhabitants of western Punjab, now in Pakistan. Women wore salwar kameez, along with a dupatta or a piece of long cloth to cover their shoulders or head, and a shawl to keep them warm. The tall and handsome men wore colourful turbans, tehmet and kurta with matching tilleh-wali juttis or embroidered slippers. After sunset, almost everyone had a bottle of whisky in their hands and they wore a leather strap across their chest with a kirpan, or dagger; they also displayed a double-barrel gun in the other hand or had it propped over the shoulder. Unfortunately, this trip soon had to be cut short because I received news of my inclusion in the Indian team, the starting XI, for the sixth Test match in Kanpur.

I smiled and thanked the Almighty for this deliverance! At one point of time, I was toying with the idea of giving up the game and now I was recalled to play for the Indian team! Still, it was hard to forget the harsh treatment I had endured. In my cynicism, I suspected everyone, including the captain. To expect any words of reassurance or encouragement would have been foolish. Throughout my innings, the non-striker hardly spoke a word and I simply focused on the milestone without wavering for a moment. Having achieved it, I closed my eyes and thanked two of the most precious souls in my life: my wife, Bickoo, and Papaji.

When I returned to the dressing room, however, I was greeted by silence. There was no celebration, no pats on the back, no words of congratulation, not even a smile or a nod of the head to acknowledge the achievement! But, if I'm going to be perfectly honest, I didn't really expect any gracious remarks from my teammates either! Immediately after the end of the series, Gavaskar flummoxed everyone with the announcement that he was stepping down as captain because 'he was not in the right frame of mind' to lead India in England. It surprised many because he'd been sailing so smoothly with the bat; he'd had a great series against Pakistan and amassed runs against Kallicharran's West Indies side. If anything at all, he ought to be looking forward to the England tour as a captain! Maybe he was some sort of clairvoyant, and he could predict the fate of the Indian team in the World Cup and against England in the Test series.

With the burden of uncertainty removed, I could relax and play freely in the knockout matches of the Ranji Trophy. Although Bishan Singh Bedi was still leading Delhi, he was going through a great deal of mental distress at having lost his place in the Indian team after his previous poor showing as captain. He too had become rather cynical about his and the team's prospects, and extremely anti-Bombay in his attitude. He perceived that the malevolent Bombay lobby had sidelined the seniors on purpose. Defeating the Bombay team in its backyard gradually became an obsession for him. Delhi achieved the goal with scant respect. On the last day of the match, it was clear that Delhi had won the semi-final of the Ranji Trophy with a first innings lead, yet Bishan rubbed salt in Bombay's wounds by mercilessly prolonging the innings till the tea break.

The crowd expected a declaration and wanted to watch Gavaskar bat again in the last session. Much to their dismay, Madan Lal and I resumed batting. The crowd reacted with angry slogans and subsequently invaded the field. Caught in a melee, Madan Lal swatted at them with his bat, but immediately realized it was an expensive English Crown bat. Thereafter, it became more precious than his own life! We dashed towards the pavilion for safety. It was not quite the culmination we'd hoped for in the most important semi-final of the domestic calendar. Yet, we cherished it! Delhi played like a true champion team against Karnataka in the finals. We excelled in all the departments of the game. In the first innings, our batting revolved around two Surinders, my brother and Surinder Khanna, both managing to score a century each. In the second innings, my brother was unfortunately dismissed in the worst possible way—he was run out. I had missed out in the first innings, but I was compensated with 178 not out in the second; Surinder Khanna repeated his performance from the first innings with another century in the second. Later, Madan Lal took five wickets to seal the game for our side, and soon the Delhi cricket team made history and lifted the Ranji Trophy for the first time.

Coming back to the Indian team, Gavaskar had declined the captaincy for the England tour and Bishan was, in any case, out of the reckoning. Venkataraghavan was the senior-most player, for which he was deemed most appropriate to take the mantle. My back-to-back centuries ensured me a place in the team for the England tour. With the cricket season in India over, I went to England to join my family, and continued my training and practice. But my serenity with my family and the sport I loved was soon disturbed by the news of my brother Surinder's omission from the Indian team—yet again. I couldn't understand what was going. He was the best left-handed batsman in India and would have been an invaluable asset in limited-overs cricket. The reason for his omission was mind-boggling; he played too many strokes to put the selectors at ease and therefore he was deemed 'too risky'.

Bengaluru, renowned for its pleasant weather, was where we held a short preparation camp. My request to join the team in England was turned down. I made a long journey to attend the camp and practise in alien conditions. Furthermore, there was no trace of seriousness amongst the players and, even worse, there was no outline of a strategy. Four years after the first World Cup in 1975, the selectors had not the slightest clue about one-day cricket. It seemed as if we were heading for another holiday package.

While some teams came prepared to replicate their earlier performances, others desired to put up a better show. However, I simply wanted to forget the past. An ugly scene in the dressing room at Headingley in 1975 refused to leave me. A mere argument in the field between two senior members of the team was carried into the dressing room, which almost resulted in grave injuries. They acted most immaturely, abusing each other and throwing punches. In the scuffle, shirts were torn and buttons flew in different directions. No one dared to intervene till the team manager separated them. The youngsters were terrified by this unusual drama.

If World Cup matches raised the adrenaline of most teams, we remained indifferent. During a match against Sri Lanka, half the team was in the rival team's dressing room watching the telecast of the West Indies versus Australia match. Such was their involvement that we could hear high-pitched discussions outside the dressing room! The seriousness of the team management could also be gauged by the absence of the team manager. We were not expected to do well and, lo and behold—we did not do well!

Shifting gears from limited overs to longer versions hardly bothered the Indian team. The World Cup matches and constant travelling by road did, of course, lead to some fatigue. The formal tour commenced with several county matches, which certainly tested our skills. Before the first Test match at Edgbaston, we played against Leicestershire. I bowled a long spell and, after each over, felt a strain in my lower back, which I ignored. What a blunder!

After losing the first test match at Edgbaston, the next test match at Lord's was important to me because I was suffering from back pain. The manager arranged an appointment with a specialist at Harley Street, London. I travelled alone in the local black taxi to his clinic and undertook the treatment for several days. Unfortunately, my condition did not improve. Then the doctor tried to give me relief with painkiller injections, but they brought little relief. Hence, I missed the next match at Lord's. Nevertheless, I got to watch two classic innings: Vishwanath and Vengsarkar scored fine centuries to guide India to safety.

The only way to heal my back and be fit for the next match was to give myself complete rest. On the contrary, the captain made me go through a long session in the nets, which further aggravated my injury. Then came a bombshell: the team management insisted that I play against Derbyshire and, if not, I should go home. Was history repeating itself? My father had faced a similar situation on the infamous England tour in 1936; the thought made me shudder! I needed rest, but the team management arranged a fitness test for me.

Determined to stay with the team, I took a precautionary step. I applied an ice pack to the tender area for forty-five minutes and subsequently took painkillers before the drill. I cleared the fitness test. However, the weather against Derbyshire brought no smile to my face. It was cold and wet, and it made my back stiff and painful. I was not sure if I would last long, defending. I adopted bold tactics, swinging the willow against all the bowlers to score a quick-fire century.

The atmosphere in the Indian dressing room remained tense thanks to the captain's obstinacy. It terrified juniors, and they had a tough time on and off the field. I remember a match against Gloucestershire where Yajurvindra Singh bowled a long spell and took five wickets. Satisfied with his accomplishment, he decided to enjoy a hot bath. When the captain announced Yajurvindra Singh's name in the batting order—I think it was in the middle order—he was missing. When the captain was informed that the concerned player was taking a bath, he was not amused. Yajurvindra was ordered to leave the tub and pad up because he was promoted. India lost an opening batsman quickly and Yajurvindra Singh replaced him for a short stint at the crease. He returned to the pavilion, tossed away his bat, gloves and pads, jumped into the hot tub once more—and got to enjoy it for even longer!

I returned to the playing XI for the third Test match at Leeds. The conditions were apt for seam bowling and I bowled a long spell to take a couple of wickets. This put considerable strain on my delicate back, which was, by now, quite sore. I was expecting to bat in the middle order like at the Edgbaston match, but was surprised to hear my slot fixed at number three. There seemed to be no set batting order for me. Before the fourth match, we were facing Nottinghamshire, and the captain asked if I would like to open the innings in the next Test. My jaw almost fell; I wondered why he would ask such an irrelevant question. Gavaskar and Chauhan were performing extremely well. For the first time in my life, I put my foot down and went against the decision of a captain: I refused to abide by his desire now.

The wicket at Nottingham was at the edge of a square, and it was prepared on purpose for Richard Hadlee and Clive Rice, two of the finest new-ball bowlers of the era. To make matches between counties and the touring team more interesting, sponsors had announced generous rewards for the winners. It created a buzz in many dressing rooms. During the game, Anshuman Gaekwad accidentally broke his spectacles and requested the captain to put him further down the order till he received a fresh pair. To his shock, he was asked to open the innings despite the handicap, and on a green-top wicket! The illogical directive could have landed the poor batsman in the grave, facing such a lethal bowling attack! How Anshuman managed to save his skin remained a mystery to me and the rest of the team.

I, however, was not so lucky. At times, it was rather difficult to see the ball because the sight screen could not be adjusted behind the bowler's arm. With pace bowlers calling the shots in the second innings, wickets tumbled. However, I remained undefeated with a half-century. The next day, Richard Hadlee opened the bowling from the far end and immediately dug the first delivery short. I had managed to successfully hook him the previous day, and I accepted the challenge. Before I could react or get into the right position, the hard red cherry hit me just above my right temple. Had it made impact just a little here or there, it could have made me another Nari Contractor.

I felt as if a thousand volts of electricity had passed through my body. I collapsed like a bag full of sand and crushed the stumps. The next thing I remember was lying on a stretcher and vomiting. I was rushed to the emergency room at a nearby hospital. The MRI revealed that I had fractured my skull; I was put under observation for the next forty-eight hours. The pain was excruciating and the thought of missing another Test match was depressing. The doctors, after a thorough check-up, advised complete rest. The hotel could not give me comfort; the doctor reluctantly relieved me. I was allowed to accompany my wife to our home in Huddersfield, Yorkshire. It was an unfortunate end to my time in the England tour.

Though the injury took a while to heal, my memory remained fresh. While the rest of the boys prepared to face a relatively weak Australian side, I stayed back at home, bedridden in England. Even the slightest movement sent spasms throughout my body. Often, late at night, I would open my eyes and prop myself up in bed to reduce the throbbing pain; it never worked. More than physical discomfort, I began worrying how I would react to the short-pitched stuff again. This started playing on a constant loop in my mind. I had, of course, been hit before on the field but I had never been knocked down.

The Indian team returned home with its prestige salvaged after a disastrous World Cup and the opening Test match. This performance almost bludgeoned home the point that despite being a good, reliable side in Test cricket, we remained greenhorns in the one-day format. As anticipated, Gavaskar regained captaincy for the home series against Australia. When I returned to India, a journalist wanted my reaction to a rumour that Gavaskar threw away his wicket at the Oval after scoring 221 and deprived India of victory. I simply laughed at this atrocious presumption and hearsay! Whatever ambitions Gavaskar may have had, he was a great team-man, a fierce competitor and a thorough professional.

By the time, the doctor gave me a clean bill of health; so I could start playing again. The first Test had already started at the Chinnaswamy Stadium in Bangalore. I reached the city of gardens with my fitness certificate and handed it to the selector, Polly Umrigar. I also confirmed my fitness and looked forward to playing the next Test, if selected. But 'Polly Kaka,' as he was fondly called, asked me to also meet the Board president, M. Chinnaswamy. The BCCI president categorically informed me that my certificate alone wouldn't do and that I must also get clearance from the board-appointed doctor.

Apparently, this gentleman was available neither in Bangalore, Bombay nor Delhi; he was in Hyderabad. With little choice or assistance from the BCCI, I was forced to travel again. Once the flight took off, I realized I wasn't alone: Yajurvindra Singh had also recovered from a recent injury and a local doctor had declared him fit. However, the BCCI official was not convinced and he sent him off to Hyderabad to consult this indispensable doctor. Due to conflicting messages, I met not one but two doctors—one to check my eyesight, the other for general fitness. I wondered if my friend ended up meeting the neurologist; I chuckled at the faux pas. Nevertheless, I underwent both tests in ten minutes and was declared fit. I was included for the next Test but failed to make it to the playing XI till the last Test in Bombay. Due to a lack of match practice, I felt rusty. I was also a bit apprehensive with my preparation. The news of my injury had travelled across the cricketing world, which impelled the Australian fast bowlers to test my nerves. Honestly, I did not expect any leniency at this level. I prepared myself in the best possible manner. I experimented with a local cricket helmet but found it too heavy. I needed something light and solid to protect my skull. The choice finally fell on the solar hat, which my father had worn against fast bowlers in Australia.

To boost my confidence, I tried it out during net practice. My timing was abysmal; alarm bells immediately started ringing in my head. Had I rushed back into international cricket too early? There was no turning around now. The way I played the first few deliveries indicated my nervousness. Around this time, Australia opted for a third new ball and Rodney Hogg came charging in to bowl. I was obsessed with bouncers and prepared myself to face them. Being proactive certainly helped my cause. I played a perfect shot. That was the happy part! But while swerving, my back foot slipped. I lost my balance and my bat hit the stumps. Without doubt, it was the most embarrassing moment of my life. As I walked back to the dressing room, 40,000 spectators taunted me. Even before this incident, critics had deemed me 'a bunny of fast bowlers'. Now, I had clearly given them a golden opportunity to brand me for life.

The period following this incident was utterly agonizing, even for my wife. She had been equally involved with my cricket and stood firmly by my side against unnecessary criticism. When this dismissal took place, she was about to enter a gurudwara where people were listening to the match commentary on the radio. 'Look, Amarnath has fallen on his stumps again!' she heard. I had to make an extra effort to reach out to her that evening.

My reputation as a batsman took some beating. Wherever or at whichever level I played, the pace bowlers took a longer run-up, ran as fast as they could and bowled the most horrible bouncers to frighten me into submission. When I look back, I think the attitude of those bowlers actually helped me. If I had to survive and be taken seriously at the international level, I had to be prepared to face six bouncers per over. Luckily for me, helmets, far lighter than the one I had tried at Bombay, soon appeared in the market.

One day, Madan Lal gave me a precious gift: a helmet. I wore it to test my comfort in the nets and match, regardless of who bowled. There were a few eyebrows raised at my new approach, but I took every comment with a pinch of salt. I simply didn't want to take another chance with an injury and terminate my career. I found that wearing a helmet increased my confidence.

As usual, I spent the summer in England, contemplating my future in Indian cricket, especially after the Hadlee and Hogg incidents. My reputation was badly tarnished and the writing was on the wall for the Australia tour. At this stage, an idea crossed my mind to play grade cricket in Australia. The emoluments were decent and the standard was good. The only obstruction was the Indian domestic season clashing with the schedule in Australia. However, the situation and the mood collectively supported me in taking a decision in favour of a new land, Australia.

I wrote to the secretary of the Western Australia Cricket Association about my desire to play as an overseas professional. Promptly, I received a response from Craig Serjeant inviting me to play for the South Perth Cricket Club. I had a month's gap between the English and Australian seasons; accordingly, I came down to Delhi to spend time with my parents. Word spread, and I was asked to play the Wills Trophy and Irani Trophy matches—the latter a selection match for Australia. I consulted friends; the consensus was that there was no way I would be picked for Australia. While I played the Wills Trophy, I decided to skip the Irani Trophy. This upset many people, including Papaji and Surinder, but my decision turned out to be the right one. Despite Surinder scoring a fluent double century (235 not out) against the entire Indian attack consisting of Kapil, Ghavri, Doshi and Yadav, he failed to find a place in the team. I guessed I would also have met the same fate.

Grade cricket in Australia was an educational experience. The standard was pretty high and the matches were tough. There were quick bowlers in every team. Playing them in the nets and matches did my confidence a world of good. Still, it hurt not to be part of the Indian team in Australia. With my confidence returning, I looked forward to re-establishing myself in the Indian team. Though the England team was touring India, I was unsure of my place in the playing XI. Fortunately, Bishan had started taking interest in the administration of Delhi cricket and it was typical of him to welcome me. Not only was I back in the Delhi team, I was appointed captain too.

It was a crucial season for me as a batsman and captain of Delhi. We managed to reach the final, but my contribution was below the general expectation. I needed a big score in the finals. Karnataka batted first and kept us on the field for almost three days, raising a mammoth total of 705. For once, I was concerned with the morale of the team and the target. Then, I saw a familiar figure from Bombay in the pavilion. He had come to support the Karnataka team. Despite the stiff target, he was heard telling the Karnataka players, 'Dismiss the Amarnath brothers early!'

The team responded in a manner befitting a champion. The young Gursharan Singh, in particular, scored a fine century to inspire the others. The five-day final had to be extended to the sixth day to complete the first innings and decide the fate of this contest. I held one end firmly but was dismissed on the sixth morning by Roger Binny at 185. There was jubilation in the Karnataka camp. However, another surprise awaited them. The determined ninth-wicket pair of Rakesh Shukla and Rajesh Peter took the wind out of Karnataka's sails, stitching an undefeated century partnership to seal the fate of the match. My cup of joy was full and I knew I couldn't have done more to regain my place in the Indian team. Still, there was no dearth of critics to snatch credit from me. One of them said that I scored a century only because it was a placid pitch. Was it a conspiracy to deny me a place in the team or did they already know the line-up? I was not part of the team. When the *Sportsworld* correspondence questioned the Indian captain about my omission, Sunil Gavaskar came out with a statement: 'What could he have been taken for? His bowling? How many Test wickets has he taken? Twenty, maybe? He could not be included as a batsman. There are any number of players better than him in that sphere; and preference should be given to the youngsters. And I cannot see him as an all-rounder in my team.'

Gavaskar was, of course, entitled to his opinion, but mocking my abilities and efforts in public left a rather poor impression of the Indian captain. When I scanned the list of players selected for England, it revived my aspiration. There were quite a few players with technical deficiencies. I knew they would be exposed against the moving ball in England. If I repeated my earlier performance in the coming domestic season, the Pakistan tour was a possibility.

With every passing year, my life span in international cricket was shrinking. I had lost three years in the wilderness and had to catch up for the years lost. I was down in the dumps and low in spirits. Adding to that, a supposedly good friend and a reputed Indian cricketer came to enjoy my hospitality in Lancaster, England. Watching me train the following morning, he almost broke my resolve with a comment: 'Jim pa, leave the hard work and enjoy life. There is no point trying another comeback. Hang up your boots!' Comments such as this left me wondering whether he was my well-wisher or an opportunist!'

I continued training as usual as I had nothing better to do. The weekend league matches kept me in touch with the game and kept alive in me a genuine hope that I would play for India again. Finding me in dire straits, Bickoo distracted me with the preview of a movie. What a blessing it turned out to be! The moment I heard the theme song of *Rocky III*, 'Eye of the tiger,' it reminded me of my struggle. 'Don't lose your grip on the dreams of the past, you must fight just to keep them alive'; that seemed so appropriate and almost identical to my story! I lost count of the hours I spent watching the film on television and listening to the soundtrack on the radio.

I felt a different sensation in my body, as if it had been infused with a fresh dose of energy. A new Jimmy had emerged; young and positive, full of vigour, ready to face any challenge. That night, I tossed and turned in bed waiting for the sun to rise to commence my new schedule for training. Despite little sleep, I was as fresh as a daisy. There was a spring in my step, strength in my voice, steadiness in my gaze.

I was obsessed with the training and attitude of Sylvester Stallone as Rocky. I walked a mile from from home to Lancaster Moor Hospital spread over fifty acres, where my wife Bickoo worked as a psychiatrist. I was carrying a three-kg medicine ball and a skipping rope for training. When the caretaker of the ground came to know that I was Dr Bickoo's spouse, he offered to help me. I ran for forty-five minutes—be it sunny, cold or wet—five days a week and without a care in the world. This was followed by one hour of exercises and 3,000 jumps with the skipping rope. Unsure of how to use the medicine ball, I pushed myself to 100 on day one. What a mistake! The next morning, I could not get up without support; my stomach muscles had contracted and I could not laugh. Knowing there was no gain without pain, I continued with the schedule. The ground staff were friendly; they offered tea or coffee after the session—a welcome break! While returning home through the fields, I never forgot to purchase 500 ml full-cream fresh milk. It restored my energy and compelled me to sing some old Hindi songs!

A few days later, another pair of Indian cricketers (Roger Binny and Anshuman Gaekwad playing in Scotland) came with their spouses to spend time with us. Their cultured discussions made the atmosphere jovial and made life seem easy. The following day, they also joined me for the training session. No doubt they took several laps and subsequently stopped due to disinterest or exhaustion. They were aghast to see my training schedule and they jokingly remarked, 'You've gone crazy!' How one song had utterly transformed my attitude!

Losing my place in the Indian team had its repercussions elsewhere too. Suddenly, my employer deducted my salary, which hit me financially. Ranji Trophy matches hardly compensated me enough for the deduction, with a meagre amount of Rs 200–300 per match. The endorsement fee from the cricket manufacturing company dried out too. At this stage, I didn't have a decent kit. The situation became so critical during the Duleep Trophy matches that I didn't have a single undamaged bat! Ultimately, I had to seek Anshuman Gaekwad's help. Luckily, the two Duleep Trophy semi-finals were held at adjacent grounds, the Brabourne Stadium and the Wankhede Stadium in Bombay. When North Zone batted at Brabourne, West Zone fielded at Wankhede. As a result, Anshuman and I could use the same bat! Every time I finished my innings, it was sent across to the other stadium for Anshuman.

I got a double century against East Zone in the semi-finals, and 80 and 67 not out in the final. After the match, Anshu presented the bat to me. Certain critics were still not happy or satisfied. They complained that I batted too slow! After the match, Bishan Bedi, now a national selector, came and cautioned me. He revealed a conspiracy to deny me another comeback. He said, 'Jimmy, you have to get a hundred in the Irani Trophy match.' I nearly threw the towel in the ring.

However, sitting alone and in deep thought, I realized Bishan's statement meant that my goal was within touching distance.

Between the two matches, I went back to Baroda and trained in solitude. I had a mission and never deviated from my goal, the India cap. However, Delhi lost the Irani Trophy, but my determination paid off. I got the century Bishan wanted from me. I recollect sitting in the dressing room, tense and out of sorts. I suddenly heard a whisper in my ears: 'You are in!' It came from the smiling face of the team manager, Gulshan Rai (now deceased).

9

PAKISTAN TOUR 1982–83
COMEBACK 2

THE PAKISTAN TOUR OF 1982 WAS DIFFERENT IN COMPARISON to my first visit in 1978. Then, I had gone high in spirits; my place in the Indian team was secure and the future looked bright. I was keen to enhance my reputation in international cricket. This time, I had come from the wilderness to mend my broken reputation.

The period from 1979 to 1982 was very traumatic for me. I had been out of international cricket for a while and, regrettably, the name 'Mohinder Amarnath' seemed ancient and lay in the discarded list of Indian cricketers. Although I was fit at thirty-two, I understood that this was probably my last chance to play international cricket.

I also realized it would be another difficult tour, keeping in mind the conditions and the dubious distinction of certain umpires. Added to it was Imran Khan, relishing his reputation as a premier fast bowler and at the height of his prowess. With India as his opponent, he was likely to push his performance a few notches higher. As for me, thanks to certain Indian cricket journalists and board officials, I had acquired a reputation of being scared of fast bowling. I knew Imran and the rest of the fast bowlers would come loaded with bouncers to take full advantage of this tag. Yet, there was one consolation: it was an away tour. I did not have to bother about the critics back home.

At times, the pressure of playing in India could be counterproductive—something only an experienced cricketer could understand. In my case, there had been an unnecessary pressure to perform or perish. Throughout my career, I was burdened with particularly scrutinous selectors. They assessed me by solitary performances, contrary to batsmen from any other zone. One bad performance meant I would be dropped and forgotten. Fortunately, this pressure was less on tour because there were only sixteen players to choose from and one or two off-colour days did not mean instant rejection. This tour was to decide my fate, once and for all.

The reception at Karachi airport was strikingly different from our previous tour. There were no massive crowds at the airport or on the streets to catch a glimpse of Indian cricketers. Maybe television provided a better option or multiple Test series between the two neighbours had removed the sheen of novelty? The next morning, we received instructions from our manager, Maharaja Fateh Singh Rao Gaekwad, to get ready for the first official engagement. As a protocol, we drove to Muhammad Ali Jinnah's tomb to lay a wreath. The local media and a large crowd awaited us. The moment I stepped out from the team coach, one person from the crowd shouted my name and said, 'YAAD HAI 1978 MEIN IMRAN NE TUMHARA

SAR PHODA THA? IS BAAR BHI HOGA (Remember how Imran knocked you with a bouncer in 1978? He will repeat it again)!' I was taken aback by this comment, yet replied with a smile. It was an open challenge to my integrity; I had to counter it with my performance on the pitch. This unexpected challenge and reminder made my resolve even greater to prove a new-found critic wrong!

Instead of being flustered, I had conviction. The main reason was that I had changed my stance from a traditional side-on stance to one that was open-chested. In 1980, I had opted to play club cricket in Australia to counter fast bowling and regain my confidence. At the onset of the season, I had an eye infection that was most tenacious and almost ruined my time in Australia. Initially, I thought there was something seriously wrong with my eyesight, till a simple test proved me wrong. By then, I had already changed my stance and found it easier to take on short-pitch deliveries.

Since the wicket at the WACA in Perth offered bounce and pace, it was a paradise for fast bowlers. Most teams preferred a lethal combination of left-and right-arm quickies, and they tested me with short-pitch deliveries. To my satisfaction, the modified stance provided me more time to judge the length and angle of their deliveries. Accordingly, I played the hook shot or left it alone. When I returned to India the following season, I continued with the square stance and in the following season too. Runs flowed easily from my blade in Indian conditions but it had little effect on those who mattered. However, facing Pakistan in their backyard was a different ball game. In addition, Imran was likely to prove a potent threat. Still, something within convinced me that I could handle him better with a square stance than a traditional side-on stance.

There were a couple of matches before the first Test at Lahore to finalize the combination. Although I had to compete for a batting slot, I was quite confident I would be part of the playing XI because I could double as the third seamer along with Kapil Dev and Madan Lal. Coming so close to my dreams was indeed exhilarating, yet nervousness caused a flurry of strange feelings within me. In retrospect, it seemed odd that a man of thirty-two, who had played the world's fastest bowlers, was susceptible to such anxiety. Maybe my three-year absence from the international circuit had something to do with my confidence. I prayed that we would field first, which would allow me to come to terms with the Test match atmosphere before padding up.

Our arrival at the venue was greeted with silence. For some strange reason, the boisterous atmosphere at Gaddafi Stadium was missing and it presented a deserted picture. All of us were baffled. Had we become less attractive and could not draw any crowds? Without them, the atmosphere and excitement were gone. It did not take long to discover the reason for their absence. We were told that the authorities had sold the rights of the match to a private promoter. Since it was an India–Pakistan contest, this company hoped to make a big profit; they had jacked up the price of the tickets beyond the grasp of the common man. This policy backfired, and most Lahoris preferred to stay home and watch it live on television. Imran won the toss and opted to bat. They kept us on the field for more than five sessions and Zaheer Abbas scored a double century to take Pakistan to 485.

When play resumed after a rest day, we lost three quick wickets, which put immediate pressure on us. At this point, I observed that Imran was getting the ball to change its course on a placid wicket with minimal effort. When I walked amongst the ruins to join Sunil Gavaskar, I was quite apprehensive of the situation. The comeback scene I had enacted in my mind for the past three years was under better conditions. Now, it seemed like a bad dream. To be honest, I was nervous and looked for a divine intervention to rescue me. For some strange reason, I recited 'shabd', or a verse from the Guru Granth Sahib, and prayed to destiny to be a little sympathetic towards me.

Coming back to the team and re-establishing my credentials had its effect on my overall mood. It does not matter how great a player you are—a fresh innings always started at zero. I had butterflies in my stomach, and hearing the opponents speak the same language added to my anxiety. Shutting my mind was not easy, so I recited the famous quote of Guru Gobind Singhji, 'Nishchay kar apni jeet karoon (Be determined, victory will be yours)', to try and overcome my nerves.

The moment I took guard, all the slip fielders and the wicketkeeper, Wasim Bari, became vocal to distract me. They understood my plight and tried to exert pressure. After each delivery, Bari shouted, 'Bahut ala hai, bahut ala' meaning splendid delivery. To keep up the momentum, the slip cordon joined the chorus while the mid-off fielder patted the bowler to inspire him. I believe my face also showed signs of nervousness, which encouraged the Pakistani fielders to react more aggressively.

True to their reading, I left alone a couple of Imran's huge inswingers, which almost shaved the off stump. Wasim Bari, the slip fielders and the bowler were foxed by my audacious decisions and my good fortune. To be honest, I did not know much about these deliveries either. My footwork was at its worst and luck probably at its best! Frustrated, Imran dug a few deliveries short in length; some sailed over my head, while others hit my left shoulder or rib cage. Each impact caused excruciating pain, but I did not rub the bruised spot; I just smiled. I seemed like a bird in a cage, attacked from all sides. Sunil Gavaskar at the non-striker's end was watching the proceedings in horror.

At this stage, Gavaskar walked down the pitch to me and said, 'I know how you must be feeling. Just relax and it will come back.' As luck would have it, the first contact with the ball off Tahir Naqqash was an inside edge. It almost kissed the leg stump, but went down to fine leg, opening my account with a boundary. Having vanquished the bloody duck, I took a deep breath and smiled! Slowly and gradually, the ball started finding the middle of the blade to release the remaining pressure and relax my muscles. It was interesting to experience how the brain plays a crucial role in controlling the heartbeat and stabilizing the pulse rate. Once my confidence increased, I freed my arms on occasion and played an attacking shot.

Gradually, the butterflies in my stomach subsided and the sweet sound of the willow hummed in my ears. It was the most beautiful music in the world! Throughout the innings, Sunil Gavaskar kept talking to me, which I thought was an excellent gesture. At that moment, my memories took me back to Trinidad, 1976, when he was confined to his own world, uttering nothing except a call for a single or more. Maybe he wanted to prove to the world what a good player he was and nothing could distract him. Having achieved his status and proved his abilities, he was more communicative.

By the end of play, I was undefeated with a half-century. I was thrilled. In the evening Papaji, along with his old friend, Brigadier Abdul Baseer Shamsi came to meet me at Hotel Hilton. Before Partition, both had played local cricket in Lahore. Later, Shamsi became a member of the Pakistan Cricket Board. An ecstatic Papaji hugged me tightly and asked for a gift. This demand took me by surprise because he had never ever demanded any gift from me. Without waiting for his choice, I gave him my word. He smiled and patted my shoulder. 'My gift is your century.' Here too he wanted nothing for himself; his gift was my accomplishment! How lucky I was to have such a magnanimous father! Before leaving the room, he asked me to get the bat and take a stance. It reminded me of my childhood when he made all three brothers demonstrate various strokes, and corrected the flow of the bat and direction of the shoulder and elbow. Once again, I was like an obedient little boy. He gave me a few tips to improve my batting. Before we parted, he applauded my efforts, thus boosting my morale even more, and he also cautioned me, 'Don't take anything on the pads.'

Unfortunately, the next day's play was washed out and there was no chance of practising in the nets either. Eager to keep my momentum intact, I asked the team doctor, Vishwas Raut, with whom I had struck a good rapport, to throw some short-pitched deliveries at me on the ground.

The following morning, Papaji wished me luck and again gave me a few tips. As advised, I used the willow to complete my century—rarely have I felt happier in my long career than on this occasion. I raised my bat in Papaji's direction as a mark of respect. It was a much-desired gift from a thankful son to his beloved father, and that too at his erstwhile home, Lahore, in front of his admirers and friends. Whatever I had achieved in cricket was due to his guidance, efforts and advice. Knowing him, he must have counted each run till the milestone and then celebrated. Later I was told, he distributed sweets in the press box. This performance sent a strong message to all my detractors that I was still 'Test match' material. No worthier opponent could have come my way to prove my abilities than Pakistan.

Although there was strong rivalry between the two teams, it was nothing compared to the 1978 series. Mohsin Khan continued to be my best friend from the opposition. Our friendship had developed in 1977, playing the Lancashire League in England, and we often met over drinks or dinner. The next Test was slated for Karachi. This was also a port city like Bombay and was quite similar in many ways, including its Bollywood-style parties. It was conveyed to me that, in the 1950s and 60s, it had plenty of bars and nightclubs, and was therefore a paradise for nocturnal folks. However, entertainment was shut in the name of religion by Zulfikar Ali Bhutto, probably to garner popular support and remain in power. This surprised me as I had heard stories of his Western lifestyle from Papaji. Before Partition, he would visit Bombay frequently to watch Test matches and sought complimentary tickets from my father. Despite the ban on liquor, the high-end parties went on unabated; drinks continued to flow like spring water.

I was surprised to notice girls in Western outfits in Karachi—an eye-opener after the conservative atmosphere in Lahore. I was told by the locals that the people of Karachi considered themselves the elite of Pakistan, with fine taste in fashion and food. They believed society here was more civilized than in Lahore, whom they considered a bunch of rustic villagers. Though these diverse views demonstrated the social fabric and rivalry of the two cities towards each other, people in both cities were cordial and warm towards me.

Having scored a century, my confidence was high, and I looked forward to the next encounter in Karachi. However, before the match, Papaji gave me a piece of advice and a warning about the umpiring. He was aware of it as a Lahore boy; he had been the manager of India's first tour to Pakistan in 1954/55. 'I know the mindset of the Pakistani umpires and the game-plan they normally indulge in better than anyone else.' He narrated an incident, which took place on the eve of the final Test match (1954) with the series undecided and Pakistan desperate to win: 'I was sitting with the Pakistan captain, Kardar, in his room when someone knocked on the door. Kardar asked the person to come in. My back was towards the door, so I did not bother to turn around to see that person. He walked in and said, "Skipper, any instructions for tomorrow's match?" These words made me suspicious and I turned around. The person standing at the door was none other than the official umpire for the last Test match, Idrees Baig. I asked him what sort of instructions he wanted. Seeing me, he panicked and fled from the room. I asked Kardar, "What instructions will you provide?" Visibly shaken, Kardar tried to find an excuse, but without conviction.

'I went back to my room and called the Pakistan Cricket Board officials and demanded the removal of Idrees Baig, failing which India would boycott the last Test match. I was damn serious. The issue went past midnight to find a solution, yet nothing concrete came about. The local officials were trying to wear me down with delay tactics, hoping I would give up my demand. They conveyed it was not possible to get a replacement for Idrees Baig at such a short notice; there are no first-class umpires available in Karachi and getting someone from Lahore was not possible. Finding me adamant, one of the officials jokingly said, there is one, but you will not agree: his name is Masood Salahuddin and he is a Pakistan selector. Much to their surprise and dismay, I accepted the offer. He gave Kardar stumped out in the nineties, which no other umpire in Pakistan would have dared to do. India returned without losing a single Test match.' What an interesting episode! But I wondered why he was telling me this now. Sensing my curiosity, he said, 'According to the information, after the Lahore Test match, you are a threat to the plans of the home team, so you're on the hit list!' He told me to be careful and to prevent the ball hitting my pad.

The prophecy was fulfilled sooner than anticipated. In both the innings, I was declared LBW in a pathetic fashion. Disappointed, I wondered whether these umpires had enough knowledge of the rules or were pawns of a bigger plan. With unconditional support like this, Pakistan didn't have to work hard to win. Another phenomenon we noticed in Karachi was Imran making the ball fly in the air and dance off the pitch. It bamboozled us; even a player of Vishwanath's class struggled to play with the meat of the blade. This unique swing and movement of the ball bewildered us no end.

What baffled us further was when Sarfraz Nawaz and Mudassar Nazar made the ball talk. We studied this phenomenon very closely and discovered that it happened immediately after lunch or tea intervals. We felt that either the home team was changing the ball during the break or applying something on it, as had happened with John Lever's Vaseline episode during the Delhi Test match; in identical conditions, Kapil could not move the ball as substantially as the Pakistani bowlers, which made us suspicious. Did they work on the old ball, polishing it on one side and scratching the other part with something potent? On the field, the fielders periodically lifted the seam and scratched the leather with their fingernails or a soda cap. This action created two different surfaces on the ball to give an undue advantage to the Pakistani bowlers. The impact of the atmosphere on two different surfaces did the trick.

However, I must admit that, irrespective of ball tampering, the Pakistani fast bowlers were more dedicated than other bowlers around the world. They had an inspiring fast bowler to look up to and no better role model could have come their way than Imran Khan. I was told that he had learned his art from Sarfraz, whom I considered one of the truly great bowlers of the world. Since then, Imran has been an outstanding exponent of this art. He led by example in terms of fitness and performance for the rest to follow. This was a major reason why Pakistan emerged as a potent force; consistently playing above their perceived potential.

Sadly, our team did not carry the same spirit. There had been no controlling power like Imran in the team. As a result, we were short of discipline. Often, players refused to run two laps, some dropped out after one and some hit the nets without training. As a side, we had been obsessed with individual performances, ignoring the collective effort, and ultimately we suffered. Many in the ranks were satisfied achieving personal goals. If we'd had someone like Imran to lift the fighting spirits beyond merely individual achievements, the story of the series may have been different.

The Indian team was demoralized losing the Test match in Karachi. Pakistan had always been a difficult country to tour; there were hardly any social activities beyond the game and it added to our woes. We felt like schoolboys in a boarding school, allowed to go out for a match and then confined to a room. It became excruciatingly boring and most of us felt homesick. No wonder Ian Botham called Pakistan an ideal place to send mothers-in-law!

Most international cricket teams were used to a Western way of life and they looked forward to evening engagements with fresh faces. However, in Pakistan, there were none to bring joy. But I happened to be fortunate because people known to my father or my contacts from earlier tours invited me for dinners. The worst hit in the team were players from Bombay and South India. They could not cope with the orthodox rules and restrictions, which dampened their spirits. I can never forget the misery of Sandeep Patil. The poor guy was counting down the days to get back to Bombay and enjoy the company of his friends. The two-and-a-half-month tour felt like an eternity! However, to my surprise, another vibrant society existed in Lahore and Karachi, away from public scrutiny. People were Westernized and enjoyed parties. Officially, alcohol was banned in Pakistan but, within the four walls of high society, I saw both men and women drinking freely.

In a confused state of mind, we went to the next Test match in Faisalabad—and the situation worsened. Imran, fresh from his exploits, showcased his talent as a leading all-rounder, both with the ball and the bat. He picked more than ten wickets in the match and scored a century as well. While all Pakistani batsmen rejoiced batting on the dead surface, G.R. Vishwanath seemed a shadow of his former self. He was a classic batsman and had dominated the best bowlers all around the world. His wristy strokes had demolished the line and length of many bowlers, but now he was maybe going through some mental agony. Although he scored a half-century in the first innings, memories of the Karachi Test kept tormenting him.

At the end of the fourth day's play, Gavaskar and I remained undefeated. The following day, we had to bat well to save the game. Winning a game and bowling out the Pakistan side twice on such good surfaces seemed nothing less than a dream to us. At 78, Imran surprised me with a banana inswing that struck my front pad outside the off-stump line. Imran led the chorus, followed by the slip fielders and a large crowd baying for blood; the scene was too tempting for the umpire to ignore and the 145-run partnership was broken, leaving me disappointed with the decision. Obviously, I took my own time to move from the crease, and Imran on his follow through demonstrated boorish behaviour and let out a volley of Punjabi abuse. Keeping in mind Imran's background, education and stature, his behaviour surprised me. However, I took it in my stride, because, at times, fast bowlers overreact in similar situations. Thereafter, the Indian middle order collapsed like a house of cards. A disappointed Gavaskar was left stranded at one end with a century; India ended up losing another Test match.

If the loss hurt, the four walls of the room frustrated us even more. Added to it was the erratic television signal at Hotel Ripple. I decided to visit the lobby to watch a few entertaining programmes. There, I saw some Pakistani guests watching the news when the anchor announced Pakistan's victory against India. At that moment, one of the jubilant guests conveyed the good news to his friend. The response of the other guest in Punjabi left me aghast! 'Keda Kashmir jit lay ya (Have we conquered Kashmir)?' Seeing how deep-rooted Kashmir was in the psyche of the average citizen was disturbing. I wondered if they had any clue about the history of Jammu and Kashmir. No doubt, local politicians exploited the emotions of the gullible public. I returned to my room and listened to some music instead.

Losing two Tests out of three left us in a hopeless situation. Perfect batting conditions and the average bowling power at our disposal was not enough to provide us comfort to bounce back in the series. To complicate matters, we played ODI matches between the longer version of the game. Here too we struggled to adjust to the conditions and our weaknesses were exposed in the shorter format of the game. The confusion intensified to such an extent that we could not decide which of the two formats suited us, Tests or ODIs.

Manager Fateh Singh Rao Gaekwad was a man of few words and kept his focus on official duties. The only time and place where he could be approached by the members of the team was at team meetings. However, these meetings were mere formalities. The captain and the manager exchanged a few words, had a cup of coffee or tea and then we dispersed. There were no discussions of tactics or strategies to tackle the Pakistani pace attack or curtail their batsmen. It seemed strange; maybe the captain had altogether given up on the idea of winning on such placid wickets. The team morale was low, and we were going with the flow of prevailing situations. No doubt, it was one-way traffic in favour of Pakistan.

Hotel Fatta (a queer name) in Hyderabad (Sind) was our next destination. This desolate town was not a regular venue for Test cricket, but against India, practically every city or town in Pakistan wanted to host us. With little social life available in Hyderabad, we were confined to the grounds and the hotel. The sheer boredom was getting on our nerves, affecting some of the players. They found the environment to be quite depressing and time went by with agonizing slowness. There was no place to visit and nothing to do, except to occupy the bed; occasionally thumping the wall of the adjacent room with bats or humming a few lines of some Hindi songs brought a modicum of relief from the unrelenting boredom. Emotionally drained and physically exhausted, each one of us, without exception, yearned to go back to India as soon as we could.

The inconsistency in the Indian batting order and Vishwanath's poor form became an issue of serious concern for the team. Vishwanath had been the backbone of our batting line-up. A day before the Test match, we practised hard to readjust our technique against Pakistan's potent new-ball attack. After the session, Gavaskar came to me and asked if it was possible to swap my slot from five to three. This unusual request took me by surprise because I had been doing quite well at number five, cementing my place in the team after a gap of a few years. The batsman in question was struggling against Imran Khan's swinging deliveries.

It convinced me that if the captain wanted to rescue any player from a perilous situation, he could do it easily. Here was a living example. The captain discreetly shielded this batsman from vulnerability, and hoped he would score runs and sustain his place in the team. I had never been so lucky—a single failure was good enough to push me into obscurity. Was I to become a sacrificial lamb at the number-three slot? Would I also receive the same treatment? Or would my failure at this position and success for this batsman bring about a similar change in the batting order for me too? I kept pondering these questions on a loop in my head.

I asked for some time to give him a response. Fortunately for me, Papaji was around, and so I approached him for some guidance. He gave it a good thought and then patted my back, and said, 'Don't worry. Go ahead; you are batting well.' This statement acted like a magic potion and removed the slightest doubt or apprehension I had about my ability with the bat. My confidence was high and I could concentrate at the top of the order.

Before the team meeting that evening, I had a quiet word with Gavaskar and informed him of my decision. He appreciated it and kept it to himself. The next day, it caught many players by surprise to see the batting order and my name at number three.

The Hyderabad pitch was no different to that of any small-town venue in North India. However, the outfield was grassless, dusty and brown in colour, very dry and uneven. A small area with basic facilities served as a pavilion. Temporary stands were erected to accommodate supporters. It reminded me of the atmosphere during my university matches, especially the dry and barren ground.

Apart from the match, I remember an incident in this barren city. A few Indian players were asked by my friend from the Pakistan team if they would be interested in joining him for a party. These words sounded like music to my ears and I instantly agreed. We reached a private party where music, wine and women had created a paradise. This Pakistani cricketer had played a great deal of cricket in England, so he wanted to impress everyone with his command of English and his British accent.

While I enjoyed my drink and chatted with some of the other guests, there was a commotion near the bar. I thought it could be one too many drinks and an argument between two guests. I was wrong! It was a fist fight between the host and the Pakistani cricketer. Bewildered, I did not know how to tackle the situation. By the time the two were separated, both were bleeding from their mouths. The host shouted and abused the cricketer, and the other guests for enjoying freestyle wrestling. Alas, the party was immediately cancelled before it had a chance to get started.

One of the guests apologized profusely to me for the unfortunate scene. Maybe he was embarrassed and he offered to drop us off at the hotel. On our way, I enquired about what had caused the altercation in the first place. He narrated the entire incident. 'After exchanging pleasantries with the host in Urdu, this cricketer switched to English and asked the host, "Who is that b****"?" Since the host's back was towards the guests, he did not know the person in question. To satisfy himself, the host turned around and saw a couple of ladies with drinks. Unsure, he smiled at his guest and asked which one. The cricketer pointed towards a beautiful, slim lady—who happened to be the host's wife! It was a dreadful mistake. "That is my wife," the host said curtly. The cricket replied, "So what! Introduce me to that b****!" Without wasting any time, the annoyed host landed a solid punch on the cricketer's right cheek. Down he went with a thud, while the host stood towering over him, spewing abuse. The shocked guests did not know what happened, till a few of the less inebriated attendees came forward and helped the cricketer on his feet. He dusted his trousers, acting as if he had learned his lesson. Then came the surprise attack! He landed a few quick blows to catch the host off his guard. Chaos prevailed for the next few minutes; they wrestled on the ground. Alas! The party ended too soon.'

Till that time, Madan Lal and Kapil Dev were spearheading the Indian pace attack. Unfortunately, Madan developed a heel injury which cut short his tour; he had to return to India for critical medical care. A farewell party was organized, where many players spoke highly about his fighting qualities. Hearing these compliments, Madan got emotional and his eyes became moist. Being a simple soul, he wanted to stay back, pleading his case, but in vain. Ironically, some players who had praised him had also mocked him during training sessions, calling him a 'limping horse' because his heel hurt him while running and he ended up limping in pain. However, the Amritsar boy never failed in his endeavours to contribute to the team's success.

Madan's loss was Balwinder Singh Sandhu's gain. He was a Sikh Jat, born and brought up in Bombay. He was making his debut on a flat, grassless pitch and most of us feared for his career. Yet, he surprised not only us but also Mohsin Khan and Haroon Rasheed with his ability to swing the new ball. He consumed them in quick succession. This gave us a ray of hope that we could restrict Pakistan, but we were counting our chickens before they hatched! Javed Miandad and Mudassar Nazar put up a big, threatening partnership; both scored double centuries.

Javed Miandad hit a purple patch and he could fit into any world XI. He was probably the only batsman to thrive, irritating the opposition with his antics. He often mocked bowlers, be it fast bowlers or spinners. Who could forget the infamous incident at the WACA in Perth where he was involved in a brawl with Australian fast bowler Dennis Lillee? The more he indulged in weird gamesmanship, the better he performed. His appetite for runs was legendary. Enjoying conditions tailor-made for batting, Javed Miandad was approaching his first triple century (280 not out), when Imran Khan declared the innings closed, a decision that left him thunderstruck. If he had achieved the milestone, he would have joined the elite list of Don Bradman, Len Hutton, Garfield Sobers and Hanif Mohammad to become the second Pakistan batsman to do so.

We had a mammoth on task at our hands to match the Pakistani total. When Gavaskar opened the Indian innings and Imran ran in to bowl the first ball, it was a majestic contest between batsman and bowler. Despite conditions loaded in favour of batsmen, Imran managed to extract bounce and pace from a docile pitch. In contrast, the Indian bowlers failed to get anything remotely close to it. Our deliveries barely reached the wicketkeeper at knee-level, while Imran's were routinely collected above the waist by Wasim Bari. I assume this ability came from discipline and hard work. Being a leading bowler and captain, he led by example and the others followed him.

The deadly duo of Imran and Sarfraz created ripples in our camp. Once Gavaskar was dismissed early in the innings, I witnessed the catastrophe from the other end. Wickets tumbled at regular intervals for no apparent reason. The way in which batsmen lost their wickets exposed their mental make-up. It seemed as if they were tired of this long tour and simply wanted to go back home. Having been promoted in the batting order, I managed to score another half-century. Later, I stitched a fruitful partnership with the debutant, Sandhu, who also scored a half-century. In my attempt to score freely against Iqbal Qasim, my bat got entangled in my pads and the ball made its way to Wasim Bari; I was out stumped.

Finally, we were bundled out for a rather measly total of 189, and Imran capitalized on the situation without hesitation and immediately enforced a follow-on.

Time and a huge lead favoured the home team; India had to gather all its resources and fight for a draw. Unfortunately, the start was dismal; we lost an early wicket. I came out at number three to join Gavaskar. We managed to steady the innings. With runs flowing easily from my bat, I was in an attacking mode to counter Imran and Sarfraz. The welcome delivery tested me and I responded in the manner expected from me. I missed the ball but Gavaskar was not happy with my attempt. The reaction was most unusual; most probably, the pressure to save the match weighed heavily on his mind. His words of caution and concentration seemed unreal, yet pleasing to my ears.

We put up 125 runs for the second wicket, complementing each other after scoring half-centuries. Both of us looked comfortable till a lapse in concentration cost us dearly. Gavaskar was dismissed caught and bowled, and I perished trying to hoist the ball over mid-off. I cursed myself for having missed another opportunity to get three figures. Subsequently, the Pakistani pace bowlers became unplayable with the reverse swing. The bewildered Indian batsmen lost faith in their abilities and crumbled like overbaked cookies.

Two interesting incidents from this match remain etched in my memory to this day: the dismissal of Kapil Dev by Sarfraz, bowled neck and crop—all three stumps lay sprawled on the ground; second, Sandeep Patil, another hard-hitting batsman, had pulled both hamstring muscles while chasing the ball on the hard outfield. He could not bat higher in the batting order and had to take a call later in the innings.

When the situation became critical to save the match, I watched him strap both legs—reminiscent of an injured warrior preparing for a battle he could not wage for too long. Unable to run, he asked for a runner, and it was legitimate. Although the situation was alarming, Patil's presentation made it comical. As he buckled his pads, I sat next to him and whispered, 'What about the other?' He looked bewildered at my question! Unable to hold back, I smiled and said, 'If you were a maharaja, you could have had the liberty to take a runner each for both your injured legs!' We smiled at each other to make light of the situation. The brave batsman was on his toes but stiff, like a puppet, and he needed the support of his bat to walk. He hobbled and wobbled from the comfort of the pavilion into the sun, looking rather like a marionette without strings as he walked gingerly towards the battlefield, ready for combat, for warfare. But, despite his best efforts, he could not conquer the enemy!

The team performance became a nightmare for the captain. He was performing exceptionally well but received little support from his long and reliable batting line-up, barring a few. We lost the Test before lunch on the final day of the match. Cricket is a game of confidence and playing against a team like Pakistan not only required technique but guts to perform on the field; while some faced it bravely and took a few knocks, others simply caved without putting up any kind of resistance at all.

Having tucked the series neatly into their pockets, the attitude of the Pakistani players changed for the better. Once hostile opponents were now more affable in their approach and attitude. They became friendly both on and off the field. While the home team could relax and enjoy the competition, we had to fight hard to retrieve our lost prestige and dignity. Karachi and Lahore hosted two Test matches each, and Faisalabad and Hyderabad were the two other venues that made us fly across Pakistan on numerous occasions.

T. Sekhar from Tamil Nadu replaced Madan Lal for the remaining Test matches of the series. He made his debut in Lahore in the fifth match. He was a quality medium fast bowler but, being flat-footed, he didn't have a smooth run-up to the wicket. Yet, he bowled impressively in the match. However, the butterfingers of some of our fielders denied him the success he deserved for his excellent spell and unfortunately a great many catches were dropped off his bowling.

The Pakistani team had no dearth of court jesters, but none could beat Sarfraz Nawaz—this time, as a batsman. He was unusually amusing and, if he had Miandad as his partner, they would have made a distinct mark on the world stage as the two best comedians. They were so funny that they would, in fact, have made the most reputed comedians run for cover.

The moment Sekhar took a few steps and gathered momentum to bowl, Sarfraz invariably turned up the volume of his commentary in Punjabi-style Urdu, 'Dekho, registan vich oonth dorr raha hai, ya toh dukka ya phir chokka (A flat-footed camel is running in the desert; either I will get two runs or hit a boundary)!' I was standing in the slip and I found it quite amusing. Added to his commentary were unorthodox shots, fetching him the results he desired!

Both the fifth Test in Lahore and the sixth in Karachi were high-scoring games. In these matches, I scored a century each to complete the series on a high note, becoming the highest scorer for India. I remember the Lahore and Karachi Tests for different reasons: a century at each venue; Papaji's response to a local supporter with classic Lahori dialogues; a fiasco at a cocktail party and the umpire's advice to Imran Khan. Not to forget Mudassar Nazar carrying the bat with an unbeaten century (152 not out) at Lahore, thus emulating his father, Nazar Mohammad (124 not out), scored at Lucknow in 1952. Kapil Dev also came up with his best performance in Lahore, taking eight wickets in an innings.

Apart from successful outings on the cricket pitch, there had been many interesting incidents on this tour. Lahore was known for its hospitality and the city threw a few surprises our way. The Indian team accepted an invitation for a late-night party because the next day of the Test match happened to be a rest day. Since Papaji was also staying with Brigadier Shamsi, he asked me to join them for a family dinner and later go on to the party.

I did exactly that, and had a wonderful evening with Brig. Shamsi and his family. At around ten at night, I took my leave from the hosts. However, Brig. Shamsi insisted on dropping me off at the party. When we reached the given address, we were greeted by a deserted house, pitch-dark and not a soul in sight. 'Are you sure this is the address?' he enquired. Maybe we were early, he thought. 'Let's take a round of the cantonment and I'll drop you here.'

When we returned, the house was still desolate, but thankfully there was a sentry at the gate. Brig. Shamsi walked up to him and introduced himself. The big Pathan in his shalwar-kameez and turla turban immediately saluted him. The brigadier showed him the address and he confirmed it. 'There was supposed to be a party here, where is everyone?' 'Janab,' the Pathan replied, 'it was cancelled.'

The Pathan went on to explain, 'Sir, there was a big gathering of cricket stars from India and Pakistan. Amongst the guests were members of affluent families. Everything was normal; drinks, dance and loud music made the evening lively! Suddenly, military police raided the place and stopped the celebrations. There was total commotion. Now, all the guests have gone home.'

Disappointed by the turn of events, I was dropped off at my hotel.

While waiting for the lift, I spotted some members of the team in the lobby and asked them about the party. 'Where were you?' they asked. Finally, they related the entire story to me. 'We were having a gala time; suddenly, the military police gatecrashed the party with AK-47s. They yelled at us to stop the music. Who is the host? They wanted to know. Before the host could respond, one of the officers looked around, and discovered liquor bottles on the counter and half-filled glasses on the tables. The situation was getting grim and tense! Then came the bombshell! "You are drinking liquor; it is banned under Islamic law in Pakistan." Everyone was stunned! Then, another army man spotted Pakistani players holding wine glasses! "Round up the hosts and Pakistan players, and put them behind bars!" It was a hopeless situation but, fortunately, there was a smart person amongst the guests. He walked confidently to the officer and said, "Take us to the police station too." Startled by his approach, the army man said, "We cannot do that; you are our guest!" Finally, the brave man's persuasion paved the way for everyone's release. While the much-relieved guests hopped in their cars for safety, crates of liquor were confiscated and transported to a secret destination.'

Why did military police raid this party when everyone in the cantonment knew about it? And who was the brave man? Well! The raid came about because of an oversight by the host. He forgot to invite the general officer commanding (GOC), under whose jurisdiction lay the cantonment (and the party); the GOC was not amused by the faux pas. In the cantonment nothing moved without his consent.

What about the brave man? He was none other than the Indian captain, Sunil Gavaskar. He knew the arrest of the Indian players would have severe political repercussions and jeopardize the tour. His action saved many from a silly fault of the host's. But what about the crates of liquor? Speculation abounded on this subject. Maybe the liquor ended up at a place not too far from the venue for others to enjoy!

Let us carry on with the account of the Test match. Batting at 80-plus in the second innings in Karachi and an hour to go, I looked set for another century. As per the rules, the fielding side had to bowl twenty mandatory overs. In case of a result, it had to be completed, otherwise batsmen and the fielding captain could reach a consensus and call off the game early.

However, after bowling maybe ten overs, Imran realized the chances of a result were remote, so he trooped towards the pavilion with his teammates. Because he did not consult me, I stood my ground. I stayed back because another three-figure score was within my reach. I had missed a few centuries in this series and did not wish to lose another. When Imran Khan and his teammates reached the boundary rope, umpire Khizer Hayat called out loudly to him and said, 'Khan sahib, kahan ja rahe ho? Agar aap boundary ko paar kar do gay toh match India ko dey diya jai ga (Where are you going, Khan sir? If you cross the boundary, the match will be awarded to India)!' Imran was not pleased and reluctantly returned to the pitch and confronted Khizer Hayat in Punjabi. Nevertheless, the match resumed and I did not take much time to complete my century.

Although the match ended in a draw on the field, another contest continued off the field between the Pakistani captain and the umpire. I was told that Imran was not pleased with umpire Khizer Hayat's attitude and had an altercation with him in the dressing room, accusing the umpire of siding with India and not Pakistan. It may sound queer, but those days, the umpires' room was adjacent to Pakistan's dressing room and they had easy mutual access. This fact came to our notice much later in the series. Did they fiddle with the ball during the breaks? But with no concrete evidence, it was difficult to confront them. Yet, it left a big question mark: what if they did?

This tour also showed how personal guidance could influence the performance of struggling players. If one had to equate the leadership capabilities of Imran and Gavaskar, though both were great in their domain, the former scored over the latter in man-management. Imran led by example to get the best from his boys. He reached out to every player and offered advice. He never shied away from sharing his mantra for success, ultimately becoming the Pied Piper of the Pakistan team.

Gavaskar, on the other hand, never felt it necessary to get close to his players. He was not a fitness freak and hardly took interest in it. In batting, his talent had no parallel, hence all his energy went in concentration and endurance. He worked extremely hard to solve his batting problems, and expected other players at the international level to be as mature as he was and to follow the same principle. I often noticed that when great players take charge, they expect similar results from others. Gavaskar hardly reached out or understood the problems of his players the way Imran perceived them. I wish he had been a lot stricter on this tour with respect to fitness and net practice. Gavaskar handled Imran and the rest of the Pakistan bowling attack so comfortably that batting looked utterly simple and productive. I wish he understood the capability of other players; I wish he had taken a few moments to sit down with the struggling batsmen and show them the way. The Test series might have been a different story.

If the performance of Imran and Gavaskar were par excellence, the efforts of another all-time great, Vishwanath, aroused tremendous emotions. Throughout the series he struggled, unable to deal with Imran's swinging deliveries. I remember the sixth Test; I was padded at number three, while Vishwanath sat all by himself, smoking furiously. Quite likely, he was aware that the final Test match offered him the last opportunity to salvage his reputation. The team for the West Indies tour was due for announcement. I remember talking to his wife, Kavita, during the match and she was also tense. She kept asking me whether 'Vishy' (Vishwanath) would make it to the West Indies. This reflected the concern of a wife about her husband's career. Although Vishwanath occupied the crease for almost two hours, the legendary batsman looked a shadow of his former self, timing deserting him. Thus ended the fabulous career of one of India's finest batsmen and gentleman cricketers.

I felt not picking Vishwanath for the West Indies tour was a blunder. He had already created a world record of playing eighty-seven consecutive Test matches, leaving behind the great Garfield Sobers. Apart from Sunil Gavaskar, he was the finest batsman against fast bowling; in the West Indies, moreover, the ball did not swing. He could have regained his magic touch and added value to the Indian team. Knowing his calibre, he could have served Indian cricket for a few more years.

Another casualty was Dilip Doshi. He had performed well in domestic cricket, like Rajinder Goel of Delhi/Haryana and Padma Shivalkar of Bombay, but the presence of Bishan Bedi had sidelined him too. However, destiny smiled on him. He served Indian cricket extremely well. Doshi seemed genial and a harmless bowler; but he deceived many on the field; he was every inch a fighter.

He was immaculately dressed and used the finest available equipment: the best bat, pads, gloves. However, in this series, he rarely used it because the moment he picked up his bat, Imran stood with the ball. The contest was predictable: Dilip Doshi's backward movement was too late to protect the stumps and Imran happily collected his sweater from the umpire! Yet, there is no doubt, the coming of Dilip Doshi on the international scene after the Pakistan tour (1978) helped Indian cricket. Unfortunately, he too followed the same path after four years. This theory gave credence to the belief that Pakistan was a graveyard for Indian spinners.

I had many wonderful memories of the tour but one incident in Peshawar stumped me, when after a day's play against the North-West Frontier XI, I was invited to partake in a Frontier party by a member of the opposition team. Expecting it to be fun, I accepted the invitation on the condition that I would be dropped at my hotel early. We jumped into the waiting jeeps and drove past the mud houses and deserted streets. I soon realized my folly when we left the last remnants of civilization behind and drove deep into the wilderness. The driver spoke in a dialect that I could not understand, which made me more nervous. Suddenly fear gripped me and I thought to myself if I was being kidnapped! After an hour-long drive, I saw bonfires and around them, Pathans in traditional attire and headgear dancing to the rustic folk tunes, while others were firing guns in the air in the spirit of revelry. The host hugged me tightly to give me a traditional welcome, but I was still apprehensive from the last hour and kept thinking of the headline 'Mohinder Amarnath Kidnapped'. I could not enjoy the food, drinks or the music and the worst of it was that the local cricketer who had accompanied me passed out after a few drinks. I was forced to spend the night in the wild without a wink of sleep. The first rays of the sun brought immense relief and we drove back to the hotel. Some experience!

If I was pleased with my performance, Papaji was over the moon. Leaving a mark in his native town of Lahore meant a lot to him. He felt as if he had been transported back to his playing days. Then came a remark at Gaddafi Stadium that brought tears to his eyes and made him proud of me. I had scored my second century in Lahore when he entered the pavilion. Someone from the gallery shouted, 'Look, Mohinder Amarnath's father has come!' Papaji then said to me, 'This was the day I had been waiting for!'

10

CALYPSO MUSIC AND FAST BOWLING
WEST INDIES 1983

IN THE WEST INDIES, THE ACTION ON THE CRICKET FIELD AND the vibrant crowds in the stands were truly awesome. The sight of fearsome fast bowlers and the carefree attitude of the West Indian batsmen kept the temperature at a boiling point. The release of adrenaline in the bodies of the fast bowlers, Andy Roberts, Michael Holding, Malcolm Marshall and Joel Garner charged them up for the contest. The diehard fans encouraged each to hurl thunderbolts repeatedly at the Indian batsmen with no remorse. Equally merciless were the batsmen; Viv Richards, Clive Lloyd, Desmond Haynes, Gordon Greenidge et al. hit the Indian bowlers with brutal power and glee. If Caribbean fast bowlers loved to see batsmen duck for cover, the exhibition by the home batsmen was equally tormenting for the opposition bowlers. The red cherry was shredded to pieces. Be it domestic matches or international contests, cricket was played with equal enthusiasm in whichever format of the game. No wonder, it was like a big carnival enjoyed with the bat, ball and rum! The beating of drums, thumping of feet and clapping made the atmosphere almost unbearably vibrant.

In 1976, we faced a barrage of bouncers from Andy Roberts and Michael Holding (thankfully, no beamers) to leave us black and blue with bruises. Then came the bloodbath in the last Test match to maim us into submission. However, by now, they had matured into a team better than the Australians. They seemed unstoppable, subjugating their opponents with little or no sympathy.

The life of batsmen around the world was not easy, countering the fiery spells of Calypso fast bowlers or Dennis Lillee and Jeff Thomson or the swing of Richard Hadlee, Ian Botham, Kapil Dev, Imran Khan and Sarfraz Nawaz. If any batsman managed to rein them in and piled runs against them, he was labelled 'courageous'. After performing well in Pakistan, I was a lot more confident of repeating my performance against the West Indies attack too.

There wasn't much break between the Pakistan and West Indies tours. Whatever little time I had was spent with my wife, Bickoo, and our daughter, Nikki, in Bombay. A cricketer's life is not easy—we mostly live out of our suitcases. Unlike the 1976 tour, we flew from Bombay to the West Indies with a stopover in New York for a much-needed break. However, the city was covered under a white blanket. This unusual and heavy snowfall forced us to stay indoors. All our plans to go sightseeing were cancelled. We remained confined to our rooms for the next two days. The only time we ventured out during our short stay was to go to the airport and board the aircraft for Jamaica, and it turned out to be a very long flight indeed.

Pakistan tours have always been a nightmare for Indian captains. Bishan Bedi lost the captaincy to Sunil Gavaskar in 1978 and now Gavaskar to Kapil Dev. This change surprised me more because Sunil Gavaskar had done well with the bat, and Kapil was still raw and not ready to shoulder this responsibility.

When we arrived at the Jamaica airport, the customs officer looked at the height of several players and was amused. The Indian team consisted of several short-statured players (Ashok Malhotra, Kiran More, Gursharan Singh and a few others), which gave the impression of a schoolboys' team. In comparison, the West Indian players were tall and well-built. The immigration officer, the porters and the customs officers wondered how we would tackle the current crop of fast bowlers, especially Holding, Roberts, Marshall and 'Big Bird' Joel Garner. Jamaica still remembered the bloodbath of the 1976 test.

The Jamaican crowd loved good, hard cricket contests. With rum flowing freely at the ground, excitement was already at fever-pitch even before the first ball of the match. Sunil Gavaskar was a big name in the Caribbean islands. However, the adverse remarks in his book pertaining to the West Indian tactics during the Jamaica Test match of 1976 received an angry reaction from locals. They didn't want him to do well in the first Test. The love for the little master was replaced with hatred, on the field and in the gallery.

The Jamaican venue had changed drastically since 1976. The rickety wooden benches were replaced with comfortable seats in a new concrete stadium. The only reminder of the bygone era was the old wooden pavilion and the area around it. Though pleasing, we were more concerned with the pitch; however, we were relieved at the sight of it. The whitish glossy texture indicated that there would be less bounce and pace than we expected.

Earlier India had faced the full-strength West Indian team during the 1979 World Cup at Edgbaston in Birmingham. They were angry with Gavaskar's 'barbarian' remark and wanted to settle the score on the field. The West Indian quartet, consisting of Holding, Roberts, Garner and Colin Croft, unleashed a barrage of short-pitched deliveries at Gavaskar. The direction and the length of each delivery on a green-top pitch was to cause physical discomfort and pain instead of capturing a prized wicket. They couldn't achieve their goal because Gavaskar was much smarter. Aware of the intention of the fast bowlers, he played an uncharacteristic shot and got dismissed; he had therefore achieved his goal of returning to the pavilion without any bruises.

The Indian batsmen had a good run against the Jamaicans, though none of us scored a century. Unfortunately, Gavaskar missed this match because of prior commitments in India, arriving late. Our performance replaced superstition with confidence and self-belief. There remained a few players from the last tour to remember the bloodbath and the fiery spell of Michael Holding. From the injured list of batsmen (Vishwanath, Brijesh Patel and Gaekwad), only the last name remained in the team to relive those horrible moments.

My successful performances in Pakistan had given me a lot of confidence. I knew it would be easier to counter the West Indies pace bowlers due to the nature of the pitches and grounds. Accordingly, I changed my approach. I was determined to fight Caribbean firepower with a strong heart and aggressive strokes. This attitude brought me the desired results against Jamaica. However, I knew these Test matches would be different; they would be an endless battle against four lethal fast bowlers with equally strong willpower.

While planning my innings, I compared Pakistan's pace attack with that of the West Indian team. Imran's artful reverse swing bowling kept me focused on the front foot. Once he completed his spell, other bowlers seemed like easy pickings. But here, there was no respite from the fury of four fast bowlers. Even without the swing, the speed of Michael Holding, Malcolm Marshall, Andy Roberts and Joel Garner, bowling at 90 miles an hour or higher, was a major threat!

If I had to survive, I had to have a flexible game plan, formulated well in advance. To counter the threat, I had to catch them off-guard with aggression from the beginning of my innings. While batting against Jamaica, especially against Courtney Walsh (also drafted in the squad), I noticed the length of the fast bowlers. This length was a psychological reminder to us of the horror of the 1976 Jamaica match.

When the West Indies players opted for the Kerry Packer World Series in Australia, the depleted West Indies team toured India under Alvin Kallicharran and was easily subjugated. A compromise formula was reached across the ICC, which revived the world and West Indies cricket. Clive Lloyd regained control and conquered every opponent at the international level. This was our first time since the World Cup facing a battery of fast bowlers.

Both teams stayed at Hotel Jamaica Pegasus. The body language of the West Indies team was aggressive, hardly exchanging any pleasantries with us. Quite likely, they were instructed to stay aloof and not mingle with the Indian team, both on and off the field. Whenever any Indian player approached them for conversation, they stared at him or simply nodded their heads. Even if there was any scope to exchange words, I am not sure how many boys from our team grasped their accent, leave alone meeting the eyes of the towering West Indian players.

Yet, there was an exception. Jeff Dujon was the friendliest player in the West Indies camp. He became a good friend during the Jamaican game. However, the senior players of the 1976 West Indian team kept their distance from us. An evening before the Test match, I happened to go past a room with its door wide open and saw feet resting on an extension of the bed, probably a single-seater sofa, to make this guest comfortable. It was clear that he did not fit the large bed. The person was none other than the 'big bird' or 'gentle giant' Joel Garner, height 6'8. He had a huge body; even his hands and feet were exceptionally large. The cricket ball in his hand appeared like a ping pong ball!

The shape and size of the West Indies pace bowling line-up was impressive enough to intimidate any batsman. Joel Garner was 6'8; Michael Holding was around 6'4; Courtney Walsh and Andy Roberts were around the same height and were both incredibly strong. The shortest of them was Malcolm Marshall—and he might indeed have been the most lethal of them all!

The West Indies team was fit, strong and talented. The hard work and discipline were worth emulating for all other teams and the Australian trainer Denis Waight was no walkover. He had been with the West Indies team for a long time. He had set high standards for fitness and led by example. While the West Indies team took the coach from the hotel to the ground, Dennis Waight ran the distance to prove his fitness.

For the past five years, the balanced and determined West Indies team had ruled the world of cricket. Their aggressive attitude combined with their calypso approach entertained large galleries and viewers on the television across the globe. Their success lay with their battery of fast bowlers who adapted quickly to all kinds of surfaces. Imagine, a talented fast bowler like Courtney Walsh could not find a regular place in the playing XI! Clive Lloyd would show no mercy to Indian batsmen.

Both teams planned their respective strategies, and each was aware of the other's strengths and weaknesses. The West Indies knew the Indian team's weakness against short-pitch rising deliveries and they would exploit it without mercy. The loss of the recent series against Pakistan and the appointment of a new captain in Kapil Dev favoured the home team even more. What kind of pressure and effect the hostile bowling would have on the Indian batsmen, of course, remained to be seen.

Quietly, I made plans to counter the hostility of the four fast bowlers. The best mode of defence was to attack and remove pressure. I rewound my thoughts and dissected the innings of the Pakistan tour. I did not have a high bat lift nor did I shuffle too much, which allowed me to pick the line and length early and use the pace of the fast bowlers to pull or hook with a calculated risk.

In the West Indies, I realized that perseverance was one of the keys to survival and success. Everyone in the team was aware that if Michael Holding didn't dismiss you, then Malcolm Marshall, Andy Roberts or Joel Garner would. These fast bowlers were like professional heavyweight boxers, ruthless and relentless. There was every chance of taking a few nasty blows from their deliveries. This factor was nothing new to me; I had been hit on the head by fast bowlers Richard Hadlee and Imran Khan; my finger had been broken and my ribs bruised facing Jeff Thomson in Australia. I knew nothing worse could happen, and, if it was to happen, I was prepared to spill my blood and not give away my wicket.

I was basically a front-foot player and ready to move forward even to a short-of-a-length delivery. I had learned this theory from my father. To reduce the distance and pace of the ball, it was important to go on the front foot. I had applied this technique against Jeff Thomson in Australia, and it had worked in my favour on the hard and fast Australian wickets. Pull and hook shots remained my strength. However, I was not a great cutter of the ball, so I left it alone, even if it happened to be a juicy delivery. To avoid committing a mistake, I kept talking to myself. This kept my brain active and ticking. The credit undoubtedly lay with my father's guidance.

Ever since our childhood, we three brothers practised regularly, and played matches both with tennis and cricket balls on the bitumen road at home. It was hard cricket in the scorching heat of the afternoon sun. The plan to tackle short-pitch balls worked well then and I was confident it would produce similar results here too. The open-chested stance restricted my movement across the stumps, which allowed me to play straight. A little stride forward gave me enough time to judge the line and length, and accordingly play different shots. After every aggressive stroke, I thumped my back and silently said shabaash, or well done!

Majority of the front-line batsmen in our team were confident of doing well. Yet, memories of the bloodbath continued to affect certain members of the team. They wondered, if two fast bowlers could do such damage in 1976, what would happen if all four fast bowlers took that route? Joel Garner was like a giant, anxious to hammer the Indian batsmen into submission; Marshall was nothing short of a cyclone; Michael Holding's rhythm and consistency reminded one of the smoothness of Rolls-Royce engines; Andy Roberts was expressionless and determined not to allow even an inch of comfort. All of them were hungry for scalps. Though all of them were different in style, one factor bound them together: consistency. I kept avoiding unnecessary discussion with my opponents or teammates and prepared myself for the battle ahead, not recalling the past. I understood the value of the first match of the series and wanted to continue with my performance from Pakistan.

There was plenty of excitement in the city as a large crowd moved towards the stadium to witness the first Test match. Seven years down, those feelings had not subsided. It was fresh with the players and the crowd. We knew what was in store for Gavaskar and the rest of the team. The attitude seemed no less than a war. They wanted to strike hard and consolidate their position. At the beginning of the innings, the aggressive West Indian fast bowlers had an attacking field placement of four slips and a gully; a silly mid-on and a leg gully felt like a beehive to put psychological pressure on the Indian batters. The solitary fielder at cover point was Gus Logie and fine leg was manned by one of the fast bowlers.

The Test match is all about skill and psychology, though temperament plays an important role. To put fear in the mind of Indian batsmen on the field and in the dressing room, the fast bowlers bowled a series of short-pitch deliveries at Sunil Gavaskar. They felt that an early dismissal, particularly the scalp of Gavaskar, would demoralize the rest of the Indian batting order.

Malcolm Marshall took a leaf out of Michael Holding's book and he bowled round the wicket. Young and eager to make an impact, he made life hell for our batsmen. His thunderbolts repeatedly crushed the ribcage or flew past their heads. This ploy of Clive Lloyd kept pressure on the batsmen throughout the innings and he was subsequently rewarded for this remorseless strategy with many important scalps.

The first innings of both the teams were well matched. It was difficult to say who played better. If the West Indies fast bowlers got the better of the Indian batting, then the Indian medium-pacers and spinners responded well. There was no exceptional individual performance, except half-centuries by Yashpal Sharma and Balwinder Sandhu. I could not convert my good start of 29 into a big score, which annoyed me. My plan had worked against short-pitched deliveries. I could pull or hook, and even allowed the bouncers to sail comfortably over my head.

When India started the second innings, the entire stadium was packed to capacity. The warm, humid conditions had little effect on the crowd wearing colourful caps, shorts and vests, dancing away. Others in Rastafarian hairstyles akin to Bob Marley happily drank beer or rum, while some smoked marijuana. Despite the disparity, one thing was common: the ruckus in the stands. Everyone supported the local hero, Michael Holding. No matter how many runs or wickets any cricketer had against his name, the boisterous crowd did not hesitate to give advice and share their wisdom.

The Indian opening pair took ten minutes to get ready and face the fast bowlers. However, I took my own sweet time. As soon as the West Indian team stepped on the field, followed by Gavaskar and Gaekwad, the entire stadium erupted in a crescendo. If one stand played the steel band and people dancedto its tunes, the other spectator's stand played loud music from the huge two-in-one radio cassette players; the battery horns were operating loudly; some blew large conch shells to indicate the continuation of a battle royale between bat and ball.

Gavaskar's first innings failure brought a ray of hope to our team, because he hardly failed in both innings. Michael Holding had a long run-up, starting not too far from the sight screen. When he cruised up to the bowling crease to deliver the first thunderbolt, he seemed to be floating in the air. I had not even fastened the first buckle of the front pad, when there was a collective reverberation in the stadium, as if the battle was won. I could not see anything from the dressing room. Hence, I rushed towards the window and saw people dancing in the stands. There was not an inch of space in the stands or in the balcony where spectators were not celebrating. To my horror, some overexcited supporters jumped from the balcony and landed on the ground, (thankfully without any injury) to celebrate the success.

The reason: Holding had cleaned up Gavaskar round his leg with the first delivery. The stump cartwheeled almost up till the wicketkeeper, Jeff Dujon. The noise of the 20,000 strong crowd was more deafening than Eden Gardens. They could not have asked for a better revenge—a twin failure for the great Sunil Gavaskar.

Before I could grasp the situation, Gavaskar had already covered two-thirds of the distance back to the dressing room. I started fastening the buckles as quickly as I could. The quicker I tried, the more I fumbled. Gavaskar entered the dressing room, disappointed and mourning his dismissal off the first ball. The situation in the dressing room was grim and I was struggling with the equipment. At the same time, the West Indies team gathered around the pitch waiting for the next batsman to arrive. If they had appealed against the incoming batsman, surely, I would have been given a time out. To avoid it, I ran a good twenty yards to occupy the crease. After the completion of the over, one of the players jokingly said, 'Jimmy, before you emerged, we thought India had conceded the match like in 1976!'

Holding was bowling at a lethal pace and he had the full support of his incredible home crowd, demanding more scalps. With each stride, the crowd screamed and shouted, making the umpire more nervous than me. What if there was a snick and he failed to hear the sound in the charged atmosphere? I had never experienced such noisy support before or after in my career. Cricket is a game of chance. It can change destiny with one delivery or with a single stroke. At the onset of my innings, I pulled Andy Roberts' short-pitched delivery with excellent control. This attitude convinced me that if I remained positive, everything would fall in place for me to enjoy a long and reliable stint in the middle.

Faoud Bacchus had toured India with Kallicharran's West Indies team in 1979 and had scored a double century at Kanpur, but he'd failed to find a place in the playing XI. He was twelfth man and of Indian origin; he conveyed to me during the drinks break that my bat looked broader while facing the fast bowlers. This gave me more confidence. Bacchus' statement revealed that I had more time to face the Windies' bowlers than others. The reason was that I got into position early, thanks to childhood coaching by Papaji and his fruitful advice to us brothers. Many times, during the discourse, he advocated a simple formula. If you had to succeed against fast bowlers, it was imperative to do one thing as much as possible: move early, play late.

On the last day, it looked as if we were heading for a draw, but one destructive over from Andy Roberts changed the complexion of the game. He ran through the Indian batting like a hot knife through butter, especially with the second new ball. When Venkataraghavan came to bat at number ten, the bowler's attitude had not changed. He welcomed him with a lightning-fast bouncer that struck him on the helmet. After a few more terrifying deliveries, Venkataraghavan succumbed and returned to the pavilion. While stepping into the dressing room, he was badly shaken. He remarked, 'Now they don't even spare the tailenders!' Cricket had changed, obliterating the ethics of the 'gentleman's game'. It didn't matter whether the batsman was opening the innings or if it was just the feeble number eleven at the crease. The idea was to win at all costs, to demolish the batting line-up. The West Indies won the match with a few wickets in hand to lead the series. Thankfully, there were no injuries in the Indian camp. I was the top scorer with 40 runs, and I was overall quite pleased with myself for how I'd handled all those highly dangerous fast bowlers.

TRINIDAD TEST

For the second Test match, we travelled to our favourite hunting ground, Queen's Park Oval, Trinidad. We had stunned the home team twice in 1976 and were confident of repeating similar performances on this tour too. With such terrific support, it seemed we were the home team and West Indies the touring party! The scenario in Trinidad has been identical ever since the first tour of the West Indies in 1952. Any new face in the team received immense attention and love from the Indian Trinidadians. This was one centre in the West Indies where the crowd did not hesitate to heckle the West Indies team against the Indians.

Of all the West Indian cricketers combined, Vivian Richards left an indelible mark on the young Indian players. They imitated Viv Richards in the way he walked and talked, which plunged us into bouts of laughter. Encouraged, one of them captivated the burly West Indian players too. Before and after the game, we found Siva in the company of Joel Garner, Michael Holding, Clive Lloyd and Viv Richards, all more than six-feet tall.

The records of 1971 and 1976 were testimony to Gavaskar's success in Trinidad. Whenever he went out to bat, there was a palpable change in the atmosphere. He had a strong influence over the Indian community. The arrival of the Indian team in Trinidad spread like wildfire. The hotel lobby was packed with the Indian diaspora for a glimpse of Indian players.

Surprisingly, nothing had changed in the last seven years in the city or at the ground. It seemed as if Trinidad had been frozen in time.

To relax, I spent my evenings sitting at the balcony, enjoying the breeze, Indian music and a few cans of beer with my roommate, Anshuman Gaekwad. I always carried a two-in-one cassette player and a collection of Hindi songs. After a hard day on the field, there was nothing better than listening to fine lyrics sung by the melodious voices of Lata, Asha, Mukesh, Rafi or Kishore Kumar, while applying ice to our bruised bodies to dull the pain of various impacts. Runa Laila's famous song 'Damma dam mast kalandar' was my favourite. Music had become the best way for us to tune out of cricket and tune into some semblance of normal life. Since a couple of one-day matches were held between the Tests, it allowed us to camp at one centre and not rush from one island to another. I knew the West Indies bowlers would come even harder at us after the first Test match.

Such was the magic of Trinidad; India was yet to lose any Test match here. This record bolstered our confidence even further. Unlike the 1976 Test, the nature of the pitch had drastically transformed. The brown barren pitch gave way to a green-top wicket, which made few players uncomfortable and triggered an allergic reaction. Given a choice, they would have preferred to shave it.

The stands were packed like sardines. Amongst them was a special Indian supporter called Birju, and for him, Sunil Gavaskar was nothing short of the Lord of Cricket. He laid a bet that Gavaskar alone would outscore Haynes and Greenidge in this match. Both the Indian and Caribbean supporters sat together to enjoy this contest. With a few beers or rum down their throats, friendly banter evolved into serious discussions.

All the Indian supporters wanted us to perform well and their loyalty was evinced by the Indian flags they waved in their hands. Despite failing to speak any Indian language, their support for the Indian team never wavered. Surprisingly, even an Indian-origin West Indies board official prayed for our success. I loved the way his family spoke in a typical Trinidadian accent about their loyalty towards India, which was indeed music to my ears. Trinidad was a cosmopolitan society; yet, this gentleman wanted his sons to marry girls of Indian origin.

India lost the toss and Lloyd rightly asked us to bat first. The green-top wicket had plenty of moisture and presented ideal conditions for the pace bowlers. Surprisingly, silence greeted the West Indies team on the field, and the moment Gavaskar and Gaekwad emerged, the atmosphere changed. The deafening sound of drums, the unfurling of the tricolour along with banners supporting the Indian team appeared from nowhere. It was a testing time for the opening pair and both did not last long. First, Gaekwad was run out for no score and then Gavaskar, at his individual score of one, departed to expose the middle order. India's supporters were shell-shocked with Gavaskar's departure; the West Indian fans danced and indulged in a few extra drinks. Poor Birju was mobbed and taunted by the intoxicated and ebullient home crowd.

Our batsmen struggled on a bowler-friendly pitch and we were bundled out by teatime for 175. The demanding conditions forced me to change my approach in comparison to Jamaica. I played late and close to the body against the seaming deliveries. Whenever there was an opportunity, I did not hesitate to hit the short balls to the fence. I was the top scorer with a half-century. Each innings enhanced my confidence and boosted my morale to face fast bowlers. I made 'courage is my destiny' the motto for this tour; I took repeated blows on my body, especially the ribcage, without wincing. This wasn't something new to me. Even while playing school matches on a coir-matting wicket, the ball would bounce awkwardly and hit the ribcage. I was clear in my mind that in a five-Test series, we were going to get more or less two innings per match and, of course, get battered black and blue.

When the West Indies opened the innings with the strong duo of Greenidge and Haynes, poor Birju was thronged by the West Indian fans. Even before a ball was bowled, the excited West Indian fans waited to collect the gambling amount from Birju. Everything seemed loaded in favour of the local batsmen. Fortunately for us, the wicket was still conducive for pace bowling. There was plenty of movement in the air as well as from the surface. Though Kapil and Sandhu did not have the same pace as the West Indian fast bowlers, they got plenty of movement off the surface to make life rather rough going for the batsmen of the home team.

Balwinder Singh Sandhu got rid of Haynes to raise hopes for Birju and his bet. Yet, an experienced Greenidge remained a big threat for him and for us. Greenidge had done well against the best bowlers in the world, but he found the swinging deliveries of a medium-pace bowler extremely difficult to handle. The moment Sandhu dismissed Gordon Greenidge for a duck, a single-digit score won a handsome bet for Birju. The celebration in the stands was equalled by the joy on the field; Sandhu, in his pink patka, entertained everyone with the Punjabi bhangra. Each step was appreciated by the large Indian diaspora.

When the West Indies lost the third wicket of Richards, out for just 1, we stood taller and stronger than the home team. There was plenty of excitement on the field, in the gallery and in the Indian dressing room. Sandhu bowled a magic spell, but poor fielding denied him further success. And, unfortunately, poor umpiring denied us critical opportunities to make further inroads into their batting line-up.

The bright sunshine on day two caused the moisture to evaporate and eased the wicket. With conditions loaded for batting, it helped the West Indies in their innings. They batted well—at times, aided by inept catching and lack of depth in our pace bowling. Centuries from Larry Gomes and Clive Lloyd helped the West Indies take a decent first-innings lead. There was plenty of time left in the match and we were expecting Gavaskar to repeat his past performance at the Queen's Park Oval. He started off aggressively, driving Malcolm Marshall through the cover on the off side to bring joy in the dressing room and the gallery, where Birju was sitting like a king, all by himself. After all, he had won an incredible bet!

The wicket was a beauty. The only thing that could have marred or mauled it were the spike marks of the fast bowlers. We required courage and strength, plus a good strategy to handle the bowlers. For a change, a solid opening partnership gave us a cushion to build a good score. Gavaskar stayed for a while before he was caught behind by Dujon off Garner. It was left to the rest to save the game. Vengsarkar and I played out the remaining time comfortably to continue our innings the following day.

Unfortunately, by evening, dark clouds began to gather on the horizon; the prospect of rain was a cause for concern. This was the last thing we wanted to deal with. We needed sunshine to ensure a smooth wicket. The thin sheet of tarpaulin used by the ground staff to cover the pitch was likely to prove ineffective against strong winds and heavy rain. The prospect of interrupted play, the hostile fast bowling and a lead of over 200 runs weighed heavily on our minds. Though India had an experienced batting line-up, it was an uphill task to bat for two days and save the game. On a lighter note, when the clouds cleared, we wanted the game to be washed out to keep the series alive and India's record intact at this hallowed venue.

Since I was one of the two not-out batsmen, I had an early dinner and went to sleep. In the early hours of the morning, I was rudely woken by a call I assumed to be a wake-up call. However, the operator informed me that it was from India. I thought it would be Papaji. But the voice was different and so was the enquiry. The person neither wished me nor introduced himself. On the contrary, he enquired about the weather. Though I was sleepy, it immediately made me suspicious: what if this person on the other end of the line was in fact a bookie, trying to get a leg up on the competition? I replied curtly and hung up the phone, never to be disturbed again.

The fourth day's play was affected by rain and gave us a glimmer of hope to save the Test. When the covers were removed, our biggest fear stared us in the face. There were quite a few damp patches in the short-of-a-length area. This was an ideal spot for Malcom Marshall and other fast bowlers to exploit. Thankfully, both umpires decided to delay the start of the day with another inspection. Under the prevailing conditions, we felt the spots would take some time to dry on this kind of pitch. Nevertheless, to our disappointment, we were disabused of that assumption.

When I went to bat with Vengsarkar, we were surprised to notice dark spots. Both of us were concerned and wondered how we were going to face the hostile bowling attack. I immediately lodged a complaint with the umpires. Unfortunately, it had little effect on either of them. In their opinion, the spots had dried 'enough' to start the match. We were going to face the music. We felt like sitting ducks in these ominous conditions. I walked around the wet area umpteen times to convey to the umpires my displeasure about their rather dubious decision. I even delayed taking my guard and murmured a few invectives out of sheer frustration.

My last hope to bail us out from this hopeless situation was the West Indian captain and the spirit of the game. Normally, I would never question the wisdom of umpires, but here, I felt the decision was unfair. I turned to Clive Lloyd, who was at the slips, and said, 'Skipper, do you think the wicket is good enough or even fit for a game?' I also asked, what if he was batting, would he have been satisfied to bat? The bowlers and the umpires were shocked by my direct approach to this issue. Even Lloyd, standing in the slips with his legs spread apart and hands on his hips, was taken by surprise. The bewildered fielders, including Viv Richards and Gordon Greenidge, had shell-shocked expressions, waiting for their skipper's response.

Clive Lloyd did not utter a word, but instead walked slowly to the wet spots where I was standing. He knelt and touched the area with his index finger. While he examined the spot, I held my breath. Many different questions rushed through my mind. What next? Lloyd remained quiet for a moment; then he walked up to the umpires and said the wicket wasn't fit enough to play. The umpire immediately decided to suspend the day's play; we would have to wait for another inspection.

It was an amazing gesture and perhaps the only in Test cricket history where the fielding-side captain agreed with the batsman to declare the pitch unfit to play. I don't think any other captain in his place would have taken a similar decision. Was he the same captain who had unleashed the bodyline tactics against us in 1976? At this moment, he stood for fair play and his earlier reputation stood vanquished. This gesture demonstrated his belief in sportsmanship and the spirit of the game.

This incident made me realize that the spirit of the game stood higher than winning. I had always admired Clive Lloyd for his cricket skills but his support for fair play made us respect his character. I continued with my good form. Malcolm

Marshall continued operating round the stumps to the right-hand batsmen, while the rest of the attack bowled over the wicket to swing most of their deliveries into the right-hand batsmen and make life thoroughly miserable. Everyone had to concentrate hard to save the game. My strategy against the short-pitched delivery was simple: if I had a chance to counter-attack, I hooked or pulled, or ducked under particularly hard bouncers. If caught in two minds, I took the blow on my body. Desmond Haynes, with a huge grin at short leg, exposed his pearl teeth and reminded us of his presence. He never shied away from performing various antics to distract the batsmen.

Many people asked me about the conversation between two batsmen after each over. To be honest, it normally revolved around a few encouraging words. However, it changed depending upon the partner and the comfort they shared with one another. Occasionally some batsmen cracked jokes or he narrated a funny anecdote to release some pressure. However, I hardly recall any partner seeking technical advice. But yes, some batsmen were clever and stayed rooted at the bowler's end when the fast bowlers became too hot to handle, thus saving their own skin in the face of lethal pace attacks.

When I was in the eighties, I tried to play a leg-glance to a delivery from Michael Holding. Did it take an inside edge or not, I was not sure because Dujon collected the ball and tossed it to a fielder. Since Holding didn't react, there was no appeal. I earned my 100 by hooking Andy Roberts at 99 to complete my first century of the series. Still, the fast bowlers did not allow me to relax. Marshall had bowled a long spell of seventeen overs and he returned with an old, soft ball that caught me on the wrong foot with a lightning-fast delivery. Before I could react, it hit my helmet and sailed over the wicketkeeper's head, a couple of bounces and over the rope. The wake-up call forced me to concentrate even harder to remain undefeated till teatime.

A few overs after the tea break, a new ball was due. I was prepared for the fast bowlers to try something different with the third new ball. To give them a little rest from one end, Viv Richards bowled off spin round the wicket. I missed an easy flick and only Viv appealed half-heartedly. To my surprise, the umpire's finger was already up. Though disappointed, I took this in my stride. Kapil took over from me and scored a fine, entertaining century in rather testing conditions.

When India lost Kirmani in the last session of the game, Balwinder Singh Sandhu replaced him. He tried to emulate Sunil Gavaskar in appearance (not in skills), discarding his helmet to show off his colourful cotton patka. Had Sandhu gone mad or lost his bearings to challenge the authority of fast bowlers on a reasonably hard wicket? Maybe one good innings in Jamaica had made him comfortable and he was not afraid to face fast bowlers without a helmet? Whatever it was, the audacity of such a gesture offended the attack, particularly Joel Garner.

The first delivery flew past Sandhu's head. Somehow, he managed to avoid it. The next four deliveries were equally fast. Oh boy, Sandhu's expression after each delivery was painfully hilarious! He finally saw reason and asked for a helmet.

Against all odds, we managed to hold the opposition to a draw. Each player had contributed his best. The Trinidad Indians were absolutely thrilled with our efforts. They gathered outside the dressing room, and cheered as if we had won the game and not merely salvaged a draw. The hotel lobby was packed with Indian supporters. The moment the Indian players arrived at the hotel, they surrounded them for autographs and snaps. An excited group of young girls hugged and kissed me all over my face, leaving lipstick marks everywhere. They kept repeating 'You have saved us from embarrassment; otherwise, the locals would have tormented us for days if not weeks!' I had never realized that cricket meant so much to the Indian Trinidadians.

BARBADOS TEST

India played a side game against Guyana before the Test match under bright sunshine on a breezy day. I enjoyed the conditions and scored a century to add to my confidence. The large Indian diaspora looked for a similar performance in the Test match but continuous rain disappointed them. Much like the 1976 tour, it played havoc with the Test. While not a single delivery was possible in 1976, fortunately, this time, we manage to get in some cricket. With conditions suitable for batting, Gavaskar added another century to his name. There was no joy for the others as the remaining days were regrettably washed out.

It had been a productive series for me and I looked forward to the next match against Barbados, followed by a Test. These first-class matches tested our batting skills. The home side bowling attack included Joel Garner and Hartley Alleyne, and a handful of rookies eager to impress the selectors with their pace. Since I had missed a big score at Guyana, I was keen to practice and prepare for the fourth Test match.

India batted for a day, followed by the home side for almost two days. On the final day of India's second innings, I decided to bat lower down the order, and give other batsmen the feel of the wicket and gain some confidence. Both the captain and the manager agreed with my suggestion. The press box was in the proximity of the pavilion, accommodating Indian journalists known to me. I decided to spend time with them and watch the game. I had hardly exchanged greetings, when India lost an opener. Before I could settle down for some comfort, a few more wickets tumbled in quick succession. Assessing the scene, I rushed to the dressing room.

By the time I padded up, the situation had become precarious with seven batsmen cooling their heels. Finally, I went out to bat at number nine. What was supposedly a relaxing morning had rapidly spiralled into a nightmare. I was in the middle facing a barrage of bouncers. Prepared as I was, I took the challenge in my stride. The young Gursharan Singh also batted well for his half-century and, together, we ensured a draw. I walked back to the pavilion, with another century tucked under my belt!

There was a break of a few days before the Test. We were invited to a boat party by the local association. *Jolly Roger* was made of oak trees with a huge sail in the middle, which made it resemble an old pirate ship. The full moon added romance to the party and it was a fun time for all of us. The steel band and Bob Marley songs forced us to occupy the floor. Soon, other guests joined in the fun and the party livened up after a few drinks. Amongst the guests was a high-ranking dignitary from the Indian High Commission. Unable to hold his drinks, he became an embarrassment for us. He could have given Donald Trump a run for his money! The country's reputation was at stake, which obviously mattered little to this gentleman. As we were in the middle of the sea, he could not be offloaded.

When this dignitary's conduct crossed the limits of decency, I decided to teach him a lesson. He was dancing barefoot and did not notice me picking up one of his shoes. My first reaction was to hit him with it, but better sense prevailed. I tossed it into the sea. The party got over after midnight and we waited for the boat to anchor. This gentleman, though inebriated, searched everywhere for his missing shoe. Unable to locate it, he became very angry. For some strange reason, he blamed Sunil Gavaskar for this episode. Gavaskar was famous for playing pranks, but this time he was entirely innocent. Everyone laughed; the mystery of the missing shoe remained unsolved.

While travelling to the resort by coach, Gavaskar was unable to come to terms with this incident. He kept pleading ignorance and kept asking me who could be behind it. I kept quiet to enjoy the fun. Unable to find his other shoe, this official followed us to our resort. He met the manager, Hanumant Singh, and blamed Sunil Gavaskar for his missing shoe. He threatened to take strict punitive action, though without success.

Many years after our retirement, I met Gavaskar in 2012 on the eve of the New Zealand series in Bangalore. It was fun meeting old pals, including Vishwanath, over a few drinks and remembering the good old days. Suddenly, the *Jolly Roger* incident came up.

I asked Gavaskar, 'Did you manage to find the culprit of the boat party episode?'

'No, Jumbo,' he replied.

Keeping a straight face, I said, 'I know the person.'

Gavaskar got excited. However, my tone and smile spilled the beans. In utter disbelief, he gasped and said, 'No! No! No! It can't be you!'

I grinned and said, quite simply, 'Yes!'

Gavaskar laughed, shook his head, and gave me a soft punch on the shoulder, and said, 'You wicked man, it never crossed my mind!'

All of us laughed our sides out!

Travelling in the West Indies was always fun. People at the airports and hotels were friendly—at times, too friendly! We flew from one island nation to another by BWIA. The crew greeted us like rockstars and the hostesses made an extra effort to make our flights comfortable. While seniors were offered beer or wine, our shy and tight-lipped youngsters on their maiden tour felt cheated. To compensate, the tall and elegant hostesses flirted and giggled, serving them Coca-Cola with a remark, 'For young boys only!' I am not sure if our young ambassadors understood their intention and accent, and they were left speechless!

The weather in all the island nations remained ideal for rest and recovery. I loved listening to music or visiting the beach to watch the locals play beach volleyball or cricket. Each sport had its own charm. While beach volleyball was an all-girls, affair, cricket was a man's game. If volleyball teams presented slim and beautiful girls, muscles and six packs were showcased by the youths playing cricket in shorts. Three twigs of different sizes and shapes acted as stumps; an old willow in strong hands and muscular arms made each batsman behave like Viv Richards! They carried his confidence and swag, and they hit the ball hard, and ran singles and doubles like their icon! Wristbands and necklaces made from colourful beads added to their vibrant character.

Another interesting observation was fast bowlers running a good forty yards–plus comfortably. Running barefoot on the loose sand is never easy but their rhythm was majestic. The fielders were equally swift; they ran fast and dived on the soft sand to take a catch.

By the middle of this tour, Bickoo and three-year-old Nikki decided to join me. It was a welcome break for them from the cold and miserable English winter. Since I had been constantly travelling, we now had the opportunity to enjoy a perfect holiday in the beautiful Caribbean islands.

They took a British Airways flight and landed in Barbados. While going through immigration, an official enquired about the purpose of her visit. She nonchalantly said that she was visiting to watch her husband play this Test match. Suddenly, the reaction of this official changed to astonishment. 'Who is your husband?' he asked politely. She replied, 'Mohinder Amarnath.' The official grinned and whispered, 'He must have West Indian blood!' Bickoo was taken by surprise, and asked, 'Why?' The officer replied, 'Maan, because he bats like us!'

Bickoo took this as a compliment and collected her passport. Before she left the counter, she had one last glance at the officer, smiled and said, 'He does not have West Indian blood, but he has Punjabi genes for sure!'

The perplexed officer could not understand her meaning; he simply shrugged his shoulders and grinned!

Bickoo was a caring, practical and determined wife. As soon as she arrived at Rockley Resort, which had cooking facilities in my room, she prepared some Indian food for me, which I had been sorely missing. Later, Romi, Pammi and Manali joined her, allowing Kapil, Gavaskar, Vengsarkar and a few other members to savour Indian curries. They provided us with hot cups of masala chai and pakoras in the evenings by the poolside. The change in atmosphere did wonders to our spirits and bellies. Later, Indian music and the company helped me relax, and forget the intimidating deliveries of the Caribbean bowlers.

We were aware of the hard bouncy track of Barbados and our past track record did not augur well. We had also struggled against the Barbadian pace and didn't need a fortune teller to tell us what lay ahead for us. Before leaving for the Test match, I happened to ask Nikki, 'How many runs would I score?' In a typical Yorkshire accent she quipped, 'Ninety-one.' I laughed, and gave her a big hug and left.

Before the match, both teams used the same area for exercises to limber up. Out of courtesy, some players wished the West Indian players good luck but received a cold stare in response. Only Dujon and Haynes responded to the greetings with a smile and a few words. Was it part of a strategy or competitiveness to apply pressure? We weren't sure, but the message came across clearly that they meant business.

The West Indies won the toss and put us in to bat on a slightly moist wicket. The conditions were loaded in favour of fast bowlers and they rubbed their hands in glee. The Indian batsmen had a tough time against four genuine fast bowlers. The juice aided bounce and the movement delighted them. My innings against Barbados had given me a lot of confidence, but it was history. I planned my innings against more potent short-pitched stuff from the dressing room. To relieve pressure, it was important to follow three principles: counter-attack, move the scoreboard and stare into the eyes of the fast bowlers. I knew a few powerful punches would unsettle their rhythm and bruise their egos. They were absolutely brutal in response. I kept repeating the lyrics of the famous Hindi song *'Jaaye toh jaaye kahan'* with reference to the merciless fast bowling.

While the top-order batsmen defended or ducked under the short-pitched stuff, I responded aggressively, picking the ball a fraction of a second early; at times, hitting good length deliveries, maybe because I was riding high on confidence. I remember a certain pull shot against Michael Holding. The bowler had not even completed the follow through and the ball crashed into the stands; it travelled under eight feet from the pitch at a lightning speed. Holding smiled and shook his head in disbelief; was it in appreciation or a signal for more thunderbolts to come my way?

Just before the lunch interval, Malcolm Marshall operated round the wicket and tested me with a fast bouncer. I accepted the challenge; fortunately, it took the top edge and landed into the stand. Possibly, fortune favours the brave; I shrugged and smiled. After lunch, I tried to pull Andy Roberts and missed the ball. It hit me on my right thigh, jolting me with a sharp burst of pain. No amount of rubbing gave me any respite till my hand accidently touched my groin. To my horror, I was not wearing an abdominal guard. A little here and there would have left me incapacitated—and without my precious jewels! When I signalled for protection, one of the West Indian players came up to me and said, 'Jimmy don't worry, carry on—we won't target the jewels!' And he burst out laughing.

At 91, I lost my focus because a prophecy returned to haunt me. I tried to brush it off but it kept coming back for some strange reason. Was it my happy childhood memories at bungalow no. 91 in New Delhi, or my daughter's prediction? Confused, I faced Marshall. This time, he bowled a short rising delivery with minimum effort; the ball caught me by surprise. It brushed my left glove for an easy catch to Dujon. Disappointed at missing another century, I later replayed the delivery in my mind so I could ponder how to tackle such situations in the future. The rest of the batsmen buckled under the blistering West Indian attack.

The West Indies responded with a healthy opening partnership. To break it, Ravi Shastri was introduced instead of the veteran Tamil Nadu spinner. This ignited Venkataraghavan's short fuse. He showed his displeasure with a remark that he wasn't here on holiday. Such remarks were the last thing we needed.

Gus Logie facing Shastri seemed nervous because he repeatedly pushed forward to defend till one ball hit his glove and went towards Venkat in the slip. The supposedly safe fielder stood resting both his hands on each knee, joined his hands in anticipation to take the catch. Suddenly, our excitement turned into horror when an easy catch went through his arms, failing to touch his hands, which gave Logie a great reprieve. This lucky escape proved very costly for India; he went on to score an impressive century. The West Indies put up a huge total to put pressure on us. I knew we had to bat well to save the Test match or pray to Lord Indra for rain, a faint possibility in the warm sultry weather.

India needed a sound start from an experienced batsman, Gavaskar. So far, in the three Tests played, he had done well only at Guyana. These bowlers gave us little time to relax. Their ominous deliveries could have had serious repercussions if the batsmen had not used their protective gear. Although the blows did not cause any serious damage, the pace attack gave a few players sleepless nights. The situation gave us no joy; every moment seemed like we were out of the frying pan and into the fire!

Most Indian cricketers are superstitious, and I was no different. For me, the most important part of my apparel was my lucky charm, a red hanky, which I tucked into my hip pocket. Whenever I packed my kitbag, the first thing I folded carefully was my hanky. Without it, my kit was incomplete and I would not step on the field. Also, despite the wear and tear, I had not changed my helmet for the past four years. To keep it wearable, I repaired it with a white plaster tape.

The half-sleeve shirt presented to me in the exhibition match in Australia in 1981 also became an integral part of my apparel. I loved this shirt because of the comfort. Even on the hottest day, the air-cool fabric mitigated the heat. I had been using it for the past two years in every game and it had proved lucky for me. It was wrinkle-free and I washed it every day in the dressing room for subsequent use. I wore the same pair of gloves that I had been wearing since the Pakistan tour and Madan Lal's pads, despite having my own. I had bought a slightly long thigh pad and abdominal guard from Morrant Sports in England for protection. The only things I changed and discarded frequently were my jockstraps and socks.

Losing Gavaskar early in the innings was a rarity. After his dismissal, I walked onto the field and was greeted with cold vibes from the West Indian fielding unit—an indication that they meant business. Determined as I was, reading the bowlers' mind was not an easy task. My memories took me to my fearless childhood battles in the backyard with wet tennis balls against Surinder and Rajender, and how I enjoyed hooking those rising deliveries with ease. I smiled at the flashback and took my guard to baffle many fielders around me. They thought I was taunting them. The first delivery was a bouncer, which did not surprise me. The fast bowlers kept bowling short stuff; it seemed like a wet tennis ball contest at home. Whenever I executed a hook or pull shot, the crowd went crazy. They loved the heavyweight bout and appreciated each stroke with a thunderous round of applause.

Marshall kept bowling round the wicket, creating an awkward angle for me and other batsmen. His express deliveries targeted the ribcage or rose consistently above the shoulder towards us. The consistent pace and precision left each batsman wondering if these bowlers would ever slow down. However, there was no sign of fatigue in their run-up, action or deliveries. Each seemed demonically possessed with the desire to shake and subjugate the Indian batsmen, to hammer us into submission.

Although I was middling the ball quite well, I knew a slight lapse in concentration or a misjudgement of length would prove fatal. To repeat another big shot, I got into position to hook but the ball came onto me quicker than anticipated. The red cherry travelling at over ninety miles per hour kissed my glove and crashed into my face. The impact was severe; it felt as if a blacksmith had put a burning-hot iron rod on my upper lip. The pain travelled rapidly through my face to other parts of my body. I was not sure of the extent of damage till I noticed blood oozing out of my mouth. It covered my glove and shirt in a few seconds. For a change, all the close-in fielders were concerned and they came running up to me to check if I was all right.

The Indian twelfth man, Sivaramakrishnan, rushed out to the field to check on me; he seemed more worried and apprehensive than I was. I covered my mouth with the red hanky; I was more concerned about the bloodstains on my lucky shirt than the injury. As soon as I reached the dressing room, I removed my shirt and started washing it. The entire sink was covered with blood dripping from my wound. The ambulance arrived a little later and the doctor was shocked to see the big gash on my upper lip; he took a call to convey me to the nearby hospital. I received twelve stitches to sew the wound. My jaw was intact but my front tooth had split in half.

Bickoo and Nikki were sitting in the VIP pavilion, unsettled by this event. This was not the first time I had been injured on the field. Jeff Thomson had almost broken my rib cage at the WACA, Perth in 1977. The impact was so deep that I desperately gasped for oxygen. I thought I would choke to death. Then, Imran's bouncer struck my head at Lahore, followed by Richard Hadlee, knocking me unconscious in England.

Once again, Bickoo was attending to me both as a wife and as an experienced doctor. Recuperating in the hotel room, I was given plenty of painkillers. However, the dosage had little effect. I had the choice to retire hurt and skip the rest of the match. But the thought of abandoning my team weighed heavily on my mind. Then Papaji's words of wisdom propped me up. He always prophesied, 'Fight fear with determination and injury with performance.' I decided to get back to the ground.

Before the fourth day's play, I accompanied the team, not knowing whether I would be able to participate in the game any further. Nevertheless, I continued to think about the strategy of the West Indian fast bowlers, especially Malcolm Marshall, who had hit me on the mouth the previous evening. On reaching the ground, I made eye contact with some West Indian players but no words were exchanged. My mouth was swollen, and my upper lip stitched and covered with an antiseptic tape to present a gory picture of a wounded warrior. I was unable to talk or walk comfortably, let alone engage in any kind of training. Every movement caused excruciating pain around my mouth.

I sat on the wooden bench outside the dressing room and watched my teammates complete pre-match formalities. The warm weather made me thirsty but I could not drink water or tea because it hurt my stitched lip. With no solid food consumed since the injury, my stomach churned with hunger. I was not sure if I would be able to bat again. Disappointed, I closed my eyes and tried to think of what I could do next. Suddenly, I was transported to my childhood training sessions with Papaji. Not only was he a great cricketer, he was also a great psychologist. His priceless counselling became part of my character. I remembered his golden words: 'Injuries are part and parcel of the game; never shy away from them.'

When all the players returned to the pavilion, I joined them in the dressing room. I picked up my half-sleeved white T-shirt, which I had washed the previous evening; I changed into my whites and started buckling my pads. Once done, I pulled the tape from my wound and let out a groan. Everyone turned to look at me, thinking I had gone crazy. Kapil came to me and asked how I was feeling. I barely managed to whisper that I was okay. I knew the night watchman Balwinder Sandhu would not survive for too long against the hostile West Indian attack.

Once he was dismissed, it was my turn to take the crease. Before stepping out of the dressing room, I told Kapil to keep someone ready, in case I needed a runner. I was not sure how I would feel sprinting for a single or more. The sight of me walking to replace Sandhu brought cheers from the stands, some in appreciation, others at the prospect of Marshall taking another wicket. To get to the crease, I had to walk past almost the entire West Indian fielding unit, who stared at me in amazement.

When I made eye contact with the West Indian fielders standing in a huddle, they smirked at my courage. Like my teammates, they also thought I was crazy! When I took my guard, I noticed four slips, a gully, the wicketkeeper, a leg gully and a silly mid-on anticipating a catch. There were only two fielders stationed in the outfield, Gus Logie at cover point and Andy Roberts at fine leg. The slip cordon had Clive Lloyd, Viv Richards, Gordon Greenidge, Michael Holding and Joel Garner, and Desmond Haynes at leg gully and Larry Gomes at silly mid-on. The field placement seemed like a beehive, with bees buzzing around me. This also meant Marshall would be targeting me with short deliveries. The boisterous slip cordon, especially Viv Richards, was very vocal; in typical West Indian accent, he said, 'Maaku, show him, maan!'

After marking the guard, I walked a few steps and tapped a few areas on the pitch with my bat to calm my nerves. I could hear the roar of the crowd expecting action. I knew what to expect from Malcolm Marshall. Since he had injured me the previous evening, nothing but a short-pitched delivery would greet me. There was no sympathy or mercy at this level of cricket. Marshall did not care about my injury; he was playing to get my scalp. I admired his commitment and ruthlessness.

Marshall ran in quicker than his normal run-up; coming round the wicket, he bowled a quick bouncer from the edge of the crease. Before I could get into any position, the ball whizzed past my nose, almost grazing it. The ball reached Jeffrey Dujon, standing thirty yards behind the stumps, high above his head. I thanked my lucky stars for saving me from another injury, potentially career-ending.

I knew there was no escape for me and I had to do something quickly to counter it. I walked a few steps, squatted down and then kicked my legs hard. Without wasting any more time, I sprinted back to the crease. With my mind ticking and blood flowing faster, I knew my reflexes would support me. Another short-pitch delivery was hurled at me; I moved quickly and hooked it perfectly to fine leg. My eyes followed the ball till it crossed the boundary line. The satisfaction of the shot nullified the pain and I forgot my injury; I was reborn. The crowd appreciated my response with loud cheers and clapping; the entire stadium was alive.

I felt light on my feet; I forgot about the runner I wanted a few minutes ago. I was normal and confident, as if there was no injury, and I started to enjoy my innings. I had played against several hostile attacks and made good scores, but this was totally different! It was one of the most satisfying innings of my career. I had never played so many hook shots in any inning before. The four fast bowlers, Holding, Roberts, Marshall and Garner, bowled short, fiery spells from both ends, failing to pin me down. Every shot from my blade forced Clive Lloyd to step in with some reactive captaincy and thin out the slip cordon a bit, which showed their concern about my batting; I was certainly motivated by their reaction!

While wickets tumbled at the other end, I kept the scoreboard ticking to score another half-century. When I reached 80 and the team total was 277, Venkataraghavan was the non-striker, indicating a hopeless situation. My only chance to reach a century was to attack all the deliveries. Andy Roberts dug one short and I tried to hit it hard, but managed to glove it; I missed yet another three-figure milestone. However, the West Indian players appreciated my performance with genuine compliments.

Before I reached the pavilion, I saw my daughter, Nikki, sitting next to Bickoo, smiling and waving at me. Later in the hotel, Bickoo told me that my brave innings was universally lauded. We lost the match by ten wickets; although I missed three-figure mark in both innings, I was declared Man of the Match, a rare honour for a player from the losing side! However, the biggest compliment and reward was receiving a telegram from Papaji. It read, 'Well played, my son, proud of you.' I was choked with emotion and tears of happiness rolled down my cheeks; I had achieved my ultimate goal; I had made my father proud of me!

Antigua Test

The last Test match of the series at Antigua was preceded by a four-day match at St Kitts. I got some much sought-after rest after the Barbados Test match. I needed time to recover after removing the stitches from my upper lip. What could have been better for me than having the company of my wife and three-year-old daughter, whose constant chirping kept me amused and diluted the pain?

The four-day break from cricket was transformed into a wonderful little holiday with my family. We visited a small island, St. Martin, once divided between the Dutch and the French. Most of the shops here were owned by the enterprising Sindhi business community, especially the boutiques and diamond shops. Antigua itself was a beautiful island, and, of course, was the home of Viv Richards and Andy Roberts. I was told that when Richards got married, almost the whole population of Antigua attended his wedding.

Though we had lost the series, it was important for our self-respect to do well in the last Test. Prior to the Test, news of Gordon Greenidge's daughter's serious illness reached us.

Calypso Music and Fast Bowling

Conditions at Antigua were ideal for batting, but the Indian openers faltered. My form continued to prosper and I enjoyed my stint in the middle. Dilip Vengsarkar also relished the conditions till he got embroiled in a verbal spat with Malcolm Marshall. The reason was Dilip's complaint to the umpire that Marshall was overstepping; that reached the bowler's ears. When the umpire did not respond to the complaint, there was a heated argument between the batman and the bowler. At this stage, Viv Richards ran from the slips to support the fast bowler, temporarily halting the proceedings.

In this melee, Clive Lloyd opted for a second new ball and tossed it to Marshall, operating from the pavilion end for revenge. Contrary to expectations, the first three deliveries were dispatched for boundaries. After each stroke, Vengsarkar mocked the fast bowler, who retorted with unparliamentary language. The twin action showcased cricket at its best, and the exchange was loved and appreciated by the large crowd. Seething, Marshall made a few changes in the field placement and dug the next delivery short. Dilip went for another big hit, but miscued the stroke and was caught at the deep square leg boundary. While the bowler celebrated the dismissal with the choicest abuse, Dilip walked back to the pavilion in silence. An unnecessary brawl and loss in concentration had cost him dearly. It would have been the icing on the cake if he had managed to score a century.

While India put up 457, I was wondering about the mindset and feelings of Gordon Greenidge. It is never easy to concentrate after the disheartening news of a beloved child's condition. When he came in to bat, I was amazed by his focus. He displayed impeccable concentration and technique, as if the news had never been conveyed to him. While he flourished, his daughter battled for her life. He had to retire after making 154 with his blade and take the next available flight. As there were no frequent flights from Antigua to Barbados, he was stranded.

The craze for cricket had brought many Indian doctors and businessmen from the USA to watch India play in the West Indies. They had come here by a private plane to watch this match. When a gentleman called Mr Shankar came to know about Gordon's daughter and her condition, he offered the private aircraft to take the West Indian batsman to Barbados. This fine gesture proved that humanity had no colour, caste, religion or nationality. It further strengthened my belief in Indian culture and its values.

The West Indies went past our score and took a vital lead of 93 runs to bring back the pressure. We needed to bat well to save the game. Gavaskar had a miserable tour, failing once more. My half-century in the first innings and a century in the second helped the cause; we ended up drawing the match. Later, I was about to board the bus when a burly West Indian supporter held me back with his strong grip and said, 'Maan you must be having some West Indian blood in you.' I laughed and replied, 'No, even better, Punjabi Indian blood!'

The West Indian crowd loved cricketers with an aggressive approach to counter short-pitched deliveries; hook or pull shots were their favourites. I won many hearts and proved that determination, discipline and talent can help achieve any goal. My hard work and single-minded devotion proved my critics wrong.

The journey from November 1982 to May 1983 was a fantasy, a tale of a ship sailing through cyclones, tsunamis and other obstacles to reach its destination. In these six months, I had achieved everything I had lost over the years. God had showered his blessings and given me more than I had expected. This was another successful tour for me in terms of runs (598), more than any other batsman from both sides.

My success against the fearsome four led to many theories being floated, but the best came from the manager of the team, Hanumant Singh. He felt the main reason for my success was a psychiatrist's pep talk. Bickoo, being a doctor, had provided me with special therapy sessions that helped me cope with the hostile bowling. With no such help available to the rest of the members, they struggled. Hence, he approached Bickoo to rescue the team. However, she denied possessing any such skill, dismissing it as a rumour. Instead, she gave full credit to the courage and iron will of her husband.

I had received an early lesson about the psyche of fast bowlers from my father in my youth. He always prophesied, 'No matter how great a bowler is, once he is taken by surprise and attacked, he is likely to become defensive and protect his reputation. This applies to pace as well as spin. If one has to spoil the rhythm of a bowler, attack is the best policy.' All great players around the world had done this successfully in the past. I adopted the same approach throughout the series.

With six or seven close-in fielders in the slip and short leg area, there were plenty of gaps to exploit. A mere push for a single, or a full-blooded hook or pull shot, enabled me to reap a rich harvest. With a solitary fine leg fielder on the leg side, I was unlikely to lose my wicket to a miscued hook shot. Once I made quick runs in the first few overs, it boosted my confidence. Still, the fast bowlers did not alter the field maybe because they believed in their abilities as strike bowlers.

I had missed nine years of international cricket between 1969 and 1983. Was it destiny or conspiracy? In fact, every successful innings encouraged me to forget my past performance and concentrate to prove myself a worthy son of a great father. I was declared Man of the Series.

This period changed the world's opinion about me. It gave me greater satisfaction and joy to read another statement after this series by none other than Sunil Gavaskar. 'Mohinder is technically the most accomplished batsmen we have. He is, in my opinion, for whatever it's worth, the best batsman in the world. Nobody plays fast bowling better than him.'

11

WORLD CUP 1983

ONE VISUALIZES THE FULFILMENT OF HIS DREAMS WHEN HE achieves them. It marks the end of being plagued by several emotions and the beginning of much happiness.

The occasion was the 1975 World Cup finals between Australia and West Indies at Lord's. Like many other players of the participating teams, I also watched the new tournament and dreamed of playing in the finals. The next World Cup of 1979 was equally disappointing. However, I kept my hopes and dreams intact, waiting for a miracle to happen. The 1983 World Cup preparation was no different from the previous World Cups. However, my wildest dream was to come true in the third attempt, which was something I had never contemplated.

The concept of one-day cricket in most parts of India had not yet developed. The longer version of the game was undoubtedly popular in the western, southern and eastern regions of India. Only North India, especially Delhi, encouraged limited-overs matches. There were quite a few local tournaments in the summers and each was hotly contested. Players from the neighbouring states, especially Punjab, Haryana, UP and the Union Territory of Chandigarh flocked to Delhi in the months of May and June. While playing such matches, many youngsters became more mature in their technique and temperament. Subsequently, the more talented ones went on to represent their own state associations in the Ranji Trophy.

The two previous World Cup performances raised serious concerns about whether India was good enough to play cricket in the limited-overs format. Whenever the Indian team participated in any ODI competition, we suffered defeat. The limited-overs series against Pakistan in 1978 exposed our slow bowlers and defensive batsmen; we had no clue how to change gears. Also, the Indian selectors were outdated in their approach towards this format. In addition, many senior cricketers concentrated on their individual performances, even if it bogged down the team. This kind of lackadaisical approach, combined with truly appalling fielding standards, made the task easy for opponents. No wonder India stood quite low in the international ranking. We did win a few one-day matches, but our record was certainly not good enough to be considered a threat to anyone.

The recent tour of the West Indies hardened our stance against fast bowlers. Although we did not win any of the Test matches, the only silver lining was a solitary victory in the limited-overs match against the mighty West Indians in Berbice. This was a small town in Guyana, close to Kurupukari, which was near Suriname. The population of this town was dominated by the Indian diaspora. The stands were decorated with vibrant Indian colours because it happened to be the festival of colours, Holi. Interestingly, we travelled to the ground not by road or sea but by air. Both teams flew in army helicopters for about half an hour to reach the venue; the chopper made several sorties to ferry us back and forth in small batches.

After the West Indies tour, I flew to England with Bickoo and Nikki for a much-needed break. As I had not signed a contract with any local club, I chalked out a timetable to concentrate on my fitness. Luckily, there was plenty of open space around the cottage in Lancaster for physical training and I enjoyed the regimen.

The World Cup was around the corner and my focus shifted to the biggest event in England. The names of players from international teams caught the attention of local newspapers but there was no news from India. When the Indian team was finally announced, I had no idea about the squad. I received the news of my selection not from the BCCI, but through a friend in England! The general atmosphere around the event indicated little interest from the BCCI. For them, this World Cup was a mere formality and no more. Worst of all, they did not find it appropriate to inform me personally either. The Indian cricketers (Sunil Gavaskar, Yashpal Sharma, Dilip Vengsarkar, Ravi Shastri, Sandeep Patil, Balwinder Sandhu, Roger Binny, Syed Kirmani, Krishnamachari Srikkanth and manager P.R. Mansingh) boarded the plane for Heathrow; I believe there was no farewell function or even any token encouragement from the higher-ups!

The preparation for this event was the board's last priority, so they didn't bother holding any sort of conditioning camp. They felt it was an unnecessary expenditure. The press, cricket board and the general feelings amongst the cricket fraternity and followers was identical. They had little faith in the team due to their poor track record in the previous World Cups. No one expected any miracles from this team.

Before the start of the World Cup, it was customary for all the teams to assemble at Lord's for a get-together and photographs. Different shades of blazers made this event colourful. However, the BCCI created an embarrassing situation for the captain and vice-captain. Ours was the only team that exhibited the title of captain and vice-captain embroidered on the blazers in block letters. When I met Dennis Lillee, he seemed rather amused with the title and said, 'Oh, so you are the vice-captain of the Indian team?' The remark made me uncomfortable. To be honest, there was no need for the brilliant mind who conceived this idea to tell the world who was the captain and the vice-captain of the side. Maybe the BCCI officials enjoyed displaying their positions on blazers. No other team had this disparity in their rank and file except us. After Lillee's comment, humorous as it may have been, I covered the pocket of my blazer with my left hand, fearing a similar question from someone else. When all the participating teams lined up for a group picture, I told Sunil Gavaskar to stand behind the captain, though it was designated for the vice-captain, because of his contribution to Indian cricket.

Before the 1983 World Cup competition, the organizers decided to discontinue the social functions. In 1975, the participating teams had been invited to Buckingham Palace for tea and met Queen Elizabeth. However, the MCC arranged a few preliminary games for each team. This was a God-sent opportunity for us to fine-tune our skills and test our abilities in these conditions. We played matches against teams from other groups and minor counties. The absence of Kapil Dev raised several questions about the seriousness of the Indian team; it was I who led the team in the first practice match against New Zealand. During this match, the BBC interviewed me, curious about our chances of winning the cup. My simple reply was that our chances were as good as the other teams in the World Cup. At that moment, I didn't have the slightest belief that this prophecy would eventually come true!

However, I wanted the team to start afresh and take on each opponent as a new challenge to accomplish the desired results. The combination of youth and experience balanced the team quite well. Sunil Gavaskar, Madan Lal, Syed Kirmani and I had been part of the 1975 World Cup squad—retaining our places amongst a happy band of cricketers. Despite our poor showing in limited-overs games, I think our preparation for this World Cup was much better than that of many other teams. We had played hard cricket against two top teams, Pakistan and West Indies. The West Indies remained the best bet for winning the tournament this time too. If so, they would create history—winning the title three times in a row despite changes in the team from 1975 and 1979. This incredible rise of the West Indies left many pundits speechless!

Before the tournament, we performed below our potential in the practice matches. We lost to New Zealand and Sri Lanka, and made a hash of ourselves against the combined Minor County XI. The body language and deadpan expressions of the Indian team reflected our plight. There was gloom and despair in the team dressing room. I had never witnessed such dejection and disappointments on the faces of the Indian players. The loss against Minor County was like a harsh, unwanted knockout punch, much like the Finchley Cricket Club match in 1975, which hurt our pride.

The track record of the Indian team in the World Cup had been quite dismal. This discouraged Indian fans from spending their hard-earned money on us. However, a member of the Air India ground staff, Praveen Shah, wanted to watch our games. When the Indian team landed at Heathrow Airport, he handled the players' baggage. This impressed the manager. When Man Singh came to know that he did not have enough money to bear boarding and lodging expenses, and was still willing to offer his services, the manager solved his problems.

Praveen knew the requirements of the cricketers; he packed our kit bags, carried them to the coach, and organized food and drinks. The players affectionately addressed him 'Praveen bhai'. Little did we know that this small gesture from our side would be rewarded later. Praveen bhai ultimately became our lucky mascot!

India's first match of the World Cup was against the favourites, the West Indies. The conditions at Old Trafford, Manchester, were like the Indian subcontinent! Although it raised our hopes, our earlier performances at Old Trafford were not encouraging. However, the solitary victory in the ODI in the West Indies raised our morale.

The World Cup competition was sixty overs a side and a quota of twelve overs for each bowler. It was possible to complete 120 overs in a day because of the long daylight hours in the Northern Hemisphere. Although floodlights introduced in the Kerry Packer World Series had allowed for day-night matches, England remained tied to tradition. The World Cup continued in white flannels with a red cricket ball. We knew the West Indies were going to be tough customers and we prepared ourselves accordingly. No one gave us a chance to perform miracles and the odds were, of course, heavily loaded in favour of the West Indies.

Fortunately, the low bounce and lack of pace at Old Trafford suited us better than the pitches in the West Indies. Yashpal Sharma played a gutsy innings and the rest contributed to the total. We bowled better than our opponents to capture eight wickets, but inclement weather extended the match to the reserve day. The sight of bright sunshine made us cheerful and we toppled the apple cart. This result sent shockwaves and gave other teams a ray of hope in light of the lethal reputation of the West Indies. The supposedly invincible favourites had chinks in their armour!

The defeat of the West Indies surprised all the cricket-playing nations. This result transformed the attitude of the journalists, commentators, officials and other teams towards India! Soon, the Indian diaspora made a beeline for us. For the first time, we saw the Indian tricolour fluttering atop cars driven by Indian supporters around Manchester. We continued with our good form against Zimbabwe to score another victory in Leicester. However, the Australians proved a tough nut to crack; they absolutely mauled us at Nottinghamshire. This was a major setback for us—a reality check after such a positive start to the tournament.

Kapil and I had a free hand as far as the final selection of the team was concerned. The manager had played cricket in Hyderabad and he understood the requirements of the game. Although he was part of the team selection, he hardly interfered in the final composition of the team. He was supportive and gave his consent for the betterment of the team's performance. This defeat forced us to take a hard decision. The opening pair hadn't performed well, so the team management took a call to experiment with the opening slot.

The rules of the World Cup allowed group teams to play against each other twice. The next game against the West Indies was scheduled at the Oval. The nature of this pitch was entirely different from what we'd dealt with so far. It was hard, fast and bouncy—ideal for pace. The West Indies could not have asked for a better venue, with Garner, Marshall, Roberts and Holding. With their pride badly hurt, we knew what was in store for us from this ever-lethal pace battery.

The West Indies won the toss and put up 9/282 in the allotted 60 overs. Viv Richards loved the pitch and demonstrated awesome power in his strokes. While he remained at the batting crease, the West Indies controlled the proceedings. When I started my bowling spell, I was amazed at the pace and bounce of the wicket. At times, the ball bounced chest-high to the wicketkeeper, Kirmani, forcing him to move a couple of yards back. He was an ideal wicketkeeper for the bowlers. He appreciated good deliveries with a smile and a nod of his head. On this occasion it was more than that. After collecting each delivery, he said, 'Bahut aala', meaning 'perfect delivery'. When Clive Lloyd was beaten a couple of times outside the off stump on my deliveries, he looked amazed, and acknowledged my skill with a nod and smile. Then, he tapped the pitch, had a few words with the non-striker and returned, visibly pleased. He foresaw our plight in the second innings.

The required run rate of 4.7 runs per over was certainly achievable. To get it, we needed a good start with the opening pair. The stadium was packed with Indian and West Indian supporters, each as vociferous as the other. True to our expectation, the West Indian fast bowlers relished the bouncy wicket. Our fears soon turned into reality; first Srikkanth and then Shastri followed his partner to the pavilion, leaving the middle order exposed. Dilip Vengsarkar joined me and, together, we put up a solid partnership. The true pace and consistent bounce made the contest between bat and ball most interesting. We knew, of course, that any lapse in concentration would lead to our downfall and any loose delivery had to be capitalized on without mercy; our stroke play was aided by a thankfully lightning-fast outfield.

Clive Lloyd kept shuffling his fast bowlers with short spells, attempting to break this partnership. Finally, he asked Marshall to charge in from the Vauxhall End. The sight of Vengsarkar at the crease brought out the best from Marshall. His eyes lit up and he stormed in, like a tiger eager to pounce on his prey. The memories of their spat at Antigua had not yet faded. Suddenly, the ball developed wings and flew up to Vengsarkar's face, forcing him to rise on his toes and defend. However, one delivery rose menacingly towards his terrified face. He tried his best to bring his gloves in the line of the ball and save his face, but it was too little too late. The ball came at supersonic speed, went past his glove and hit him on the chin.

The impact forced Vengsarkar to drop his bat. Next, he threw his gloves in pain and, in desperation, covered the bleeding wound with his hand. No one was sure of the damage except Marshall; he stood by the batsman after his follow through. Without any remorse or even a token word of sympathy, he looked at the batsman writhing in pain, simply picked up the ball and slowly walked back towards his end.

As he passed me, I saw him removing a piece of Vengsarkar's tissue from the seam of the ball and tossing it away. This was typical of a fast bowler's attitude. It was a big blow for the Indian team because Vengsarkar had been batting exceptionally well through the innings; he was forced to retire midway through our fruitful partnership. Due to this chin injury, he could not take part in the remaining matches of the World Cup. He had to take a few stitches to seal the wound. The pain was gone, but not the scar.

I held one end and looked set to continue with my good form against the West Indies. However, a slight lapse in concentration was enough for me to lose my wicket to Michael Holding. At 80, I tried to hoist him over midwicket, but I ended up sending the ball straight into the hands of Clive Lloyd. The lower-order batsmen failed to click and the West Indies won comfortably by 66 runs.

So far, India had won two and lost two matches to leave us in a precarious position in the group table. The next two games naturally became critical for us. To qualify, we had to beat both Zimbabwe and Australia. We were certainly confident of defeating Zimbabwe as we had done previously, but Australia was a question mark.

The World Cup schedule was meticulously planned with sufficient breaks between matches for all the teams. We made use of them for practice sessions; they were not intense, rather, they were relaxing. Even team meetings were informal and there were hardly any intense discussions. The atmosphere remained congenial and everyone was aware of his role in the team's success. However, we did sit down on multiple occasions to study and dissect the opponents' batsmen and bowlers, so we could go in to the next two matches armed and ready.

As for fielding, emphasis was placed upon one-bounce throws from the boundary. This became necessary because, except for a few players, most did not have strong arms. One-bounce throws reached the wicketkeeper much faster and stopped batsmen from stealing an extra run. I do not recall any other discussion. As for the final XI, we discontinued the policy of suspense; we announced the names in advance and prepared them for the contest. Once done, we had a cup of tea or coffee, bid goodbye and good luck to the players making the final XI.

The game against Zimbabwe was scheduled at a relatively unknown venue called Tunbridge Wells, a small town in Kent County. It was indeed a big occasion for the local population to enjoy an international match. Only a hospitality tent and a couple of marquees were erected around the ground for locals to enjoy the match and the pleasantly sunny weather. Many Indian supporters travelled from different counties with dhols or drums to cheer us on in the contest. Some wealthy Indian doctors chartered a flight from America with their video recorders to capture the action on the field and, of course, get a few glimpses of the Indian players with them.

The dressing room was in the basement of the main pavilion. The exterior of the bar was adorned with hanging baskets full of flowers, and wooden benches were placed to it to allow people to enjoy their drinks and spectate in comfort.

This ground resembled a rugby or football field with open space and tall trees. For the players, a small marquee with a few chairs was pitched near the pavilion. The atmosphere seemed somewhat like that of a village carnival.

Zimbabwe won the toss and invited India to bat on a slightly damp wicket. We knew the first hour was critical but were confident to fight it out with a strong batting line-up. However, the Zimbabwe pace bowlers surprised us. In the first few overs, we lost our top five batsmen for a paltry score of 17. This unusual display wiped the smiles clean off our faces. One jolt after another felt like the blow of a sledgehammer, rapidly erasing our chances of making it to the next round of the World Cup. There was complete, almost deathly, silence in the bunker dressing room.

Was it the end of the journey for us in the World Cup? I had never witnessed such a silent dressing room until now. None of us felt the desire to watch the game, expecting an even worse drubbing than what we were witnessing now. Once Kapil started dominating the Zimbabwe bowlers, however, the players started moving out of the basement to the marquee upstairs to watch the game. With the way Kapil was demolishing them, we found ourselves more optimistic, and we looked up to the lower-order batsmen for support and a total of at least 150 to make the game more competitive and to give us a real chance.

The situation, much to our delight, took a drastic turn for the better, and the scoreboard started ticking faster and faster. Smiles returned to the faces of the Indian camp. As the match progressed, we found ourselves even more confident of a competitive score and we revised the target to 200. The sitting area became lighter and the players looked more relaxed; we started joking and pulling each other's legs.

The sombre atmosphere changed to jovial when Man Singh joined other players to crack jokes. Each took a dig at the other, but in a friendly manner. The manager came in for most attacks. It was a known fact that he had poor eyesight, yet insisted on driving his car in Hyderabad. However, his concentration was limited to the bonnet of the car instead of the traffic ahead. Whenever he came too close to a car in front, the person sitting next to him would yell, 'Maan Bacho' or brace for an impact! Due to this handicap, he could not see the scoreboard clearly and had to ask the nearest player for the score. If it was Srikkanth, it was in Tamil, and others in English or Hindi. Gradually, pressure receded on the pitch and in the marquee.

Now, a score of 200 seemed too modest for the Indian team. With Kapil playing a marvellous innings, we could not set a target for our opponents. It was a rare treat to watch such an exhibition of batting (175 not out). One had to give credit to Madan Lal, Roger Binny and Syed Kirmani for their solid support. Unfortunately, the BBC did not cover this match due to a strike; millions of people missed this first-class display. Later, the Indian bowlers did a wonderful job to achieve a comfortable victory.

Having removed the first hurdle, our morale was high. Still, Australia remained a bigger challenge in our way to the semi-finals. I wasn't thinking of the semis; in fact, we were taking the simple approach of dealing with the tournament one game at a time. In the evenings, we had a few drinks in the bar, cracked jokes and relaxed with discussions about everything under the sun—except cricket.

Lady Luck was smiling down on us. The game against the Aussies at Chelmsford was crucial for both teams. Our previous defeat against them had taught us a lesson. We did not wish to repeat our mistakes. However, the media and the public favoured the Aussies. The winning team was destined to play England in the semi-finals at Old Trafford; everyone looked forward to a contest between the world's oldest rivals. The overconfidence of the Australian team was reflected in the captain giving their strike bowler Dennis Lillee a rest in this crucial match!

In a tight game, no Indian batsman dominated the bowlers; yet, everyone contributed something to the total of 247 and presented a sufficient challenge to the Aussies. The conditions were still conducive for seam bowling and we bowled up to the batsmen. This length provided movement in the air and off the wicket. As anticipated, the Aussies faltered in their approach to dominate the proceedings, giving us an early breakthrough. Subsequently, we changed our tactics and denied them scoring opportunities to keep up the pressure. Unable to break the shackles, the Australian batsmen fell into our traps and collapsed like a house of cards. Roger Binny and Madan Lal snagged four wickets each, and Sandhu another two. India won the game by 118 runs, causing another major upset in the tournament. This anti-climax brought mixed reactions from the critics. They were shocked at first but later quite pleased with the result; England's task had apparently become simpler because they wouldn't need to deal with their dangerous arch-rivals. It seemed to the English fans and media alike that they would simply stroll over to Lord's for the finals.

We had been in England for a long time. Unlike previous Indian teams, we made our opponents sweat till the end. The Indian diaspora encouraged us by holding up the national flag, waving it after every success. We pushed ourselves beyond our limits and played for the pride of the nation.

After the game, we joined the Indian supporters to celebrate our victory. As I passed through the large crowd to board the coach, someone pushed a small bundle of notes (English pounds) in my pocket to enjoy more drinks. Simultaneously, someone from the crowd shouted, 'Don't forget us! I hope we can join the celebrations, maybe next time. Go and enjoy on our behalf!' While we left the sea of Indian supporters behind, how I wished they could have been with us and enjoyed the celebration!

I closed my eyes and wondered how destiny had changed its course. Before the World Cup, we were considered a walkover and now we had defeated two strong contenders for the title in our group. While the West Indies remained in the reckoning for the title, the Australians were knocked out. With our confidence peaking, we eagerly looked forward to the semi-finals against England at Old Trafford.

The journey till the knockout stage had been a rollercoaster ride, with each match worth remembering. Old Trafford reminded us of the encounter against the mighty West Indians and how we had proved the pundits wrong. We knew conditions were unlikely to change. Also, the support for the Indian team in Manchester and at the Old Trafford ground was likely to grow to put pressure on the home side. Suddenly, the word 'can' morphed into 'will'! I smiled at the prospect of changing the script and marching to Lord's for the finals, beating England on English soil in a tournament where they were slated as one of the favourites for the hallowed trophy.

India's matches during the 1975 and 1979 World Cup showed poor attendance. However, the situation had changed for the better this time around, and young Indians born and brought up in Britain were emotionally attached to us. Their parents had migrated to England in the 1950s or 1960s for greener pastures. Despite a hard life, they maintained close contact with their villages, towns or cities, and also kept their traditional culture intact. Another revelation during the World Cup of 1983 was the presence of the tricolour—not one or two, but literally hundreds fluttering amongst the large crowd; we hardly saw it even in India while playing international cricket matches! When we qualified for the semi-finals, the atmosphere was utterly transformed. Indians residing in Manchester, Leeds and Birmingham drove to Old Trafford in Manchester in large numbers to cheer us on in the hope of victory.

At the same time, I received a letter from the caretaker and the ground staff of the Lancaster Moor Hospital, where Bickoo worked as a psychiatrist. The staff members played a crucial role in my fitness, especially with the heavy medicine ball. One of them raised my morale with a statement: 'One day, your dreams will come true and you will achieve your desired goal.' Was the prophecy coming true? Every blessing and good wish added to my determination to prove them correct!

Praveen bhai's dedication and hard work had made him part of the team. He was always with us in the team coach, dressing room and hotel. At functions, the ICC officials thought he was one of the officials with the team. No wonder, he was present in every historic picture of the World Cup. How an unknown person became an integral part of a touring party was a classic example of Indian culture and the inclusive, vibrant spirit of the Indian cricket team!

The weather in Manchester was perfect for the big occasion. It wasn't only the pitch that reminded me of home conditions, it was also the atmosphere. Large numbers of Indian supporters waved tricolours and shouted national slogans to drown out the voices of English supporters. The ratio in the gallery stood 2:1 in favour of India. However, the critics and pundits, as usual, gave us little chance against the home team, thus entirely missing one of the most vital points in our favour: our massive confidence. Little did they realize Indians were aspiring for a bigger goal than just defeating England.

The night before the game, we went to an Indian restaurant for a meal. Sandeep Patil asked me to play two more innings of substance. He said, 'Jimmy, if you do that, we will win the

World Cup!' I replied, 'Sure, Sandy! I would like you to do the same.' We finished up our meal and parted on a high note, laughing!

England won the toss, and Graeme Fowler and Chris Tavaré made batting look so simple and effective; a big total seemed imminent. Kapil, Sandhu and Madan Lal proved ineffective. Roger Binny remained our last hope. His action and ability to move the ball in both directions had already fetched him loads of wickets, and he provided a much-needed breakthrough. However, Mike Gatting and David Gower kept the scoreboard ticking for their side.

The 1983 World Cup rules offered teams two breaks, lunch and tea, during the match. With lunch approaching, Kapil asked if I could bowl. Although I was nursing a sore right shoulder, I said I would try. I had avoided bowling thus far due to an injury, concentrating instead on my batting. As luck would have it, in my first over, Gower played a rash stroke and Kirmani dived to his left, taking a brilliant catch. It was my first wicket and a huge bonus for us to get Gower before lunch.

Kirti Azad and I bowled a full quota of twelve overs each, and picked three wickets amongst us. I got Gower and Gatting, while Kirti dismissed Ian Botham. While bowlers cast magic spells on the English batsmen, the brilliant minds of Gavaskar and Yashpal came into action as well. They swapped positions without informing the captain. Allan Lamb and Gatting did not notice it either; they tried to steal another quick single, a decision that proved suicidal. Yashpal Sharma's direct throw at the bowler's end got rid of the dangerous Allan Lamb. After a brilliant start, England was crippled by our performance and managed to put up a rather modest total of 213.

For a change, Gavaskar and Srikkanth set the ball rolling with an opening partnership of 46 runs before both perished in quick succession. When Yashpal Sharma joined me, the runs dried to a trickle, which caused a great deal of panic in the dressing room. However, I had made my own plan of not losing another wicket before the break and was satisfied with the slow run rate. When we walked into the dressing room, there was pin-drop silence. When tea was offered to me, I could sense uneasiness amongst the batsmen to follow. No one said a word. Even the captain looked uncomfortable and he just kept quiet the whole time.

After tea, I told Yashpal to stick around because I was going to take some risks. I came down the wicket and lofted Ian Botham over mid-off for a boundary. The message was loud and clear. I was hoping Yashpal would rotate the strike and allow me to continue with a bold approach. To my surprise, he too lofted Paul Allott in his typical style for a much-needed boundary.

When Bob Willis returned for his second spell, I instructed Yashpal to relax and not play any risky shots. On the contrary, he threw caution to the wind, exposed all three stumps and played an amazing flick. The ball landed amongst the Indian supporters in the stands. The unexpected opening of the floodgates gave the Indian dressing room some much-needed relief! I complimented his stroke play, but wondered aloud why he was taking such risks. Yashpal responded in typical Punjabi fashion, 'I have a score to settle with Willis; in the last Test match in India, he had abused me with four-letter words and I want to take revenge now.'

In the tense moments of the semi-final, Derek Randall, acting as a substitute fielder, showed the spirit of a true sportsman. I played an uppish stroke against off spinner Vic Marks towards midwicket. Derek Randall dived forward to take a catch. While the others celebrated my dismissal, the gentleman cricketer told the umpire that he had not taken the catch cleanly. Despite the vociferous appeals of the other fielders, the umpire agreed with the fielder in question and denied England a crucial breakthrough in a do-or-die situation.

We were cruising comfortably towards the target when a communication gap led to my dismissal and I was run out at 46. Sandeep Patil replaced me and instantly attacked Bob Willis, bringing back old memories of hitting Willis for six boundaries in an over. No English bowler could curtail him–he scored a quick-fire 51 and sealed the fate of the match. As India inched closer to the target, the numerous Indian supporters grew more voluble than ever. Holding the tricolour, waving it fiercely, they waited impatiently to storm the field. When Patil ran two instead of three runs for victory, the excited fans miscalculated the total and rushed onto the field to celebrate, temporarily halting the match. The writing was on the wall.

Willis simply completed the formality, bowled the last ball and charged towards the pavilion with his teammates. No one looked to see where Patil played the ball. The batsmen completed the victory run and dashed away for safety. The Indian batsmen and the English players had to dodge the crowd descending like a plague of locusts from all directions. It was an unusual sight, players in their cricket whites dodging frenzied spectators in different shades of colours. I had never witnessed such an amazing sight. All of us hugged each other and rejoiced at our triumph! Later, a small ceremony was held on the balcony of the pavilion to conclude the match and I was named 'Man of the Match'.

The atmosphere in the dressing room gave one the impression of an Indian wedding: the dressing room floor reverberated with the pounding beats of bhangra music; there was the sound of corks popping from champagne bottles; some players took sips while others sprayed it over other team members dancing on the floor.

Subsequently, our attention was drawn to the thousands of supporters below the dressing room. The entire team emerged on the balcony to thank them for their support. They kept chanting 'India, India!' It was a big day for Indian cricket; we'd qualified for the finals at Lord's. I felt proud to be an Indian and part of this team.

The British sports media was baffled by this result. They couldn't believe India could ever defeat England. My dreams were coming true. I had watched the 1975 World Cup final at Lord's and, ever since then, I'd dreamed of playing the finals at this venue. I pinched myself to check if it was all true. The newspaper reports, discussions on television, cables and calls from friends and relatives proved beyond doubt that this was all very real, and that we, the Indian team, were going to play the finals at Lord's!

Hotel Westmoreland was walking distance from Lord's; it became our last destination for the World Cup. Being the vice-captain, I got a single room. It wasn't big enough to accommodate two people and all our baggage. The moment I checked in, the telephone rang incessantly and each call was for tickets or complimentary passes. Unfortunately, each player had limited resources and the demand was soaring every minute. It was embarrassing to decline requests. A night before the finals, Bickoo, Nikki and Samina arrived at the hotel. To allow the ladies the comfort of a soft bed, I spread a few blankets on the carpet to make myself comfortable.

The World Cup final was a complete sell-off because English fans had been utterly confident of playing the final. Disappointed with the semi-final result, many English supporters put their tickets up for sale. This news spread like wildfire; there was a mad scramble amongst Indian supporters to lay their hands on the tickets and witness the historic match. Every ticket for the final was sold at a premium.

We had a two-day break before the final. I decided to give my mind and body a complete break. Music was the best way to revive the exhausted mind and muscles. The next day, I overslept and almost missed the morning practice session! Even the captain reported late for the session. It was such a coincidence that both the captain and vice-captain overslept! I had always been a stickler for discipline, but now I arrived quite late for practice. I apologized and explained the reason. Then I went to the team coach to get my lucky bat. It was missing, which shocked me. This bat had fetched me more than eleven hundred runs in the last one year. With great difficulty I found a replacement. Since net practice at the 'Nursery' (practice ground adjoining Lord's) was not so arduous or extended, all was forgotten and taken in a good spirit. The session even ended with a few jokes!

The West Indies team was also at the Nursery for the same purpose. The session ended simultaneously for both teams. I picked up my bat, pads, gloves and spikes, and I headed for the dressing room when Viv Richards crossed my path. We wished each other all the best and chatted about our experiences at this World Cup. As we entered Lord's cricket ground, I failed to locate the centre pitch. The strip for the final at Lord's was almost lost in the green cover of the outfield. I found it a bit surprising to see so much grass on the wicket for a one-day match.

A well-known BBC commentator, Peter West, was at the pitch, busy with a shoot. I asked Viv if he would like to see the strip. He smiled and said, 'I'm fine, you carry on.' The body language of Viv Richards said it all. Peter West saw me and waved. Soon, he joined us but only wished me good luck. It was strange that neither Viv nor Peter exchanged any pleasantries. I thanked Peter but had not forgotten his comments at the fag end of the semi-finals against England. With the scores level, he had chided the exuberant Indian supporters with a little comment: 'The chickens have not yet hatched!' It had not gone down well with the Indian team.

Once again, Viv and I walked towards the Lord's pavilion. We talked about everything: the good, bad and ugly moments on the cricket field, and how cricket had developed around the world. Happy as he was, he remarked in a typical West Indies style, 'Isn't it great that the two establishments of cricket [Australia and England] are not in the final; instead the two Indies—India and West Indies—are contesting the final!' Happily, we entered the empty Long Room and took the flight of steps towards the individual dressing rooms. Once there, we shook hands and wished each other the very best for this big, historic match. It had never really occurred to me just how historic the occasion was. Now it truly sank in for the first time and made me feel proud that our national flag would be hoisted on the famous pavilion!

In the evening, we had our customary team meeting. As usual, we hardly discussed anything specific regarding tactics or strategies for the final. The mood was buoyant and each of us wanted to continue with the good work from the previous game. The body language indicated our resolve to give our best shot in the final and hope for the best. I had a quiet dinner in the hotel with my wife, daughter and a friend, Samina. Later, I spread a blanket on the floor to sleep, while the ladies occupied the bed. Due to the excitement of the finals, I could not shut my eyes, no matter how hard I tried. My journey over the last year kept flashing back to me and the challenge lying ahead kept my brain ticking. Even my heartbeat was abnormally fast; did I have a premonition of something historic, something cataclysmic on the horizon?

The general stands were crammed with West Indians, Indians and English cricket enthusiasts. However, the passive

Englishmen seemed a little odd amongst the vociferous supporters of both the competing teams. It was an ideal wicket for pace bowlers, a hard surface with a green top. The setting, under the shining sun, compelled me to paint the scene on canvas, but I was no artist!

We lost the toss and Clive Lloyd asked us to bat on a juicy fast bowler's paradise. The West Indies' bowlers were stimulated and excited playing their third consecutive World Cup final. Clive Lloyd wanted to go down in history with three World Cup trophies in a row. The conditions were ripe for pace bowling and the bowlers charged in with hostility.

We could not get a decent start. Sunil Gavaskar hardly managed to leave an impression on this occasion too. I joined Srikkanth quite early in the innings. It was quite a sight to see the fidgety yet confident newcomer from Tamil Nadu stay stationary at the non-striker's end. Was it nervousness, pressure or just his style? I ignored it with a smile and got ready to face the music on a blistering pitch.

Srikkanth was baffled by Garner's bounce, but he somehow managed to survive. In the next over, he confessed to me, 'Jimmy, would it be okay if you face him [Garner] for a while, before I get used to him from the non-striker's end?' It was undoubtedly a difficult request, but as a senior player I accepted the plea. To keep Srikkanth's morale high, I made a passing remark, 'Just go ahead and play your natural game!' I was reminded of Venkataraghavan's encouraging words to me in Madras in 1969. There was a total transformation in Srikkanth's attitude after this. First, he hit Garner for a boundary and, in the following over, Andy Roberts. Srikkanth's brisk 38 was a valuable contribution while the rest of the order struggled against the pace.

We were disappointed with our performance; we failed to last the full 60 overs and were bowled out for 183. Before going to the field, Kapil addressed the team in a typical Punjabi accent: 'Chalo, jawano, ladte hain (Come on, boys, let's fight it out)!' Akin to soldiers, we marched out of the dressing room and through the packed Long Room at Lord's. Here, the elite list consisted of former cricketers, politicians, diplomats, senior citizens et al. in suits and MCC ties, welcoming us with thunderous applause to boost our morale. This experience will remain etched in my memory forever. The moment we stepped on the green grass, flashes of 1975 came back to me. My dream to play the final had turned into reality! Would the prophecy of the staff at Lancaster Hospital come true?

Although we were defending a modest total, our success hung on two crucial hinges: denying the West Indies a flying start and making early inroads to expose the middle order. Balwinder Singh Sandhu had troubled Gordon Greenidge with his inswingers in the West Indies and earlier in this World Cup. For some strange reason, Gordon could not pick his big inswingers. He had the same effect on Greenidge that Eknath Solkar had on Geoffrey Boycott.

Gordon Greenidge's weakness was soon exposed; he misjudged Sandhu's inswinger, offering no stroke. His stumps were shattered. The young South Hall Sikhs in the audience beat the drums as never before. It felt like we were back in Punjab, celebrating Baisakhi. The joy was intense; each one of us embraced Sandhu and congratulated him.

Vivian Richards wearing a maroon cap entered the field and was greeted in a typical West Indian style. He swayed his hips like a samba dancer, flexed his muscles and strong arms like a heavyweight boxer; the West Indian supporters jumped in joy, pumping the air with their fists. Each step reflected his certainty of putting fear in the bowler's mind. The heavy Stuart Surridge bat looked like a fly swatter in his hand. Even at Lord's, he was no less than a veritable king of the ring!

He immediately dominated the bowling and started hitting boundaries around the park. This kind of stroke play displayed his arrogance and authority with minimum effort. It seemed he was in a hurry to fly back home; he wanted to finish the proceedings quickly and celebrate a third West Indian World Cup victory! This overconfidence and awesome display gave us a glimmer of hope; what if he misjudged the line and length? Sure enough, the tide changed and destiny smiled on us when Viv Richards mistimed a pull stroke off Madan Lal, fetching us the prized wicket!

Still, the West Indians possessed a strong batting line-up, even though Viv's dismissal had boosted our confidence. The green-top wicket assisted the Indian medium-pacers. As wickets started tumbling, the pressure took a heavy toll on every new batsman. From a situation of strength the West Indian batsmen suddenly found themselves backed in a corner. They found the atmosphere too demanding for their comfort.

On the other hand, the Indian bowling and fielding were at their zenith. A classic example was Kirmani's superlative work behind the stumps. He took an amazing diving catch to fetch us the wicket of Bacchus. To celebrate this effort, the entire team surrounded him; some patted him, others hugged him. Instead of looking elated, he suddenly groaned in pain and pointed to his foot. We saw an exuberant Srikkanth repeatedly jumping on Kirmani's foot! Thankfully, the injury was not too serious.

After losing six wickets, Jeff Dujon and Malcolm Marshall put together a fruitful, although from our standpoint, potentially dangerous partnership. With the scoreboard ticking, each run became precious. At this stage, Kapil handed me the ball. My first delivery was innocuous, pitched outside the off stump. But it turned out to yield ripe fruit for us. Unsure whether to play or let it go, my friend Dujon dragged the ball to the wicket and obliged us with a much-needed breakthrough!

This hesitancy reflected the tremendous pressure on each batsman at this stage of the game. With Dujon's dismissal, we could smell victory the way a lion smells a wounded gazelle; but the task was not done yet. There could be many a slip between the cup and the lip!

With success under my belt, my rhythm returned. I told Kapil to place a slip for me. It did raise a few eyebrows. Seeing my confidence, the request was obliged. While walking to my bowling mark, I knew we had to capture the remaining wickets quickly; I kept one eye on the scoreboard, the other on the field placement and, lastly, I also looked out for the initial movement of the batsman. My lazy run-up forced Marshall to edge the swinging delivery into the safe hands of Gavaskar and then Kapil got rid of Andy Roberts. When the last pair of Holding and Garner occupied the crease, we sensed history in the making. We, the underdogs of the tournament, casually dismissed by pundits and critics, and the public, could see the shores of the promised land!

The last pair kept us waiting for some time. When Kapil operated from the pavilion end, I muttered a prayer: 'God, please don't let Kapil take the last wicket!' This was not for reasons of personal glory but for safety. I wondered how I would cover the distance from the point boundary to the pavilion through the excited crowd! The frenzied images of the Manchester semi-final flashed back to me.

I started a fresh over to Michael Holding with a strong offside field. I changed my line and bowled a slightly short delivery in line with the stumps; Holding tried to pull it to midwicket. My deceptive action brought the ball quicker off the wicket to hit Holding's pad. The moment Dicky Bird raised his finger in the air, the crowd invaded the field. I rushed towards the stumps to grab one of them as a memento. However, they were stuck deep in the earth and I just could not pull it out!

I could have picked the ball or bails, but got so nervous seeing the tsunami of people running towards the pitch. I left everything and ran for my life like Carl Lewis. My mad dash to the pavilion was probably the fastest 100-metre sprint of my life! I ran through the Long Room, up the stairs and, on reaching the dressing room, took a deep breath. The entire dressing room was filled with board officials, staff from the Indian High Commission and several friends.

I sat on my seat; I couldn't believe it. We had created history! The players hugged each other like long lost friends and champagne flowed like the waters of a Biblical flood. Many hands reached to congratulate me for my efforts. The dressing room was like an open house; hundreds of people thronged to greet us. I did not recognize half of them, each eager to hug the nearest player. The celebrations continued outside the pavilion too. Thousands of Indian supporters gathered below the Lord's dressing room's balcony, waving their Indian flags and repeatedly chanting, 'India! India!'

Both teams were escorted to the Lord's balcony for the prize distribution ceremony. The body language and expressions said it all. The ceremony commenced with a Man of the Match award for the World Cup final. Amid thunderous applause, the name announced was ... Mohinder Amarnath! I was giddy, ecstatic, delirious! It thrilled me no end. My dream was realized—and then some! I was presented a gold medal and a big bottle of Magnum Champagne. It was followed by Kapil Dev lifting the Prudential Cup. The beaming team returned to the dressing room for further celebrations. Winning the World Cup was like conquering Mount Everest!

Having lost a precious memento on the field (the stumps), I decided to go to the West Indies' dressing room for team autographs. When I entered the dressing room, there was pin-drop silence. The entire team was in shock! They just sat there in utter dejection, as if they had lost everything in life. A few faces failed to control their emotions; tears rolled down their cheeks. I also noticed a crate of champagne in the corner, left untouched. These had been stacked in anticipation to celebrate another title. Unfortunately for them, fortune had favoured us. Seeing an unwanted guest, they composed themselves and obliged me with autographs. Whilst signing the autograph bats, each of the players demonstrated great maturity and congratulated me. However, their expressions failed to hide their sorrow. It seemed like a bad dream, especially when the odds had been so greatly in their favour right from the outset. I was told that some people became richer, while others poorer!

Later, Jeff Dujon and a few other West Indian players came to the Indian dressing room to have a drink and congratulate us. Since our dressing room was so overcrowded, poor Jeff Dujon lost his wallet and a few hundred pounds. The poor guy not only lost the finals, but money as well!

The celebration continued unabated till some sane advice forced all the guests to leave the dressing room. Once serenity returned, I closed my eyes to feel the truth and the gravity of the achievement. It had indeed been a long, arduous journey from 1969 to 1983. During this roller-coaster period, I had observed the character of cricket board officials and the men in whites. Ecstasy made brief yet repeated appearances, while desolation ran in parallel like an ever-present shadow. The Indian cap was extended to fit players with little or no skills. The journey from the general stands watching the World Cup in 1975 to the batting crease at the 1983 World Cup final was like a truly epic novel reaching its earth-shattering climax! With God's grace, I proved myself a worthy son of a great cricketer. It gave me immense satisfaction, to say the least!

Although Hotel Westmoreland was at walking distance from Lord's, it was thought best to travel by coach. The street across the hotel was inundated with Indian supporters and Indian flags. No sooner had we descended from the coach than we were mobbed by the enthusiastic crowd. The scene resembled a Bollywood show or political rally. The hotel lobby and the bar was flooded with Indian supporters beating drums and dancing to its beat!

Earlier, Bickoo and Nikki left the ground when Viv Richards started battering the Indian bowlers and the West Indian supporters started shouting biting remarks. Unknown to them, the wheel of fortune had changed. Samina woke them up to witness the miracle! How they enjoyed my three-wicket bowling spell, including the last wicket to lift the World Cup. They remained glued to the television till the ceremony concluded. The sound of drums in the lobby made them watch the celebrations from a vantage point. The serene atmosphere of the hotel was transformed to resemble the Blackpool Carnival and, for a change, the hotel management didn't object. I believe the bar was thrown open till the last drop of alcohol and beer was consumed. The sales that day was no less than winning a jackpot for the management!

As soon as I reached the lobby, carrying my award, the bottle of champagne in my hand, I saw Bickoo and Nikki waiting for me. Before I could move towards them, the big crowd encircled me. Subsequently, I was lifted like a feather on many waiting shoulders and transported to a huge bar. The atmosphere resembled a Punjabi festival being celebrated. Liquor flowed uninterruptedly and the floor reverberated with the beat of dhols or drums. Soon, my wife and daughter joined in the fun. I lifted my three-year-old daughter on my shoulders so she could enjoy the scene. Drinks were free but with a rider: those coming to the bar had to join the floor and dance to the beat of the drums!

The Man of the Match Magnum bottle was something I wanted to share with Bickoo over a candlelight dinner; it was opened and consumed within seconds! Later, cricketers' wives and some Pakistani players staying at the same hotel joined in the fun. Famished as I was for missing lunch, I ventured out in my grey tracksuit with family and friends. It was around five in the morning; I was totally sozzled with the effect of the champagne and I searched for food across London. After much exploration, we found some snacks opposite Victoria Station!

There were many hilarious and absurd tales connected to India's victory. The most amusing was about one man sacrificing all his crockery. Watching the intense contest in the finals, the glass from a Sardarji's hand slipped and broke. Immediately, India captured another wicket. Thinking it to be a good omen, he started smashing one glass after another against the wall! Finding himself short of glasses, he allegedly broke the rest of the crockery at home. The proud fellow was sure that it was his great, noble sacrifice that had blessed India and enabled us to win the World Cup!

While the entire nation rejoiced in this victory, the Prime Minister of India, Indira Gandhi, declared the next day a public holiday. The celebrations were not confined to the ground; we continued rejoicing in the sky at 35,000 feet. A special cake was arranged and cut on the flight, and the champagne flowed like never before. A high-ranking BCCI official was also travelling with the team. For a change, we were upgraded from economy class to business class to get some much-needed sleep till Bombay. As soon as the seat belt sign was switched off, the BCCI official jumped up from his seat and dropped his pants. It shocked everyone, including the ladies. Without a care in the world, he pulled on his pajamas and fell asleep!

The Bombay airport was filled to the brim. There was a mad scramble to catch a glimpse of the triumphant squad. Thousands of hands stretched out to garland us. Some managed to do so, while others threw them in the air to reach us. Despite police bandobast, or arrangements, we barely moved an inch; we jostled through the thick crowd to the safety of the waiting coach.

The drive from the airport to Wankhede Stadium was another memorable journey; people stood on both sides of the road to greet us and the large crowd on the balconies of the flats along the way showered us with roses or marigold flowers. The civic reception at Wankhede Stadium was delayed by a few hours due to the slow ride from the airport. The sight at Wankhede was phenomenal. Thousands had gathered to welcome us. The moment we arrived, there was a crescendo of applause. For a change, this victory was not confined to the cricket team alone; it belonged to hundreds of millions of Indians who had dreamed of such a day! Our great nation of India was united as never before with this marvellous achievement.

My journey over the last twelve months was too astonishing even for me to believe. Here was a cricketer who had been struggling to find a permanent place in the team before the Pakistan tour of 1982. And now I had won the Man of the Match award in the most historic game of Indian cricket!

My case happened to be a classic example of zero to hero! One year down the line and victory in the World Cup had changed everyone's behaviour towards me. Now I had become a 'role model' for the new generation.

12

THE LUCKY BREAK
COMEBACK 3

THE EUPHORIA OF INDIA WINNING THE 1983 WORLD CUP, MY contribution in the semi-final and final, and the celebrations that followed gradually gave way to a nightmare. The wounds of the West Indians had not yet healed when they landed in India in full strength. The cricket season in India was packed with two series against two equally strong sides: Pakistan and the West Indies. I was confident of doing well because of my recent performance against them. India hosted Pakistan for three Tests and two ODIs. The tour started with the ODI series and I was the Man of the Match in the first ODI in Hyderabad with an unbeaten 60. This performance did not surprise many because of my recent performances. I was more than pleased because it happened in India. The next match in Jaipur was won by India too. The first two Test matches in Bangalore and

Jalandhar provided me one innings each. For the first time, an unusual weakness set in. I could not take it anymore, so I opted out of the Nagpur Test.

The first ODI against the West Indies was held in Srinagar, in the Kashmir Valley, and my condition had not yet improved. Expectations were high but there was something drastically wrong with me. Accordingly, I consulted Dr Kamal Pathak, dean of Medical College, Baroda; he gave me medicine and advised complete rest for a longer period. Doctors spoke about burnout syndrome, which I could not understand. My symptoms were fatigue, exhaustion and reduced performance. My condition and the doctors' advice left me confused. However, I informed the BCCI of my inability to play the first ODI.

The match in Srinagar was televised. I watched the tourists romping home with minimal effort. Since I was selected for the Kanpur Test match, I spoke to the doctors for advice. They recommended more rest but I overlooked their suggestion. In Kanpur, I happened to meet a journalist to get the details of the Srinagar match. Apart from the match, he informed me, the Indian team was fighting a twin battle. If the West Indies gave no respite to India on the ground, the anti-India slogans chanted by Kashmiri separatists compounded the pressure greatly, which ruined the atmosphere.

The conditions at Green Park, Kanpur, astonished both teams. For reasons best known to the curator, the wicket wore a green blanket, which suited the battery of West Indian fast bowlers. No wonder they wrapped up the match within four days. The next Test was at Feroz Shah Kotla, New Delhi. I had developed a fever by then and felt very weak. I conveyed my hopeless condition to the selectors and the captain before the match and on the morning of the Test, but got little support.

India won the toss and elected to bat. Although I had batted at number three for the past one year, I was in no position to bat at the same number in this match. Such was my condition, but the management felt I would recover later and placed me at number seven. When I got up to bat, my legs were unable to bear the weight of my body. Even the 2.6-pound cricket bat seemed heavier to lift. I realized the mistake of overlooking the advice of the doctor, but it was too late. No wonder, I hardly lasted. Seeing my condition, the management advised me to take rest in the hotel. I did not take part in the proceedings when the tourists batted. When India commenced the second innings, I was still confined to the four walls of the hotel room.

At that time, my brother-in-law, Gurinder Kahlon, participating in the Himalayan Car Rally, happened to drive through Delhi. He, along with his girlfriend, called on me at the hotel to enquire about my health. At that moment, the local manager also arrived with a message from the team manager. Without using the intercom of the hotel, he rushed to my room and knocked on my door. As Gurinder was using the bathroom and I was confined to bed, the door was answered by the third person, Gurinder's girlfriend. The face of a pretty girl startled the official—and seeing me lying there in bed probably gave him the wrong idea. Nevertheless, he asked me to accompany him to the ground.

Miserable as I was with a fever, I reached Feroz Shah Kotla and waited for my turn. My eyes were burning and body aching. I was easy prey for the pace attack. Annoyed as I was, I received another shock. Spicy rumours linking me with a girl hit the social circle. Fortunately, the selectors paid little attention to it and understood my condition; they rested me for the next two matches in Ahmedabad and Bombay.

Distraught and confused by my loss of form, I decided to take a complete break from cricket. To keep a low profile, I flew to Goa to revive my flagging spirits. I did not touch the cricket bat and, to be honest, did not miss it very much, nor did I miss the hullaballoo of the cricket stadiums either. I wilfully kept away from the game, avoiding listening to match analyses on television or the radio. The long walks I took along the pristine beaches were very refreshing and I greatly enjoyed my solitude. After two days of complete rest, I was given an unexpected message: I had been selected for the Indore and Jamshedpur ODIs. My first reaction was to decline the offer but Papaji's earlier advice changed my mind. Remembering the Jalandhar match against the West Indies in 1979, I felt hope in the midst of overwhelming underconfidence. I accepted the invitation with little preparation and no expectations. Free from any tension, I scored a half-century at Indore to keep my reputation intact.

Happy with my return to form, the selectors showed faith in me. I was picked for the Calcutta Test. On entering the lobby of Grand Hotel at Chowringhee, I noticed a palmist surrounded by foreigners. Ignoring them, I went through with the basic formalities at the check-in desk and took my room key. I was pleasantly surprised to see the palmist standing behind me. He smiled and insisted on telling me my future. Vulnerable as I was, I took the bait. He predicted a memorable Test match for me. Simultaneously, he requested me for a few complimentary passes, a request I readily obliged. There was no divine intervention and my wretched form continued without a run against my name. Dejected, I entered the hotel lobby to see the palmist making quick money from gullible foreigners. I walked towards him angrily, but before I could utter a word, he said, 'The best is yet to come!' I felt relieved and spent the evening with my family.

As I walked out to bat in the second innings, predictions kept humming in my ear; this innings would change my fortune—and it did! Indeed. I was cleaned up by Michael Holding for a duck, so now I had a pair of ducks to my name!

My misery was no different than that of most batsmen in the second innings that day. The large crowd was livid and waited outside the pavilion with stones to welcome us. We waited for a long while but the crowd refused to disperse. Finally, most of the players decided to wear helmets to protect their skulls and the police escorted us safely to the hotel. The moment I entered the lobby, my eyes searched for the palmist; he had clearly abandoned his profession and fled. In the evening, there was a cocktail party, in which I met Michael Holding. He was most sympathetic about my horrible form. He said, 'Jimmy, we wanted to get you out early, but not for so little! I hope your career is not jeopardized.' These words came from his heart.

By the time the series ended, I took a deep breath and sat down for some introspection. With no cricket being played in the summer months in India, I flew to England to spend some time with my family.

The domestic season was to commence with the Pakistan tour in September. As much as I would have loved to be part of the team, I gave myself no reasonable chance for selection. In 1982, I had scored loads of runs in domestic cricket, but this time, there were just a few trial matches for the selection of the national team. True to my expectation, my name did not figure anywhere, not even amongst the probables. When I returned to Delhi after completing another successful cricket season in England, I prepared myself for another challenge and recall. I knew it would only happen after the Pakistan tour. While I landed safely at the Delhi airport, my baggage was inexplicably diverted to Bombay by Air India; without it, there was little I could do in Delhi.

All my plans to hit the nets were delayed. It was then that I decided to go across to where trial games were being held and meet the Indian players. The first person to welcome me was Sunil Gavaskar. He was already elected captain for the Pakistan tour. He casually asked me the reason for my visit. I gave an honest reply that it was purely a courtesy call. The next question took me by surprise: 'Are you carrying your kit?' I said no because I wasn't even on the list of probables. I also told him my kitbag had gone to Bombay by mistake and I had no equipment.

Gavaskar paused for a moment, then said, 'Try someone's kit and bat.' Happy with this unexpected opportunity, I acceded to his request and approached Anshuman Gaekwad. I borrowed his entire kit, right down to his socks. As I got ready to bat, I wondered if I was in some kind of a dream world—I was not used to getting breaks like this! I played a couple of deliveries before lunch. Watching me bat, Gavaskar was impressed. When I returned to the dressing room, a player told me Gavaskar's reaction: 'This is my man!' The news of my selection for the Pakistan tour took many people by surprise, including me. My selection reminded me of the Vengsarkar episode before the Hyderabad (Pakistan) Test match. For a change, I was to experience a similar rescue by the same man—Gavaskar! I was told that he insisted on including my name in the team during the selection committee meeting, which therewith paved the way for my third trip to Pakistan in 1984.

When the local manager Gulshan Rai came and hugged me for my selection, I was taken back down the memory lane to a meeting with an astrologer in Delhi, Ramesh Chander, living in Gole Market, near Bangla Sweet House. The intermediary for this meeting was the former Railways wicketkeeper-batsman Dina Bandu. He regarded Papaji as his godfather and had come to pay his respects. I was there too and he spoke about the predictions of this astrologer. Papaji's first reaction was dismissive and my memories of Calcutta were not pleasant either. When he requested permission repeatedly, my father reluctantly gave his consent.

We hired an autorickshaw and reached Gole Market. The flat was on the second floor. We climbed about twenty-odd steps and reached the terrace. I was expecting an old man with grey hair and a flowing saffron gown. However, to my surprise, I saw a young man in his thirties, wearing jeans and a white shirt, surrounded by women. We were received with a big smile, a handshake and a cup of tea. After a while, he asked me to lie down on the floor and felt my body. Instantly, he said, 'You're a victim of black magic!' I not only felt embarrassed but stupid to have come this far to hear such nonsense. But then he startled me with his prediction: 'You are going to Pakistan.' I smiled sheepishly and said that I hadn't even been listed among the probables. He told me not to worry. He scribbled something on a piece of paper and asked me to go to a particular jeweller in Karol Bagh. Now I felt I was being ensnared in some quack's money-making scheme!

However, Dina Bandu was convinced; he took me to a certain jeweller's shop in Karol Bagh. The owner saw the paper and asked me to wait while he attended to my order. I was expecting a hefty bill, so I checked my wallet to see how I would pay for it. After an hour or so, one of his staff members brought a packet wrapped in red paper. He opened it and gave me a slim silver bracelet. It fitted my left wrist perfectly. I asked the jeweller for the invoice but he declined. He even refused to accept payment. Dina Bandu and I parted ways; I reached home to enjoy a meal prepared by my mother. After lunch, I went to Feroz Shah Kotla to meet a few friends. The rest is history!

When news of my selection reached me, I felt obligated to Ramesh Chander. Once again, Dina Bandu picked me up from home, and this time the joyride was on his old Vespa scooter.

He must have spoken non-stop but I heard nothing; I was lost in my thoughts and the astrologer's prediction. This time, our meeting was confined to the Pakistan tour and I was keen to know about my performance. 'You will score a century, a predicted score of 101.' Hearing this, all my worries vanished and I returned home happier than before. Was it destiny or plain dumb luck that I met someone who had the power to open a closed door?

I was overjoyed with my selection but suspense engulfed me more than before. I could not believe that such a rare stroke of luck could come my way. All my life, I had to convince selectors that I was good enough to be part of the squad and I consistently performed to impress, receiving little support and sympathy. However, here I was, not expecting to be selected and, out of the blue, I received this pleasant news. This gesture bolstered my conviction that if the captain wanted someone on his side, he rarely failed to get what he wanted—or was it, in fact, a kind of divine intervention?

As my jubilation faded, logic took the reins. Was it my past performances in the earlier tour of 1982, familiarity with the conditions or my temperament that went in my favour? To test these and be doubly sure, the genius that Gavaskar was, he pushed me out to bat halfway through a trial match in Delhi without any preparation. Once he found me comfortable in a tense atmosphere at short notice, he knew I would survive on this tour too. Pakistan probably remained the toughest place on and off the field to play and relax. He wanted someone with experience to anchor one end and I fitted quite well in his scheme. Since Gavaskar had replaced Kapil, he did not wish to lose the captaincy after the Pakistan tour. Memories of the 1982 tour and its fallout had not yet deserted his memory. After all, Pakistan had proved to be something of a Waterloo for Indian captains, including Gavaskar himself. When all was said and done, it was, nonetheless, a fine gesture to accommodate me in the team.

The 1984 tour was streamlined for six weeks, the shortest till date with three Test matches and an equal number of one-day contests. There wasn't much time available to fine-tune our technique before the crucial first Test in Lahore, except an ODI at Quetta and a charity match for handicapped children in Rawalpindi. Sunil Gavaskar opted out of the charity match, instead, going on a brief visit to Murree, a scenic hill station.

Before the tea interval, the team manager informed us that we would be meeting the President of Pakistan, General Zia-ul-Haq. I thought it was an ideal time to play a prank. Gavaskar had been in a rather relaxed mood and he'd taken off his shoes. I picked up his shoes when he wasn't looking, locked them in a closet and joined the others for the introduction. The Indian captain searched heaven and earth for his shoes, under the bench and all corners, but had to give up. He was introduced to the President of Pakistan wearing slip-ons!

For many players, this tour was like the beginning of the domestic season. Due to little or no cricket available in the summer months, followed by monsoon rains, most of the players seemed a little rusty. Fortunately for me, the English summer had provided me with enough match practice in the Central Lancashire league. As soon as we landed in Pakistan, Gavaskar had confided in me, 'No matter what combination is picked for the one-dayers, let me assure you: you'll be part of the playing XI in the first Test.' These words increased my confidence enormously. Imagine a captain giving such an assurance at the beginning of a tour.

Batting first, Pakistan put up a large total due to another fine century by Pakistan's new captain, Zaheer Abbas. It felt as though the cosmic clock had frozen time in Pakistan, with

Abbas continuing his tremendous form from the 1978 series. Ever so elegant and productive against Indian bowlers, he was a treat to watch. India responded well but lost a couple of quick wickets. When I strode down to bat, I was still nervous. Even though Gavaskar had placed his confidence in me, it did not take away the fact that I was still on another comeback trail. I was placed at number four and the Pakistan bowling attack without Imran and Sarfraz did not look as potent as before. However, Pakistan had always surprised international teams by unleashing untested products to spring a nasty surprise on them. Lahore had a rich history of producing fast bowlers and I looked forward to seeing new faces. This time, it was the young left-arm pace bowler Azeem Hafeez who wrecked the Indian party. Several dubious LBW decisions against Indian batsmen left us aghast. I stood perplexed at the non-striker's end, witnessing these strange umpiring decisions.

In retrospect, the umpiring 'performances' of Shakoor Rana and Khizer Hayat (God bless their souls) in this match did more harm than good to their reputation. Roger Binny suffered the most. He was unceremoniously evicted in both innings, once by Shakoor Rana and subsequently by Khizer Hayat, perhaps the only umpires to carry the distinction of hunting in pairs, similar to fast bowlers, enjoying giving whimsical decisions. At that moment, I remembered my conversation with these gentlemen during a train journey in 1982. Pakistan had drubbed Australia 3-0. How Shakoor Rana and Khizer Hayat, in rustic Punjabi, had mocked the Australian batsmen's inability to read Abdul Qadir's spin and Imran's swing! Was it to demoralize and put the fear of the unknown in our hearts? Boastful as Lahoris are, Shakoor Rana, a big bulky man, described Imran's swing to me. 'Mhindar [Mohinder],' he said, 'Imran swung the ball not in inches ...' He paused, got up in excitement from his seat and literally stretched his large arms apart, '... but this much!'

Then Khizer Hayat chimed in, 'Jimmy, after Imran rattled them, Abdul Qadir foxed them. You know, he purchased an unusual turn [spin] not in inches, but in yards!' And he theatrically stretched his arms like his partner. None of this had any effect on my psychology; on the contrary, I pretended to agree with them. Honestly, it was fun, listening to these exaggerations. Unknown to them, I was quite accustomed to such loose descriptions and exaggerations in Amritsar, Ludhiana, Jalandhar and Patiala. This belt had so much in common before and after 1947, which made me realize that nothing had changed on either side of the Punjab border. I took each word with a pinch of salt and enjoyed the conversation with simple expressions of amazement: 'My God! Wow! That's incredible!' And so forth.

Invariably, both bowlers were successful. Once Imran ran through the Australian top order, Qadir rattled the middle order. The two umpires laughed uproariously and took the conversation to the next level. 'When maybe one or two batsmen were left to be dismissed, we wasted no time, simply sending them off.' My jaw dropped hearing their recollection and wondered if they were seriously, conveying their intentions or pulling my leg! They were dead serious then and even now.

Their love for Roger became evident, when they wasted little time and instantly raised their index fingers. When Maninder Singh's bat took the inside edge on the pad and landed safely in the silly point fielder's hand, the umpire simply smiled and declared him not out. It was a clever ploy because they knew Maninder wouldn't last too long. I occupied the crease for a reasonable length of time to judge the nature of the pitch, till I was dismissed last at my personal score of 36.

Due to the huge deficit, Zaheer Abbas enforced a follow-on. We had to bat for two days to save the Test. I convinced myself to play the role of a saviour. During our second innings, I sensed mistrust between Zaheer Abbas and Javed Miandad, pertaining to the captaincy. Zaheer was not feeling well and he often left the field to take rest; Miandad then assumed responsibility for leading the team. Instantly, luck favoured Pakistan. I always held Miandad's cricketing sense and shrewdness above that of other Pakistani players. He was a street-smart and proactive cricketer. Zaheer realized that a win for Pakistan under Miandad's leadership would jeopardize his captaincy and he returned to the field to take charge. His bowling changes and field placements could not yield similar fruit.

To achieve success, I couldn't afford to take anything on my pads. I found in Shastri someone temperamentally suited to play a similar innings. We stitched together a good partnership to keep our hopes alive and achieve an honourable draw. After tea on the last day, I remember telling him, 'This is a crucial period. We have ninety minutes to play, and they need five wickets. They will be desperate. Don't allow anything to hit your pads.' Shastri was batting well on 71 and he looked comfortable at the crease. However, the first ball after tea from Salim Malik hit his front pad; he was gone.

It was a wake-up call for me too. The scenario around my bat was comical; each player was trying to ruin my concentration with jokes and slang in Punjabi, especially the wicketkeeper, Ashraf Ali. Despite middling the ball, the bowler, fielders and wicketkeeper jumped in the air in excitement and exclaimed, 'Bach gaya, bat ball par lag gaya. Koi baat nahi, agli baari out hai (He's saved because he played the ball with his bat. Don't worry, we will get him with the next delivery)!' I smiled and replied, 'Lage raho, bachchon (Carry on, kids)!'

Roger Binny replaced Ravi Shastri and we fought hard to save the Test match. Roger understood the situation and used the willow till he missed an innocuous delivery from Wasim

Raja and stretched forward. He was struck on the front pad and the bowler exclaimed, 'Aah!' There was not even a semblance of an appeal from him or the wicketkeeper, yet Hayat's finger went straight up without a moment's delay. It was the most hideous decision of the match. I was disgusted; I threw my bat down at the non-striker's end. At that moment, Hayat tried to calm me down: 'Don't get upset, Jimmy. It hit his back leg!' My jaw dropped in astonishment; the ball had clearly hit the front pad. No wonder, Hayat and Rana's partnership contributed towards Roger's absence in the next match!

How we managed to save the Test match was nothing short of divine justice. At the close of play, I had scored another century in Lahore. When I returned to the dressing room, the atmosphere was buoyant and no one was happier than the Indian captain. His faith in me had proved correct and India had come out unscathed. However, Sunil Gavaskar was livid with the umpiring standards and gave a strong statement. 'Despite the best efforts of the Pakistan umpires to favour the home team, we have managed to draw the Test, and that is a miracle. Before embarking on the tour of Pakistan, we expected close decisions, but what happened in the Lahore Test was pre-planned and pre-determined.' The comment did not go down well with the local authorities. This statement eventually led to a strong call for neutral umpires.

While everyone celebrated this feat, I was lost in my thoughts. The prediction had come true even in the most minute details. I had remained undefeated at 101, a figure predicted by the soothsayer in Delhi. I shook my head in disbelief, nevertheless happy to have left another impression in Lahore and carried back wonderful memories. I received great attention and love from Papaji's friends and well-wishers. Now I understood why he missed Lahore and cherished such fond memories of growing up in the city!

The next Test match was in Faisalabad; we travelled by coach to our new accommodation, a decent guest house. Here we noticed a fakir squatting by the side of the hotel entrance. His posture and character drew everyone's attention: long grey hair flowing till his shoulders and his left hand resting on his left thigh, his right hand raised high, index finger pointing at the sky. Before anyone could say anything, Roger Binny, in his Anglo-Indian accent, said, 'Bloody Shakoor Rana is already here.' Everyone burst out laughing! The high-scoring match ended in a draw. It rained centuries for both the teams, Ravi Shastri and Sandeep Patil for India; Mudassar Nazar, Saleem Malik and Qasim Umar for Pakistan. For a change, the two great run machines, Sunil Gavaskar and Zaheer Abbas, were missing from the list.

From here, we moved to Sialkot for an ODI match. One night before the match, the captain and his deputy reported health issues and opted out. At the team meeting, Gavaskar informed me that I would be the captain. This turn of events was quite pleasing for someone like me. I was not destined to be part of the team and here I was, getting the honour of captaincy! Destiny was kind to me, but I couldn't be sure for how long!

After dinner, I decided to take a stroll in the garden; I met a security guard. He saluted me and asked for medicine for a bad throat. Fortunately, I had a few tablets of Strepsils, which I offered him. 'No! No! Sir, not this; the bottle one! It makes the body warm and the mind tipsy.' I understood he was referring to whisky! His happiness knew no bounds when I gave him some.

Batting first, India posted a decent total. However, it was cut short by the sad news of Indira Gandhi's assassination, conveyed to us by the manager. We were stunned; we had fond memories of our last meeting with the Prime Minister in Delhi.

Destiny could be so cruel. I remembered meeting her at Hyderabad House and Rashtrapati Bhawan over tea. The President, Giani Zail Singh, had invited her, a council of ministers, some diplomats and a few of society's elite citizens to honour the world champions. By the time I joined the celebrations, and was introduced to the President and other important citizens of the country, I noticed Papaji talking to Prime Minister Gandhi. I walked towards them and greeted the graceful lady with folded hands.

Before I could utter a word, my father introduced me.

'You have a handsome son,' said Mrs Gandhi.

'All my sons are handsome,' Papaji replied.

A little embarrassed, I took my leave from them and joined the other guests, while they stayed busy with their conversation. Papaji's body language reflected his personality. He spoke at length and the Prime Minister listened.

After a long chat with the elegant PM, Papaji called me aside and said rather wickedly, 'You silly boy, you should have stuck by her side a little longer!'

'Who?' I asked. 'The PM?'

'Yes!' he snapped. 'If I was in your place, I wouldn't have moved anywhere.'

He was talking from experience. He'd maintained long-lasting relationships with the most powerful people of his time. After all, he had rubbed shoulders with maharajas, governor generals, viceroys, Presidents and Prime Ministers.

Out of curiosity, I asked him if he knew the PM and the President personally. He smiled and said, 'I have known both for a long time. Indira had met me in 1948 when I was the captain of the Indian team and her father, Prime Minister Nehru, had come to inaugurate the first Test match at Feroz Shah Kotla. It was probably at teatime that Nehru introduced me to Indira. I have known her since then. As for Zail Singh, you go and ask him for yourself. Just tell him you are Lala Amarnath's son and from Patiala. Observe his reaction!'

I did as suggested. The moment I told the President about my background, his smile froze and he seemed uncomfortable, as if something about him would be revealed. While I was confused, Papaji had a hearty laugh! Was there some secret they shared? I was most curious!

13

ENGLAND IN INDIA
1984–85

INDIA REGISTERED A COMPREHENSIVE VICTORY IN THE FIRST Test match in Bombay. There emerged on the horizon a lean young boy from Madras. He tormented the English batsmen with his leg spin, taking ten wickets in this match. This boy had been with the team a few years, and how well he mingled with the seniors and how well he performed at the highest level of the game reflected his strength of character. The newbie had a rather long name even by Indian standards: Laxman Sivaramakrishnan, which was simply shortened to LS. This boy was unlike other mild players from his region; he was smart and aggressive, and, at times, he crossed the line and taunted the English batsmen with harsh words to put pressure on them. This unusual sight provoked serious bouts of laughter among the senior players.

When the British occupied the southern parts of India, the entire region was termed as Madras Presidency. The inhabitants of different states in southern India lost their identity. People from Travancore (Kerala), Mysore (Karnataka), Vijayanagaram in what is in today's Andhra Pradesh, etc., all came under the direct control and supervision of Madras Presidency, hence referred to as 'Madrasis'. Even when I was growing up, all south Indians were referred to as 'Madrasis'. It was strange; even after Independence, we knew very little about the rich culture of South India. Thankfully, during cricket tours and matches, with consistent interaction between the players and people from different states, I understood and appreciated their history far better than most from other parts of India.

For me, the series began with luck firmly on my side. I snicked the first ball of the innings into the gloves of the wicketkeeper, but, to my great relief, it turned out to be a no ball. This strange phenomenon made me aware that destiny was kind to me and good times lay ahead. Though I did not play a big innings, the way I middled the ball gave me tremendous satisfaction and confidence. I was sure of occupying the crease for a longer period and returning with fruitful results.

The result of the first Test provided plenty of fodder for the Indian media. They did not think much of the English team and labelled them an ordinary side. The Indian team was also overconfident after Bombay. We were convinced that the English team would not be able to handle Indian spinners in Indian conditions. How we misjudged the potential of certain English players! They handled Indian spinners extremely well at Feroz Shah Kotla, except for LS. Other than Tim Robinson's century, the rest of the English batsmen were clueless. The first four days were without much excitement; the match was fading to a draw. On the last day, we were sitting pretty with just two wickets down; Sunil Gavaskar and I were batting comfortably.

The good partnership continued the next day too without any hindrance.

However, after my dismissal, wickets started tumbling for no apparent reason on a good batting track. We never expected the English spinners to get the better of us. Suddenly, the Indian batsmen struggled to break free from the tight grip of the English spinners. The pressure became evident when Kapil played an aggressive stroke against off spinner Paddock and gave away his wicket. The mistimed stroke received an adverse reaction from the dressing room, including from the captain. He was incensed with this attitude. From a position of strength, we were reduced to a sorry condition, committing hara-kiri. The Indian innings folded quickly on a good batting pitch and provided sufficient time to the English team to score the required runs and level the series. We lost a game that we should have easily drawn. It was indeed a classic example of Test cricket's unpredictable nature!

The team for the next Test was due for announcement that evening and everyone was expecting a few changes. However, we didn't know who would be pushed to the altar for sacrifice! The selectors decided to send a strong message that no player was indispensable; accountability mattered most to them. Kapil Dev and Sandeep Patil were dropped for their lackadaisical and slipshod approach in the ill-fated match.

Suddenly, a cauldron of rumours engulfed the Indian media. Several theories appeared on different platforms; apart from the selection committee, they felt there was someone else behind this decision. Since Sunil Gavaskar was at the helm of affairs, accusing fingers were pointed at him. Was he settling old scores? Then emerged the old North–West rivalry to give credence to several articles, which added fuel to the burgeoning fire. Last, but not the least, many critics and observers of the situation felt that Kapil Dev's decision to drop Gavaskar in the

1983 World Cup during the India-Australia contest was the last straw in their strained relationship. Surely, the media was agog with such rumours and people lapped them up gleefully!

The next test was in the City of Joy—Calcutta. Its rich culture and cricket history had been a delight for players and cricket afficionados, and everyone looked forward to playing here. Christmas and New Year parties in this city had no parallel in India. The city was decked with lights and parties continued till the early hours of the mornings. The cricket-crazy Bengalis understood cricket politics better than most Indians. They may not have produced many top-ranking cricketers, but they possessed a deep knowledge of the game and its finer points. This was my third visit to Eden Gardens with the Indian team and, honestly, little had changed. The VIP area in the pavilion was filled with a well-dressed crowd, both men and women. The fragrance of ladies' perfumes, the colour of their sarees and dresses was captivating—a true feast for the senses.

Playing at Eden Gardens was a fascinating experience for all international teams. The large crowd had been supportive. Any milestone by a batsman or a bowler from the home team or even the opponents was appreciated. Imagine, one lakh voices from the gallery appealing with the same intensity as the Indian bowler for LBW or a catch, which indeed put immense pressure on the umpire. This relentless involvement kept the atmosphere electric and the umpires on their toes. Even after the day's play, many enthusiasts carried home debatable umpiring decisions for late-night discussions. I have never experienced such excitement elsewhere in the world. This tradition continued without interruption since the first official Test match at Eden Gardens against England in the 1933-34 test series. The heroes in Calcutta may have changed from Lala Amarnath to Mansoor Ali Khan Pataudi; Sachin Tendulkar to Virat Kohli. But the love for the game remained constant in every generation.

This match heralded another cricketer on the scene—a simple boy with a taveez (locket) attached to a black thread around his neck like a devout Muslim. Mohammad Azharuddin was well-mannered, soft-spoken—and destructive with the bat. He was an elegant stroke player from Hyderabad, a city with a rich cricket history. To me, he reflected the grace and style of M.L. Jaisimha, an exceptionally talented batsman of yore. Eden Gardens remains one of the best cricket centres of the world. It provides a typical Indian pitch, brown in colour and barren to make it a paradise for batsmen and an inferno for pacers. However, Sunil Gavaskar was not in the best of form and several articles in the local dailies pertaining to the selection of the team for this match added needless pressure.

Mohammad Azharuddin, in the presence of almost one lakh spectators, scored a delightful century. He joined the elite list of the few Indian Test batsmen to score a century on debut, beginning with my father, Lala Amarnath, in 1933 against England. One could see his enormous talent and a bright future for Azharuddin. Apart from batting, he was a brilliant fielder, a safe pair of hands in practically any position.

The game was heading towards a draw. However, the large crowd desired some sort of entertainment. Unaware of the growing restlessness of the large gathering, Sunil Gavaskar went to the Doordarshan / All India Radio box for an interview. While returning to the dressing room, people sitting in the VIP enclosure and nearby stands started shouting slogans. Unable to get any reaction from Gavaskar, some people became frustrated and resorted to showing their anger by throwing orange peels. This was most unlike Bengali culture and the great tradition of cricket in Calcutta. The annoyed Indian captain, on entering the dressing room, announced that he would never play in Calcutta again.

The episode reminded me of the 1966 Calcutta Test match against the West Indies, led by Garfield Sobers, when a violent crowd burned the North Stand, and chased the policemen and local officials alike. Despite violence and tear gas shells exploding all around, the large crowd showed immense courtesy to the players of both teams and escorted them to safety. I know it is difficult to control a mob, but witnessing some disgruntled elements at Eden Gardens hijacking the match left a poor impression of the otherwise cheerful and educated Calcutta crowd.

The next Test was in Madras, and Kapil returned to the team. Did the selectors buckle under adverse publicity? Nothing substantial had happened in domestic cricket between the two Test matches. I felt sorry for Sandeep Patil for not getting a similar reprieve. In the recently concluded series against Pakistan, he had scored a century and he played reasonably well in Delhi too. While one player continued to play international cricket, the other was sidelined forever.

The return of Kapil Dev led to a peculiar situation as well as a daunting task for the manager to find a suitable cricketer to share a room with him. He could not accommodate him with any player from the West Zone, due to mistrust. This mindset reflected the cricket rivalry between the West and North Zone players. Finally, the manager took me into his confidence and asked me to find a way to help him out. I had no issues with anyone in the team, so I gave my consent.

Having solved one ticklish problem, I received another strange request from the selection committee. They asked me to pacify Kapil and make him understand that, in the best interest of the team, the past should be forgotten. Let bygones be bygones and henceforth concentrate on the game at hand. It was easier said than done! I was amused with this indirect

DECEMBER 11-17, 1988

THE ILLUSTRATED WEEKLY OF INDIA

THE FEATURES MAGAZINE

RS 5

MOHINDER AMARNATH BECOMES THE FIRST INDIAN CRICKETER TO CHALLENGE THE MIGHT OF THE SELECTORS

"I won't take any more Bullshit"

Mohinder Amarnath punching Mudassar Nazarr of Pakistan bowler (not in picture); scored 60 runs during the first Charminar Challenge One Day International (ODI) cricket tournament between India and Pakistan at Hyderabad on September 10, 1983.
Photo: The Hindu Archives

'Heads I win, tails you lose,' Zaheer Abbas seems to be remarking to acting captain Mohinder Amarnath at the start of the Sialkot one-day cricket match on October 31, 1984.
Photo: The Hindu Archives

Mohinder Amarnath, the Board President XI skipper proudly holding the Wills trophy flanked by his team members after beating Karnataka at Bangalore on February 12, 1984.
Photo: The Hindu Archives

Indian team on Pakistan tour in 1984, celebrating Diwali

Mohinder Amarnath drives England bowler Edmonds (not in picture) in the first innings being watched by the wicket-keeper Paul Downton and Allan Lamp at slips on the first day of the second cricket test match between India and England at Feroz Shah Kotla.
Photo: The Hindu Archives

Mohinder Amarnath through the ages

Mohinder Amarnath hooks Norman Cowans of England for a six; during the fourth Test match between India and England at Chepauk, Madras on January 13, 1985.
Photo: The Hindu Archives

The Indian cricket team pose for photo session with the Sri Lankan President J.R. Jayewardene in Colombo on August 21, 1985.
Photo: The Hindu Archives

The Delhi team with the Ranji Trophy after beating Haryana in the final at New Delhi on April 01, 1986.
Photo: The Hindu Archives

Mohinder Amarnath gets a special treatment from Kapil Dev and a cool pick-me-up from Rajinder Singh Ghai in the first innings during the third test match between India and Australia at Sydney on January 03, 1986.
Photo: The Hindu Archives

Hooking Wasim Akram, Pakistan vs India at Eden Gardens, 1987
Courtesy: Srenik Sett

Mohinder Amarnath plays a hook shot in the third Test cricket match between Australia and India at Sydney on January 02, 1986.
Photo: The Hindu Archives

A rare sight: Mohinder Amarnath losing composure vs New Zealand at Sharjah, 1988

Mohinder Amarnath seen with his lawyer Haresh Jagtiani in New Delhi after he walked out of the disciplinary committee meeting on January 29, 1989.
Photo: The Hindu Archives

The Indian cricket team for Asia Cup 1989, Dhaka

Mohinder Amarnath along with Peter Walker, the award-winning TV producer, and Sir Garfield Sobers during India's tour of West Indies from March 02 to May 03, 1989.
Photo: N. Sridharan / The Hindu Archives

Mohinder Amarnath seen in action during the six nation MRF World Series (Nehru Cup) one day international (ODI) semi-final cricket match between India and West Indies at Bombay on October 30, 1989.
Photo: The Hindu Archives

Abdul Qadir, Mohsin Khan and Mohinder Amarnath at Sharjah

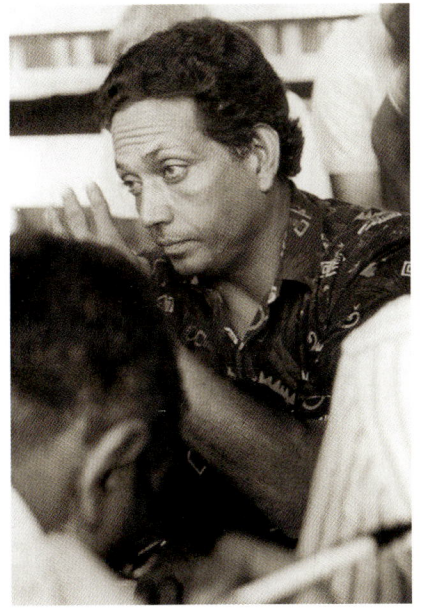

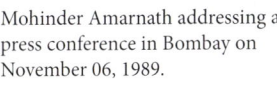

New challenges: As commentator with Sachin Tendulkar in Sri Lanka

Mohinder Amarnath addressing a press conference in Bombay on November 06, 1989.
Photo: The Hindu Archives

With Rajiv Dani and Dwarka Nath

With famous singer Jagjit Singh, 1996

Mohinder Amarnath receiving a cheque from Manohar Joshi, Mumbai Cricket Association at the end of the Pepsi Challenge Mohinder Amarnath Benefit one-day international cricket match between India and South Africa held at Wankhede Stadium, Bombay on December 14, 1996. India won the match.
Photo: V.V. Krishnan / The Hindu Archives

Recipient of CEAT Life Time achievement award, Mohinder Amarnath with Sunil Gavaskar and Harsh Goenka in Mumbai on May 13, 2019.
Photo: Vivek Bendre / The Hindu Archives

Sir Don Bradman (third from left) in the Indian team's dressing room, 1947. Lala Amarnath is in the centre in his whites.

Sir Donald Bradman and Lala Amarnath, Australia, 1947-48

Mohinder Amarnath with his legendary father and guru, 87-year-old Lala Amarnath at Mohali, Punjab, 1998

Mohinder and Surinder on their maiden tour to New Zealand, 1976

After completing the wedding formalities, standing outside the Registrar's office in Dewsbury, England; August 25, 1977

Jimmy's wedding reception in Delhi, 1978
From left to right: Mother-in-law Prakash Kahlon, Bickoo, Col. Daljeet S. Kahlon, Jimmy

Jimmy's wedding reception in Delhi, 1978
From left to right: Jimmy, Bickoo, Pt. Haveli Ram, Lala Amarnath, sister-in-law Harshad Amarnath, Surinder Amarnath, uncle Raj Kumar

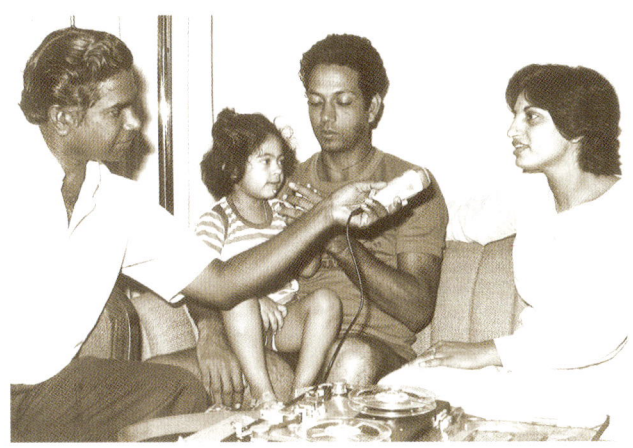
Bickoo gets the credit! An interview after winning the World Cup 1983

With Bickoo, 1984

Diwali, 1990, with Bickoo

Jimmy and Bickoo at Sun and Sand, Juhu, Bombay, 2003

Jimmy's 50th birthday celebrations with family, in Paris, 2000

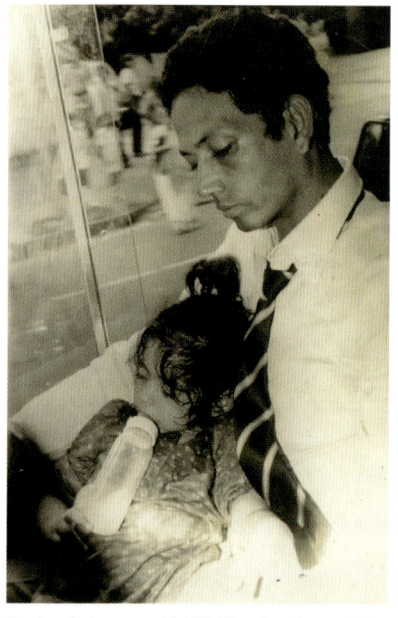
Doting father ... with Nikki at Bombay, 1983

With mummyji and Nikki

Winter in England with Nikki

Jimmy, Bickoo and Nikki at Taj Mahal 2002

Nostalgic ... Jimmy visiting his school in Jalandhar in 2002.
In frame: Principal, Bickoo and a staff member

With Bickoo and Nikki 2009

Jimmy's 60th birthday celebrations, 2010

Karan Amarnath (nephew) in front of the Mohinder Amarnath stand at its inauguration in November 2017

Life after retirement; with friends in London, 2019

Visit to the Golden Temple

Chilling at Restaurant Dhishoom, Canary Wharf, London, July 2024

communication. Why not have a direct dialogue and sort out all the issues in person? I was not the kind of man to touch anyone's raw nerves, so I allowed my roommate to take his time opening up to me whenever he wanted.

During the practice session, the two Indian stars hardly exchanged any words. For some strange reason, the selection committee also avoided any contact with them. The atmosphere in the dressing room remained tense; it was devoid of jokes or pranks. The situation was quite alien to me—I'd never come across anything like this in my long career. I observed that players could not relax after sweating it out in the hot and humid conditions for want of a congenial atmosphere. It made me wonder how we would tackle our opponents when we stood divided amongst ourselves!

I had scored a few 40s and 50s, but was unable to convert them into big scores. However, I was satisfied and confident of another good performance in this match too. The hard and bouncy pitch at Chepauk was to my liking. I always enjoyed the ball coming rapidly on to the bat. I had been more successful on the hard and fast tracks outside the country, and scored more runs compared to home conditions.

On the eve of the match, it was customary to have a team meeting, where the captain discussed strategy and tactics; several players responded with their input and the manager announced twelve names for the Test match. However, the scenario at this meeting was different; there was hardly any discussion on strategy or anything of importance related to the match, probably due to the recent episodes in Delhi and Calcutta. Furthermore, Gavaskar was going through a harrowing time; he needed some space to concentrate on his game. He had scored a solitary 50 in the last four Test matches and his consistently poor performance had shaken his confidence.

Cricket is a great leveller, a lesson I had experienced in my long career, but I'd never thought it would apply to Sunil Gavaskar. His concentration had always been the hallmark of his batting, but it had now somehow abandoned him. To make matters worse, several incidents aggravated the situation even more. He looked a shadow of his former self—struggling to grope his way out of this wretched form. A batsman who had dominated world cricket was now consulting any player he could talk to for advice. With his confidence at the lowest point possible, he was desperate to command respect with his batting performance. With the old Midas touch missing and his confidence thoroughly shaken, the little master seemed to be no more than a mere mortal. This was an important game for India, but we didn't have the means to pin down the English batsmen twice on a good surface.

During the match, the Indian captain left the field briefly; he asked me to take charge, which took me by surprise. It seemed I had become an indispensable member of the unit. The selectors were to announce the team for the remaining ODIs. I had played the first ODI at Cuttack and, for some strange reason, batted in the middle order, facing only one ball and bowling a solitary over. To send a strong message to the selectors about my abilities as a limited-overs player, I got 72 runs in the first innings. I was pleased with my form and looked forward to the remaining ODI matches.

The team announcement left me puzzled; except for me, the rest of the team remained untouched. I failed to understand the logic or reasons to drop me. They never gave any indication as to why they did that. I decided to ignore all the selectors, and adopt my father's advice and words of wisdom: 'Those who feel they have achieved their goal by dropping you should get a befitting reply; even better to show them in a poorer light. Let your bat do the talking!' I had another innings in this match and, surprisingly, felt no pressure; I was in rather light spirits!

But my fear about our bowling attack proved correct when Gatting and Fowler made mincemeat of the Indian bowlers. Both scored double centuries to give the tourists a large lead. India responded disastrously, losing Gavaskar, Srikkanth and Vengsarkar with 22 runs on the board. England won the game quite easily due to their overall performance. The redeeming feature of the Indian batting was another century by Mohammad Azharuddin in the second innings. I missed the same milestone by a narrow margin when Cowan plucked the ball over his head at deep fine leg, leaving me stranded at 95. The entire English team was surprised by this bonus because both of us were going strong and a draw had seemed to be very much on the cards.

Kapil didn't achieve much with his bowling but managed to score a few runs. The interesting part of his batting in both innings was the number of strokes played in the air, some clearing the fielders and others falling in no man's land. Had he played that way on purpose to send a message to someone in the team or on the selection committee? In any case, India lost the series after a dull draw in Kanpur. Nonetheless, Mohammad Azharuddin created a sensation by scoring another century and a new record against England. A simple soul from Hyderabad had followed the Hyderabadi tradition, emulating players like M.L. Jaisimha and Abbas Ali Baig, and he was now a bigger star. His brilliant batting and outstanding fielding were a revelation. Sivaramakrishnan, another simple boy from Madras, also surprised everyone with his aggressive approach and harvest. Though India lost the series, we had discovered two talented cricketers from Hyderabad and Madras.

Most selectors had little sympathy for the losing captain. The poor chap never saw the light the following morning. It did not matter to the selectors whether the loss was at home or abroad. Bishan Singh Bedi lost his coveted post after the Pakistan tour in 1978; Venkataraghavan after the England tour in 1979; Sunil Gavaskar after losing the series to Pakistan in 1982-83, and Kapil Dev, after winning the World Cup, lost the home series to the West Indies in 1983-84 and was sacked.

The dark clouds kept hovering threateningly over Gavaskar's head. Given the past record, anything was possible. For once, the selection committee showed a modicum of maturity and retained him at the helm of affairs for the Australia tour.

14

AUSTRALIA, SHARJAH AND SRI LANKA

1985

SUNIL GAVASKAR CONTINUED AS CAPTAIN, WHICH SURPRISED many. However, I felt it was a mature decision by the selection committee to discard the musical chairs contest it held for captaincy. Gavaskar understood the conditions in Australia quite well, and his insistence on including LS in the team proved to be a masterstroke. I also returned to the team after playing a solitary ODI against England. I remembered the encouraging words of the new chairman of the selection committee, Chandu Borde: 'The doors are not shut for your return to the one-day team.' That statement proved his vast knowledge of the game and his ability to judge a player. The chairman's faith in me undoubtedly resurrected my career in the shorter format. The

BCCI organized a camp for a few days—a mere formality before the tour.

The World Championship sponsored by Benson & Hedges was expected to be nothing short of the Prudential World Cup. It was to showcase Australian cricket in all its grandeur and to mark the centenary celebration of the Victoria Cricket Association. Earlier, two big events had captivated the Australians. In 1971, the Australia Cricket Board cancelled South Africa's tour of Australia because of their apartheid regime and substituted the tour with unofficial Test matches against the World XI. The galaxy of stars that descended on the Australian continent, led by Gary Sobers, included Rohan Kanhai, Clive Lloyd, Zaheer Abbas, Intikhab Alam, Sunil Gavaskar, Bishan Bedi, Tony Greig, the Pollock brothers and many more to present different shades of world cricket. Australia was led by Ian Chappell, and the team included Greg Chappell, Doug Walters, Ian Redpath, Graham McKenzie, Dennis Lillee and Bob Massie, among others, to raise an equally strong team.

A few years later, a packed house at the MCG witnessed an absorbing centenary Test match between England and Australia. To ensure a similar response from the crowd for the Benson & Hedges World Championship, the Australian Cricket Board (ACB) planned this event quite meticulously. Most games were scheduled under floodlights at the MCG and a few at the SCG in Sydney. The ACB invited the top international teams to compete in this tournament: England, New Zealand, Pakistan, Sri Lanka, India and the West Indies. South Africa, still facing a ban for its policy of apartheid, was not invited.

Before the grand opening ceremony at the MCG, most of the teams were accommodated at the Melbourne Hilton. We attended various functions, signed cricket bats and, if free, enjoyed ourselves at the hotel disco, Juliana. Loud music, colourful lights, heady aromas, pretty faces and drinks made it a favourite place for all the players to enjoy the lively atmosphere. The news of international players visiting it spread like wildfire, attracting the locals to rub shoulders with their favourite stars. Suddenly, Juliana became the most sought-after discotheque in the city, with the West Indian players being particularly popular among the younger generation.

The Indian team had no experience of playing under floodlights, nevertheless, we were excited. I had watched the day-night matches of the Kerry Packer World Series in 1977, and everything looked colourful and easy from the stands. Now, we were to experience this phenomenon for ourselves. Unlike other tournaments with tight schedules, there were long breaks between matches here. In the league stage, two out of three matches were held at the MCG. This enabled us to explore the beautiful city of gardens and monuments, and interact with the local people. We walked around in small groups, discovered different restaurants and developed new tastes. Our familiar faces soon made us honorary citizens of Melbourne!

While life was enjoyable off the cricket field, conditions on the field were demanding—beginning with the practice wickets. They were hard, fast and bouncy compared to the slow and low-bounce pitches in India. We were used to facing red cherries, but here, the organizers provided us with white balls. The hard new ball with an upright seam astonished batsmen and bowlers alike. While pace bowlers enjoyed the movement and carry, batsmen had a torrid time. The rule of two white balls for the allotted fifty overs was likely to leave the cricket ball hard and seam intact to bounce more. Except for Australia, every team required hard work to get used to the unusual bounce.

No doubt India had discovered immense talent in the batting of Mohammad Azharuddin and the spin bowling of LS, and the wicketkeeping by Sadanand Viswanath, but they remained untested in Australia. After the 1983 World Cup, the Indians had struggled against the West Indies, followed by a similar performance against England in the home series. We had talent and resources, but would we perform in the limited-overs matches? That certainly remained the million-dollar question.

If adjusting to the bounce and pace was difficult, spotting the white ball under the dark sky and floodlights was even more demanding. We had to work extremely hard to take high catches and throw hard from the outfield to the wicketkeeper. Each one of us fumbled with the catches and, at times, failed to throw the ball accurately to the stumps. We practised till no ice cubes were needed to relieve our bruised fingers.

Interestingly, every player took the initiative at fielding practice. To compensate for the strength of our shoulders and the big boundaries, we adopted a policy of a one bounce flat throw to cover the distance quickly. The only exception was Roger Binny; he was a champion javelin thrower, and he could throw the ball to the keeper with ease.

The concept of a professional trainer for the Indian team had not yet crossed the mind of the BCCI. This left us with one common drill: run a few laps around the ground together and sprint a little distance for speed work. Subsequently, each player was left to do his own exercise. From an early age, my father had instilled in me the value of fitness, so exercises became an integral part of my training. Since I was a willing teacher, it suited the team to have me as a trainer.

The Indian team was residing in the proximity of the MCG; we took the decision to walk through the huge park to the cricket ground. This routine not only kept us fit but also warmed our bodies before practice. After the practice session, we walked back, but for a different reason—to get some Chinese takeout and feed our empty bellies in the hotel.

At times, a bottle of red or white wine or a can of chilled lager changed the taste of the meal for the better and revitalized our exhausted limbs!

When the other teams moved out of Melbourne, we became Juliana's primary patrons. We had maximum matches at the MCG and Juliana gave us comfort. The team spirit was amazing and the youngsters were terrific. They were favourites with the girls of all ages, sizes and heights on the dancing floor. Watching their energy on the field and then later in the evening left us speechless.

On this tour, all the players received a meagre weekly allowance and were forced to stick to their budget; but one of the players was an exception. He preferred to live a luxurious lifestyle, leaving deep holes in his pocket. I had heard stories of the maharajas of yore and their lifestyles but never witnessed it till I saw this boy. He was certainly equivalent to a maharaja in habit, if not status. He spent his entire allowance in a few days and subsequently knocked on teammates' doors to borrow money; nobody refused because he always returned it the following week. Once, he borrowed my music system with a promise to return it by evening, but it took several reminders over many days to get it back. The excuse was always polite: 'I am rehearsing a love song!' I later came to know that he'd impressed half of the girls in Melbourne!

Once, this player wanted a haircut; he found an expensive salon. To win the hearts of the pretty hairdressers, he carried chocolates and a bouquet of flowers, and he floored everyone. He travelled by cab for dinner or shopping, and never failed to pay a tip to the driver. While dining at a restaurant, he ordered expensive wine and enjoyed it with the meal. Later, he also tipped the waiter in a regal manner. His love for clothes and shoes made us wonder if they would fit in his suitcase or if he would purchase a few more. He was always smiling and perfectly dressed for the occasion. His habit of living like a maharaja continued even after this tour.

Srikkanth was another interesting character in the team. He was strictly vegetarian; it was always challenging for him to find a decent South Indian meal suiting his taste. The varieties of salads and cheese failed to satiate his hunger, and he simply yearned for rice, sambar and curd! While we enjoyed North Indian dishes, he preferred rice and curd. Finally, one day, he came across a South Indian couple at an Indian restaurant and exchanged words in Tamil. He came back to the table rubbing his hands, grinning broadly. We knew he had hit a jackpot. Thereafter, Srikkanth was out to dine with his new friends nearly every day.

However, he soon suffered a sort of burnout and, one evening, he surprised me with an electric rice cooker. I thought it was a weird gift from an admirer. 'No,' he said; he had apparently bought it, which baffled me further! Then he dropped a bombshell, 'Jumbo, do you know how to cook rice?' I knew Srikkanth was capable of throwing surprises but this was off the wall. I certainly had experience with cooking, but this device and how it worked was beyond me. I really had no idea. We sat down and read the instructions. Soon, his room smelled of rice and the spices he sprinkled over his curd. No amount of deodorant spray could make the smell go. I remember, on one occasion, after helping him make rice, I was walking towards my room and noticed a housekeeping lady standing in the corridor smiling at me. Maybe the pungent aromas of the South Indian spices had stuck to my clothes.

The World Championship matches were telecast by Channel 9, which proved that the acrimonious past (the duel between the Australian Cricket Board and Kerry Packer) had been laid to rest. Interestingly, the Indian government owned the

Doordarshan TV channel and had also signed an agreement with Channel 9 to take a direct feed of the matches, especially when India played. This transformation came after India's historic victory in the World Cup at Lord's, and the increase in public demand to watch the Indian team compete in another high-profile tournament.

We were placed in a group with Pakistan, Australia and England—all equally strong and talented teams. Sadly, there was no practice game for us before the tournament to test the raw talent and finalize the composition of the team. Nonetheless, there were quite a few players from the 1983 winning team to make up for this loss.

Roger Binny was my roommate for the entire tour, and what a roommate he was! One could share concerns and emotions with him with the least fear of disclosure to the public or teammates, which was a boon. He was quite content with himself, to such an extent that I always made bed tea and offered it to him. I loved his Anglo-Carnatic accent, while he was handicapped with Hindi, the language I simply adored. There was little or no discussion about cricket in the room, allowing us to relax and enjoy each other's company. His love for chilled beer was matched by my love for Hindi music, a perfect combination! However, he still revelled in his ancestral hobby, fishing for relaxation. He was genuinely one of the nicest people in the team.

Our first game was against our nemesis Pakistan at the MCG. Interestingly, we were facing Pakistan for the first time in a limited-overs match at a neutral venue. Our earlier experiences were confined to either country or in Sharjah with dead pitches. However, the pitches in Australia were quite the opposite, hard and bouncy. India versus Pakistan contests always raised the adrenaline of the players and charged the atmosphere of both dressing rooms; it was no different here.

However, we were buoyant with the presence of neutral umpires to ease the pressure.

The tournament commenced with a victory for the hosts beating England by seven wickets. The next game between India and Pakistan was similar in nature and hundreds of millions of people in the two countries were holding their breath in anticipation. Due to time differences, the subcontinent public was comfortably placed at home to enjoy the live telecast. Both teams were loaded with all-rounders and reputed batsmen. However, Pakistan had an edge in their pace attack. To compensate, we depended heavily on our line, length and movement. This factor became potent given the conditions suiting our style. Our confidence received a further boost with two white balls. Roger Binny had proved in the Prudential Cup how lethal he could be with the movement and he became an ideal partner for Kapil. Madan Lal, Shastri and Sivaramakrishnan were expected to bowl the middle overs. In case of an emergency, I was readily available.

The good news for Pakistan was the return of Imran Khan. In the past, he had inspired the team with his leadership till he relinquished it. He was replaced by Javed Miandad. The new captain's first stint was marred by a revolt by the senior cricketers. Was it because he was considerably junior to them or was it because he lacked the communication skills to command respect from his fellow cricketers? Whatever little I had observed on my earlier tours to Pakistan showed that there remained a wedge between the societies of Karachi and Lahore. Did it percolate to the cricket field too? Miandad had a rather torrid time controlling the flock.

Pakistan had always produced quality fast bowlers and Miandad found in Wasim Akram an outstanding left arm bowler to partner with Imran Khan. He had impressed everyone with his performance against New Zealand. Both the Indian and Pakistani were staying in the same hotel and we relived memories of earlier contests. Fortunately, frequent series between us had removed animosity, and replaced it with mutual admiration and friendship. I had a good understanding with many Pakistani cricketers from Lahore due to our common language, Punjabi. As for Karachi players, only Mohsin Khan had something in common with me to become a good friend during the 1982 tour of Pakistan. Nevertheless, camaraderie took a backseat when we represented our nation—no quarter was offered or expected; it was tough cricket all the way.

This Pakistan team may have carried happy memories of the 1982-83 series against us, but, surprisingly, they seemed to be a pale shadow of their former selves. As for us, most had done well against England, apart from the captain. Once home pressure was removed, he was at ease in a new environment, looking a different batsman in the nets; the old spark was back. However, he surprised everyone with his decision to bat in the middle order, a rare sight for sure!

Winning the toss and batting first, Pakistan faced a stiff test. Roger Binny found the conditions to his liking. It seemed as if he had carried the English strip to Melbourne. Since Doordarshan took direct feed from Channel 9, it had little scope to block any visuals. Every home was glued to their TV sets watching this important match against Pakistan. The ball moved and bounced to find edges; Roger was undoubtedly the pick of the Indian bowlers with four scalps. The debutant L. Sivaramakrishnan took two wickets. Zaheer Abbas and Qasim Umar were both beaten by the flight and spin, and their mistimed shots offered return catches to the leggy. Every dismissal was watched in India with utter glee.

However, there was embarrassment for the elders and excitement for the youth when the cameras focused on the crowd. The bikini-clad girls and bare-chested boys in shorts drinking beer was a rare sight for most Indians. I was told the viewership of this match and subsequent ones achieved new heights. For a change, there was no protest or questions raised in Parliament for indecent exposure!

A target of 184 may have looked small but conditions still suited the seam bowlers. An early burst by Imran reduced us to 3/27 till Javed Miandad made a faux pas, replacing him with another bowler and giving India some breathing space. Gavaskar justified his decision to bat in the middle order with a solid half-century. The combination of experience with India's new batting sensation, Mohammad Azharuddin, added a crucial match-winning century partnership. Azhar won the hearts of the Indian public with his wristy strokes, remaining unbeaten with a half-century.

The next game against England was at the SCG. If Melbourne had been auspicious for us, Sydney also ladened us with blissful memories to cherish. The Indian team was beaming with confidence and playing as a fine unit. The pace bowlers and spinners were in good form; brave batsmen and outstanding work in the field made us a potent force. It reminded me of the 1983 World Cup team.

The final match of the league was against the hosts. It was very important for us to win and qualify. Failing this, we would be placed with Australia and Pakistan on the points table. Around 50,000 diehard Australian supporters converged at the famous MCG. It still looked empty because of its vast capacity of 90,000. They came with big ice boxes full of beer, a variety of snacks and fluttering national flags to support the home team and enjoy the atmosphere. However, the picnic was spoiled by the tourists—especially Roger Binny and Srikkanth.

Roger Binny had a high success rate against left-handers; he simply didn't falter. His accuracy and movement proved lethal, and he took three wickets. He was well supported by the other bowlers. The Indian fielding was outstanding as well; Azharuddin, Roger Binny and Kapil matched some of the known fielders from other teams. Roger Binny, especially, was a complete athlete, throwing the ball flat from the edge of the boundary of the MCG into the hands of the wicketkeeper. Australia slumped to their lowest total of the tournament (163).

The pitch was still assisting pace bowlers and Australia, hoping to make an early dent, received a rude shock. Srikkanth's strokes left the Aussie pace battery bruised if not battered. This display left the gallery, media and commentators overawed; they loved his style. The century opening partnership with Ravi Shastri (51) sealed the fate of the match; Srikkanth made an unbeaten 93. However, for some strange reason, he wasn't given the Man of the Match award.

At this stage, I observed a change in the attitude of the Australian cricketers. Earlier, they had been renowned for their sportsmanship both in victory and defeat. I had witnessed it on the 1977 tour when the losing team, led by the captain, visited the counterparts' dressing room, congratulated them and stayed for a drink. Neither the tradition nor the spirit of camaraderie existed anymore. The loss had thrown the hosts along with England out of the competition. The performance of the Indian team was truly magnificent. We behaved like a typhoon, decimating every opponent. We had played the best possible cricket after the Prudential Cup of 1983. We clicked together like a well-oiled engine, supremely in control, whether batting or bowling or fielding!

Our next destination was Sydney to face New Zealand in the semi-final. Both teams had played a game each at this venue; we had beaten England, while the New Zealand versus West Indies match had been washed out. New Zealand was a good team without big names, apart from Richard Hadlee, one of the best all-rounders in the game. He had the ability to turn the tide even in rough weather.

The toss was vital for us because we had chased all the targets with ease. Once again, Gavaskar was lucky and India elected to field. Roger Binny and Kapil Dev had been consistently providing us with early breakthroughs and did not disappoint, picking a wicket each to give us a perfect start. Yet, we knew the batting capabilities of John Reid, Geoff Howarth, Martin Crowe, Ian Smith, Jeremy Coney, Lance Cairns and Richard Hadlee. Much to our delight, Madan Lal produced a magic spell, taking four wickets; Ravi Shastri took three and the Kiwis were ultimately restricted to just 206.

While fielding, I remember a hilarious incident involving Srikkanth. I had never seen anyone belting the ball the way Lance Cairns did; his massive sixes were loaded with ferocious power and travelled some distance. Knowing the strength and abilities of this rather dangerous batsman, Sunil Gavaskar placed Srikkanth at the deep midwicket boundary. Much to the Indian captain's delight, Cairns responded with a massive mis-hit towards Srikkanth. The ball took a flight to eternity, challenging the height of the floodlight towers.

The white ball kept rising under the dark sky till it resembled a table tennis ball. The entire Indian team stood with their hands on their hips and jaws hanging to the ground. However, both batsmen scrambled hard to collect runs in case of a reprieve. Srikkanth was like a buzzy bee, hovering under the ball to confirm the line of descent. I can tell you from experience that it is never easy to take high catches with blazing floodlights in the background, no matter how easy it looks. Srikkanth's neck was locked and head thrown back for a long time, watching the tiny ball in the sky. No matter how hard he tried to judge the path of descent, the strong breeze altered its course a few times. Srikkanth's reaction confirmed that he had lost the flight and, of course, dropped the catch. This was probably the first catch we dropped in the competition and that too of a big hitter capable of changing the course of a match. Gavaskar knew Cairns would repeat the stroke, so he replaced Srikkanth with another fielder, Azharuddin, at deep midwicket; he put Srikkanth at the square leg fence.

As luck would have it, the big, burly Cairns smashed Madan Lal once more, this time to square leg where Srikkanth was stationed. The flat pull shot, loaded with thundering power, flew towards Srikkanth. While the bowler and fielders held their breath, I was not sure about Srikkanth. He stood frozen and hardly moved an inch; could he even see the ball? Much to everyone's delight, Srikkanth held the catch over his head, rather calmly. Astonished and amused, Gavaskar held his stomach and doubled over in laughter. Holding the ball in his hand, Srikkanth walked up to the captain and produced a typical one-liner, 'What? I never drop difficult catches!' Everyone joined in the hilarity and lit the field with their laughter!

Chasing a modest total, India looked at Srikkanth for an explosive start but lost him quite early in the innings. Thereafter, Shastri and Azharuddin found pace bowling a bit of a challenge; runs came at a pedestrian pace, which, of course, increased the required run rate. Shastri crawled to his 50, leaving the dressing room restless. Gavaskar and I were padded up; we checked the scoreboard and the asking rate more often than the innings. At this stage, Gavaskar asked Kapil to pad up too. When Shastri was dismissed, there was a sigh of relief, and a ray of hope for us. Kapil was promoted with a licence to swing the willow in any manner he deemed fit. His arrival at the crease made Vengsarkar feel more confident, and he too joined in the fireworks and launched his own assault on the bowling attack from the other end.

The change in tactics took the opponents by surprise. The competition between Kapil and Vengsarkar produced a variety of strokes, which perplexed the Kiwis. What was once an immaculate line suddenly looked innocuous. The asking rate plummeted to change the mood in the Indian dressing room. The silence and frustration gave way to joy; palms ached with constant applause and throats became hoarse with shouts of delight. By nature, Indian cricketers remained superstitious; nobody moved or changed their seats. Even using the toilet was forbidden during the over and, if one was desperate to heed the call of nature, he could only do so between the overs. As we moved closer to the target, Kapil's strike rate surged past 150 and Vengsarkar's past 100; both batsmen made a half-century. India cruised to another victory, but not without hiccups, winning the match by seven wickets. Pakistan defeated West Indies in the other semi-final with a similar margin to meet us in the grand finale at the MCG.

There was celebration in the Indian dressing room and in the stands by many Indian supporters. With one too many drinks down their throats, the fans remained boisterous and wanted one last glimpse, standing by our coach. While the Indian players made a beeline for the coach, I completed the formalities of getting the autographs of both teams. As I walked towards the coach, I saw Kapil evading the aggressive posture of a few Indian supporters. I presumed he was having fun till one of them tried to grab him. I realized at once that the situation had turned out to be more serious than anticipated. I dropped my kit bag and ran with two autographed cricket bats; I tossed one to Kapil and held the other. Before taking any punitive action, I asked Kapil the reason for the commotion. He replied, 'These people are forcing me to accompany them and I am not interested.' Looking at Kapil, I smiled and said, 'Let's do it.' We swung the bats in the air to scare them. It had some effect but the inebriated supporters, in fact, grew even more vocal and abusive.

The commotion attracted young Chetan Sharma; he came running to rescue us. Without uttering a word, he launched a bloody attack and landed a few blows with his bat. The effect was instant and the hecklers begged for mercy. Having tamed them, Chetan asked us in Punjabi, 'Ki hoya si (What happened)?' I was taken aback by his statement; he had joined a fight without even knowing the reason. I couldn't help smiling at the commitment of the young warrior! Such was the spirit of the team, especially the youngsters. Thankfully, there was no police complaint filed against us. We decided to forget it like a bad dream and enjoyed the celebration with champagne!

All the players were thrilled with the prospect of returning to Melbourne, and none was happier than Srikkanth. During the long flight from Sydney to Melbourne, we cracked jokes and pulled each other's legs, but Srikkanth remained silent. He was lost in his own thoughts, looking forward to the company of the South Indian doctors he'd befriended—no doubt relishing the prospect of idli and sambar.

The day before the finals, we had a customary team meeting in team manager E.A.S. Prasanna's room. Instead of strategy, valuable time was spent discussing the Man of the Series award and how to split the proceeds. Srikkanth, Roger Binny, Kapil Dev and Ravi Shastri were strong contenders for the prize. We knew if India won the finals, one of them would get an Audi as the Man of the Series award. However, some players, including a star performer, were emphatic that the car should be sold and proceeds distributed equally. I strongly objected and suggested that it should remain with the winner to enjoy. We were unable to come to any rational conclusion; we abandoned the discussion till the trophy was won and the car was awarded.

I had hardly contributed anything substantial batting at number six because India had cruised to victories one after another before I even had a chance to occupy the crease. If I did get a chance, it was for a brief period. Gavaskar used me as the sixth bowler to plug the flow of runs and was not disappointed.

On the day of the final, Roger Binny was down with strong symptoms of flu and a high temperature. It was a big blow for us losing our strike bowler. He was replaced by the little dynamite Chetan Sharma. We had seen what he could do outside the field but whether he would rise to the occasion remained untested. Pakistan also suffered a big blow. Wasim Akram was ruled out due to poor health. The absence of two wicket-taking bowlers from either side brought relief to many batsmen.

About 50,000 people turned up to enjoy the finals involving India and Pakistan. A few disgruntled locals joined the supporters, not out of love for either team but compulsion; they had bought their tickets for the final in the hope of seeing Australia or England. Disappointed, they carried big banners to tease us: 'Finals between bus conductors and drivers.' The slogan amused me, and I showed the thumb-up sign as a moral victory for beating Australia and England in this competition.

It was indeed a big occasion for both teams playing the final for the first time, and what a stage it was: the Benson & Hedges World Championship at the MCG. This match raised the aspiration of thousands of fans at the ground and millions watching on television across the world. Knowing the mentality of the people from both countries, this match seemed no less than a war and our izzat, or honour, depended on the result. Business houses and shops were likely to remain shut, schools and colleges given a holiday, and families chanting prayers more frequently than ever in life. Even streets would remain deserted with little or no traffic. Realizing these sentiments, I was also inflamed with feelings of patriotism.

Sunil Gavaskar had been lucky with the toss, or he had mastered the art of winning the toss in this tournament. However, luck deserted him on the big stage and Pakistan decided to bat first. Kapil had a new partner from the city of Chandigarh in Chetan Sharma. He was short yet strongly built, and he could surprise batsmen with his pace.

Kapil produced another good spell, taking three wickets. He was ably supported by Chetan Sharma with one wicket to reduce Pakistan to 4/33. When Imran Khan came to bat, I moved to mid-off to give Chetan a few words of encouragement and share my experiences with him. Knowing Imran's propensity to hook in the air, I told Chetan to test him with a bouncer. The youngster bowled a perfect bouncer and Imran gloved the ball to the wicketkeeper S. Viswanath. The chorus of appeals had little impact on the umpire or the batsman. However, the replays on the huge MCG electronic screen proved us correct. Although disappointed, it did not dampen our spirits. After the over, I wondered about Imran's reluctance to walk off the pitch before the umpire's decision. Maybe it was because this was no ordinary contest. The aspirations of millions of Pakistanis depended on him. If it meant sacrificing the spirit of the game, so be it! Nevertheless, we continued to apply pressure on Pakistan.

The introduction of the leg spinner LS in the middle overs yielded fruit. He had mesmerized many batsmen with his guile, causing destruction on the pitch and headache in the opponents' dressing room. Short and thin, with dark glossy skin and hair, he had almost become a cult figure amongst the cricket-loving Aussies.

Javed Miandad and Imran Khan had been good players of spin bowling, but they also struggled with LS's immaculate length. After dismissing Imran run out with a neat piece of fielding, Javed Miandad remained the only threat for us. However, his dismissal was a classic combination involving LS, and the wicketkeeper. These juniors wrote a beautiful script and executed it to perfection.

Sadanand Vishwanath was a hyperactive wicketkeeper behind the stumps. He was chirpy and backed all the bowlers to the hilt. He not only irritated Javed Miandad, but also got the better of him in a verbal duel, which left the Pakistan captain speechless. This unusual drama had an enormous impact on the batsman. Miandad not only lost his concentration, but also his wicket. A target of 177 runs was even lower than what it had been in our previous encounter.

This tournament seemed like a corporate event. Cricket Australia in general and the Victoria Cricket Association in particular took note of the team's requirements and handled them professionally. Dinner was served between the innings, this time a bit early. Every team placed orders in advance from the long list provided to us. The Indian players preferred lamb or pork chops, grilled chicken, while a few wanted Aussie steaks with boiled vegetables or French fries. The odd man out was Srikkanth, wanting only a South Indian meal. This problem was sorted out by his doctor friends.

Dinner was served in the dining room for both teams, except the opening batsmen. They had the privilege of enjoying it in the dressing room. Srikkanth always relished his steaming rice with hot and spicy sambar, curd and papadum, cooked fresh and delivered by his friends. This gesture lifted his spirits and mood. The aroma of various spices pervaded the atmosphere of the dressing room, forcing a few of us to dig into his box too. Before walking out of the dressing room to bat, Srikkanth would invariably let out a big burp to indicate his satisfied stomach—yet he was perennially hungry for runs! Another noticeable action of his while walking towards the crease was to look at the sun for blessings, obviously hard to find at night, but he did indulge in a brief glance at the floodlights!

India possessed a long batting line-up and the mood was buoyant, chasing a modest target of 177 in 50 overs. However, Gavaskar sitting next to me eating was a little perturbed. He said, 'Jimmy, please ask him [Srikkanth] to take it easy.'

I replied, 'Leave him alone; don't say anything to him.'

Srikkanth knew only one way of batting and that was simply attacking. He was in good form and advising him at this juncture meant confusing him. And asking him to play the role of an anchor was like beating one's head against a brick wall.

Right from the word go, he attacked the Pakistani bowlers. He effortlessly lofted Hafeez into the stand, and let out a big burp to draw the attention of the bowler and the fielders. How he surprised everyone, including us, with his hits! Here was a man, who ate nothing but rice and sambar, generating so much strength that it left everyone utterly baffled!

We played like a champion side; the closer we got to the target, the louder the dressing room became. It was great to see the two youngsters LS and Viswanath jumping like toddlers. Once the target was achieved, the popping sound of champagne bottles filled the dressing room. We hugged and danced to begin the celebration, and later we did a victory lap in the Audi at the MCG.

The celebration at the hotel was no less. It was filled with fans, friends and more champagne. When I got up the next morning, I went to fetch the newspaper outside the door but found a bottle of champagne there, neatly wrapped as a gift. I've been part of three of the greatest achievements by the Indian team: rewriting Test history with a victory against the West Indies in Trinidad in 1976, World Cup victory at Lord's in 1983 and now at the MCG in 1985. In my long career, I found this one the sweetest!

If I had to summarize the success of this tour, many factors come to mind. Gavaskar's captaincy played an important role. How he judged the weakness of the opponent batsmen and laid traps to dismiss them speaks volumes about his planning and execution. The rapport amongst the players was also noteworthy. The team was devoid of pettiness and quarrels. Instead, love and care bound us together in a spirit of camaraderie, which helped us overcome many hurdles and achieve success.

Team meetings were mere formalities. There was hardly any plan discussed in detail or strategies drawn on a blackboard. The captain and the senior players shouldered the responsibility of guiding the juniors, and they responded with enthusiasm.

Sunil Gavaskar was a remarkable opening batsman and judge of form. After an inconsistent performance against England, he promptly demoted himself to the middle order. This batting reshuffle enabled Srikkanth and Shastri to form an ideal opening pair; aggressive and defensive in approach, they provided us with good starts. Another secret characteristic of Gavaskar remained hidden from most players, and it was his ability to play a prank and then feign ignorance. He wore a thoroughly convincing poker face to fool many, though he always acted in good spirit!

If Kapil Dev, Roger Binny and Madan Lal were outstanding with the new ball, Ravi Shastri and Laxman Sivaramakrishnan were equally effective, and posed a grave threat to the opposing batsmen. Their never-say-die spirits became the backbone of our attack. However, it was amusing to see Kapil and Madan congratulating Binny with pats and laughter and the barest of compliments. How body language jelled and lifted the team spirit was easily noticeable during our rambunctious celebrations!

The four exceptionally talented players from South India—Srikkanth, Azharuddin, Sivaramakrishnan and Sadanand Viswanath—were all unique characters: Srikkanth, reckless but funny; Azharuddin, a simple, God-fearing man from Hyderabad, doing namaz five times a day; S. Vishwanath and L. Sivaramakrishnan undoubtedly remained the lifeline of the dressing room and livewires on the dancing floor, and they remained the seniors' favourites.

The World Championship of 1985 not only provided stability to Indian cricket, but it also brought respect. The 1983 World Cup success was complemented with the victory at the MCG. These triumphs opened the doors for the next generations to conquer new frontiers! The team returned to India as inconspicuously as it had boarded the plane to Australia. No receptions, no bouquets or garlands to welcome us, which proved repeating history was not as sweet as creating it! India's next destination was for the Rothmans Cup at Sharjah. Everything seemed to be in place till Sunil Gavaskar dropped a bombshell and relinquished his captaincy. The selectors, media and the players were taken by surprise. To play it safe, the selectors reverted to Kapil Dev.

After a few days' break in India, we landed at Sharjah, oozing confidence. Much to our surprise, the local media had already built an atmosphere of rivalry between India and Pakistan. It was a clever ploy to attract large crowds at the venue. Simultaneously, it touched the raw nerves of thousands in the streets, shops, offices and hotels to put psychological pressure on the large diaspora of the two countries. With the warm welcome came a plea: 'Please don't lose to Pakistan!' I was sure it remained the same for our rivals too. Often, these pleading souls followed us to our rooms and repeated their requests when they met us in the dining halls for breakfast. Thank God the local bus driver left us alone!

In the past, pitches here were barren, which assisted the batsmen and spin bowlers. However, this time, the nature of the pitch had changed. It was helping pace bowlers, especially Imran. Watching him bowl with hostility was a lesson for other fast bowlers, which, fortunately for us, they could not emulate. Within no time, India was tottering, losing five early wickets. At this crucial stage, the Pakistani captain committed a grave mistake and removed the successful Imran from the attack. India managed to post 125, to leave the large Indian diaspora disappointed and the Pakistan fans thrilled. Imran Khan produced the best spell of his career, taking 6/14.

As the Indian innings had terminated ahead of the scheduled time, the organizers extended the designated break. We went to nap in the dressing room. On resumption, the Pakistan innings commenced in an aggressive manner till a call for a tight single brought us a much-desired breakthrough. My direct throw from mid-off found the target. Thus began a drama, pushing Pakistan on the back foot. Once the spinners came into operation, the Pakistan batsmen danced to their tune, especially Miandad to LS. At this stage, a confident Imran walked ahead of the established batsmen because he had allegedly boasted, 'Main abhi match khatam kar kay aata hoon (I will finish the game in no time)'; he lasted only two balls.

Panic seized the rank and file of the Pakistan camp, and they crumbled like overbaked cookies. Defending a modest total brought back those precious memories of the World Cup. Kapil, Shastri and LS were outstanding with the ball; Gavaskar compensated for his failure with the bat with golden catches. He dived, rolled and jumped in glee, which added another dimension to the happy atmosphere. India bamboozled the strong Pakistan batting line-up and dismissed them for a paltry 87 to achieve a spectacular victory in a low-scoring match. The agony of the Pakistani team did not end here; they were trolled and subjected to shouts of abuse from the large Pakistani diaspora, an unfortunate reaction that ruined the spirit of the game.

The next day, we were invited by the Indian Consulate to Abu Dhabi, about 145 kilometres from Sharjah, for a party. The evening ended on a high note; we cracked jokes, laughed and sang songs on our return. The following day being free, we went shopping. When we returned to the hotel in small groups, we faced a peculiar situation. Local policemen were waiting to interrogate us against a complaint filed by the previous evening's bus driver that his vehicle has been vandalized by the Indian team. Even though some of us contested the complaint, the police officers refused to believe us and insisted that we accompany them to the police station.

Finding the situation going out of hand, we frantically contacted Asif Iqbal, the organizer of the tournament. On his intervention, the charges were dropped. However, we were eager to know the truth, and it emerged sooner rather than later. The driver of the bus that had ferried us to Abu Dhabi was of Pakistani origin. He was annoyed with us because we had bested his home country's team and our high spirits after the party only made him angrier. To take revenge, he damaged the seats with a knife and tore the ceiling of the bus. Later, he lodged a complaint with the police, demanding action and compensation from the Indian team.

Our victory also had an adverse impact on the officials of the tournament. There was no warm send-off. Cricketers were used as a golden goose to make money, but our comfort was last on the list of priorities. Unlike the BCCI officials, enjoying the facilities of five-star hotels and first-class ambiance in the air, we were booked in economy class. While Indian players on the off day hired local cabs to go out, the BCCI officials were pampered with chauffeur-driven limousines.

The effect of our victory continued to follow us till the airport. The ground staff at the check-in counter of the local airline was uncooperative. They shocked some players by demanding excess baggage charges. Since players were paid a pittance, it became challenging to dish out these additional charges. No amount of persuasion had any impact on the staff till a Mr Khimji from Oman, a cricket enthusiast, happened to pass by, witnessing the plight of the players. He came forward and paid for our excess baggage by credit card, a noble gesture!

Although the Rothmans Cup at Sharjah was gruelling, victory gave us tremendous satisfaction. There was no cricket played in India after the Sharjah tournament. However, I was fortunate to continue with the game in England, fulfilling my contract with a club. The Indian team for the Sri Lanka series was selected based on players' performance at the Sharjah Cup. At this stage, the island nation was going through a turbulent period due to strained relations between the Sri Lankan government and the Tamil United Liberation Front. I had read a few articles in England about Sri Lanka's political situation but didn't comprehend its gravity.

Unaware of the the ground reality in Sri Lanka, we prepared ourselves for a tough series. Srikkanth and L. Sivaramkrishnan were the two Tamil players in the squad and their presence at the immigration counter caused some concern. The attitude of the immigration official towards him was discourteous, probably due to the ground reality in Sri Lanka, the Tamil Nadu government's support to the ethnic Tamil movement in Sri Lanka. Little did we realize that anti-India feelings had percolated down to the cricket ground, which affected the umpires too. Fortunately, cricket fans kept themselves away from politics and followed us with undiminished enthusiasm.

I did not play the first Test match in Colombo due to health issues. The Indian team for a change had a new opening pair, despite Gavaskar's presence. For some strange reason, he opted to bat in the middle order, leaving the top order exposed. The effect of the political reverberations was also felt on the ground. The men in white coats left no stone unturned in expressing their dislike for the tourists. Cricket rules became the first casualty, mauled beyond repair. I returned to the team in the following Test and scored a half-century to cement my place in the playing XI. However, India faltered against the pace bowling of Rumesh Ratnayake to lose the second Test.

The last Test was at Kandy. The conditions here were a little better than Colombo, where weather had disrupted the game on a few occasions. However, the clearly prejudiced umpiring continued to test our patience. A classic example was an LBW decision against Srikkanth; he was midway down the pitch to complete a single when the umpire raised his finger. The bewildered batsman expressed his disappointment, shaking his head in disbelief. Then the impossible happened. Finding Srikkanth out of the crease, the fielder shattered the stumps with a direct throw and appealed for a run out. The square leg umpire happily obliged and lifted his finger too, a comical exhibition of camaraderie. Nonetheless, I continued with my form. I scored a solitary century for the Indian team, and in fact, registered the highest number of runs. Chetan Sharma was the pick of the Indian bowlers.

Apart from cricket, I remember the presence of one of my childhood heroes, M.L. Jaisimha, acting as our manager on this tour. His debonair personality and appeal, even at this age, was envied by us. He was loved, respected and adored by everyone. In his heyday, he had charmed more maidens than Pataudi, Durrani, Engineer and many more put together, with his flair on and off the field.

We lost only one Test and drew the ODI series, which was in itself no less than an achievement for us. We had battled the combined efforts of the umpires and the conditions to upturn our momentum like seasoned professionals. The Australia tour was round the corner and this trip had certainly prepared us well.

AUSTRALIA TEST SERIES: 1985–86

It was a rare sight for the Aussies to see the Indian team on its soil twice in a year. However, this time, the Indian team bore a new look. Sunil Gavaskar had resigned as captain after winning the World Championship; the selectors brought back Kapil Dev at the helm of affairs. Erapalli Prasanna was also replaced by Venkataraghavan as manager. There were, in addition, a few new faces. The last time we were here, India had little or no support from the critics. How we surprised everyone and won the finals brought us great joy. However, this tour was different in terms of the format. The three-Test series against Australia was followed by a Tri-Series involving New Zealand and the host.

This was my fourth tour of Australia, beginning with the Indian Schoolboys' team in 1968, the Indian team in 1977 and the third a few months ago. Every tour left a deep impression and created fond memories. I loved playing on lively pitches and facing the aggressive Australian players. Cricket was tough and sledging was part and parcel of the game. It was undoubtedly demanding on each occasion.

Although memories of the last tour remained intact, we missed the presence of the bubbly Sadanand Viswanath. He was outstanding during the World Championship and the Sharjah tournament. I loved his attitude; he spared no batsman from behind the stumps, talking non-stop and encouraging the bowler.

The return of Syed Kirmani in place of Sadanand Viswanath to the team brought back memories of our earlier tours, the earliest being in 1967 to England with the Indian Schoolboys' team. The difference in this long journey was Kiri's appearance. Once upon a time, he had nice, thick black hair styled like the film star Dev Anand, but now he resembled the Hollywood star Yul Brynner. However, Kiri's mimicry of the evergreen actor and dialogue delivery remained intact. He stayed smart and had a great sense of humour. He too carried a heavy suitcase. His sunglasses and bright casual shirts lifted the spirits of people around him. Kiri still fit in his 1967 England tour blazer, which spoke volumes about his fitness.

We dismissed memories of the Sri Lanka tour as a bad dream and looked forward to new challenges in Australia. Before we departed, news of a rebel tour by Australian international cricketers to South Africa jolted the ACB once more, leaving them in a hopeless situation. Except for Allan Border, they had no known face, which was reminiscent of the situation back in 1977. It seemed as if the Springboks had sucked the life out of Australian cricket. Left at a crossroads, public opinion didn't fancy Australia's chances against us. We were pleasantly surprised to hear the magic words from an immigration officer at the airport: 'Don't worry! You will have an easy time.'

A few days later, I went to a pub and asked the bartender about Australia's chances against India. 'Rubbish,' he muttered. 'The Indians will get them easily.' These words were soothing because the bartender had no clue that I was part of the Indian team. Clearly our performance in the World Championship had impressed the Australians, and the local media backed us as favourites to win the Test series. The unhappy memories of Sri Lanka were forgotten but the scars remained, no matter how hard we tried to cover them.

There were a few warm-up matches scheduled before the first Test. The tour commenced with a one-day match at Canberra, followed by serious cricket against South Australia. The four-day match provided Indian players many opportunities to excel with the bat and ball. After the match, I met an elderly gentleman who had witnessed the marvellous batting skills of two former captains, Don Bradman and Lala Amarnath, at this venue in 1947. Bradman scored a brilliant 156 in the first innings and was matched by an aggressive 144 by Lala Amarnath. While Bradman was dismissed for 12 by Vinoo Mankad in the second innings, Lala Amarnath dominated the bowlers, remaining unbeaten on 94, adding 175 runs with opening batsman Vinoo Mankad (116 not out) in approximately two hours.

The match against Victoria, though marred by rain, nevertheless announced the arrival of Merv Hughes on the international scene. The first sight of this bowler was overwhelming. He was tall with strong, broad shoulders and had a thick moustache. However, an extra bit of flesh around the waistline presented a strange sight for a fast bowler. He had performed well and impressed the selectors enough to be part of the Australian team for the first Test at Adelaide. After selection, he gave a few interviews running down the Indian batsmen and boasting about his abilities.

A night before the Test, we held a customary team meeting in the manager's room to discuss the finer points and composition of the final XI. Most players had proved their abilities except LS; his form was a matter of grave concern. While the discussion was on, a senior member of the team took the liberty of ordering some snacks. He knew both the manager and captain received additional entertainment allowance on foreign tours. Shortly, there was a knock on the door. One of the players attended to it. A young waitress in a white dress and red apron rolled the trolley full of snacks into the room. The waitress presented the bill to the manager, as it happened to be his room. He simply ignored her. The situation became awfully embarrassing—the waitress stood with a bill, waiting for someone to sign while players helped themselves to the snacks. Finally, the Indian captain signed the bill.

The Adelaide pitch was known to be a batsman's paradise, and presented enormous challenges to bowlers of both pace and spin. Australia batted first and enjoyed the conditions, especially David Boon and Greg Ritchie, notching a century each. Despite that, Kapil bowled brilliant spells and caused hiccups in the Aussie camp, taking eight wickets. Chetan Sharma also bowled his heart out, but without any success. However, he was involved in a verbal duel with Greg Ritchie. Both players adopted an aggressive attitude, one as a batsman and the other as a bowler. Every time Chetan Sharma bowled a bouncer, Ritchie ducked under it, stretched his right arm and bent his elbow to indicate to the umpire that the bowler was bowling illegitimate deliveries. It did not go down well with the young rookie and he reacted in typical pace bowler style. While Ritchie used his typical Aussie expressions, Chetan mixed English with Punjabi invectives to convey his annoyance.

After a tough day's play, each of us got busy removing spikes when my attention was drawn by Sunny's expression. His sense of humour and ability to play pranks was known to me; I saw the same wicked smile covering his face. I knew he was up to something—but what? I waited for him to make a move! He casually approached Chetan and, with a rather innocent face, said, 'Won't you do anything about that incident with Greg Ritchie?' These words ignited Chetan Sharma's fuse and he took the bait. He got up in a huff and marched out of the dressing room wearing spikes; the raw wounds stood exposed. The Australian dressing room was adjacent to ours; Chetan stood in front of it flaunting an aggressive posture and swearing, even threatening Ritchie with dire consequences.

The entire Indian team was eager to witness this drama, so we came out to the sitting area outside the dressing room, each player hustling for space to get a clearer view. The sight of his teammates excited Chetan even more. Taking everyone's presence as support, he raised his pitch even higher. When there was no response, he looked back at us, and the master prankster gestured him to continue and then ducked behind us. After a brief lull, I think it was Bobby Simpson who came out. He asked Chetan why he was making such a fuss in front of their dressing room. Taken by surprise, Chetan was momentarily speechless, till he remembered his motive. He repeated his demand: 'Send Ritchie out! I have to settle scores with him.' He thumped his foot hard on the concrete floor. Bobby Simpson gave him one last look and said, 'We are having a team meeting and you are disturbing us.' He followed this up with a few objectionable expressions.

This response took the steam out of Chetan's fury and he retracted his steps. All of us spectators rushed back to our original seats as if nothing was heard or seen. The dejected bowler walked quietly to his seat and removed his spikes, looking a bit disappointed, till Gavaskar patted his shoulder and said, 'Well done!' Practically everyone in the dressing room nodded their head and gave a thumbs-up.

When the Indian openers occupied the crease, Merv Hughes hoped to emulate the Indian bowlers, but received a rude shock from the Indian batting. It was good to see Gavaskar returning to his favourite slot, looking calm and confident. Why he opted to bat in the middle order in Sri Lanka remained a mystery. Srikkanth and Gavaskar gave India a fine start and the former, in his usual style, scored a half-century. On his dismissal, Chetan Sharma occupied the crease as a night watchman. No matter how hard Merv Hughes tried, he failed to get any purchase from the pitch or dislodge Chetan Sharma.

While Gavaskar looked solid, Chetan Sharma provided entertainment as a batsman. He batted in the most unorthodox fashion, beaten occasionally and edged a few times; given an opportunity, he slashed hard over the slips to get boundaries. This irritated Merv Hughes even further; he kept swearing at both the batsmen. Unmindful, Chetan Sharma piled on the runs. Then there was a rare misjudgement by Gavaskar; the rising ball from Craig McDermott hit his forearm and he retired hurt. When he returned to bat, he looked more determined. New to international cricket, Merv Hughes thought it was an appropriate time to bully Gavaskar into submission with harsh words and bouncers, but received the shock of his life. The maestro scored a brilliant hundred and Chetan Sharma an entertaining half-century. The rest chipped in with a decent score to pile up a huge total. Though this Test ended in a draw, Merv Hughes was dropped for the remaining matches.

I was supposed to bat at number three but had to shift down to the middle order because my eyelids had suddenly swollen. It became difficult to open them in the sunshine. It was my worst nightmare; I thought I had some serious issue and feared for my career. I told the manager about my condition and requested an appointment with an ophthalmologist. While India continued batting, I was ushered into a clinic for a check-up. To my utter relief, the ophthalmologist found the root cause; my eyes were extremely dry. The doctor prescribed eye drops to lubricate my eyes, which brought instant relief.

The next Test at the MCG brought back memories of the World Championship and that great time. Once again, we were accommodated at the Melbourne Hilton. The Test at Melbourne always started on Boxing Day and memories of the 1977 tour came flooding back to us. We beat Australia at this venue for the first time and the celebration that followed was most delightful. Quite a few of us remained part of this squad too. The tradition of the Boxing Day match invariably brought a good crowd on 26 December; maybe it was part of Christmas celebrations there.

Melbourne was known for its notorious weather; one could experience different conditions in a day—pleasant, hot, cold and wet. The Indian team was still without a trainer and I continued to do the honorary job. After the warm-up, we decided to inspect the wicket. It was unlike the MCG wicket. It was soft to an extent; my index finger slipped easily into the turf. I was sure that no amount of sunshine or strong breeze could remove the moisture from underneath the surface. With a day to go, Kapil was himself unsure of what to do if he won the toss, and he sought the opinion of senior players and was left more confused. Some wanted to bat, others preferred to field.

I was glad that after winning the toss, we opted to field. The soft surface aided the bowlers and made stroke play difficult. Although the Australians struggled against the Indian seamers, it brought little success. The spinners brought greater joy to us, taking nine wickets between themselves. Steve Waugh made his debut and lasted for a short while, falling to LS, back in the Indian side. However, Greg Matthews had a different idea; he adopted an aggressive attitude and belted each spinner to score a fine century on a spinner's paradise. Watching the plight of the Indian spinners, memories of the 1977-78 series returned; I recalled the class of Bishan, Chandra and Prasanna. I remembered Chandra ripping through the Australian batting at the MCG with six wickets in each innings and Bishan Bedi's magical spell of five wickets at the Gabba in Brisbane. Unfortunately, here, we gave the Kangaroos a free run from 6/127 to 262. The Indian captaincy came under the scanner once Matthews and the tailenders became effective.

India lost Gavaskar early in the innings and I occupied my position at one down to enjoy the conditions, stitching a century partnership with Srikkanth. My partner was quite severe on short deliveries, entertaining the gallery and the commentators. Bill Lawry, the former Australian opening batsman and captain in the 1960s and 1970s, simply loved Srikkanth's style. While Richie Benaud remained soft and precise in his commentary, Bill Lawry was excited. Tony Greig and Ian Chappell added flair to give TV commentary a new lease of life. The cameramen also gave shape to splendid angles; the highlights of the day's play were worth watching and I loved every minute of it.

India responded with 445 runs—with a lead of 183, and two days remaining in the Test put us in a commanding position. Once again, we pinned down the Australians and reduced them to 5/126 with only Allan Border, the last recognized batsman at the crease. He was one of the finest batsmen of spin bowling, and he shielded the tailenders and dominated the spinners on a helpful wicket. Instead of learning from the first innings' mistakes, we committed similar blunders. Precious time was compromised and opportunities lost relying on one particular spinner for too long. If relevant bowlers were given the chance and field placements rectified, we could have brought down the curtains on the fourth day itself. Australia survived the day, fighting hard at 8/228, with a slender lead of 45 runs.

The Melbourne weather remained a source of concern and a big challenge for the teams. It changed its character faster than a chameleon. The morning bulletin predicted heavy rains at teatime and, if true, we had only two sessions to win this match. When we took the field, I expected Kapil to operate from one end and a spinner from the other to quickly finish off the innings, but I was appalled to see the opposite. The Indian captain's approach was baffling. It was a repeat of the first innings' mistake when Matthews, in the company of the tailenders, had consumed precious time and scored a century, and now Allan Border was in the same mode.

The Australian captain continued to dominate the spinners, controlling the proceedings and gathering runs at will; he also held the strike for the majority of the time. The first session extended into the second; probably after an hour, Yadav dismissed Border at 163. By then, valuable time had been lost and Australia had also managed to consolidate a priceless 77-run partnership for the last wicket. Time was of the essence; could we achieve the target of 126 before divine intervention? I kept my fingers crossed.

By teatime, India could manage only 59 runs (for the loss of two wickets) due to the slowness of the pitch, defensive tactics and Border's faith in the weather prediction. Still short of 67 runs to win the match, I walked back to the pavilion and saw dark clouds forming on the horizon. The forecast of heavy rains came racing to my mind. I had a gut feeling that we had missed the bus. While I sipped tea in the dressing room, there was the loud sound of thunder, followed by applause and voluble cheers from the Australian dressing room. The weather forecast had come true. Within no time, the clouds poured forth to wash out the entire third session. Was it a miracle or uninspired leadership that had robbed India of victory?

Disappointed with the lost opportunity, we landed in Sydney and checked into Hotel Boulevard at William Street. It was in the vicinity of Kings Cross, a delight for tourists. The area boasted nightclubs, bars, restaurants and other places of entertainment, which lifted our spirits. Hungry as we were, we marched out of the hotel in travel attire (blazers and ties) for lunch. Soon, we were surrounded by pretty girls offering to give us company, which made a few players' eyes light up. The excitement turned into a nightmare when it was found that they were escort professionals. All was not yet over. When one of the players said, 'We are from the Indian team—how about a discount?' we were left thoroughly embarrassed!

The Indian team in comparison to Australia in the last two Tests seemed more settled and confident. The hosts were still struggling to find a composite eleven to rely upon. For the

Sydney Test, Australia included leg spinner Bob Holland; he had done pretty well against the West Indies.

The SCG had a reputation for producing a pitch similar to those typically found in the Indian subcontinent. It did not favour pace and bounce. It played true to reputation on the first two days and later helped the spinners. When we inspected the strip, it had not changed its character, and it certainly looked marvellous for batting. India won the toss and naturally elected to bat. The two openers, Gavaskar and Srikkanth, both in solid form, could not have asked for a better platform. After the pace bowlers failed to yield fruit, Allan Border turned to Bob Holland for respite. However, Srikkanth had his own plan; he unleashed a series of attacks, and demolished Holland's confidence and the Australian captain's calculations. The two Indian batsmen put up 191 runs for the opening partnership before Srikkanth was dismissed, having scored a fine century.

I could not have asked for a better platform to bat at number three. I also relished the conditions and remained undefeated at 72 in the company of centurion Gavaskar. This was India's best performance of the series, and mine too. The next morning, I completed my century (137) and Gavaskar (172) added 224 runs for the second wicket. India declared the innings closed at 4/600.

During this big partnership, I noticed a sea change in Sunny's behaviour. He was more relaxed during this innings than I had seen in the past. It was a welcome change; he was enjoying cricket and was no longer indifferent to the presence of the non-striker. When I completed my half-century, he came down the wicket and said, 'Well done, OT! You have booked your seat for the England tour.' I started laughing loudly and, for a change, he looked worried. To calm my emotions, he gestured and whispered, 'Jimmy! Take it easy.' It was genuine concern for me. He thought I would lose my concentration and my wicket as well. It was rare for him to interact with the non-striker in such an intimate manner. Sunny, Roger, Yadav and I took pride in being part of the 'OT Brigade'. OT stood for 'Over Thirty' and this expression stuck because a former captain of India, and now a selector, had made an unnecessary remark on television that players over thirty should be dropped. I was surprised by his remark because batsmen mature in their late twenties and are at the very peak of their powers in their thirties.

If there were light moments, there happened to be tense moments as well during the partnership. In the early part of my innings, there was a loud appeal of a catch, which the umpire negated. A star player of Australia fielding, placed at silly point, was not amused; he exploded, 'You Indians are cheats! And that goes for your captain too!' Such language, I thought, showed the fielding side's frustration, despair and plight. Normally, I wouldn't respond to such behaviour, but abusing my countrymen did not go down well with me and I became equally vocal to put him in his place. However, the fielders continued passing snide remarks. Instead of responding, I decided to concentrate on my batting and score runs. Gradually, the situation changed; there were no further comments directed at me.

The Australian opening pair of Boon and Marsh also relished the batting conditions and added over 200 runs for the first wicket. It was important for us to make a breakthrough and get back into the game. However, for some strange reason, the Indian captain became overly cautious and adopted a defensive field with a solitary slip. A senior player standing at first slip was not amused with the field placement, especially the vacant slip cordon. Every time an edge flew at a catchable height through this vacant area, he threw his floppy hat on the ground in frustration. Interestingly, two Indian stars were not on talking terms after recent incidents and there was a perpetual undercurrent of tension. They hardly made eye contact or exchanged any words.

During the water break, a senior member of the team walked up to me and shared his thoughts about the match. He seemed quite upset with the attitude of the captain. 'What sort of a field placement is this? Are we playing for a draw or a win?' Knowing my relationship with the captain, he pleaded with me, 'Why don't you tell him to set a more attacking field?'

I smiled and said, 'Why are you telling me? Talk to him!' There was no response. Still, I took a call and asked Kapil, 'Are we playing for a draw?' He seemed astounded by my question and said, 'Why, why? What happened?' I shared those concerns, and convinced him to attack and get the much-desired breakthrough so we could wrap up the innings and enforce a follow-on. If runs leaked, we would still not lose this match.

After the drinks break, the mode changed from defensive to attacking. There was a ring of fielders around the bat and the captain stationed himself at silly point to the bowling of Shivlal Yadav. After the over, I walked up to him and said, 'Well done, but you should not be fielding at silly point.' That confused him. I told him he was the team's premier bowler and any injury could hamper our chances; I persuaded him to move to a safer position in the slips.

The sudden transformation worked in our favour. Both Shivlal Yadav and Shastri ran through the Australian batting to enforce a follow-on. The aggressive posture brought dividends in the second innings too. We ran through the cream of Australia's batting but time constraints and the benevolent attitude of the gentlemen in white coats denied us the joy of tasting victory. The three-Test series ended without a result, which disappointed us greatly. We had chances, of course, but guidance, weather and umpiring deprived us of victory! We had a break of a few days to change gears from the longest to the shorter version of the game.

BENSON & HEDGES TRI-SERIES: 1986

After doing well in the recently concluded series, we looked forward to the Tri-Series. The memories and our performance of the 1985 World Championship gave us an edge over the hosts and New Zealand. However, we were aware that fresh contests could not be won by earlier performances, so we naturally prepared ourselves to match the youthful Aussies, and the might of Richard Hadlee with the ball and Martin Crowe and company with the willow.

The cricketers of my era or earlier hardly consulted any legal luminary; hence, the BCCI contract and its clauses for overseas tours remained strictly one-sided. They were drafted by a BCCI-appointed lawyer to control the players. Neither did they have any knowledge about the stress and loneliness of overseas tours, but they also denied cricketers the company of their spouses. The players had no choice but to sign on the dotted lines. However, when senior players held a private parley with an influential official, the BCCI showed magnanimity and allowed spouses to join their partners in the second half of the Australia tour. The board also made it quite clear that all the expenses of the spouses would be borne by the respective players.

Although this decision was welcomed, it did dent many pockets while paying for international and domestic flights. To survive with an additional partner on a meagre weekly allowance was quite challenging and securing supplementary foreign exchange was not easy by any stretch. Under these circumstances, paying for a room in the same hotel became next to impossible. While team members shared rooms, the manager and the captain were privileged to get single rooms and faced no such difficulty. This led to privacy problems for couples. Finally, a compromise was devised and adopted. The junior players agreed to accommodate the seniors; they moved out and shared rooms with fellow cricketers. However, players moving down the hall carrying pillows and blankets in the evening did not go unnoticed. The housekeeping staff was first to spot this movement and, on several occasions, asked me if these boys played with pillows all night. My smile left them very confused indeed!

This tournament was most unlike any Tri-Series; it was long and arduous. It was scheduled from 9 January to 2 February 1986, including a best of three finals. We were to play five matches each against New Zealand and host Australia at Brisbane, Melbourne, Sydney, Perth, Adelaide and Tasmania. Travelling from one venue to another was likely to be time-consuming and exhausting.

Our first game was at the Gabba in Brisbane against New Zealand. We were in the thick of our practice session when I noticed a large group of Australian mediapersons arriving at the ground. It was quite evident that they were looking for some juicy remarks from us to make their articles more exciting. My observation was spot on; one of the journalists questioned my abilities against Richard Hadlee on fast tracks in Australia, getting no reaction from me. Not to be bogged down by my silence, the cheeky journalist threw a bouncer, reminding me of the match against Nottinghamshire (England) in 1979 and the hairline fracture that I'd suffered. I had already forgotten that incident but this chap was needling me on purpose. My response was calm: 'I take it one day at a time and do not believe in living in the past.' However, I wanted to settle the score with this impudent journalist with a good performance. Not only did we win the match against New Zealand, but I was also the top scorer with 61 to settle the issue forever.

Gavaskar's return to his favourite spot with Srikkanth in the Test matches had produced two centuries, settling the issue of the opening pair for India in the Tri-Series too. The day after the match against New Zealand we faced the hosts at the same venue. With little time to recharge our batteries, we performed worse than the much fresher Australians. This pattern was evident on a few occasions in the series, where one team was put at a disadvantage playing consecutive matches at the same venue.

However, we rectified the result against Australia at the MCG, winning the match by eight wickets. I continued with my good form and added another unbeaten half-century. However, I was in great pain; an old injury had resurfaced. The ligament of my right foot had swollen, so I was forced to take a cortisone injection and strap the area tightly for temporary relief. After the match, I used hot and cold water therapy to reduce the swelling and took anti-inflammatory ibuprofen tablets for pain relief. I conveyed the problem to the team management but they wanted me to continue playing.

We flew to Perth for the second encounter against New Zealand. The last time I played here was against Thomson and company on a wicket that was hard, bouncy and fast. I had both painful and happy memories of this venue. I was hit on the forehead by left-arm fast bowler Sam Gannon and briefly retired hurt. This time too the nature of the pitch remained the same, except for the colour, which had gone from brownish to green. The New Zealand captain won the toss and put us to bat on a juicy fast bowler's paradise. Ewen Chatfield, Richard Hadlee and Martin Snedden cut through our batting in no time. I managed to score 30 out of India's total of 113. The Indian bowlers responded with equal vigour but could not defend such a modest total. We lost the game by three wickets. The roller-coaster performance by all the teams kept the competition even and alive.

However, this match could best be remembered for the one and only Srikkanth. He was known to be accident-prone and fellow cricketers kept him at bay. While tying his pads, the space around him remained deserted; there was fear he may elbow the player next to him or accidentally step on his toe. While leaving the dressing room, he invariably tucked his bat under his armpit, knocking the closest head on his way out! To remain safe, the opening batsman preferred to walk behind him. However, many times, his bat got stuck in the door or he would kick the door backwards to hit an unprepared target! Chaos would reign in the dressing room, till he occupied the crease and started the action on the field. Even doing exercises with him was not safe. I remember doing a warm-up lap and Srikkanth running behind me. Suddenly, he kicked my heel and I almost tripped. I turned around and curtly said, 'What's wrong with you, Chikka?'

He was unaware of his action and said, 'What happened, Jumbo?'

'You just kicked me!' I replied. 'Be careful!'

He was astonished; he had no idea whatsoever. I just shook my head in disbelief!

Most Indian batsmen carried two different sets of batting shoes, ripple or rubber studs, with them. Only players with experience of damp conditions in England felt comfortable with spike shoes for batting, but not Srikkanth. He preferred batting with rubber-sole shoes on the green pitch at the WACA in Perth too, which was a cardinal mistake!

Srikkanth was always eager to get off the mark, but conditions at the WACA were demanding. After a few dot balls, he managed to hit the ball hard to the square leg fielder near the umpire and called for a tight single. To gather extra momentum, he pushed harder but slipped and fell on the pitch. Before the ball could be fielded, Srikkanth rose in a flash to run again, but failed; it seemed like he was spot-running on a greasy surface. The scene resembled the best of Charlie Chaplin movies! The fielder, holding the ball, was distracted too; he was unsure whether to go for a direct hit at the bowler's end or lob the ball to the bowler standing near the panic-stricken batsman some distance from the stumps. Taking advantage of the predicament, Srikkanth started crawling on his knees and hands towards safety. It was too little too late; he could not beat the bowler running in with the ball to dismiss him and he was run out in the most comical fashion!

The scene on the pitch caught the attention of the teammates in the dressing room too. Everyone was in splits—some holding their stomach, others rolling on the floor. I also could not hold back and I just burst out laughing, feeling sorry for Srikkanth! Even when I crossed him on the field on my way to bat, I was still giggling. An amused Sunil Gavaskar was also affected by this unique display and chuckled, 'Jumbo, hope you're wearing spikes!' This was not the first time Srikkanth was dismissed, run out in such an extraordinary fashion. It had happened earlier and it also happened later in his career.

Srikkanth started his international career on a not quite happy note; a duck in the first innings against England in Bombay left little mark on spectators. However, he redeemed himself in the second innings—till he almost edged the ball to the safe hands of John Emburey at gully. Relieved that it wasn't a catch, he looked up at the sky, closed his eyes in prayer and wandered around thinking he was walking towards short leg, a customary habit. Finding Srikkanth out of the crease, Emburey broke the stumps and ran him out! Pataudi, covering the match, reacted with, 'Srikkanth should know this is not Juhu beach but a Test match!'

Another unforgettable dismissal came a few years after the Australia tour. India was playing the MRF Cup match against

Pakistan at Eden Gardens in Calcutta. Srikkanth swept Abdul Qadir to deep square leg for a comfortable two runs. He ran the first run hard and turned for the second, momentarily looked at the fielder to judge the throw, and managed to tangle his bat between his pads and tripped, run out once again. It would be unfair not to give the award of 'best run out category player' to Srikkanth, though years later Inzamam-ul-Haq of Pakistan became the closest competitor. Their ingenuity to dismiss themselves in the most bizarre fashion stumped the best of brains!

Sydney had been a happy hunting ground for the Indians, who were at the receiving end against Australia. After winning the toss, for some strange reason, India allowed the Aussies the first use of a placid pitch. Marsh and Boon gave a flying start to ruin our day. Australia put up a huge total and India lost the match by a margin of 100 runs. Two back-to-back defeats shook us badly and made our progress to the finals more difficult.

Our next match at the MCG against New Zealand was crucial. By now, all three teams were aware of each other's strengths and weaknesses. Sunil Gavaskar, who had been in good form, was ruled out for this crucial match; that was certainly a big setback. Shastri had been batting lower in the order—he looked out of touch at the opening slot and India lost wickets at regular intervals. I continued with my form and scored a third half-century; the Indian innings folded at 238. The bowler to wreck our innings was not Hadlee but Ewen Chatfield.

The New Zealand response was slow but steady. The Indian bowlers also adopted a safety-first policy to dry the flow of runs, forcing the Kiwis to commit mistakes and lose wickets, leading to an even contest. While New Zealand held back wickets for one last assault, we steadily moved to complete the quota of overs to strangulate their plan. This led to an alarming situation, where runs and wickets mattered to both teams. However, New Zealand won the tantalizing match with just one ball to spare. It was arguably the best match of the tournament.

With four more matches to go, we had to win at least three to qualify for the best of three finals against Australia, sitting pretty in the driver's seat. We beat New Zealand but lost to Australia at Adelaide to leave our spot in the finals undecided. The next match between Australia and New Zealand was also important for us. To our dismay, Australia lost to New Zealand. Suddenly, winning the remaining matches became critical for the Indian team. I had been struggling with my ankle for a long time and could barely walk. I had to sit out the match at the MCG and applaud my teammates' efforts.

The last match against New Zealand at Launceston in Tasmania was to decide the fate of both teams. My condition had not improved due to non-availability of the team physio. Even minor injuries took a rather long time to heal; mine, alas, was major. Whatever little help we got came from Cricket Australia.

During the practice session at Launceston, I was struggling to put my body weight on the right foot. I told the manager about my hopeless condition. He looked unhappy and frustrated because another prominent batsman had opted out of this match due to a bruised thigh and there seemed to be no worthy replacement for me. The manager pleaded for me to reconsider. I was caught in an awkward position. On one hand was the honour of the Indian team and, on the other, my fitness; I supported the former but with a caveat: I shouldn't be pressed to bowl. Battered, bruised and apprehensive about my fitness, I relied on a cortisone injection, ibuprofen tablets, crepe bandage and sheer willpower to support my decision.

After finishing the practice session, everyone prepared for the biggest test. The team spirit touched the nerves and heart of the manager. Venkataraghavan called for everyone's attention and declared that if India won the match against New Zealand, he would treat the entire team for dinner. Was it a bait, blunder or a joke? Everyone knew how tight-fisted our manager was with his additional allowance. Nevertheless, this statement took one and all by surprise. No one could believe what they heard and, in a chorus, asked him to repeat what he'd just said. Venkataraghavan repeated the offer, though with a reluctant smile. Each one of us applauded him and smiled at his generous offer.

The setting at Launceston brought back memories of England, especially the minor county grounds. In addition, I had seen a picture of my father playing here in 1947 and that structure seemed to have survived the scourge of time. The small pavilion looked cute and the ground had plenty of open space around it for people to enjoy cricket. The pitch matched the green outfield and convinced me that it would not be a high-scoring match. Ever since the Tri-Series commenced, we had adjusted well to play day-and-night matches. However, here, we were exposed to play under the blue sky and bright sunshine; soon, it changed to cloudy and damp conditions. Engrossed, we forgot about the manager's generous offer.

Put to bat, India struggled in bowler-friendly conditions. There were no big innings from any batsman, including me. However, each made a small contribution to raise the score to 202. The pick of the Indian batsmen was undoubtedly Chetan Sharma. He played a cameo role to help India cross the psychological barrier of 200 runs, which, at times, had looked impossible to get!

The target did not look too ominous, but the conditions suited our pace bowlers well. A brief rain interruption revised the target to 190 from 45 overs. India needed early wickets and Roger Binny bowled his usual self to remove the Crowe brothers to apply pressure. Kapil and he shared three wickets each to seal the fate of the match; India ended up winning by 22 runs! It was indeed a team effort that helped us to clear the last obstacle and march into the final stage of the tournament.

Once we returned to the dressing room, I recollected the generous offer made by Venkataraghavan. I raised my hand and reminded the manager of his gracious promise. He not only extended the invitation to the team members, but spouses were invited too. The venue was a comfortable hotel restaurant.

We assembled at a given time in the lobby for this much-awaited and rare treat from the manager. Different tables accommodated small groups. This restaurant served only à la carte. Gavaskar and I took a call to enjoy the evening with popular dishes and wine. To commemorate the occasion, we ordered the best wine and gave the manager's room number to the waitress to settle the bill. By the time we vacated the table, each one of us was in high spirits. We thanked the manager for his generosity and the wonderful meal.

The next day, we were booked for a late afternoon flight to Sydney to play the first of the three finals at the SCG. Accordingly, I had placed a morning tea order. The next morning, I heard a knock at the door. When I opened it, I saw the Indian captain standing with some money in his hand. I was pleasantly surprised; were we getting a bonus for reaching the finals? Before I could utter a word, Kapil said 'You have to give me twenty dollars for dinner.' I blinked in astonishment and said, 'What?'

Then I invited Kapil into the room for an explanation. He narrated his entire conversation with the manager. The previous night's dinner bill had exceeded the manager's expectation; therefore, Venkat had asked him to collect money from the players and pay the bill. Kapil went from one room to another to collect $20 from everyone who had come to the dinner party.

However, when he went to Roger Binny's room and asked for $60 dollars, Roger slumped on his bed in disbelief. No amount of reasoning had its effect. Reluctantly, he shelled out $60, paying for both his wife and son Stuart, who probably had a spoonful from his mom's plate. The next day, he shared the experience with me and bemoaned accepting the invitation for dinner. He would have been far better ordering the meal to his room and saved precious dollars than attending an 'invitational dinner'!

The SCG happened to be sacred soil for Gavaskar, Srikkanth and me; all of us had scored centuries, a rare feat for India in a Test match in Australia. After winning the World Championship in 1985, India were the favourites to lift another trophy. However, destiny had something else scripted for us. A packed house greeted us for the first final. The atmosphere was nothing short of a carnival; the multicoloured clothes and boisterous Aussies enlivened the spectacle.

Due to inclement weather, the match was reduced to 44 overs. India won the toss and fielded; the bowlers hit an impeccable line and length to worry the Australian batsmen. Except for a half-century from David Boon, the rest crumbled under pressure. The surprise package was Mohammad Azharuddin emerging as a bowler. He was known for his wristy batting and outstanding fielding, but he now also bowled a magical spell and picked took 2/26 in nine overs.

Chasing a modest target of 170 was certainly within our grasp, but the Aussies had done their homework too. They understood our weakness against pace—but opted for Simon Davis, a swing bowler, in the line-up. He surprised Srikkanth with a banana inswinger to shatter his stumps. It was one of the three shocks he gave us. The absence of Gavaskar at the opening slot proved a disaster for India. Later, Allan Border sprung another surprise, swinging his arm as an orthodox left-arm spinner. The last time I saw him bowling a few overs was in the Lancashire league. After the game, I had enquired why he wasn't using his talent as a bowler; he seemed a bit apprehensive and unsure about it. However, here, he completed the full quota of nine overs and also took wickets to maintain pressure on our batsmen.

Simon, Border and Matthews took three wickets each to turn the tables. Although Vengsarkar and Gavaskar tried their best, India lost the match by 11 runs. Did we take our opponents lightly and become complacent, or did Sunny batting in the middle order deprive us of a good start? We were disappointed with the result but looked forward to retrieving our honour in the next final.

The MCG had been auspicious for the Amarnaths, beginning with my father in 1947. However, I left this tour with the strangest of dismissals. I played a defensive shot to a sharply spinning delivery from Greg Matthews; the ball hit the pitch hard and bounced backward towards the stumps. According to the rules, I could have stopped it with my foot, body or bat. However, in a reflex action, I committed a cardinal mistake, using my hand to stop the ball from hitting the stumps. Instantly, I realized my mistake. There was jubilation on the ground and in the gallery when the wicketkeeper and bowler appealed. The commentators also had a field day replaying this rare footage and capturing my reaction! Sheepishly, I smiled and shook my head in embarrassment; I walked off the field before the umpire had a chance to even raise his finger. I was dismissed for handling the ball. The Australians outplayed us at the MCG to lift the Benson & Hedges trophy.

A few years later, I was dismissed in another freak manner to complete the list of different dismissals! This time, it was against Sri Lanka in the MRF Cup (1989) in Ahmedabad, India. At the MCG, I had been embarrassed, but here I was furious. Facing Sri Lanka's captain Arjuna Ranatunga, I moved a few steps down the pitch to hit the delivery, but changed my mind and blocked it. Since there was no chance of taking a run or being run out, I wanted to toss the ball back to the bowler but refrained, fearing another decision of handling the ball; instead, I kicked the ball gently back to the bowler.

However, I was horrified by the bowler's reaction; he appealed and I was declared out under an obsolete MCC law: obstructing the fielder. I was livid! I reprimanded the bowler for his pathetic sportsmanship. Little did anyone, including me, realize that I had set a world record! I became the only batsman in the history of cricket to be dismissed in every conceivable manner except a time out on the cricket field. I had been bowled, caught, caught and bowled, LBW, run out, hit wicket, handling the ball—and now, obstructing the fielder. Some distinction!

The double tour of Australia left me with a bagful of memories. A happy one stuck after winning the Benson & Hedges World Championship, emulating the Prudential Cup. Frustration followed for not winning the Test series and pain for losing the Tri-Series! As a cricketer, this was also my last tour of a wonderful country, thus ending a long journey that had commenced as a schoolboy in 1968. I had cherished every moment both on and off the cricket field.

15

ENGLAND 1986

AFTER DISAPPOINTING TEST AND TRI-SERIES RESULTS IN Australia, there was a likelihood of one or more heads rolling. Little did I realize that putting the interest of the team ahead of my injury would cost me dearly! The only change for the Sharjah Cup was me. Was I dropped because of my performance, injury or machination? Most likely machination—because no member of the selection committee enquired about my fitness. It would be an understatement to say I was not hurt by my exclusion.

The loss to Pakistan in the Sharjah Cup final revealed a silver lining called reliability and experience. When the team for England was announced, I was pleased to find my name in the list. It was most likely the century in the Sydney Test match that had sealed my place for the England tour. But I didn't really celebrate my inclusion; I had got used to the whimsical sense of humour of the selectors.

The Indian team assembled at President Hotel, in Cuffe Parade, Bombay. Before our departure for Holland and the UK, the BCCI organized a farewell dinner at the hotel. Out of courtesy, the organizers invited the team manager to talk about the forthcoming English tour and the Indian team's prospects. During the address, he shocked everyone by rebuking one player; he held him responsible for India's defeat in Sharjah. Why on earth was he admonishing and demoralizing this young bowler before an important tour? I found it odd.

The twin tour commenced with a couple of limited-overs matches against Holland. This tour was part of the ICC promotional scheme to popularize cricket in Holland and other European countries. I was taken aback by the history of cricket in Holland; some clubs were established more than a hundred years ago and had played regular cricket ever since then. Former South African and West Indian international cricketers accepted regular assignments to coach and play in the local leagues. Rotterdam had a substantial Pakistani presence and they came in huge numbers to watch us play. It was a cold day with a grey sky, indicating what was in store for us in England. The match was played on an AstroTurf pitch, maybe because of the wet weather conditions and the lack of seasoned ground staff to maintain turf pitches.

Sunil Gavaskar's exploits on earlier Pakistan tours excited the South Asian crowd. To enjoy the attention of the Pakistani fans, Gavaskar opted to field at deep fine leg boundary and obliged them with autographs. However, his honeymoon period with the crowd was brief. I noticed a change in his behaviour towards them from my position at cover. The Indian star seemed unhappy with a section of the crowd laughing at him, which led to a heated argument. After the over, I enquired from him about the commotion. He said they spoke in Punjabi, which he could not understand, except that they repeatedly called him Chacha, meaning uncle. In utter confusion, Sunny said, 'I am not related to them!'

I swapped places with him. Since I spoke Punjabi, chatting with the crowd was smooth. When I asked about the Sunny situation, the crowd revealed they called him Chacha not to tease him but out of respect! I had to laugh, now aware that Sunny's misunderstanding had just been a language barrier.

We concluded the tour on a happy note and reached London to commence a much more difficult tour. The first engagement was a fifty-over match against Lavinia, Duchess of Norfolk's XI, at Arundel Castle Cricket Ground. The picturesque ground with a castle in the background was a delight to the eyes but the cold breeze of early May was not comforting. Yet, a small crowd braved the weather to enjoy the run feast. Unlike us, many spectators were wrapped in blankets, and wore woollen hats and gloves to keep warm. They also carried personal folding chairs and sat at vantage points. Some also spread out blankets on the green grass and opened picnic baskets. As the match progressed, they ate sandwiches, cookies and sipped hot coffee. Result-wise, there was no joy for us: we lost the match by five wickets.

The tour was packed with first-class matches against Gloucestershire, Worcestershire, Hampshire, Kent and Northamptonshire, as well as a limited-overs match against Surrey. To keep our spirits high under depressing weather conditions, Raj Singh, the team manager, decided to introduce a 'Sunday Club'. The concept was first mooted by Lala Amarnath on the Australia tour in 1947-48. Friday evenings were marked special; the informal atmosphere allowed the players to crack jokes and eat dinner with an unaccustomed hand—right-handers had to eat with their left hand and vice versa. Any player found guilty of not following the rule was fined. The collection was deposited with the manager Pankaj Gupta for Sunday picnics in the countryside. Bishan Bedi revived this tradition on the 1977-78 tour to Australia by organizing a fancy-dress contest; at times, our costumes left the hotel guests guffawing!

It was probably on the second day of the match against Gloucestershire that Raj Singh announced the formation of the Sunday Club. He asked everyone to assemble in his room after the match. Except for Gavaskar and me, no one had any idea and none had the audacity to ask the manager to explain what this was about. The confused team reached his room at the appointed hour. Raj Singh welcomed everyone with a broad smile and explained the rules like a schoolteacher. He said, 'It is an informal gathering; players can crack jokes and say anything under the sun without any fear of retribution.'

The atmosphere was light and everyone enjoyed the hospitality. Raj Singh had already related some anecdotes and was in high spirits. Suddenly, Srikkanth raised his hand and sought permission to speak. He said, 'Sir, anything under the sun? I have something to say but I am not sure if I should say it or not.'

'Go on, Sri; anything under the sun,' said Raj Singh.

Looking at Srikkanth, I knew something unusual was forthcoming. He walked towards the manager and said, 'Sir, when you walk, your buttock reminds me of an elephant!' Raj Singh did not know how to react; even the team members were stunned. There was complete silence in the room. Finally, Raj Singh laughed loudly and said, 'Is that so?'

This was the first and last Sunday Club gathering.

After India's debacle against Pakistan at Sharjah and my return to the team, I was pretty sure of a spot in the playing XI in both formats. However, I got a rude shock when I was left out for the limited-overs match against Surrey before the ODIs. Neither the captain nor the manager had a word with me about my exclusion, a basic courtesy followed in the past!

I knew instantly that I was not part of the ODI team, and when the Indian XI was announced for the ODI at the Oval, I hardly took any notice of it.

The next day, I reached the Oval and trained as usual. Later, I met Mike Gatting and we exchanged greetings. We talked about the cold weather and the pitch. Before we parted, Gatting said, 'See you in the middle.' I laughed and said, 'Sure, during the Test series. I haven't been selected for this game!' He retracted his steps and said, 'You must be joking!'

Selecting the final XI remained the prerogative of the captain in consultation with the tour committee, consisting of the vice-captain and the manager. This match was covered by BBC and our manager was invited for an interview. During the conversation, the anchor raised the question of my omission and reminded him about my performance in the recent World Cup. For some strange reason, the manager questioned my credentials and raised doubts about my capabilities.

After both teams won a match each to draw the ODI series, we prepared for the Test matches with a warm-up game against Northamptonshire. I had not forgotten the manager's remarks questioning my abilities in the shorter format, so I decided to settle the issue with my performance. I batted at number three, and scored a century before lunch to send a strong signal to any critics and doubters.

The first Test was at Lord's, which brought back happy memories beginning with my father's five-wicket haul in 1946 and my Man of the Match performance in the final of the Prudential World Cup a few years ago. Unlike the casual dress code, tradition and formality remained the hallmark at Lord's. Much like tennis players at Wimbledon, cricketers also practised in their whites.

The first half of the England tour remained mostly wet and cold, and the conditions here could really test the skills of the touring teams. Many players in our team also faced similar challenges. However, I was quite at home with the conditions; I had played league cricket in Durham and Lancashire for a considerable period, and, at times, spent long winters with my family in Yorkshire.

On the eve of the Test, I walked from the hotel to the closest red telephone booth and made an international call to Papaji. Speaking to him brought immense joy and loads of blessings. On a serious note, he would enquire about the nature of the pitch and the weather. Sitting thousands of miles away, he would caution and encourage me, with advice that invariably helped me sail through difficult situations. Aware of the manager's interview and my response against Northamptonshire, he advised me to put aside the incident and concentrate on the Test match. In the same breath, he said that he wished to see my name on the board of honour: 'You would make me ten years younger if you scored a century at Lord's!'

Lunch at Lord's was served in the dining room and all the players wore blazers atop their cricket whites to abide by the formality of the event. On the morning of the match, a special duty was assigned to a reserve player to note down the choice of meal for each player and convey it to the officials. Soup was common; grilled chicken, fried/steamed fish or lamb chops for non-vegetarians; salad, steamed vegetables and the chef's bland Indian curry for the vegetarians among us. Dessert was then followed by hot tea and coffee.

The tea interval tested our fitness, choice and appetite due to paucity of time. The table in the dining hall was already set with sandwiches, fruit cakes and biscuits. Cups and saucers were placed near hot tea/coffee pots, and glasses near a couple of jugs filled with orange squash. There was also a provision to enjoy country milk in half-and one-litre bottles. This I drank mostly after the match.

England had an experienced batting line-up in Graham Gooch, David Gower, Allan Lamb and Mike Gatting; Graham Dilley, Richard Ellison and Derek Pringle were all set to challenge us with the new ball. In Phil Edmonds and John Emburey, England had two experienced spinners. The English summer was underway, but it felt very cold for the month of June. I remember wearing a track bottom under my cricket trousers and a couple of woollen jumpers provided by the local sponsor to keep us warm. I wondered about our plight if we had worn flimsy BCCI sweaters meant for Bombay 'winters'!

India won the toss and decided to exploit the conditions ripe for pace bowling. Roger Binny and Chetan Sharma wreaked havoc with the new ball; only Graham Gooch stood solid among the collapsing English line-up with a fine century. Frequent showers led to many interruptions and, before end of play on day two, India lost Srikkanth. I walked to the crease at an odd time to fight a twin battle against the opponents and those in our dressing room! Gavaskar and I survived the day.

The following morning, batting was comparatively easier, till India lost Gavaskar. The arrival of Vengsarkar changed the complexion of the innings and the match. Both of us took the attack to the opponents' camp and scored half-centuries each. Right through the innings, I focused on the milestone for two reasons. This was probably my last chance to play at Lord's—and to realize my father's dream. However, this dream was shattered by poor shot selection. On 69, I tried to play a premeditated inside-out shot over mid-off against left-arm spinner Edmonds, a misjudgement that cost me my wicket. I was caught at mid-on. How I cursed myself for letting down Papaji and my team! However, Vengsarkar continued his honeymoon with this ground and he scored another century.

India kept England on their toes for the first three days, but Sunday brought respite to the hosts; Lord's continued to follow the age-old tradition, observing Sunday as a rest day. This tradition, according to my father, was in place during the 1932, 1936 and 1946 tours, and even in the 1950s. Sunday remained a pious day and families, dressed in formal wear, went to church for prayers. However, the trend had now changed; boys and girls visited beaches while the elders attended to their gardening duties. Shops remained shut then and even now. Interestingly, pubs remained the most sought-after destination for all ages from the afternoon to late into the night. As for us, we preferred to laze in bed and we ventured out in the afternoon to a nearby Indian restaurant to enjoy some steaming curries.

On the fourth day of the test, Kapil Dev polished off the top order, while Chetan Sharma and Roger Binny played a supporting role to put pressure on England. Later, another emerging spinner, Maninder Singh, made important dents with the ball. He bowled a long spell of 20.4 overs, conceding just nine runs and taking three wickets. England were bowled out for 180; we now had to chase a target of 134. We won the game comfortably, by five wickets, to lead the series.

Before the second Test at Leeds, Leicestershire hosted India. This venue brought back unhappy memories of the 1979 match, which still haunted me. I bowled a long spell of twenty-one overs and with 3/39. I was quite pleased with my performance. The next day, however, when I tried to get out of the bed, I had a shooting pain in my lower back. Since I was batting well, I did not wish to miss the next Test. To check my condition, I decided to give it one last chance; I tossed a painkiller in my mouth and occupied the crease. But the discomfort continued and I had to retire at 10.

Although the Leicester game ended in a draw, the presence of a policeman in our dressing room led to confusion. He was accompanied by an Indian supporter holding a flag and his shirt was soaked in blood. The policeman wished to interrogate a certain player because a complaint was filed against him by the injured supporter. The sight of blood shocked us. Manhandling leading to an injury was a serious offence in England and, if convicted, could lead to grave consequences. However, the manager handled the entire incident with maturity and brought about a compromise to save the player.

Once everything was settled, everyone was eager to know the truth. Finally, it came to light, though reluctantly. This incident was an exhibition of Punjabi character—react first and repent later. This player was dismissed cheaply and, before entering the pavilion, encountered a few overexcited and tipsy supporters. Their constant taunts led to an exchange of a few harsh words in Punjabi. Unable to control his instincts, he hit the closest spectator and took refuge in the dressing room, hoping this incident would be overlooked, till the policeman showed up!

After the match, I spoke to the manager and informed him about the condition of my back. The next day, I underwent some medical treatment but it failed to bring any relief. I conveyed to the manager that my back might not take the load of a Test match, and I expressed my desire to make way for another player. I knew two days' rest was too short a period to get into shape. This led to a peculiar situation because most teams, after winning a Test match, avoided changing the line-up, either out of inertia or superstition. Raj Singh also followed this principle and insisted that I play. He comforted me with a promise that he would tell the captain to keep me in the slip cordon and put no pressure on me to bowl.

However, I had burned my hands once keeping the interest of the team above my fitness, so I said no to the suggestion and opted out of the next Test. Little did I realize that rumour-mongers within the team would have a field day. A classic comment that humoured me most was: 'Jimmy had chickened out seeing the green-top wicket!' Taking little notice of this comment, I thought of an obvious replacement for me. It was young Manoj Prabhakar. He had the ability to move the ball and was a decent batsman too. When Chetan Sharma was also declared unfit due to injury, the Delhi lad seemed the best possible option for either of us.

The team management had a job on their hands to fill two vacant spots before the second Test at Leeds. There was an established batsman capable of replacing me but his confidence was currently at its lowest ebb. Still, the manager was keen to include him. To help him regain confidence, the manager spoke to a local club, enabling him to play in the local league. However, the move failed to get the desired result. I felt sorry for the free-flowing batsman; he was going through a rough patch.

Before the Test, an Indian doctor, Bhasin, invited us for a meal at his residence in Huddersfield. He was known to most Indian cricketers playing in the league and in the Indian squad too. While we were enjoying snacks, the familiar face of Madan Lal appeared. He was playing in the neighbouring league. He mingled with the crowd quite easily, and was seen talking intimately with the captain and, later, the manager. These conversations raised little or no interest in anyone.

However, when Madan Lal joined the touring team for a practice session, most members were curious but unreactive. However, on the day of the match, I saw him carrying a kit bag and boarding the coach. The mystery of his inclusion baffled some of us because there were enough replacements for Chetan and me in the team. The scenario reminded me of the 1936 tour of England by the Indian team. The Indian captain, the maharajkumar of Vizianagaram, replaced wicketkeeper Dattaram Hindlekar with Dilawar Hussain in the Test match. Incidentally, Dilawar too was not part of the touring team. Was history repeating itself after fifty years?

While the second Test was in progress, I was following the instructions of the doctor and trained in right earnest. I did not wish to repeat the mistake of the 1979 tour of applying ice to merely numb the pain and suffer further. Now, I took an extended hot tub bath, at least three times a day, applied ice as many times as possible, and took anti-inflammatory tablets to fight the pain and get back into shape. By the time we reached Birmingham, I had developed another problem: my vision was blurry. Was it a reoccurrence of dry eyes or something worse? There happened to be an ophthalmologist near the hotel and I immediately sought his professional advice. Different eye drops did the trick and I looked forward to the next match.

Chandrakant Pandit replaced me while Madan Lal played for the injured Chetan Sharma. The second decision left one particular player with deep wounds and frustration. India won this Test too and sealed the fate of the series. There were a couple of outstanding performances; a classic century by Dilip Vengsarkar in the second innings, a five-wicket haul by Roger Binny and another fine spell by Maninder Singh on an unresponsive track. Madan Lal justified his inclusion with three wickets—but would he continue to be part of the team for the next Test?

The Edgbaston pitch was known to assist batsmen; my fitness was only at 80 per cent. Should I take the chance or miss the opportunity? I deliberated for a while and came to the conclusion that if I missed two Tests on the trot on account of fitness, I might end up being permanently sidelined! I informed the tour committee that I was fit to play, but with a rider that I should not be pressed to bowl. The request was accepted because all the seamers were performing well and were being ably supported by the two spinners, especially Maninder Singh. Once Chetan Sharma was declared fit, Madan Lal was not invited to be part of the playing XI for this tour.

After our success in the first two Test matches, the Indian team was in demand. There was a likelihood, not of a whitewash, but a brownwash, and it excited the large Indian population in Birmingham. Apart from cricket fever, the presence of Bollywood stars caught the imagination of young and old alike. A group of artistes, including the actress Rekha, were performing in the city. The organizers invited the Indian team to add glamour to the show. It was an era when there were no hard and fast rules or restrictions on attending such functions; we obliged the organizers. It was a cocktail of cricketers and Bollywood on the stage; everyone in the crowd enjoyed this rare spectacle.

The last Test was important for me to establish my credentials and put a lid on the murmurs of my ineptitude. My performance would decide my fate for the upcoming series at home. I batted comfortably in the nets, thanks to having undergone regular physiotherapy sessions and ice treatment. I was still unsure how I would react to pain if it erupted during the innings. However, one look at the condition of the Edgbaston pitch brought an instant smile to my face and I forgot all about my injury. Our seamers hardly got any assistance from the pitch, which suited Mike Gatting.

Before going in to bat, I applied an ointment on the sensitive area to keep my back warm. The moment I middled the ball, my confidence returned and the pain vanished. I was involved in fruitful partnerships with Vengsarkar and Azharuddin, and I looked set for a big score. However, at 79, I tried to play a cut shot against Phil Edmonds. The ball failed to rise; it hit the bottom of the off stump to leave me distraught. I had missed yet another opportunity to score a century. The only consolation was that I was the highest scorer for India. The Test ended in a tame draw.

Winning the series so convincingly after 1971 gave us immense satisfaction. All the seamers and Maninder Singh bowled exceptionally well. In batting, Dilip Vengsarkar dominated the proceedings with two centuries. For me, there were mixed feelings; although I amassed runs, it hurt me that I couldn't convert my half-centuries into three figures.

Foreign tours usually ended with an international match, but, for some odd reason, we had the last fixture against Yorkshire at Scarborough. On the eve of this match, the manager asked me to lead the team. I was stumped! On enquiring, I was told that the senior players were released to play an exhibition game, which left me wondering about their commitment towards the Indian team. Nevertheless, I enjoyed the atmosphere and the proceedings as a captain. India won the match by five wickets to wrap up the tour on a high note. Raman Lamba had warmed different benches during the entire tour and he scored a century to remain in the reckoning.

Having finished the tour on this note, everyone was quite happy. At this stage, we received a request for a charity match. Our response was quick and positive. It was organized by my good friend Tanvir Ahmed at Harrogate against the Pakistan team. Tanvir was known for his generosity and always helped cricketers in need with placements in his restaurants, Shabab, at Harrogate and Huddersfield. A large crowd of Pakistani supporters occupied the ground to enjoy carnival cricket. However, the mood of the crowd changed for the worse when they realized India was about to win the match. They shouted anti-India slogans and invaded the field, uprooted the stumps and dug the pitch. Later, the unruly crowd vandalized the ground and tore up various posters. I couldn't understand their psyche. Tanvir, himself a Pakistani from Lahore, was disgusted with the crowd's behaviour!

Looking back at this tour, I observed many things, both on and off the field. The players' behaviour, especially while travelling across the British Isles, caught my attention. We had a permanent luxury coach at our disposal, loaded with a music system, video facilities, a small pantry and comfortable seats to stretch out. The large windowpanes gave us a view of the beautiful countryside.

On most occasions, I noticed Maninder Singh and Kapil engrossed in a game of chess, while Chetan Sharma watched them intently. Sunil Gavaskar was an avid reader, enjoying a book till he dozed off. For a change, Srikkanth, the most fidgety of all the players, was content, sleeping through the journey. Raman Lamba and Manoj Prabhakar enjoyed each other's company, and the Bombay boys felt at home amongst themselves—speaking Marathi, cracking jokes and laughing. Ravi Shastri loved listening to music and was lost in his own world. Sandeep Patil kept us entertained with his jokes and anecdotes. Roger Binny kept mostly to himself, but would occasionally smile and exchanged a few words. Many times, we watched movies, till Sandeep Patil recommended a Hindi movie, *Andheri Raat Mein Diya Tere Haath Mein*, which had us in splits. The acting of Dada Kondke was outstanding.

This team was indeed a group of happy cricketers!

16

TIED TEST MATCH
MADRAS, 1986

THE LIFE OF A CRICKETER MAY SEEM GLAMOROUS, BUT IT requires sacrifice and dedication. I had been living out of my suitcase ever since I started playing first-class cricket at the age of sixteen. The last five years had been hectic—especially after the home series, followed by the tours of Sri Lanka, Australia and England. Therefore, after the England Test series, I took permission from the BCCI and stayed back. I looked forward to spending quality time with my family in Yorkshire.

The countryside of West Yorkshire was captivating and the views of the meadows from our hilltop cottage at Denby Dale would have thrilled any painter. It was simply beautiful and ready for canvas! The village was self-sufficient. It had a post office with a stationery shop and a butcher's shop adjoining it, managed by a well-built Yorkshireman. The barber shop was operated by enterprising young girls, and it had customers from other villages too. A decent-sized grocery store owned by a Sikh gentleman came in handy for many products, particularly last-minute requirements and the spices we needed to cook curries.

The colourful bakery shop attracted one and all to savour delicious cakes, cupcakes, pastries, sandwiches, chicken pies in hot white sauce and much more. It was managed by ladies of different ages, wearing red caps and aprons. Fish and chips, the most famous dish, was in great demand. The traditional pub was always overflowing on weekends. Not far was a Chinese takeaway and an Indian restaurant, probably run by a local Pakistani, which did brisk business on the weekends too.

Throughout the week, the old library was frequented by avid readers. A small pavilion added romance to the Cricket Club and the area. The club's team participated in village cricket while the Bowling Green was in high demand with senior citizens, both men and women. The tennis courts drew the younger lot. Since the population of the village was not high, all the inhabitants knew each other. Furthermore, a small vintage railway station and regular bus service connected Denby Dale to the town of Huddersfield. The motorway (M1) nearby let us travel freely to other counties.

To keep myself fit for the coming season in India, the countryside offered me more than enough space to walk, jog and exercise. To enjoy the scenic beauty of the woods behind our cottage, I wandered around for hours. The freshness of the woods transported me back to my childhood when I spent summers in the mountains of Chail. For jogging, I took a shortcut, and ran through a narrow grass and sand path all the way to the village council football ground and trained by myself. After exhausting all my energy, I walked back home. The workout lasted a couple of hours each day.

To cover the long distance back and enjoy the atmosphere, I purchased a farm-fresh bottle of milk and relished the flavour. I also loudly sang a few Hindi songs to glory! The frequency of my walks allowed me to interact with the locals and develop friendships with them. I was recognized not as a cricketer but as the husband of Dr Bickoo. She worked as a psychiatrist at Storthes Hall Hospital, Huddersfield, and many people in the area had seen us together at the hospital or in the town, purchasing groceries. I regularly cooked breakfast and lunch, organized barbeques in our back garden, drank red wine and watched the sun set behind the tall fern trees. I felt like a free bird! Other than that, I indulged my little daughter to make up for the precious time lost on cricket tours. I also shared my experiences with my better half. Life beyond the boundaries of the cricket field was indeed bliss!

Although I had not touched the willow, my physical and mental condition was tickety-boo! The season in India was commencing with six ODIs and three Test matches against Australia. Normally, a couple of domestic matches provided cricketers a platform to perform and gain confidence, but I had no such option. To fine-tune my skills and get ready for the Tests, I had to sweat it out in the nets. The first Test was scheduled for Madras on 18 September.

I had fond memories of Chepauk because of my debut. My last Test innings against England also brought back a smile to my face and I looked forward to this match too. However, after the monsoon, the temperature and humidity rose considerably in Madras, which tested the nerves and fitness of all the cricketers. The ground was a furnace. The moment we stepped out on the field, our T-shirts were soaked in sweat.

Chepauk of the earlier days was most unlike today; the free flow of the sea breeze kept all parts of the ground pleasant. I recall my debut and the temporary stands around it, not very high, which allowed the late afternoon breeze to rejuvenate the exhausted players. The curator at Chepauk had the ability to play with the character of the pitch—either it was a square turner or a batting paradise!

This time, it looked like a beautiful batting strip. There was no grass, no pace, and yet bounce was even, which allowed the batsmen to play their strokes with confidence. Australia batted first and piled up 574 runs for the loss of seven wickets, before Allan Border declared the innings closed. We were stuck on the field for nearly two days, bowling 170.5 overs. It was so hot under the blazing sun that one could feel the heat seeping through the soles of our shoes and baking our feet. Dean Jones played an amazing innings under incredibly adverse conditions, a testament to his fitness.

During the lunch and tea breaks, the Aussie physio met Dean Jones and measured his water intake by collecting his urine to decide how best to keep him hydrated. However, the long innings eventually took a toll on him. The heat and loss of fluids caused cramps and he vomited several times on the field. After scoring a memorable double century, exhaustion forced him to make a mistake. On reaching the dressing room, his condition became alarming and he collapsed; he was rushed to a hospital and put on a drip for recovery. Border recalled, 'When I returned to the pavilion after scoring a century, I enquired about Dean's health. I was so worried that I wondered if I'd killed him!'

David Boon also had a piece of the pie and scored a century. The Indian seamers and spinners toiled hard for wickets on the unresponsive surface. Walking and running on the hot, grassless outfield intensified our misery. Honestly, all of us looked forward to lunch and tea to give rest to our tired legs. Once the shadows lengthened on the hot field, shade near the stands provided welcome relief to the lucky fielder in the deep.

While the Australian batsmen received massages and health drinks during the breaks, we took cold showers to regain some strength. However, there was no respite from the hot and humid conditions of the dressing room thanks to the concrete structure above and around us. The ceiling fans became ineffective—they circulated hot air. Consumption of excessive fluids robbed us of our appetite. Despite the variety of choice, most players preferred curd rice to keep the body temperature under control, but failed miserably!

The third day's play was crucial for us; we had to bat well to avoid a follow-on. Unfortunately, I got run out in a mix-up with Srikkanth, while the other batters lost wickets playing rash strokes—probably emulating the Aussies. India finished the day at 7/270, desperately requiring dedication from the rest of the batsmen to avoid a follow-on. Kapil was unbeaten at 33, and he wasn't happy with the team performance. During the team meeting in the evening, he blamed the batsmen for playing a Test match like a limited-overs match.

On the fourth day of the Test, the two overnight batsmen were required to adopt a cautious approach. However, the first ball Kapil faced went over the mid-off fielder's head, followed by a similar stroke over mid-on and so forth. The red cherry seemed to have grown wings and it flew in all directions, contrary to the Indian captain's speech. His approach was in no way different from that of the batsmen dismissed the previous day. So much for his unhappiness the previous evening! We couldn't help but chuckle at what we were witnessing. The stroke-filled century helped India sail through the critical juncture and avoid a follow-on. When Kapil returned to the pavilion, everyone appreciated his innings—and, of course, reminded him of his own words last evening; everyone had a good laugh!

In the second innings, the Australian batsmen adopted a bold approach and went for quick runs to put pressure on

India once again. By the end of day four, the lead had galloped to 347. By now, the pitch had started assisting spinners and Australia had a good combination in Greg Matthews and Ray Bright to exploit the surface on the last day. Would Border take the heavy roller the next morning and break the surface further? On the morning of the fifth day, we were getting ready to take the field when we heard a knock on the door of our dressing room. When it opened, we saw Allan Border. He was quick with his words about Australia's declaration and left the Indian dressing room in disarray. We were caught on the wrong foot. Surely, a lot of thoughts must have gone into Border's decision!

Discarding their spikes, the two openers now had to pad up. There was no time to discuss any strategy nor any instruction offered by the captain. Gavaskar was playing his hundredth consecutive Test match and was yet to set the stands on fire, and his partner, the local boy Srikkanth, was like an untamed leopard capable of destroying any attack. However, scoring more than hundred runs per session was not an easy task on a surface showing signs of crumbling.

True to his reputation, Srikkanth led an all-out attack and set the ball rolling early in the opening partnership. The first wicket added 51 runs in no time before Srikkanth perished. I had not contributed anything in the first innings and was keen to put up a score now. Runs came at a normal pace without any undue risks. The heat and humidity, along with the fielders chirping away to get under our skin, made for a most challenging situation. Further, there was no respite from the turning deliveries of Bright and Matthews. At one stage, India was sitting pretty; both Gavaskar and I had scored half-centuries.

After tea, however, wickets started tumbling. Gavaskar missed another milestone by 10 runs. If this wicket brought joy to the Australian camp, a rearguard action by Azharuddin and

Chandrakant Pandit caused panic. The pendulum swung from one extreme to the other. The large crowd at Chepauk could not have asked for anything better; it was certainly Test cricket at its best. The reaction in the Indian and Australian dressing rooms brought opposite reactions of joy and misery. The gallery was also not left emotionally untouched.

When Ravi Shastri and Chetan Sharma were scoring freely and India was at 6/331, victory was within our grasp. Panic and frustration forced the Aussies to adopt another tactic: sledging. Pressure was building on both sides, and Chetan Sharma got involved in a verbal bout with Ray Bright and the close-in fielders; he lost his cool and played a rash stroke to lose his wicket. Victory seemed so near and yet so far. India lost another two wickets in a nerve-wracking situation.

Finally, Maninder Singh walked out to the crease, anxiety writ large on the face of the bowler, fielders and the last batsman. Even the players and managers of the two dressing rooms were affected. They stood in complete silence, awaiting the decisive moment to celebrate. There was tension all round while Allan Border repeatedly changed the field to test the nerves of the batsman and the patience of the umpire. Ravi Shastri was a seasoned campaigner, cool as a cucumber, and he was indeed our last hope for victory. With four runs required to win, there was a rare misfield to fetch us two runs. The entire stadium erupted in joy and people rose to their feet in anticipation, awaiting the moment of victory.

To keep the suspense intact, Ravi took a single to level the score. This brought Maninder Singh to face Matthews and a ring of fielders breathing down his neck. The pressure was unbearably intense; should he go for a big hit and give India victory? But what if he mistimed his shot? Confusion prevailed and Maninder decided to defend. The ball missed the bat and hit the pad. The eleven Aussies on the field and the entire Australian enclosure, consisting of the team management and reserve players in the pavilion, jumped simultaneously in the air in excitement. Much to their delight, the umpire, V. Vikramraju, raised his finger—and the match ended in a tie!

Although we were disappointed with the result, little did we realize that we had emulated a unique record in the history of Test cricket. Since 1877, there had been only one instance of a Test match ending in a tie. That was between Australia and the West Indies at the Gabba in Brisbane in 1960—and now, our Chepauk duel had put us in the same page of the record books. Only one person had witnessed both these historic moments for Australia. It was Bobby Simpson—first as a player in 1960 and now as a coach in 1986.

17

PAKISTAN IN INDIA 1987

THE 1986-87 SEASON WAS CRAMMED WITH DOMESTIC matches, and two Test series against Sri Lanka and Pakistan. However, the most debated and eagerly awaited event in India was the World Cup (known as the Reliance Cup) from 8 October to 8 November 1987. The earlier World Cups were held in England and the last was a game changer for Indian cricket, on and off the field. Why was the fourth World Cup not held in England? That was an interesting story. After India romped home with a victory over England in the semi-finals, many BCCI officials rushed to London to witness the historic final.

A mere request for two additional tickets by the BCCI president, N.K.P Salve, got a stiff upper lip from the Marylebone Cricket Club official; that changed the face of world cricket. Air Marshal Nur Khan, attending the event on behalf of the Pakistan Cricket Board (PCB), met Salve over lunch, and both decided to take the bull by the horns and shift the World Cup out of England—by no means an easy task. After several meetings and threats, the members of the ICC ultimately agreed to allow India and Pakistan to jointly host the tournament. It was the end of the MCC's hegemony over international cricket.

If Salve and Nur Khan played an important role in persuading the members of the ICC, including the associate members, to shift the tournament out of England, Dhirubhai Ambani, the chairman of Reliance Group, also played a prominent role in the success of the 1987 World Cup, sponsoring the event. The cricket boards of both countries had developed a fine relationship, which had begun after India's tour of Pakistan in 1978. However, politically, both countries remained at loggerheads, unable to agree on several issues. Despite this handicap, the mature heads of the organizational committee, which included I.S. Bindra, Jagmohan Dalmiya and Arif Ali Khan Abbasi, remained on the same page.

Fresh from our exploits in England in 1986, I looked forward to a packed home season, including international matches. The Sri Lankans by no means carried the irresistible tag of Pakistan or the West Indies, nor the attraction of the Aussies or the English cricketers; they were, nevertheless, a potent force. They had earlier surprised many international teams with their abilities and performances. I missed the first Test match because of a fractured index finger sustained during the Irani Trophy. However, I returned to the team for the second Test at Nagpur and scored a century to prove my fitness. India won the three-Test series 2-0 to set the tempo for the next, and more important, series against Pakistan.

India–Pakistan series always generated mass hysteria, and this touring team was no different from Abdul Hafeez Kardar's 1952 or Fazal Mahmood's 1960 teams. The presence of a flamboyant cricketer at the helm of affairs added colour to this series. Imran's Casanova reputation from the 1979 tour had not yet faded. This time too the social fraternity was agog. However, Imran's familiarity with the opposite sex did not augur well with a distinct Pakistani player from Karachi. He developed an inferiority complex due to his limitation with the English language. How he disdained his captain and often complained about him! He shared his feelings with an Indian friend, 'If only I could speak fluent English like him, I would have had the company of at least half of those beautiful ladies!'

Few players survived from the 1978 series, except Imran and Miandad from Pakistan, and Gavaskar, Kapil Dev, Vengsarkar and me from India. Both teams respected each other's capabilities and played hard cricket. The intensity with which these matches were contested raised everyone's adrenaline, not only on the field but even in the galleries of the stadium. It was probably the mother of all battles—bigger and more meaningful than the Ashes. The result meant a lot to people on both sides of the border.

The first Test was played at Chepauk in Madras. The pitch seemed to be a batsman's paradise. Even a blind man would have regained his sight thanks to its sparkling sheen. It was whitish in colour, hard as a rock and had not a blade of grass on its surface.

If it was joy for batsmen, it was a nightmare for bowlers. The first over proved the batting-friendliness of the pitch. The Pakistani batsmen enjoyed the outing on a placid wicket and exploited the conditions to their benefit. Shoaib Mohammad, in particular, and later, Imran relished the conditions and excelled with the bat. The way Shoaib batted reminded me of the stories I'd heard of his legendary father, Hanif Mohammad. I was told that he never counted time, runs or sessions, but instead believed in occupying the crease forever. His memorable innings of 337 against the West Indies at Bridgetown in 1958 took a mammoth 970 minutes, which spoke volumes about his concentration and love for batting. Thereafter, he was referred to as 'Little Master'. This quality was noticeable in his son too. If, given a choice, he would have slept on the pitch all night.

Many Pakistani batsmen who didn't make use of the opportunity must have kicked themselves for having missed out. From an Indian perspective, there was no relief for the home bowlers, whether spin or pace. After piling up a huge total, Pakistan hoped to make early inroads against our strong batting line-up; they declared the innings closed in the dying moments of play on day two. However, India survived the tension of the day's end without losing a wicket.

India had an interesting opening pair: Sunil Gavaskar was a master grafter, calm and calculating, and, of course, technically sound. His partner Srikkanth, on the contrary, was a queer combination of many streaks. He was a carefree and restless attacking batsman, who bamboozled many bowlers with unsuspecting strokes. There was always an element of excitement and drama during his stay at the crease. His stance may not have been ideal for the coaching manual but his strokes created confusion among bowlers. As he himself admitted, he had no control over his instinct, so did not know what stroke he would unleash next.

Once he completed a half-century, he could hardly stay motionless. He moved his head consistently from left to right, stretched his legs, twitched his nose, looked at the sky, shutting his eyes several times causing a khalbali, or commotion, in the otherwise serene atmosphere of the dressing room. No one knew what to expect from him in the following over. He seemed in a tearing hurry to complete a century within the next few overs. In his pursuit, he often took too many risks, which usually led to his downfall. This was one reason why he did not have many more centuries to his name. That was Srikkanth for you!

However, at Chepauk, he set the stadium on fire with a truly brilliant century. After his dismissal, I walked out to replace him with the team score on 200; I hoped the batting would be comfortable against Imran and Wasim Akram. Well, it wasn't; they gave me a torrid time with short-pitched deliveries. Batting is not only about mindset and technique, but also about the ability to learn quickly from your partner, especially when you happen to be in dire straits. At this moment, I had Sunil Gavaskar as partner. His sound technique helped him deal with short-pitched deliveries. It was a lesson not only for me but also for all the youngsters in both teams. How he watched the ball go past him to the wicketkeeper's gloves disheartening the fast bowlers. This exhibition gave me the confidence to face both fast bowlers and dictate terms in my own way, without being intimidated by their pace and length.

In my opinion, Gavaskar was the most self-disciplined and unselfish partner to bat with. Through my career I had quite a few big partnerships with him; both of us scored heavily and responded instantly to each other's call. He never spoke much but always appreciated the efforts of his partner. He had amazing concentration and unbelievable talent, probably one of the fittest batsmen of all time. He loved to bat for days without the slightest fatigue—but ask him to run a few laps, he would be exhausted beyond imagination. Trick or truth? Hard to say!

After the end of day three, I was undefeated at 33 when Rajan Bala, a journalist friend covering this match, came to meet me at the Taj Connemara. He wanted to evaluate the Indian response after Pakistan's big total. Normally, I never boasted, but now I was sure that I would even get a double century!

Gavaskar looked set for another coveted milestone, but missed it by a mere 9 runs, a very unusual sight. Dilip

Vengsarkar, nicknamed 'Colonel', had the ability to hit huge sixes like the former Indian captain of 1932-33, Col C.K. Nayudu. Batting with Vengsarkar was always challenging. Unlike Gavaskar, he often ignored his partner's call. However, he ran like a gazelle to collect runs on his own strokes.

I was comfortably placed at 88, and I looked forward to keeping my promise. I flicked Wasim Akram to deep fine leg and immediately called for two; I ran the first run hard, keeping my eyes on Ramiz Raja, the fielder, and I covered more than half the pitch to retain the strike, but was aghast to see Vengsarkar standing like a statue in the crease with no expression or response. I tried my best to return to the bowler's end, but it was too late. I got run out and I was beyond livid!

I trudged back towards the dressing room and threw my bat on the floor in disgust, and, for a change, let my emotions get the better of me. This was most unlike me. I was like a wounded tiger, pacing up and down in a cage, full of rage and with my pads still on. The players were silent; they had never witnessed this sort of behaviour from me. They kept to themselves and left me alone. My inability to keep my promise was devastating!

The next Test was at Eden Gardens in Calcutta, and Sunil Gavaskar opted out of the match due to personal reasons. His decision not to play in such an important match had its genesis in an ugly incident during the 1984-85 series against England. This fact was known to the selection committee, yet none of the members persuaded him to change his mind.

Cricketers, by nature, are superstitious. The dressing room at Eden Gardens had cane chairs, and the players preferred to occupy the same chair they had sat on during the previous Test match as a good luck charm. All the chairs were occupied, except one. The vacant chair belonged to Sunil Gavaskar and was used during the England Test match. Nobody dared to sit on it, fearing an adverse reaction from the crowd. This match also ended in a draw.

After the match and a day's break, both teams assembled for the second ODI. There were no floodlights at Eden Gardens, so the match was confined to forty overs for each side. I was not part of the squad; I stayed back to watch it before flying to Delhi and later to Jaipur for the next Test. I occupied a seat in the VIP area below the team dressing rooms when I was spotted by the Pakistani players from Lahore. It was hard to believe they still carried a soft corner for me because of Papaji's link with Lahore. They insisted I join them and I could not say no. This invitation gave me a rare opportunity to get a feel of their dressing room atmosphere. I observed that only a few spoke in English, which was an indication of their background and education. Most players felt at home with Urdu and it bound them together. However, interacting with the Punjabi players left me with tears of laughter because of their sense of humour. Mudassar Nazar the pick of the comedians with his slapstick remarks.

His best comment was fired at Younis Ahmed, making his ODI debut at the age of over forty. In a true Lahori dialect and accent, he left everyone rolling in laughter. Younis had sprinted quite a few times to collect cheeky singles and doubles, and eventually scored a half-century. After his dismissal, he had a long walk back to the pavilion and climbed forty-odd steps to reach the dressing room, which left him completely exhausted. Taking a dig at him, Mudassar said, 'Look at your condition! Did you bat or just complete a marathon? Hope you don't have a heart attack. Please save us the agony of finding a place for your burial!' Younis simply smiled and pinched his cheek.

Politics and cricket go hand in hand in the subcontinent. No one could have used it better than President. Zia-ul-Haq. He invited himself to witness the next Test in Jaipur, which the BCCI could not refuse. His itinerary included a visit to Ajmer Sharif Dargah. No doubt, he surprised many brains in South Block, but not for too long. Because he was on a private visit, the Government of India was not obliged to present a ceremonial welcome; they deputed an official from the Ministry of Foreign Affairs to receive him. Was it a move to thaw the frigid relationship between the two nations or simply to watch a Test match? Only he could have answered that.

Papaji always watched me play in Delhi and later discussed my flaws, if any. He expressed his desire to watch the Jaipur Test and meet General Zia as well. His Lahore connections and Papaji's previous visit to Pakistan had helped him develop a good rapport with the President. Ever since then, General Zia sent Papaji a personally signed New Year's greeting, delivered by an official from the Pakistan High Commission. To thank him, he asked the local BCCI official to arrange a meeting with the President at the ground itself. For some strange reason, they did not respond. I understood his disappointment and took a call to convey his message to the President.

General Zia was the chief guest, so both teams were introduced to him. Shaking hands with me, he enquired about Papaji's health and welfare. I instantly replied, 'Why don't you ask him?' He asked, 'Is he here?' Then he immediately asked the BCCI officials to arrange a meeting with 'Lala Sahib' in his box. This took the BCCI officials by surprise, and they escorted Papaji to General Zia's box. Ignoring the presence of the BCCI officials, the two Lahoris spent most of the time conversing in Punjabi. Anecdotes of pre-Partition India, especially Papaji's Lahore days, amused General Zia and his entourage so much that they practically guffawed, which left the BCCI officials bewildered.

Maharajas, in the past, had promoted cricket, and this connection continued with the royal house of Jaipur. Maharaja

Bhawani Singh invited both teams to his palace. The drive from Rambagh Palace to the maharaja's residence presented different shades of the beautiful city, and local officials added flavour with stories of valour and the rich history of Jaipur.

We had a regal welcome; we heard drums beating to the tune of a shehnai. Two elephants were stationed at the entrance of the palace and they garlanded each player. These were made of marigold and roses. During the home series, there was no dress code, so we attended most functions in casual clothing. I was with Bickoo and seven-year-old Nikki, enjoying the evening. We were introduced to Bhawani Singh and I told my little daughter about his status, that he was a maharaja. She refused to believe me. For her, maharajas wore a crown; Bhawani Singh had none. However, he convinced Nikki that his crown was locked away for the night. He promised to wear it next time. This statement convinced my innocent little daughter. Thereafter, she did not question Bhawani Singh about his crown!

The Jaipur Test as well as the contest at the ground in Ahmedabad ended without any result. However, at Ahmedabad, Sunil Gavaskar became the first player in history to cross the hallowed figure of 10,000 international runs in Test cricket.

Bangalore was the venue for the final Test match of the series. It had a reputation for providing a good Test wicket, which initially helped batsmen and later spinners. I expected a good track to finish the series. However, the first look at the surface got identical reactions from all the batsmen: disappointment. The pitch looked like a barren piece of land, most unlike a Bangalore wicket. It was dry with cracks. One look at it made me realize that it was not an easy pitch to bat on. It would get worse with each passing day. Why prepare such a wicket in the last Test when previous Tests had produced no result?

Winning the toss was now of paramount importance; it was like winning half the battle. Imran had not played the specialist leg spinner, Abdul Qadir, after the Madras Test. I had always rated him highly. He had won many games for his country. However, his success rate against India was low because Indian batsmen had the ability to read him well. We found him to be no threat on a good batting track at Chepauk in Madras. But now, looking at the condition of the pitch here in Bangalore, I had the sneaking suspicion that Abdul Qadir would become Pakistan's trump card. How relieved we were to see his name missing from the playing XI! Instead, Saleem Jaffar took his place to strengthen the pace attack.

Imran won the toss and elected to bat. It was a foregone conclusion that batting on this pitch last would be a Herculean task. The first over itself indicated that it was devoid of bounce, pace or movement. The pace bowler's delivery hardly carried to the wicketkeeper. The track appeared to be tailor-made for spinners.

Maninder Singh bowled a magic spell, probably the best of his life, and, most importantly, for his country. He was lethally accurate and denied the Pakistan batsmen any liberty to play their strokes. The ball bounced and spun viciously on the helpful surface. He took seven wickets and obliterated Pakistan for 116. The modest total made us feel quite confident that we would secure a vital first innings lead, no matter how big a task it was.

The wicket had already developed quite a few spots to play marbles. I knew the conditions were deplorable but I could never have guessed how obnoxious it would be. If this was happening on the first day of the match, the contest would not last too long. The Indian batsmen, with the exception of Dilip Vengsarkar, were unsure whether to attack or defend; they perished against the tight bowling of Tauseef Ahmed and Iqbal Qasim. Dilip used all his experience and batted well for his half-century, which helped India go past the Pakistani total and secure a first innings lead.

Every run was precious, but, out of the blue, Vengsarkar played an uncharacteristic stroke to lose his wicket. Unlike the Pakistani batsmen dreading Imran's retribution, Dilip seemed least remorseful. He was quite happy to be the top scorer. It reminded me of two incidents; first at a Delhi Test match against England and the aftermath. But here, life proceeded casually with no comments! The second incident involved Saleem Malik during the Jaipur Test. He played a similar rash stroke off Gopal Sharma and lost his wicket. He lamented, 'Oh! Marr gaye; Imran kha jaayega (Oh! I'm doomed; Imran will sail into me)!' Once Vengsarkar was gone, the rest fell like autumn leaves.

A slender but precious lead of 29 runs on a difficult pitch boosted our morale. If the Indian spinners could repeat the first innings' performance, our task in the fourth innings would become easier. I expected the captain to give a pep talk and charge all the bowlers before taking the field; but I was surprised that not a word was spoken. We left the dressing room quietly, hoping the tourists would buckle under pressure.

Comprehending the critical situation, Pakistan changed the batting order and promoted Javed Miandad up with Ramiz Raja. Both ran singles as if their life depended on it, an approach that gave their team a decent start. Every batsman at the top of the order or tail-end used his experience or borrowed technique to protect his wicket. Whenever they had an opportunity, they never shied away from playing a big stroke, a rarity. While wickets tumbled, runs leaked in plenty.

Bowling on moon craters requires discipline, which was missing on quite a few occasions. Too many runs were given away by the spinners. When India dismissed Imran at a team score of 198 as the eighth batsman, we were back in the game. But the ninth wicket pair of Saleem Yousuf (41 not out) and Tauseef Ahmed (10) frustrated us. While the former used his skills to score runs, the latter defended his wicket till his last breath. They added 51 golden runs to take Pakistan to a healthy score of 249.

A target of 220 runs on a decaying pitch was a huge challenge. The way the dust exploded after each delivery warned us of just how difficult this chase would be. Left-arm Iqbal Qasim and off spinner Tauseef Ahmed had made life miserable in the first innings. Thank God there was no Abdul Qadir to deal with! To avoid damaging the pitch, all the batsmen used frayed rubber-sole shoes. If we'd had the choice, we would have batted barefoot for the same purpose.

However, Pakistan's close-in fielders, wearing spikes, crossed the pitch with purpose. At times, one of them intentionally twisted his foot to damage the surface further, especially the good length area. The mastermind of this act was a street-smart batsman from Karachi. This took place after the over was completed and the umpires changed position. When we complained to the umpires, the player was reprimanded—but the damage was already done.

The stories of Pakistani groundsmen cheating were recounted to me by Papaji. He said they ingeniously hid a handful of sand mixed with tiny stones in their torn pockets. When they pulled the roller, the sand trickled down from their pockets, giving undue advantage to their own bowlers against the teams that happened to be touring. The anecdote left me speechless!

We expected a few overs from Imran but he surprised everyone. He defied expectations, and opened the bowling with Wasim Akram and Iqbal Qasim. It was a shrewd move against the right-handed batsmen. He had come with a plan to exploit the surface with a left-arm spinner and left-arm fast bowler. Imran literally guided Akram after every delivery and he changed the young man's angle from over the wicket to round the wicket. The followthrough of Akram bowling over the wicket created a bigger crater outside the off stump for the right-hand batsmen to suit the off spinner Tauseef.

Once the effect of the roller receded, the ball started gripping the surface and changing course. Wasim Akram bowled a sensational spell to put us on the back foot. He had been on the international scene for quite some time and he was a quick learner. Realizing that normal pace bowling would not bring success, he changed his grip on the ball to surprise the batsman. He mixed crossed seam with a traditional grip so well that he captured two wickets, while Iqbal and Tauseef took one each to reduce India to 4/99 by the end of day three. The saving grace for India was Gavaskar, holding the fort with a well-compiled half-century.

Day four of the Test was a rest day because of Holi, the Indian festival of colours. I loved this festival not because of its colours, but for its atmosphere of bonhomie and its history. I remember studying at Harcourt Butler School in Delhi. I treaded the narrow paths of the jungle behind the school and collected wild tesu flowers. These trees were well over thirty-feet tall, but the flowers made it to the ground courtesy birds pecking it for taste and discarding the rest. We soaked these flowers overnight in two huge tubs to change the colour of the water to a beautiful yellow and used it for the balloons to target people during the Holi festivities.

Both teams were staying at Taj West End. It was probably the first time that Pakistani players were witnessing a Hindu festival. They seemed excited—each one was covered with multicoloured powder and their faces were beyond recognition. Then came a smiling Imran to join his colleagues, and he was instantly smeared with dry and wet colours and later pushed into the pool. The fun and frolic covered the pool and area around it with different colours. Despite the mess, the hotel staff did not complain. I watched the scene from my room facing the pool and wondered if religious festivities could bring so much joy and happiness, why should there be conflict between the two neighbouring countries?

Scoring another 121 runs to win the Test felt like climbing Mount Everest with a solitary oxygen cylinder named Sunil Gavaskar. He was our lifeline and last hope in this arduous battle. I had witnessed many fine knocks from him, but the situation was different now. Here, he used all his experience to play spinners and pace bowlers from the middle of the bat; the rest of the batsmen struggled.

Despite the die cast heavily against us, the stadium was almost full on the fourth day. The first hour of the session was crucial for us. Runs dripped in singles but we lost Azharuddin and later Shastri with the scoreboard reading 6/155. However, Gavaskar kept all the Pakistan bowlers at bay with his classic technique and truly Olympian concentration.

This innings was an ultimate lesson for all the batsmen—how to bat in difficult conditions, especially when every ball played tricks on a tricky wicket. The variable bounce and turn played havoc with the brain. Negotiating it with the middle of the bat spoke volumes about Sunny. He kept scoring runs as if there was no devil in the pitch while the others looked naïve. When India lost Kapil as the seventh wicket at 161, our hope rested on the new partners to enable Gavaskar to continue scoring from the other end and achieve victory.

Imran knew that with dust exploding after every delivery, they needed one unplayable ball aimed at Gavaskar to seal the fate of the match. To his joy, the ever-vigilant batsman received one such delivery from Iqbal Qasim. It hit the glove and landed safely in the hands of Rizwan-uz-Zaman. Although Roger Binny tried his best, India lost the battle by a mere 16 runs. It was Pakistan's first-ever series win on Indian soil. The credit undoubtedly went to Imran for handling the situation with a cool mind. The way he handled his spinners in a nervy contest made Tauseef and Iqbal effective.

It was also Gavaskar's last Test innings—and what an innings! I rate this as maybe the best of his life. Hats off to his contribution to Indian cricket. During the two decades of my international career, I found him to be the best batsman of world cricket. All I can say is: 'SALAAM SUNNY!'

18

TAKEN FOR A RIDE

THE RELIANCE WORLD CUP WAS EXTREMELY SUCCESSFUL AS a tournament on its own, but bitterly disappointing for the Indian team. As the title-holders, we performed below expectations in this one. I had played three earlier World Cup tournaments quite successfully; apparently, the age factor was blown out of proportion and, to my dismay, I was denied an opportunity to play. I think a player's fitness and potential should be the prime consideration for selection, not his age.

The period immediately afterwards created a storm of confusion in Indian cricket. First, Kapil was sacked after losing the semi-final of the World Cup and, subsequently, the players refused to sign fresh contracts with the board. Time was running out for the BCCI because the West Indies team had already reached India and the selectors had not yet announced the captain or the team. Dilip Vengsarkar was slated to be the next captain, subject to signing the contract.

Away from BCCI politics, I was playing a match at Mohan Nagar (Uttar Pradesh) and I decided to spend the night at Madan Lal's house. Around midnight, I got a call from Johnny (my younger brother) to discuss something urgent. My first reaction was to ask if everyone was okay at home. He said yes and that the BCCI secretary had called, requesting my presence in Chandigarh. There was a consensus to offer me India's captaincy.

I found this news difficult to swallow because I hadn't been in the race at all. Moreover, I had reservations pertaining to certain characters in the cricket board known for their machinations. While confusion prevailed, I had to take a quick call on two accounts: the first available flight for Chandigarh left in the next few hours, and second, the BCCI secretary had made the call himself, which meant that this was serious. I reached Delhi airport at four in the morning and bumped into one of the national selectors booked on the same flight. He looked surprised, which left me perplexed and worried. Perplexed, because the secretary had called me to assume the Indian captaincy and this selector was not aware of it; worried, suspecting now that something was amiss.

My fears were confirmed; there was no official, local or from the BCCI, to receive me at Chandigarh airport! However, I reached my hotel (Shivalik View) and checked in. At half-past-eight in the morning, I received a call from the chairman of the selection committee, inviting me to his room. He greeted me warmly and called another selector through the intercom. This gesture temporarily allayed my apprehensions. Subsequently, the chairman opened the entrance door, peered out and returned to the chair quite relaxed. I thought he was checking to see if there was any media around because the India U-25 team was playing against the West Indies and the press were always around to interview any member of the Caribbean line-up.

After a few minutes, a familiar face entered the room and exchanged greetings with me. Surprisingly, it was not the chairman, but the selector who started the discussion. It was strange to see the chairman with a notepad and a pencil taking notes; I thought this was my big moment. However, the selector's opening statement cleared the picture. 'Jimmy, we are not sure whether Dilip will arrive, so we asked for you.' I could have died right there; I was not to be crowned king but to be used as a pawn!

The next sentence was even more shocking. 'So then, all the best, Jimmy. Keep your fingers crossed and hope Dilip doesn't show up.' Shell-shocked, I did not know how to react, though deep within me a bomb of fury was on the brink of detonation. Shortly thereafter, Dilip arrived and was warmly welcomed. The return flight to Delhi happened to be in the evening; I decided to watch the match at Sector 16 stadium. However, my wounds were too raw to give me comfort. I got up to go back to the hotel when I saw a local official approaching me. He said, 'The BCCI secretary wants to meet you.' This was the last name I wanted to hear, and I exploded, 'Tell him to come here if he wants to talk to me!' At about 2.30 p.m., I met the media and shared this episode. I returned home poorer, with a heavy bill and no crown!

I was selected for the first Test in Delhi but had to drop out due to a high fever. For some strange reason, the North Zone match against West Indies was shifted to Pune. I was on trial once more and had to prove my credentials for the next Test. On the eve of the match, the team manager (with whom I had opened the bowling for Punjab seventeen years ago) conveyed a message from the North Zone selector that two specific players should be part of the playing XI at the expense of two young cricketers. I tried to explain that it was the prerogative of the captain to decide the composition of the squad. The argument continued late into the night without any resolution. However, the next day I took a call, and we played Gursharan Singh and Mahesh Inder Singh. The former scored 71 and the latter took a few wickets.

I was selected for the Bombay Test but could not perform. I then looked forward to Calcutta, when the selectors sprung another surprise on me—I was selected for the Guwahati ODI. Barely three months ago, I was considered too old to play one-day cricket; now suddenly I was good enough! This baffled everyone, including me.

Calcutta was a batsman's paradise, but Winston Davis found sufficient bounce from the pitch at Eden Gardens to get one delivery to rise and hit Vengsarkar on the forearm. He was ruled out for the rest of the match. The selectors were caught in a terrible situation; who would lead India for the rest of the match? The choice was between Kapil and me. However, the selectors didn't want Kapil after the World Cup debacle and I had become persona non grata after the Chandigarh episode. Who would lead India in the absence of injured Vengsarkar? This was hotly debated.

Ravi Shastri was given the crown; he led the Indian team at Chepauk in Madras, a Test that will go down in history as Narendra Hirwani's match. He bowled a good line and showed fine temperament on a spinner-friendly pitch. The West Indian batsmen also hastened their own downfall. They perished trying to destroy Hirwani and ultimately committed hara-kiri. It felt good to hold the West Indies to 1-1 in the series.

Immediately after the series, the BCCI banned Dilip Vengsarkar for six months, for writing columns in a newspaper. For a change, the team stood by him and held several meetings to project unity; most players signed a letter to revoke the ban, and also conveyed they would not sign the contract and possibly avoid the Sharjah tournament. However, one player did not sign the letter but signed the contract; he was rewarded by the board.

This year, I was a 'beneficiary' at Sharjah but my choice was dogged in controversy. I had met Asif Iqbal, the convenor of this project, during the Lord's Test in 1986, and I asked him about Cricketers Benefit Fund Series (CBFS) selection of the beneficiaries. He explained that the player had to sign with CBFS and, thereafter, the choice was made on seniority. By the end of 1986, I was in Sharjah meeting Mr. Bakhtiar and I asked the same question; I received a similar reply. However, contrary to all the assurances, the scenario changed and a rather junior player got preference as the next beneficiary. I wondered, with some amusement, whether all conventions concluded at my doorstep!

Later in the year, General Zia-ul-Haq stunned political pundits with his decision to watch the India—Pakistan match in Jaipur. This was good news for me because of my father's closeness to General Zia and the Pakistanis' involvement in running the show at Sharjah. My father assured me that he would have a word with the Pakistani President. When they were together in Jaipur, Papaji mentioned the confusion at Sharjah and the prospect of his son being compromised. General Zia promised to look into the matter and the topic concluded with a smile. After a few weeks, the news of General Zia's death in an air crash disturbed me, but another piece of news brought relief. I received a letter from CBFS confirming my seniority. Up to this day, I don't know whether it was General Zia who paved the way for me or if CBFS simply followed the procedure.

The desert tournament continued to attract Bollywood personalities and a large crowd at the stadium, especially during India—Pakistan matches. However, when unwanted elements got involved and the match results baffled the best of brains, India decided to ignore this tournament. Without India, viewership fell and the sponsors moved away. What began as a 'desert carnival' died an unnatural death. However, before the curtain fell, CBFS had started an unparalleled trend in the cricketing world to honour former and current international cricketers with a heavy purse. This was a period when cricket boards paid a pittance to cricketers. This gesture undoubtedly helped many international players, especially those of us from the Indian subcontinent!

19

BUNCH OF JOKERS

THE 1988 SHARJAH CUP WAS SPECIAL FOR THE AMARNATH family; the organizers decided to honour my father and me as beneficiaries. The international cricket calendar was packed with limited-overs tournaments at Sharjah in April, the Asia Cup in Bangladesh in October, followed by a home series against New Zealand. With Lady Luck smiling down on me at Sharjah, I scored a century, followed by another half-century against New Zealand. India won the tri-nation cup in a close encounter.

The Asia Cup in Bangladesh was expected to be tougher competition with Sri Lanka and Pakistan as opponents. Dilip Vengsarkar returned to lead the team. India won the opening match against Bangladesh comfortably. However, the next encounter did not bring us joy. Sri Lanka proved to be a tough nut to crack; India lost the match in a tight contest. I remember this game not for our defeat but for the captain's tirade from the dressing room balcony against the batsmen occupying the crease. It left everyone aghast!

Despite the loss, the morale of the team was high. The rivalry against Pakistan brought out the best in me. Fortunately, everyone jelled with each other. Determination and enthusiasm were the key factors in our solid performance. Being the senior-most player, I remember offering advice to the captain on more than one occasion. Though the target set by Pakistan for us was modest, the conditions favoured bowlers, which tested our experience and skills. I guided India to a comfortable victory with an undefeated 74, enabling us to find a place in the finals against Sri Lanka. Ultimately, India won the Asia Cup.

Immediately after the final, Dilip and I got busy discussing New Zealand's forthcoming tour of India. I suggested that Navjot Singh Sidhu open the innings with Srikkanth; Dilip wanted me to bat onedown while he was comfortable at number four.

I went to Bombay to complete the shoot of a cricket coaching video I was producing. To focus on my cricket, I opted to train at Wankhede Stadium with a bit of knocking. On the second day, a journalist approached me and asked about the Indian team selection. I ignored both the question and the person. Nevertheless, the journalist revealed that there were two changes from the Asia Cup squad, though I was expecting one of the two keepers to be excluded. He dropped a bombshell naming Chandrakant Pandit and me as the two players omitted for the Bangalore Test match. Shocked as I was, I continued with my training without any expression or emotion. However, deep down, there was a hollow feeling. Not sure whether to believe him, I wondered why anyone would play such a cruel joke. I looked around for the truth. At that moment, I spotted Polly Umrigar; his body language and expressions confirmed my worst fear.

I went to the dressing room and sat down all by myself. The bubble burst and my emotions flowed without restraint. For the first time in nineteen years of international cricket, my eyes were moist but the pain was gone. And, at that moment, I told myself that I had enough of this nonsense (dropped for the twelfth time) and would take it no more. I decided to expose the antagonists in the way my legendary father, Lala Amarnath, would have done. After all, I was a chip off the old block. I could no longer continue to be a whipping horse; I had to become the master of my fate.

Support and sympathy poured out for me from all corners of the country. Many former Test players were equally surprised. The former national selector and Test cricketer Pankaj Roy said, 'An injustice has been done to Mohinder. I was very surprised to find his name missing from the squad. He is a very competent player.' Gavaskar's words were similar: 'Another injustice has been done to him.' The former Test cricketer from the South Zone C.R. Rangachari said, 'Absolutely unwarranted; a cricketer of such calibre should not have been kept out of the series.'

My wife and daughter were in England, and my parents in Delhi; I felt lonely. To make my next move, I had to think quickly. The next morning, I left my bed rather reluctantly to train, not as a compulsion but as a routine to remain fit and healthy. Thereafter, I hardly stepped out of my room at the Cricket Club of India, hoping this news had not travelled to England. But of course, it had. Bickoo called me with moral support to raise my spirits. She also shared my anguish. I called Papaji in Delhi to share my feelings and sought his guidance. He listened carefully, and endorsed my action of drawing a line and taking the antagonists head-on. Whatever little doubt remained vanished with his wholehearted support and one simple sentence: 'I am with you.' That was enough to give me immense strength! However, journalists known to me advised me against this approach. They felt that the establishment was too strong and would harm my career. However, their suggestion did not deter me and I flew to Bangalore on the eve of the first Test match.

The Indian team was staying at Taj West End; hence the presence of the media. It was a perfect place to express my feelings. The moment I entered the lobby, I saw the chairman of the selection committee conversing with two seasoned journalists, Dicky Rutnagur and Kishore Bhimani. My presence startled him. However, I held back my feelings and remained courteous; I exchanged greetings with the three gentlemen. I met another journalist, Debashish Datta from Calcutta; I told him about the purpose of my visit, which excited him. I told Debashish to assemble the media personnel because I wished to express my disappointment at the shabby treatment inflicted on me. The news spread like wildfire amongst the journalists and they reached the designated room for a much-awaited press conference.

I did not waste any time and said, 'I have undergone disappointments in my career, but this one takes the cake. Time has come to set the record straight and speak my mind. The present set of selectors are unfit for this job. They are a BUNCH OF JOKERS!' The journalists were taken aback by my vehemence and many jaws dropped. Here was a new Jimmy Amarnath they had never known; I responded to every query and questioned the selectors' fairness by choosing a player who had not performed in Sharjah and played no role in the Asia Cup, and another player a few years younger than me. 'If age was a criterion, only one fitted; if it was performance, the board secretary needs a refresher's course in cricket.'

I continued, 'In the past too, when the media enquired about my exclusion, the "wise men" fumbled with words and gave conflicting statements. Sometimes it was my present form, other times, the past. Sometimes, I was good only for one-day matches and, next time, suited for Test matches. I do not think they could make up their minds; they seemed confused. Also, the family surname I proudly carry played its part; the caliphs who ran Indian cricket were still allergic to it. My father's reputation and remarks continue to rattle and rankle with them.' The reporters jotted down every word and rushed back to the office to print the news. That night, I slept peacefully.

'The selectors clearly did not anticipate a ruckus. Our cricketers are not fabled for their derring-do off the pitch: they tend to spurn confrontation with the board and usually meekly accept its diktat. The criticism in the press would die down quickly, the panjandrums felt. Mohinder's fire and brimstone at Bangalore queered their pitch. The all-rounder has been a portrait of reticence in public, never flying off the handle, even though he has been dropped more times than people can remember. Attacking the selectors as a "pack of jokers", he went on to expose the games selectors often play ...' *The Illustrated Weekly of India.*

The next morning changed my entire life. Every newspaper carried the story. My phone rang continuously; the media and my friends showed sympathy and congratulated me for the courageous interview. I wanted to fly to Delhi in the morning but could only manage to get a seat for the evening flight; I decided to watch the Test match. The moment I entered the lobby of the hotel, all heads turned towards me; people smiled and waved, others took autographs.

When I reached Chinnaswamy Stadium, the response from the crowd was no less effusive. They clapped and raised newspapers in the air to show solidarity with me. I received a similar reception from spectators in the pavilion area too. However, the selectors were upset with my description; they maintained a safe distance. Ignoring them, I walked into the Indian dressing room; no one stopped me. All the players remained courteous and sympathized with me till one comment, 'Tumney bahut jaldi kar di (You've been hasty,)' surprised me.

By late afternoon, conflicting versions of team selection emerged. One selector met me and blamed the chairman for the mess. He gave a classic example of a player's selection because he happened to play 'county cricket in England'. The North Zone selector confided in me that he insisted on my name but did not get the requisite support. The captain endorsed it and added that he too wanted the same. However, in private, the North Zone selector blamed the captain while another selector blamed the North Zone selector. The media pressure and public outcry had its effect on the selectors. To broker peace, one of the officials of the host association arranged a meeting with the BCCI president, B.N. Dutt, who was watching the Test match. The meeting was brief and cordial; it failed to break the ice.

I had already tasted adulation after the famous victory in Trinidad in 1976 and the World Cup reception in Bombay in 1983; however, when I entered Bangalore airport, I was no less than a superstar! The kind of attention I received during the check-in process, aboard the flight and at Delhi airport stumped me. At that moment, I had a flashback of another prophecy of the astrologer Ramesh Chandra. He had predicted that I would become more famous with my words than with my bat!

I was received at the airport by my younger brother, Johnny, and he narrated Papaji's reaction to my comments. He said the entire media in Delhi had called him for a comment but he gave the honour to (late) Jagan Nath Rao from PTI because he was treated like a member of the family. He addressed Papaji as 'Skipper'. He asked, 'Skipper, what is your reaction to Jimmy's "bunch of jokers" remarks?' Papaji burst out laughing and said, 'You've come here for this?'

Rao sheepishly said, 'No and yes!' Papaji paused and smiled. 'Why limit the label to the selectors? The entire BCCI is a pack of jokers!' Rao jumped in excitement; he got more than he expected, contacted the PTI office at Parliament Street and asked his junior to prepare a caption: 'Lala calls the BCCI a Pack of Jokers'. When I heard that, I shouted, 'Chuk de phattey (Bowled them)!' I stayed with my parents for a few days, happy and secure like a little baby!

Before I bid goodbye to my parents, Papaji confided in me an incident pertaining to the chairman of the selection committee. 'Mushtaq Ali and I frequently played for Rajputana XI in the 1930s; we knew the royal family of Dungarpur quite well. After retirement, the Indore batsman frequented Dungarpur state and was impressed by a prince. This boy was eager to don the Indian cap but was not getting the opportunity because of stiff competition from Ramakant Desai, Surendra Nath, and a few other bowlers. Mushtaq told the Royal Highness that only Lala Amarnath could help the prince achieve his ultimate dream. Accordingly, they contacted me, but I expressed my inability because I was no longer the chairman of the selection committee. After a few days, Mushtaq called me and requested me to make a "statement" that the prince was an emerging fast bowler and good enough to play for India. I told Mushtaq that the prince was flat-footed and no fast bowler; I could not give a wrong statement. Then I asked Mushtaq, "Why don't you give a statement?" He did not answer! The prince never played for India.'

I flew to Bombay for an interview with Sandeep Patil for a Marathi magazine and *Illustrated Weekly of India*. I also played a charity match at the CCI. My interview made a deep impression on readers, raising questions about the integrity of the selectors. Since I was in town, I decided to watch the Test match at the Wankhede Stadium and feel the pulse of the public. The reaction towards the selectors was quite intense. *The Afternoon Despatch & Courier,* a local Bombay newspaper, published an article with a photograph of the five selectors captioned: 'All the Jokers!'

The loss of the second Test match at Wankhede caused a headache for the selectors. There was public outcry to bring me back. However, I was convinced that my chances to play for India were now remote. But the North Zone selector contacted me in Baroda to discuss my return to the Indian team for the ODI series. Was it because the selectors were reassessing their decision or because they were feeling guilty? I was not sure. I agreed to meet him as a friend and not as a selector. Nevertheless, the condition for my return was attached with an apology to the selectors, which I declined to consider. Since I was not part of the Indian team, I undertook an assignment with a leading newspaper to cover the ODI match at Indore; I ran into the same selector there. He divulged the support of two more selectors to strengthen my case but repeated the condition for my return: an apology. I declined the offer again.

Distraught by my attitude and the adverse publicity, the BCCI waited for the series against New Zealand to conclude.

I received a show cause notice from the BCCI within twenty-four hours of the New Zealand team leaving India, which did not surprise me. My father had fought a legal battle with the BCCI president Anthony de Mello in 1949 when he was banned from playing any class of cricket in India. My father sued the BCCI president for Rs 1 lakh and threatened other BCCI members with similar charges; this action split the cricket board vertically into two camps. A compromise was reached—he was exonerated of all the charges and played for India again. Subsequently, he led India against Pakistan in 1952; he won the series for his team and retired. Later, he became chairman of the selection committee till 1960.

I remember Papaji telling me about this case and how the secretary of the Cricket Association of Bengal, Pankaj Gupta, and other associations rallied around him, and Niren Dey, who later became Bengal's attorney general, managed his case. I was neither captain of India nor an icon like my father, and I did not have the support of any association. What I needed was the support of a good lawyer to fight my case. Lost in my thoughts, I went to the CCI lounge and ordered tea. Here, I watched kids playing tennis-ball cricket on the lawns. Some of these kids saw me and asked if I could join them too. The invitation thrilled me; I indulged them like a little boy, forgetting my crisis.

However, my attention was drawn to the tea I had ordered. Before I could taste it, two boys came, and introduced themselves as Sharan and Shom Jagtiani. They asked if I could visit their residence for tea. These boys stayed at the CCI Chambers across the club. I agreed to visit them the following evening and kept my promise. When I rang the doorbell, I was greeted by them and introduced to their father, Haresh Jagtiani, and the rest of the family. We chatted for a while and had tea. Haresh gave me his visiting card; I simply put it in my pocket and left.

After two days, I looked at the visiting card. It turned out that Haresh Jagtiani was a well-known and respected attorney in Bombay. I called his office and sought an appointment. I was later surprised to receive a call from his office confirming the time for the meeting. At his office, I showed him the BCCI show cause notice. Haresh was aghast to read the contents of the notice; the language was uncouth! Like a seasoned attorney, he read my contract with the BCCI. He said, 'It is a one-sided contract; it would not stand in a court of law, even for a moment.' He also added that this was a 'contingent contract', meaning the terms were applicable only if I was playing for India. Since I hadn't been selected for the Indian team, I was not bound by the contract! Having put my mind at ease, I asked Haresh about his fee. I knew lawyers in Bombay could be terribly expensive. He laughed, held my hand firmly and said, 'Nothing, Jimmy. It would be an honour. Anything for you!'

Haresh drafted my response to the charges and posted the letter to the BCCI office. Since I was leaving for England, I gave power of attorney to Haresh and simultaneously informed the BCCI to contact my attorney for any query, correspondence or future meetings. The BCCI did not respond; they appointed a disciplinary committee consisting of Madhavrao Scindia (the railways minister), Ghulam Ahmed (of the Hyderabad Cricket Association) and Abbas Ali Baig (a former cricketer) to settle my case. This news was flashed across India.

On my return to India from England, I received a request to play a charity match at Eden Gardens, the home turf of the BCCI president B.N. Dutt. On reaching the hotel, I received an urgent message from a journalist suggesting a meeting with Mr Dutt. Was it a back-door parley to close the chapter or a ploy to assess my attitude? I declined the offer.

After a few days, I received a letter from the BCCI to appear before the disciplinary committee on 29 January 1989 at Taj Palace, New Delhi. There was a rider that my attorney would not be permitted to attend the meeting. I wrote back that, without him, I would not be in attendance either. I received no response. I presumed they had acceded to my request.

I booked a room at the Taj Palace for Haresh and stayed at home with my family. My father was confident that the committee simply wanted an apology and no more. He insisted, 'Never apologize to these people', which strengthened my resolve. Before I reached the hotel, I received a note from Sunil Gavaskar wishing me all the best. He told me about his own experience and insisted I should be accompanied by someone dependable, or the BCCI would push me against the wall. I was quite touched by this gesture.

My father accompanied me to Taj Palace, which gave me additional strength. I had a last-minute briefing from Haresh. I asked him to wait in the room for my call before joining the meeting. The lobby was packed with mediapersons, and the sight of Papaji thrilled everyone. The news of Papaji's presence must have filtered into the committee room too. The moment I entered the room, Ghulam Ahmed told the rest of the members that he wished to speak to me in private. The former cricketer owed his international career to Papaji. He put his hand on my shoulder and gently said, 'Why are you so obstinate like your father?' The reference pleased me, but I kept quiet. I had known Ghulam uncle since my childhood and respected him. He said, 'The BCCI simply wants an apology and the matter will be closed.' I smiled and said, 'No apology, sir', which took him by surprise. I added, 'Since the BCCI has sent me a legal notice, I want to be accompanied by my attorney while facing the disciplinary committee.'

The battle line was clearly drawn. The committee members were nervous; they refused to entertain my request and we were in a deadlock. To give them comfort, I volunteered to answer all their questions—provided Haresh stayed in the room for moral and legal support. He would be consulted if there was any doubt about legal implications. The response from the BCCI remained negative and uncompromising. At this stage, I remembered Gavaskar's experience. How true was his observation! They were evaluating my patience and simultaneously pushing me to the wall, which kept us in a stalemate. After half an hour or so, I got up and wished everyone a good day, and left the meeting.

I went straight to Papaji, who was enthralling journalists with his anecdotes. They asked me about the meeting, but I preferred to stay quiet till the verdict was announced. I went to Haresh's room; he was surprised to see me because he was waiting for my phone call. I narrated the entire story to him. We went down and joined Papaji in the coffee shop. Like the members of the media, we were also waiting for the disciplinary committee's decision.

The BCCI imposed a penalty of Rs 20,000 for my 'bunch of jokers' remark. My first reaction was, 'There's no way I'm going to pay that.' I asked Haresh to respond to the media's questions.

The verdict did not stop me from ardently desiring to play for India, which left the selection committee exasperated. My friends, cricketers and journalists, were sure I would be selected for the West Indies tour, but not me. I was sceptical about a certain gentleman on the selection committee and his record. His ego was badly bruised and I knew he wanted to avenge himself by denying me another opportunity to play for India. When the team was announced, as expected, I did not figure in it.

However, I went to the West Indies in a different capacity. My absence from the Indian team presented an alternative platform to stay connected with the game I loved most. Before the tour, a private company had signed an agreement with the national television channel of India to provide match highlights of the series. This company approached me to cover the series as a commentator and journalist. This was a new experience and I thoroughly enjoyed it. True to my expectation, the Indian batting struggled against the West Indian pace battery and India ultimately lost the series.

The BCCI had always been tight-fisted with their remuneration to the Indian players, be it the Test matches or limited-overs games, forcing players to look for greener pastures and earn extra money. The large Indian diaspora in the USA travelled to the Caribbean islands to watch Indian cricketers, and they approached a former Indian star to entertain them with good cricket in the USA. In return, they offered lucrative terms. Accordingly, a few exhibition matches were arranged between India and Pakistan in the United States after the West Indies tour.

As a protocol, the Indian team approached the BCCI and sought permission to play these matches. However, some officials felt threatened by the players' action, bypassing them and taking unilateral decisions. Much to the dismay of the players, the response was contrary to their expectations. The BCCI refused to entertain the request and demanded all the players to report back to India.

However, the players stood their ground, thanks to the lucrative terms offered by the US promoters. The players felt they had fulfilled their commitments in the contract and so were free to do as they wished. The attitude and unity in the Indian camp startled the BCCI. Still, a select few played it safe and consulted legal luminaries. Once they were assured that they were not in breach of contract, everyone became complacent. They believed that the BCCI would initially throw tantrums and would eventually, after letting off steam, take a lenient view. So they went ahead with the 'cricket circus' in the USA. Unfortunately, they were in for a rude shock. The BCCI called an emergency meeting and banned players from representing India or playing domestic cricket.

The banned players sought refuge in the Supreme Court and filed a petition against the ban by the BCCI. After the top court's intervention, a Hearing Committee was formed to look into the matter, giving them a temporary reprieve. The committee met players before the 1989 domestic season at Wankhede Stadium in Bombay. All the banned players were heard individually and several conflicting versions emerged from their reports. One board official claimed that certain 'senior players' begged them for relief while the juniors blamed the seniors for their action. However, after a reprieve from the Supreme Court, the BCCI did not wish to get embroiled in the legal net.

Although I was part of the event in the USA, my case was listed in the Supreme Court for a reprieve against the disciplinary committee's verdict and payment of fine for calling the selectors a 'Bunch of Jokers'. Having received an admonition in the Supreme Court, the BCCI was in a conciliatory mode; they summoned me to Bombay. The atmosphere and attitude of the panel members came as a pleasant surprise. At the onset of our discussion, Rungta jokingly said, 'Hope we are not in the same category', referring to my now-famous statement! This opening certainly thawed the ice; we exchanged pleasant memories. I was instantly cleared by the panel to play first-class cricket!

20

CONTROVERSY AND COMEBACK 4

I HAD NOT PLAYED SERIOUS CRICKET FOR A YEAR AND DIDN'T have much time to prepare either. However, I did long net sessions at Feroze Shah Kotla and spoke to Papaji about my prospects. 'Go and enjoy the atmosphere at Baradari Gardens, and relive your childhood,' was all he said. Not a single word about cricket relaxed my mind. Kapil was appointed captain of North Zone for the Duleep Trophy, but he opted out due to personal reasons and I took over the reins. I scored an unbeaten 149 against the East Zone to get back into the reckoning for the forthcoming Sharjah Cup.

To qualify for the Sharjah Cup, Deodhar Trophy matches became more important for all the players. Kapil returned to lead the team, despite a recurring knee injury. He bowled from a shortened run-up, which raised many eyebrows. The chairman of the North Zone, a seasoned former cricketer, noticed it too. The highlight of the North Zone innings was a century by Raman Lamba, while I remained undefeated at 38 and outplayed West Zone in the semi-finals. The final match was slated for Delhi. I now had another opportunity to prove my worth. I was determined to perform in front of the ever-loving Delhi fans and well-wishers. I prayed to the Almighty to provide me the strength to perform on this critical occasion. My mantra changed to 'courage is destiny', which convinced me to adopt a different approach.

The Indian cricket board had long been a cauldron of conspiracies that sprung surprises at different levels—beginning with districts to state and then to zones, till it reached the national level. Ever since its formation, politics remained an integral part of its operations. At times, quite a few officials indulged in all sorts of machinations to feed their egos. A day before the finals, the North Zone selector called me aside and told me to lead the team. Though each word was music to my ears, I was also quite shocked. According to him, the captain was unfit and he did not wish to carry a liability on the field. However, my conscience would not support this plan. I felt it should have been discussed with the player but it was not. I politely declined the offer. I had always played fair and this opportunity felt like nothing short of stabbing a colleague in the back. Was it wise to affront a selector who had offered me a golden opportunity? I couldn't be sure.

With my conscience clear, and the tremendous support of press and local fans at my disposal, I looked forward to the crucial contest. Would it add another feather to my cap or lead me down a dark alley? My biggest foe was not the South Zone but someone in the VIP box watching the proceedings. The Indian team for the Sharjah Cup was to be announced after this match, and I wanted to perform exceedingly well and leave little scope for any discussion regarding my inclusion in the national XI.

As I walked down the famous Feroz Shah Kotla steps, I received a roaring reception from the large Delhi crowd supporting my cause. The roar seemed to come from the core of their hearts and it gave me additional strength. The gesture, their faith in my abilities, boosted my confidence in accepting the challenge. The lethal concoction of confidence and encouragement fuelled me to launch an immediate attack.

This new approach caught the South Zone bowlers on the wrong foot and delighted the large gathering at the ground. They applauded every stroke and simultaneously turned their heads in the direction of the VIP box, located on the first floor of the old pavilion, which accommodated the chairman and the selectors. The slapstick comments and thumbs-down signs kept the large crowd entertained. Later, local officials conveyed that an important member of the selection committee seemed nervous with the behaviour of the large crowd and my display on the field. While the supporters enjoyed the spectacle, he was uncomfortable. The haggling by the vociferous crowd was much like the reception he had received in Bombay or wherever he watched the first-class matches.

I took a calculated risk in hitting boundaries and sixes to apply pressure on the selectors. I contributed 90 runs to North Zone's total score, which turned out to be enough for a victory. While the selectors stayed in a huddle to finalize the team, a large crowd gathered outside the pavilion awaiting my fate. I received the news in the dressing room: I was part of the team for Sharjah! The relief and joy I felt were beyond words. My selection had proved that nothing was impossible, provided one worked hard and with sincerity. God helps those who help themselves.

After hearing the good news, my teammates congratulated me and extended their best wishes. At that moment, I noticed an unexpected person: the chairman of the selection committee! He congratulated me with a warm handshake. The gesture took me by surprise, but pleased me, nevertheless. I wondered how many times more I would have to prove my credentials. I deserved better treatment than being brazenly discarded. I had been dropped against New Zealand, despite a decent performance in the Asia Cup in Bangladesh. That was the last straw to test my patience and I could not hold back my frustration. My outburst against the system and the pervasive injustice of it found widespread support across the country. Now, destiny and luck had joined hands to support me in my mission.

During this critical match, news of Papaji's illness and admission at Willingdon (Dr Ram Manohar Lohia) Hospital disturbed me considerably. I knew he was a fighter to the core and would not abandon me. Without celebrating my inclusion in the team, I rushed to the hospital to seek his blessings! Touching his feet always brought me immense pleasure and happiness; it was no different this time too. Delighted with my performance, he smiled and said, 'God bless you, my son. May the Almighty provide you with more strength and unlimited fame.' These words lifted my spirits even higher. How lucky and blessed I was to have him around! I thanked God for giving me shelter under such parents. They remained beacons of hope even in extreme situations; they always stood by me and showed me the right path.

Although I was happy with my comeback, it felt as though the sword of Damocles was hanging precariously over my head. Any lapse in performance was a good excuse for the selectors to strike me down. I had a reasonable start against the West Indies, which I could not convert into a big score. However, against Pakistan, my form returned, and I scored 85 runs. I always fancied my chances against them, possibly being a Punjabi myself. I could relate to them and understand their psyche better than most Indian players. I remember an incident when Aaqib Javed bowled a bouncer to me and I dispatched it over the boundary. Annoyed, Imran chided the bowler in Punjabi, 'Kinoo bouncer pa raya hai (Who are you testing with a bouncer)?' and promptly removed him from the attack. As luck would have it, I fared well in the tournament.

Immediately on return, we played the Nehru Cup sponsored by MRF. This tournament was hurriedly organized to be part of the birth centenary celebrations of India's first Prime Minister, Jawaharlal Nehru. I thought this tournament was extremely taxing for all the players. The tight schedule and constant travelling left us exhausted. We were hit hard since we lacked sufficient rest before and during the tournament. The worst experience came before the crucial game against Pakistan at Eden Gardens. It exposed the professional capabilities of the BCCI.

Due to a lack of floodlights, we played day matches. So the possibility of taking an evening flight became remote. After winning a tight match against Australia at Chinnaswamy Stadium, we boarded the late-night flight for Calcutta. We reached the city in the early hours of the morning to play another important match. Tired as we were after a long flight from southern India to the eastern part of the country, we barely managed a wink of sleep. From the airport, we drove to the hotel for a brief but much needed rest. Before we could catch up on precious sleep, it was time to proceed to the venue. Our limbs were tired and our swollen eyes could barely open; we looked like zombies at the Eden Gardens. It did not surprise me that we lost the game to our arch-rival Pakistan.

Despite the loss, India qualified to play the semi-finals against the West Indies in Bombay. The bus ride from the airport to Taj Mahal Hotel consumed precious time discussing the payment pattern for players. The senior players were disappointed with the BCCI for not recognizing their contribution to Indian cricket. They felt that players should get decent emoluments for representing India, maybe by sharing the profits—sort of like an understanding between the BCCI and the state associations. Failing that, it could be like the emoluments received by international cricketers from other countries; Indian cricketers received a pittance for ODIs and Tests. The discussion concluded with an understanding that players needed to put their demands across to the BCCI for a better pay structure. In case they declined, the current team would boycott the Pakistan tour. Although Dilip Vengsarkar had opted out of the Pakistan tour due to personal reasons, he remained part of the discussion with Kapil Dev, Ravi Shastri, Mohammad Azharuddin, Srikkanth and me.

A night before the semi-finals against the West Indies, we assembled for a team meeting in manager Chandu Borde's room in the old wing of the Taj Mahal Hotel. The manager happened to be a former captain of India and former chairman of the selectors; he was a decent person and one of my childhood heroes. The topic, for a change, was not the semi-final next day but our demand for better emoluments for the forthcoming Pakistan tour. How could we approach the BCCI? The manager was flummoxed by this discussion. After a brief pause, Kapil recommended my name to represent the 'players' association', which caught me off guard. I did not wish to be projected a villain in the eyes of the board for demanding a piece of their pie. I made it clear that if at all I was to accept the responsibility, any decision following my discussion with the BCCI officials would be binding on all. Everyone nodded their heads and, in a chorus, endorsed my concerns. However, all the nitty-gritty for the Calcutta meeting had to be resolved by the president with the secretary (the secretary was not available at the Bombay meeting) before I reached Calcutta. Before parting, I repeated the condition under which I would undertake the responsibility. Everyone gave me their assurance and promised to stick by my decision.

There seemed to be little or no focus on the immediate contest against the West Indies. However, before everyone split, a few minutes were dedicated to the next day's match. This attitude left individual players to work out their respective strategies. This approach failed to bring the requisite result and India ended up losing a crucial match to the West Indies.

Free from all responsibilities, the like-minded players concentrated on the cricketers' association. The purpose was to create better understanding between the BCCI and the cricketers. Accordingly, a PoA (Power of Attorney) was prepared on behalf of the Association of Indian Cricketers and signed by the president, Kapil Dev, and vice-president, Dilip Vengsarkar, nominating me to represent them.

The BCCI representatives (the states' associations) had assembled for the annual general meeting (AGM) in Calcutta. The agenda included the forthcoming Pakistan tour. I made arrangements at my own expense to travel to Calcutta and meet the BCCI officials. However, Bickoo did not approve of me representing the other players. There were several reasons for her reservations. My family had come for a short holiday from England and wished to spend time together, away from cricket politics. I was in a hopeless situation; I had given my word, therefore, I stood by it. I took the first available flight to Calcutta carrying the trust and faith of my colleagues. According to a prior understanding, the secretary of the players' association was to receive me at Dum Dum Airport in Calcutta and join me for the meeting. Right through the flight, I kept thinking about the approach and presentation to the BCCI. The prospect of doing something worthy for the cricket fraternity excited me.

However, I received the first shock at Dum Dum. Although the secretary met me at the airport, he also conveyed that he was taking a flight to Dhaka to play a match, which rather surprised me. Did he develop cold feet? I was left with two choices—return to Bombay abandoning the project or move forward.

I decided on the latter and took a cab to Eden Gardens where the AGM was underway. A message was conveyed to Jagmohan Dalmiya, and he immediately left the important meeting and greeted me. He enquired about the purpose of my visit, leaving me speechless. The president of the players' association was expected to convey the agenda of the meeting to the BCCI officials. Dalmiya feigned ignorance about any such correspondence; he, nevertheless, invited me in for a cup of tea.

P.R. Man Singh, the manager of the 1983 World Cup winning team, was also present, probably representing the Hyderabad Cricket Association; he also enquired about the reason for my presence. I explained everything and, like true gentlemen, they ushered me into the hall where the rest of the BCCI members had assembled. Everyone gave me a patient hearing and promised to discuss our demands. However, one board member questioned the existence of the players' association and its relevance. After an hour or so, I thanked them and left for the airport, hoping they would consider the request. The BCCI refused to budge or approve any of the proposals, including the issue of better emoluments for senior players. They decided to continue with the old-fashioned system, where emoluments of the debutants were pretty much the same as those for the seniors.

When news of the BCCI decision reached me, I held a press conference on behalf of the players' association in Bombay. It was conveyed in no uncertain terms that if our demands were not accepted, the players may opt out of the Pakistan tour. This was just a ruse to exert pressure on the BCCI. We knew the importance of the tour, and hoped the board would be sympathetic towards our grievances and provide financial security to the players. Having stuck my neck out for a good cause, I became a target and was promptly dropped from the team for the Pakistan tour. The reason given was a new roadmap for Indian cricket, where seniors had to make way for newcomers. While the others escaped the wrath of the board, I was made the scapegoat for standing up and demanding a better pay packet for the team.

When the media grilled the chairman of the selectors about my exclusion, he was quick to comment on my performance in the Nehru Cup. The statement did not disappoint me as it was bound to happen sooner than later after my famous 'Bunch of Jokers' quote and my visit to Calcutta. It was a foregone conclusion: there existed two sets of rules, one for me and another for the rest. If the Indian team was selected purely on performance in the Nehru Cup, half the team needed to be replaced! However, the inclusion of one name in the team made me very happy indeed. A young boy from Bombay was part of the team for the Pakistan tour. I had watched him bat briefly during the Deodhar Trophy match against us (North Zone) in Jalandhar and I'd also witnessed him in action several times in the nets at the CCI. The boy's name was Sachin Tendulkar.

After announcing the team for the Pakistan tour, the BCCI was not sure of the players' reaction. The mistrust led to the assumption that players could still boycott the tour at the last moment. To avoid an unpleasant situation, the BCCI summoned a former Test cricketer to Delhi and sought his advice to select an alternate team for Pakistan. This news, in all probability, was leaked to test the nerves of the players. It undoubtedly set off alarm bells and put pressure on the players in the squad. In addition, the BCCI set a deadline for players to sign the contract; failing that, they would be unceremoniously dropped from the team for the Pakistan tour.

Since the Indian team had assembled in Delhi and I happened to be in Bombay, I expected the players to adhere to the unanimous decision of the Bombay meeting and refrain from signing the contract till we met. I booked the first available flight but poor weather in Delhi delayed the take-off from Bombay. I tried to contact the president of the players' association from the airport booth to convey the delay. Unfortunately, I failed in my attempts. This was a period when mobile phones did not exist and I was at the mercy of the telephone exchange. After several attempts, I managed to get through but the person in question was not available. However, I did finally get in touch with another senior player of the team at the Taj Palace Hotel in Delhi, and informed him to notify the players and also withhold the process of signing the contract till I reached Delhi. My flight was unfortunately delayed further and I reached Delhi only in the afternoon.

On my arrival at the hotel, I met the Indian captain in his room. I was shocked to hear that except for him (Srikkanth), Navjot Singh Sidhu and (the late) Raman Lamba, all other players had signed the contract provided by the BCCI some time the previous evening or that morning. Later, Raman Lamba told me that all the players apart from the three of us seemed petrified of the board's diktat. I could understand the anxiety of the newly capped players—Sachin Tendulkar, Vivek Razdan and Salil Ankola—but was dismayed to hear that even senior players had buckled under the pressure!

That evening, the entire team assembled in the captain's room. I asked everyone, especially the seniors, a simple question: 'Why didn't you wait for me?' No one had any answer and there was complete silence in the room. How I repented not listening to Papaji's advice since I started playing top-grade cricket. He had cautioned me numerous times not to trust people who made promises. My father had learned a bitter lesson during his tour of England in 1936, and how true his observation was! I was so naïve to have neglected his advice. I kept telling myself that times and people had changed for the better; well, nothing had changed.

This episode left me rather disillusioned, but I did admire the character of certain players. Undoubtedly, Srikkanth, Navjot Singh Sidhu and Raman Lamba exemplified strength of character and withstood the pressure of the cricket board. At the same time, I felt sorry for them because they were now marked players. Later, a decision was reached that the seniors would not accept tour emoluments and would continue exerting pressure on the BCCI. As for the newcomers, they would adhere to the contract in totality. Despite strong undercurrents of distrust, the tour progressed as planned.

Pakistan had long been the graveyard for Indian captains and spinners. However, the Indian team under Srikkanth emulated the 1954 team to draw the series. Unimpressed, the selection committee replaced him as captain for the New Zealand tour. To rub salt on his wounds, he was dropped from the squad altogether. The 'Sunday Club' remark came flashing back, as did the famous quote, 'Elephants never forget!' The next in line was Raman Lamba, who also met the same dismal fate. Only Navjot Singh Sidhu managed to retain his place after having put together a few fine batting performances on the tour.

The change of guard and the unceremonious exit of some players shook the confidence of the Indian players. No one wanted to join the jinxed platform. The much-touted players' association was like a monument perennially under construction, which collapsed and died an unnatural death!

At that moment, I realized that the time had come to take a hard decision. After pondering over it for a while, I took a call to say goodbye to cricket. It had been a long journey starting with fun matches against my brothers, Tom and John, at home and then taking me around the world, including to the Mecca of Cricket at Lord's. There were joys to cherish and heartbreaks to forget. I knew I would miss the buzz of the ground, the atmosphere in the dressing room and the banter of my teammates. These sweet memories would, nevertheless, stay with me till eternity.

But all my achievements would be incomplete without thanking Bharat, my motherland!

ACKNOWLEDGEMENTS

MANY HANDS AND MINDS WERE PUT TOGETHER TO SHAPE this book. The list is long and unending. However, I would like to especially thank *The Hindu* for digging into their archives and sharing the pictures of various memorable tours with me.

Additionally, my appreciation to Srenik Sett and late Amiya Tarafdar for sharing memorable pictures too.

Last but not the least, my sister-in-law Kamaljit Kahlon and brother-in-law Gurinder Kahlon for their valuable contribution in the different stages of the book.

SPECIAL PORTRAIT

MOHINDER AMARNATH BHARADWAJ: RIGHT-HAND batsman and right-arm medium pace bowler, son of Lala Amarnath and younger brother of Surinder Amarnath and elder brother of Ranji player Rajender Amarnath of Punjab and Delhi, was born on 24 September 1950 in Patiala in Punjab.

TOURS

England	in 1967	with Indian Schoolboys
	1975	for One-day Internationals (World Cup)
	1979	for World Cup & Test Series
	1983	for One-day Internationals (World Cup)
	1986	for Test Series & One-day Internationals
New Zealand	in 1975-76	for Test Series
West Indies	in 1975-76	for Test Series
	1982-83	for Test Series & One-day Internationals

Australia	in 1967-68	(with Indian Schoolboys)
	1977-78	for Test Series
	1985	for World Series
	1986	for Test Series & Triangular One-day Internationals
Pakistan	in 1978-79	for Test Series and One-day Internationals
	1982-83	for Test Series and One-day Internationals
	1984-85	for Test Series and One-day Internationals
Sri Lanka	in 1970-71	(with Indian Universities)
	1985-86	for Test Series and One-day Internationals
Sharjah	in 1985	for One-day Internationals
	1988	for One-day Internationals

AMARNATH'S CENTURIES (31) TESTS (11)

100	2nd Test v Australia at Perth, 1977-78
101*	6th Test v West Indies at Kanpur, 1978-79
109*	1st Test v Pakistan at Lahore, 1982-83
120	5th Test v Pakistan at Lahore, 1982-83
103*	6th Test v Pakistan at Karachi, 1982-83
117	2nd Test v West Indies at Port of Spain, 1982-83
116	5th Test v West Indies at St. John's, 1982-83
101*	1st Test v Pakistan at Lahore, 1984-85
116*	2nd Test v Sri Lanka at Kandy, 1985-86
138	3rd Test v Australia at Sydney, 1985-86
131	2nd Test v Sri Lanka at Nagpur, 1986-87

Ranji Trophy (8)

100* for Punjab	v Delhi 1972-73
115* for Punjab	v Services at Jalandhar, 1973-74
162* for Delhi	v Bombay at Bombay, 1978-79
178* for Delhi	v Karnataka at Bangalore, 1978-79
191 for Delhi	v Bombay at Delhi, 1979-80
185 for Delhi	v Karnataka at Delhi, 1981-82 (final)
103 for Delhi	v Bombay at Bombay, 1983-84 (final)
194 for Delhi	v Haryana at Delhi, 1985-86 (final)

Duleep Trophy (3)

207	for North Zone	v West Zone 1982-83
136	for North Zone	v West Zone 1985-86
149*	for North Zone	v East Zone 1988-89

Irani Cup (1)

127	for Delhi	v Rest of India at Delhi, 1982-83

Other First-class Matches (8)

137	against New South Wales at Sydney, I 977-7B
100*	against Punjab XI at Bahawalpur, 1978-79
140*	for North Zone v West Indies at Jalandhar, 1978-79
123	against Derbyshire at Derby, 1979
114	against Trinidad and Tobago at Pointe-A-Pierre, 1982-83
121	against Guyana at Georgetown, 1982-83
101*	against Barbados at Bridgetown, 1982-83

One-Day Internationals

debut-	M	I	NO	T	HS	Ave	100s	Ct	St	Balls	M	R	Ws	Ave	5wt	10wt
v England at Lord's, 7-6-1975 till his last appearance v West Indies at Bombay on 30-10-1989	85	75	12	1924	102*	30.54	2	24	–	2730	15	1972	46	42.87	–	–

Summary

	M	I	NO	T	HS	Ave	100s	Ct	St	Balls	M	R	Ws	Ave	5wt	10wt
Tests – 1969-70 to 1987-88	69	113	10	4378	138	42.49	11	47	–	3676	101	1782	32	55.69	–	–
Unofficial Tests 1975-76	2	4	2	54	33*	27.00	–	1	–	222	11	61	2	30.50	–	–

SPECIAL PORTRAIT

	M	I	NO	Runs	HS	Avg	100	50		Balls	Mdns	Runs	Wkts	Avg	5wi	10wm
Ranji – 1967-68 to 1988-89	76	107	15	4016	194	43.65	8	42	–	8206	353	3231	124	26.05	7	1
Duleep – 1968-69 to 1988-89	31	49	9	1692	207	42.30	3	20	–	2977	114	1367	46	29.71	1	–
Irani – 1970-71 to 1986-87	7	11	2	354	127	39.33	1	3	–	666	18	307	6	51.16	–	–
Moin-ud-Dowla Gold Cup 1966-67 to 1974-75	13	15	5	306	72	30.60	–	6	–	1398	57	571	16	35.68	–	–
Other first-class matches 1969-70 to 1987-88	52	79	18	3049	140	49.98	8	23	–	3719	137	1694	46	36.82	–	–
	250	378	61	13849	207	43.68	11	112	–	20864	791	9013	272	33.33	8	1

Career best knock of 207 was played in the Duleep Trophy match for North Zone against East Zone at Bombay in 1982-83.

Staged a comeback in Test history by scoring 584 runs @ 73.00 in the series against Pakistan in Pakistan (highest by an Indian against Pakistan), followed by 598 runs @ 66.44 in the series against West Indies in West Indies in the 1982-83 season.

Scored 1071 runs in Tests in a calendar year 1983—1065 coming by 3rd May—earliest 1000 runs in the World. Scored 2355 runs @ 81.00 during the 1982-83 season, more than anyone outside England.

Selected 'One of the Five Cricketers' of the Year 1983 by *Wisden* in 1984.

Received Arjuna Award in 1984.

INDEX

Abbasi, Arif Ali, 383
Abbas, Zaheer, 153, 154, 156, 160, 162, 192, 293–94, 295–96, 312, 319
Abu Dhabi, 332–33
ACC, 68–69
accountability, 303
Adelaide, 146–51, 338
Oval, 147
pitch, 338–39
Adhikari, Hemu, 40, 42
aggressive cricket, 41
aggressive strokes, 75, 133
Ahmadiyya community, 173
Ahmed, Ghulam, 413
Ahmed, Tanvir, 372–73
Ahmed, Tauseef, 392, 393
Ahmed, Younis, 388
Air Force Station, 40
Air India 707 aircraft, 40
Ajmeri Gate, 9
Ajmer Sharif, 389
Akram, Wasim, 103, 386, 391, 394

Alam, Intikhab, 153, 312
Alexandra cricket ground, 61
Ali, Abid, 51, 74
Ali, Ashraf, 296
Aligarh Muslim University (AMU), 59
Ali, Hyder, 38
Ali, Imtiaz, 103
Ali, Muhammad, 103
Alleyne, Hartley, 237
All India Radio, 35, 51, 123, 135
Altaf, Saleem, 159
Amarnath, Lala, 3, 337–38
advice, 118–19, 365
as friend, 22
as future star of India, 61
illness and admission at Willingdon, 420
Indian selection committee, chairman of, 6–7
passionate gardener, 21–22
private cricket tour to Pakistan, 11–12

reputation, 134–35
self-made cricketer, 20
'Sunday Club,' 362–63
Amarnath, Mohinder
Australia 1977-78, 121–51
childhood, 1–17
England
1986, 360–73
in India, 301–31
goal, 18–44
New Zealand 1975, 67–86
Pakistan
1978, 152–68
in India 1987, 382–96
tour 1982/83, 189–215
test debut and wilderness, 45–66
tied test match, 374–81
West Indies
1976, 87–120
1983, 216–54
World Cup 1983, 255–84
Amarnath, Surinder, 4, 35, 37, 38, 43, 46, 47, 50–51, 63–64, 68, 69, 78, 79, 116, 123, 124, 154, 160–61, 165, 175
counterattack, 85
at DAV College, Amritsar, 59
debut in Ahmedabad, 74–75
Delhi attack, 33
Guru Nanak University, 59–60
half-century, 123
in Jalandhar, 30
omission from Indian team, 176
as premier batsman, 32
spin attack struggle, 123

stroke of Gavaskar, 81–82
Ambani, Dhirubhai, 383
American 'Sabre Jets,' 65
Amrit Bazar Patrika, 123
Amritsar, 59–66, 92–93, 141, 295
business community, 65–66
'Hall Gate' area, 66
topography, 64–65
Amritsar Dhaba, 32
'Anand Margi,' 124–25, 146
Anglo-Carnatic accent, 317
Ankola, Salil, 426
Ansett Australia Airlines, 137–38
anti-Bombay attitude, 175
Antigua test, 250–54
anti-India slogans, 286
Arlott, John, 43
Arora, C. L., 62–63
Arundel castle cricket Ground, 362
Ashes series of 1932, 114–15
Ashok Leyland bus, 40
Asia Cup in Bangladesh, 403, 420
Asian Games, 152
'Association of Indian Cricketers,' 423
Attari border, 64
attitude, 31, 52–53
Auckland, 77, 81
Aussies, 47–48, 56, 339, 381
Australia Airlines, 19
Australia/Australian, 3, 39, 51, 59, 88, 126, 153, 161, 171, 183, 311–59

Index

1977-78, 121–51
  Adelaide, 146–51
  Melbourne, 137–43
  Perth, 131–37
  Sydney, 143–46
  cricket, 127
  itinerary, 46–47
  language, 127
  shores, 124
  team, 48
  test series 1985-86, 335–47
  tour, 124, 348
  and West Indies at Lords, 255
Australian Cricket Board (ACB), 124–25, 146, 312
Azad, Kirti, 270
Azharuddin, Mohammed, 305, 309, 313–14, 320, 357, 422
Aziz, Khalid, 157

Baig, Abbas Ali, 309
Baig, Idris, 197
Bajwa, Harcharan Singh, 173
Bala, Rajan, 386
banana inswinger, 357–58
Bandu, Dina, 290–92
Bangalore, 71–72, 123, 390
Bange, Bir Singh, 61
Bangladesh, 66
Baradari Gardens cricket ground, 4, 7, 33, 417
Barbados, 87–88, 91, 95, 241, 250
  test, 237–50
Bari, Wasim, 193, 206
'Barossa Valley Winery,' 147
Basin Reserve, 84

Batala, 172
batting capabilities, 322
BCCI, 6, 39–40, 58, 70–71, 76, 79, 84, 158, 159, 257, 283, 286, 312, 333, 348, 361, 382, 383, 389, 398, 411, 412–14, 427
  camp, 39
  contract, 348
  headquarters at Brabourne Stadium, 70
  representatives, 423
Bedi, Bishan Singh, 69–71, 90, 92, 97, 99–100, 102, 110, 122, 128, 153, 165, 167, 310, 312
  as captain, 75
  centre of attraction, 142–43
  cheering, 132
  Delhi cricket administration, 184
  destiny, 77–78
  leadership qualities, 74
  lost captaincy to Sunil Gavaskar in 1978, 218
  opportunity, 80
  organizing fancy dress contest, 363
  recovery and return to team, 83
  replaced by Sunil Gavaskar, 170
Benaud, Richie, 342–43
Bengali refugees, 64
Benson and Hedges trophy, 358
Benson & Hedges World Championship, 312, 326, 359

tri-series, 1986, 348–59
'Bhangra,' 62–63
Bhasin, A.B., 26–27
Bhimani, Kishore, 406
'Bhupindra Pavilion,' 20
Bhutta, Jeetendra, 41
Bhutto, Zulfikar Ali, 196
Bickoo (wife), 171–72, 185–86, 217–18, 240–41, 246, 250, 257, 282–83, 376, 405–6
Bihar, 90
bilateral competition, 152–53
Bimla (sister), 3
'Binaca Geet Mala,' 11
Bindra, I. S., 383
Binny, Roger, 184, 186–87, 266, 270, 298, 317, 318, 320, 325–26, 356, 366
Birla Mandir, 14
'Blackpool Carnival,' 282
'Bobby Helmet,' 118
body language and expressions, 280
Bombay (Mumbai), 34, 37, 38, 68–69, 70, 404
by Air India, 289
monsoon, 101
press, 35, 39
test, 400
Bombay Gymkhana, 35
Boon, David, 338–39, 357, 377–78
Borde, Chandu, 89, 422
Border, Allan, 337, 343, 345, 358, 377, 380
Botham, Ian, 103, 217

Bouncers, 89
bowler-friendly conditions, 355
Boxing Day match, 341
Boycott, Geoffrey, 39
Brabourne Stadium in Bombay, 35–36, 48, 70–71
Bradman, Don, 43–44, 124, 206, 337–38
Bradman, Donald, 143
Brahamcharya Ashram hostel, 27–28
Brisbane, 127
British Isles, 40
British Raj, 2
British sports media, 273
Britto Hotel, 92–93
'Bunch of Jokers' remark, 403–16
Burton Park, 47–48

Calcutta, 47–48, 123, 307, 400
Eden Gardens in, 48, 304, 306, 353, 387–88
test, 288
calypso music and fast bowling, 216–54
Camaraderie, 112
Caribbean
fast bowlers, 216–17
islands, 86, 90–91
spin bowlers, 104
tours, 97
CBFS, 401–2
'CCI' at Brabourne Stadium, 34

celebrations, 109–10
Central Lancashire league, 293
Central Secretariat Grounds, 46
Ceylon (Sri Lanka), 32, 74, 75, 79, 81
Chanakya, 49
Chander, Ramesh, 290, 291–92
Chandigarh, 326, 398
Chandini Chowk, 9
Chand, Kishen, 143
Chand, Nanak (grandfather), 2
Chandra, Ramesh, 77, 81, 83, 135, 408
Chandrashekhar, Bhagwat, 74, 80, 90, 142–43, 149, 151
Chappell, Greg, 312
Chappell, Ian, 46, 54, 147, 312
charity match, 293
Charlie Chaplin, 352
Chauhan, Chetan, 134, 144, 146, 150, 160, 161
Chepauk Stadium in Madras, 48, 50, 53, 307, 376–77, 381, 384, 386
childhood, 1–17
Childhood memories, 32–33
Chinnaswamy Stadium in Bangalore, 123, 181, 407–8
'chokri' square, 10–11
Clarke, Wayne, 128, 130, 145
Clay, Cassius, 103
'Club House,' 34
Coca Cola, 240
coir matting, 31

Colosseum in Ancient Rome, 115
comeback
four, 417–28
Pakistan tour 1982/83, 189–215
performance, 420–21
scene, 192–93
three, 285–300
confidence, 122
and swag, 240
Connaught place, 25
Connemara Hotel to Chepauk, 51
contingent contract, 412
Contractor, Nari, 94–95, 113, 116–17, 179
controversy, 417–28
Cooch-Behar Trophy, 32
cops-and-robbers game, 148
Cosier, Tony, 149
Cowdery, Colin, 39
Cricket Association of Bengal, 411
Cricket Australia, 128, 150
Cricket Club of India (CCI), 405–6
cricket whites, 79
Crime Branch, 36–37
Cuttack, 308

Dalmia, Jagmohan, 383, 424
Dalvi, Michael, 51
Daniel, Wayne, 112
Das, Charan, 69
Datta, Debashish, 406
DAV College, 60, 62–63

Davis, Simon, 357–58
Davis, Winston, 400
day-and-night matches, 355
'Deccan Queen,' 34
dejection, 59
Delhi, 33, 39–40, 122
team, 69–70
test, 122
test match, 198
Delhi Cricket Association, 70
Delhi University, 59
Deodhar Trophy matches, 417–18, 425
Desai, Ramakant, 409
determination, 59
Dev, Gokul Inder, 141–42
Dev, Kapil, 165, 192, 217, 222, 248, 280, 303, 310, 378–79, 422, 423
dismissal, 207
England 1986 tour, 367
Indian pace attack, 205
in Lahore, 209
Dey, Niren, 411
Dhabas of Punjab, 32
disbelief, 243
District Cricket Association, 33–34
Dogra, 61
Dolly, 3–4
domestic season, 56, 70
Doon School, 26
Doordarshan, 72, 319
All India Radio box, 305
TV channel, 316–17
Doshi, Dilip, 214
Doshi, Sushil, 135

Dujon, Geoffrey, 221, 226, 278
Dujon, Jeffrey, 249, 281
Duleep Trophy, 47, 124, 187, 417
in 1974, 71
Dum Dum Airport in Calcutta, 423
Durham League in England, 120, 121
Durrani, Salim, 69, 95
Dutt, B. N., 408

East Africa, 73–74
Eastern Court, 30
East Pakistan (Bangladesh), 64
Eastwood, Clint, 148–49
Eden Gardens in Calcutta, 48, 304, 306, 353, 387–88, 421, 424
Edgbaston pitch, 370–71
Edmonds, Phil, 371–72
Elahi, Amir, 154, 166–67
emotions, 67–68, 136
Engineer, Farokh, 12, 58, 74, 80, 153
England, 21, 39–40, 41, 59, 73–74, 87, 122, 183
1986, 360–73
and Australia match, 312
batting lineup, 366
in India, 301–31
memories, 355
English league, 124
enthusiasm, 31, 404
ethnic Indians, 90, 108–9
European clubs, 2

facilities in Bombay, 35
Faisalabad, 298
families, 2
Feroz Shah Kotla, New Delhi,
    286, 287, 299, 302, 417,
    419
fitness, 354
Flower, Graeme, 270
fracture, 180–81
Fredericks, Roy, 94, 120
'Friday evenings,' 362–63

Gabba in Brisbane, 127, 349
Gaddafi Stadium, 192, 215
Gaekwad, Anshuman, 114–15,
    165, 179, 186–87, 229, 290
Gaekwad, Fateh Singh Rao,
    154–55, 159, 167, 190, 200
Gandhi, Indira, 65, 283, 299
Gandhi, Mahatma, 57
Gandhi Stadium, 61, 62–63
Gannon, Sam, 134, 350
Garner, Joel, 216, 223–24,
    236, 237
Gatting, Mike, 270, 371
Gavaskar-Chauhan duo, 144
Gavaskar, Sunil, 34, 73–75,
    76, 78, 85, 90, 94, 99, 130,
    133, 153, 156–57, 159,
    211, 290, 297, 305, 312,
    386, 395
on abilities and efforts, 185
in Bangalore, meeting, 239–40
Birju, Indian supporter, 230–
    31
as captain of India, 29–330
century, 104–5

confidence and stability,
    140–41
dismissal, 108
lost captaincy to Kapil Dev,
    218
Pakistan tour 1982/83, 193–94
partner Srikkanth, 385
performances, 95, 330
resignation, 335–36
returning, 340
statement, 254
and Surinder Amarnath
    partnership, 82–83
Gen. Zia, 389–90, 401
Ghavri, Karsan, 69, 132–33,
    140, 146, 165
Ghosh, William, 38
Gilchrist, 89
Gillette Cup, 73
'gilli danda,' 10
Gloucestershire, 178, 362
'G-nat,' 65
Goel, Rajinder, 71–72, 95–96,
    214
Golden Temple, 59–66
Gomes, Larry, 232
Gower, David, 270
grade cricket in Australia, 184
Graveney, Tom, 39
Greenidge, Gordon, 231–32,
    234, 252, 277
Greig, Tony, 122–23, 312
Griffith, Charlie, 39, 89
guilty, 30
Gupta, Pankaj, 362–63, 411
Gupte, Subhash, 90
Guru Granth Sahib, 60

Guwahati ODI, 400
Guyana, 90, 101, 102

Hadlee, Richard, 76, 80, 82, 85, 86, 103, 121–22, 179, 246, 321, 349
Hall, Wesley, 39, 89
Hampshire, 362–63
Harcourt Butler School in Delhi, 7, 394–95
Hardam, 19–20
Haridwar, 123
'Harmandir Sahib,' 60
Hayat, Khizr, 211, 294, 295
Heathrow building, 40
Himalayan Car Rally, 287
Himalayan foothills, 5–6
Hindi songs, 229, 242, 376
Hindlekar, 369–70
Hirwani, Narendra, 400
Hindu Colleges, 62–63
Hogg, Rodney, 182
Holder, Vanburn, 112
Holding, Michael, 93, 94, 97, 100, 103, 104, 105–6, 107, 111, 113–14, 119, 216, 225–26, 235–36, 242–43, 278, 289
Holekars, 35
Holland, Bob, 344, 361
Hotel Fatta in Hyderabad, 202
Hotel Westmoreland, 273
Hubbert, Paul, 128
Huddersfield, Yorkshire, 180
Hughes, Merv, 340–41
humanity, 252
Hurst, Alan, 130

Hussain, Murawwat, 154, 166
Hutton, Len, 206
Hyderabad, 74–75, 90, 261, 266
Hyderabad Cricket Association, 424
Hyderabad (Pakistan) test match, 290

ICC
bankrupt, 125
promotional scheme, 361
inaugural test series, 124
India Gate, 11
India/Indian, 59
and Caribbean supporters, 230
domestic season, 183
in England, 174
schoolboys' team, 43
spinners, 104
team, losing palce in, 187
India Lahore, 47
Indian Air Force, 65
Indian Express, The, 57–58
Indian High Commission, 279
Indian international cricketers, 34
Indian Premier League (IPL) matches, 158
Indian Punjab, 60
'Indian Starlets,' 12
India-Pakistan matches, 383–84, 401
India U-25 team, 398
indirect communication, 307
Indra Gandhi Terminal 3 in Delhi, 40
inter-college contest, 62

INDEX 445

International Cricket Conference (ICC), 125
inter-railway family sports day, 11
inter-university match, 59–60
Inzamam-ul-Haq, 353
Iqbal, Asif, 154, 157, 158, 333
Irani Trophy matches, 78, 183, 187, 188, 383

Jagtiani, Haresh, 411
Jahan, Shah, 9
Jaipur test, 390
Jaisimha, M.L., 12, 305, 309, 335
Jalandhar, Punjab, 17, 27, 30, 35, 36, 37, 38, 43, 107, 295
Jamaica, 94, 111, 119, 218–19
Jama Masjid, 9–10
Jammu & Kashmir, 200
Janta Party in 1977, 153
Jardine, Douglas, 3, 61, 115
Javed, Aaqib, 421
'Jhat-Pat' studio, 14
Jimmy, 35, 186
Jinnah, Muhammad Ali, 190–91
JK Industries, 69
Joe, Smokey, 99
John Player league, 73
Julien, Bernard, 105–6, 112
Jullundur (Jalandhar), 47, 71–72
Jumadeen, 103

Kahlon, Gurinder, 287

Kallicharran, Alvin, 94, 103, 170, 174, 220
Kamla (sister), 3, 30, 56, 57
Kanhai, Rohan, 39, 89, 312
Kanitkar, Hrishikesh, 69
Kanpur, 20, 69
Kapara, 9
Kapurthala, Punjab, 2
Karachi, 154–55, 161, 194–95, 197, 318
Kardar, Abdul Hafeez, 152, 383–84
Karnail Singh Stadium, 46
Karnataka, 175, 184
Kashmir, 200
Kashmiri separatists, 286
Kennington Oval, 261
Kent, 362–63
Kerry Packer's World Series Cricket, 125, 138, 154, 157
'Kesar da Dhaba,' 60
Khan, Dilawar Hussain, 369–70
Khan, Imran, 103, 154, 217, 318, 327, 1903
 Imran's Casanova reputation, 384
 swinging deliveries, 202
Khan, Majid, 154
Khan, Mohsin, 194–95, 205, 319
Khanna, Surinder, 175
Khanna Talkies in Paharganj, 15–16
Khan, Nur, 382–83
Khan, Yahya, 66
Kinaari bazaar, 9

Kingston, 111, 119
Kirmani, Syed, 58, 78, 80, 128, 130, 150, 161, 164, 236, 261–62, 266, 278
'Kirpan,' 173
kites flying, 9–10
Kiwis, 77, 85, 353–54
spinners, 82
Kohli, Virat, 305
Kosi Kalan, 133
Kullar tea, 57
Kumari, Kailash (Mummy ji), 16

Lady Harding Medical College, 25
Lahore, 3, 47, 60, 153, 166–67, 293–94, 318
test, 297
Lal Bahadur Stadium, 39
Lal Kuan, 9
Lal, Madan, 74, 76, 83–84, 92–93, 99, 117, 120, 128–29, 146, 175, 183, 192, 266, 323, 369
heel injury, 205
Indian pace attack, 205
replacement, 208
Lamba, Raman, 372, 418, 426, 427
Lancashire Cricket Club, 58
Lancashire League in England, 3–4, 194–95
language barrier, 362
Launceston, 354
Lavinia, Duchess of Norfolk XI, 362

Lawrence School, 26
Lawry, Bill, 46, 53, 342–43
Leicestershire, 177
Lever, John, 122
Lewis, Carl, 279
life in Patiala, 5
Lillee, Dennis, 88, 145, 217, 258, 267, 312
Lloyd, Clive, 68, 71–72, 90, 95–96, 100, 103–4, 107, 110–11, 113–14, 117, 232, 234, 251, 262, 312
cricket skills, 235
Logie, Gus, 224
London, 40, 42, 125
Lords, 40
Australia and West Indies at, 255
test matches at, 177, 364
Lucknow test match, 161
lucky break, 285–300
Ludhiana, 295

Madras, 124
humidity, 51
test match, 69
tied test match, 374–81
Madras Hotel, 25
Madras Presidency, 302
Mafatlal, 68–69
magnanimity, 60–61
Magnum Champagne, 280, 282
Mahajan, Hans Raj, 43
Maharaja Bhupindra Singh of Patiala, 35–36
Mahendra, J. K., 41

Mahmood, Fazal, 154, 166, 383–84
MAK Pataudi, 69
Malhotra, Chaman Lal, 45–46
Malik, Salim, 296, 298, 392
Mallet, Ashley, 56
Manjrekar, Vijay, 34–35
Mankad, Vinoo, 34, 338
man-management, 213
Mann, Tony, 128
Mansingh, P. R., 424
Marathi magazine, 409
Marley, Bob, 91, 111
Marshall, Malcolm, 103, 171–72, 216, 224–25, 232–33, 235, 243, 247
Marshall, Marshall, 279
Marwari businessmen, 9
Masood, Asif, 153
Massie, Bob, 312
MB High School, 7
MCC match, 141
'MCC Schoolboys' team, 35, 42–43
McDermott, Craig, 341
McKenzie, Graham, 46, 55–56, 312
Mehra, Madan, 38
Mehta, R. N., 62–63
Melbourne, 137–44, 341–42, 343
Melbourne Cricket Ground (MCG), 138, 312–13, 314–15, 321, 350, 353–54, 358
Mello, Anthony De, 410–11
mental trauma, 122

Miandad, Javed, 20, 154, 156, 205, 296, 318, 327, 392–93
Milburn, Colin, 127
Mirza family, 172–73
mistrust, 70–71, 306
Mohammad, Hanif, 206, 384–85
Mohammad, Mushtaq, 154, 156
Mohammad, Nazar, 209
Mohammad, Shoaib, 384–85
Mohammed, Gul, 167
Mohammed, Hanif, 42
Mohan, Surinder, 61
Mohla, H. R., 38
Moin-ud-Dowlah Gold Cup, 32
morning walk, 11
MRF Cup
1989 in Ahmedabad, 359
match, 352–53
Mughal Empire, 9
Mukesh's songs, 81
Mummyji, 5, 7, 8, 12–14, 16, 19, 68
Murray, Derek, 119
Murtaza, 38
Mushtaq, 38
music-lovers, 11
Mysore (Karnataka), 107, 302

Naqqash, Tahir, 193–94
Nath, Surender, 409
National Relief Fund match at Poona (Pune), 34
National Stadium near India Gate, 20, 46

Nawaz, Sarfaraz, 154, 156, 198, 209, 217, 294
Nayudu, C. K., 387
Nazar, Mudassar, 156, 161, 198, 205, 298, 388
Nehru Cup, 421
Nehru, Jawahar Lal, 299, 421
New Delhi, 88
New Delhi railway station, 12–13
news transmission, 57
New York, 66
New Zealand, 39, 74–75, 76, 77, 78, 80, 121, 122, 318, 321, 353–54, 404
1975, 67–86
to India, 121
media, 76
pace bowlers, 83
series, 123
series in Bangalore, 239
tour, 427
Nicholls, Gray, 106
Nikki (daughter), 217–18, 240–41, 246, 250, 257, 282, 390
Nirlons, 68–69
Nizamuddin, 12–14
Northamptonshire, 362–63, 364
Northamptonshire County team in England, 156
Northern Punjab, 32, 33, 46
team, 45
Northern Punjab Association, 38
Northern Punjab State U-19 team, 32

Northern Punjab U-19 team, 33
North-West Frontier Region, 26
North Zone, 70–71
match, 46–47
players, 70
team, 47, 141
Nottinghamshire, 179, 261, 349
Nottingham, wicket at, 179

O' Connell, Max, 128
Ogilvy, David, 128
O'Keeffe, Kerry, 38–39
Old Delhi Railway Station, 57
Old Trafford in Manchester, 266–67, 268–69
Olympics, 89–90, 152
Omar, Qasim, 298
one-day cricket concept, 255–56
one-day international in Sahiwal, 165
opposition, strengths and weaknesses, 76–77
O'Sullivan, David, 82
outstation matches, 31
Oval, The, 81
overconfidence, 76

pace bowlers, 51
Packer, Kerry, 125, 127, 128, 170–71, 220, 260
Paharganj, 9
Pakistan/Pakistani, 16, 42, 59, 64–65, 66, 153, 158, 159, 289, 293, 297, 318, 353, 385

1978, 152–68
army, 64
attack, 160–61
forces in Dacca, 66
in India 1987, 382–96
pace bowler, 144–45
performances in, 219–20
radio, 66
at Sharjah, 363–64
tour 1982/83, 189–215
Gaddafi Stadium, 192
reception at Karachi airport, 190
social activities, 199
team morale, 201–2
test match in Faisalabad, 200
wicket at WACA, 191
Pakistan Cricket Board (PCB), 154, 165–66, 194, 382–83
Pakistan High Commission, 389
Pakistani Punjab, 60
Pakistan TV, 166
Pakram Pakrai, 11
Palam Airport, 40
Panchkuian Road, 26
Pandit, Chandrakant, 370
Pantangular Tournament, 70–71
'PARJAI,' 166
Pataudi, Mansoor Ali Khan (Indian captain), 40, 48, 50, 51, 54–55, 128, 304–5
Pataudi, Tiger, 69
Patel, Brijesh, 99, 109, 115–16
Pathak, Kamal, 286
Patiala, 6, 21, 32, 47, 295

cricket, 32–33
Patiala, Maharaja Bhupindra Singh, 61
Patil, Sandeep, 199, 207, 269–70, 272, 298, 303, 306, 373, 409
patriotism, 66, 164
Perth, 131–37
Peter, Rajesh, 184–85
physical training, 51
'Pitthu,' 10
P.J. Hindu Gymkhana, 34
'Players Association' in Bombay, 424–25
Polly Kaka, 181
Prabhakar, Manoj, 369
Prabhu, K.N., 35
Prasanna, Erapalli, 55, 74, 77, 80, 83, 90, 145, 336
President Estate, 46
Press Trust of India (PTI), 166
Principal Arora, 28
private cricket tournament, 125
professional trainer concept, 314
Promila (sister), 3
Prudential Cup of 1983, 321
Prudential World Cup, 364
punishing training, 16–17, 19, 30
Punjabi character, 368
Punjab/Punjabi, 17, 37
cricketers, 71
government, 45
Punjab Roadways, 172

Qadian, 171
via Batala, 172
Qadir, Abdul, 295, 353, 391
Qasim, Iqbal, 392, 394, 396
Queens Park Oval in Trinidad, 98–99, 102, 113
Quetta, 165

'Radio Ceylon,' 11
radio or telegrams, 57
Rafi, Mohammad, 12
Rai, Gulshan, 188, 290
railways cricket, 6–7
Railway stadium at Paharganj, 20, 24
Raja, Ramiz, 387, 392–93
Raja, Wasim, 296–97
Raj, Govind, 90
Rajinder, 3–4, 35
Raj, Inder, 42–43
Rajindra Gymkhana Club, 7, 33
Rajkumari Amrit Kaur Sports Foundation in Delhi, 6
Ram Bhaiya, 99
'Ramble Restaurant,' 29
Rana, Shakoor, 156–57, 294
Ranatunga, Arjuna, 359
Randall, Derek, 271–72
Ranji Trophy, 32, 45, 47, 69–70, 174, 175, 187, 256
Rashid, Haroon, 205
Ratnayake, Rumesh, 334
Raut, Vishwas, 194
Ravi River, 166–67
Rawalpindi, 156, 293
Razdan, Vivek, 426

Redpath, Ian, 46, 55, 312
Regal Cinema, 29
regimental training schedule, 19
reliability and experience, 360
Reliance Group, 383
Reliance World Cup, 397
reputation as batsman, 182
reserve players, 118
Rice, Clive, 179
Richards, Vivian (Viv), 94, 95, 99–100, 103, 234, 240, 251, 261, 277
Ritchie, Greg, 338–39
Rixon, Steve, 128
Roadside Romeos, 62
Roberts, Andy, 103, 216, 227, 243, 250
Robinson, Tim, 302–3
Rocky III, 186
Roger, Jolly, 237
'Rolls Royce,' 94
Rothmans Cup at Sharjah, 331, 334
Rotterdam, 361
Rowe, Lawrence, 90, 94, 99
Roy, Pankaj, 89
rumours, 287
Russia, 66
Russian MIG 21s, 65
Rutnagar, Dicky, 35, 90, 406

Safdarjung tomb, 40
Sai Dass Anglo Sanskrit Higher secondary school, 28
Salahuddin, Masood, 197
Salve, N. K. P., 382–83

Sampoorna Ramayana, 15–16, 28
Sandhu, Balwinder Singh, 205, 225, 231–32, 236, 277
Sarafa bazaar, 9
Sarbadhakari, Barry, 35
Sarfaraz, 144–45, 160, 162, 164–65
Sargent, Craig, 183
satisfaction, 68, 83
Sayani, Amin, 11
SBI, 68–69
Sekhar, T., 208
selection
to North Zone, 34
trials for the Northern Punjab team, 45
sense of tranquillity, 31
Shah Jahanabad, 9
Shah, Praveen, 259–60
Shamsi, Baseer, 210
Sharjah, 311–59
tournament, 400–401
Sharjah Cup, 360, 417–18
Sharma, Chetan, 324–25, 326–27, 335, 339, 355, 366, 370, 371, 380
Sharma, Gopal, 392
Sharma, Parthasarathy, 94
Sharma, Suresh (brother-in-law), 56–57
Sharma, Yashpal, 225, 260, 270–71
Shastri, Ravi, 243, 296–97, 321, 380, 400, 422
Sheffield Shield match, 127
Shivaji Hockey Stadium, 25

short-of-a-length deliveries, 133
short-pitch deliveries, 118–19, 134
Shroff, Binod, 49
Shukla, Rakesh, 184–85
Sialkot, 298
'Sid Cottage,' 6
Sidhu, Navjot Singh, 404, 426, 427
Sikh holy scriptures, 60
Simpson, Bobby, 127, 129, 135, 140, 149, 339–40
fielding at slips, 136
Singhania, Kamlapat, 69
Singhania, Padampat, 69
Singhania, Vijaypat, 69
Singh, Bhawani, 390
Singh, Bir, 5, 19–20, 32–33
Singh, Giani Zail, 299
Singh, Gursharan, 184, 237, 400
Singh, Hanumant, 239, 253
Singh, Laxman, 69
Singh, Mahesh Inder, 400
Singh, Man, 261, 265–66
Singh, Maninder, 295, 370–71, 373, 380, 391
Singh, Milkha, 12
Singh, Raj, 362–63, 368
Singh, Rajindra, 5–6
Singh, Sardar Karnail, 6
Singh, Surinder Pratap, 38
Singh, Yajvendra, 178, 181
Singh, Zail, 299
Sivaramakrishnan, Laxman, 301, 309, 327, 330, 338

sledging, 380
Snow, John, 39, 42
Sobers, Garfield, 43, 89, 206, 214
Sobers, Garry, 39, 103–4, 106–7, 312
Solar Hat, 182
Solkar, Eknath, 51, 76, 123
failure in Calcutta, 123
Somi, 19–20
South Africa *vs.* England contest, 1939, 146
Southern Punjab, 33, 61
South Hall Sikhs, 277
South India, 72–73
culture, 302
South Perth Club, 183
South Zone at Wilson College Gymkhana, 35
South Zone bowlers, 419
spinners, 38, 39, 52, 74, 80, 129, 132
-friendly pitch, 145
'square cut,' 147
Srikkanth, 266, 276, 315–16, 325, 329, 334, 350, 351, 353, 357–58, 379–80, 404, 422, 427
Sri Lanka, 74, 177, 311–59, 383
Stackpole, Keith, 46, 53
Stallone, Sylvester, 186
Statesman, The, 57–58
Storthes Hall Hospital, Huddersfield, 376
Strepsils, 298
Sunday Club, 362–63

superstition, 324
Surti, Rusi, 51
Sydney Cricket Ground, 143–46, 357

Taj Palace Hotel, New Delhi, 412–13, 421, 426
Talkatora Gardens, 26
Tamil Nadu government, 334
Tamil United Liberation Front, 334
Tatas, 68–69
Tavare, Chris, 270
Taylor, Lynton, 158, 170–71
team performance, 208
telefax, 57
Tendulkar, Sachin, 304–5, 425, 426
Tennekoon, Anura, 74
test debut, 45–66
test matches, 49
in Bangalore, 285–86
at Edgbaston, 178–79
in Faisalabad, 200
in Jalandhar, 285–86
in Jamaica, 218
at Kandy, 335
in Karachi, 209
in Lahore, 209
at Leeds, 367
at Lords, 177, 364
in Madras, 306, 374–81
tied, 374–81
Trinidad test, 228–37
Thomson, Jeff, 88, 103, 127, 129, 130, 132, 133, 149, 150, 217

Three W's, 88
Times of India, The, 57–58
Times Shield, 69
Toohey, Peter, 128, 129, 136, 145
training, 20–21
Travancore (Kerala), 302
Trinidad, 90, 97–98, 101–2, 112
Indians, 237
test, 228–37
turf wickets, 35

UK tour, 361
Umrigar, Polly, 87, 95, 102, 110, 116–17, 181, 404
uniformity, 79
United States, 90–91
Uttar Pradesh, 90

Vengsarkar, Dilip, 78, 129–30, 150, 233–34, 251–52, 262–63, 290, 370, 387, 392, 397, 400–401, 403–4, 410, 422, 423
Venkataraghavan, 50–51, 53, 74, 80, 175–76, 227–28, 243, 310, 336, 355, 356
Victoria Cricket Association, 312, 328
victory, 109
video recording, 25
Vijayanagram (Andhra Pradesh), 302, 369–70
Vishwanath, Gundappa, 56, 72–73, 76, 90, 106, 108, 115, 116, 130, 140, 145, 150, 157, 160–61, 165, 200, 202, 213–14
Vishwanath, Sadanand, 313–14, 327–28, 336–37

WACA, 244–45
in 1977, 246
conditions at, 133–34, 351–52
in Perth, 205
pitch at Perth, 131
Wadekar, Ajit, 51, 56, 74
Walsh, Courtney, 216
Walters, Doug, 52, 312
Wankhede Stadium in Bombay, 170, 187, 284, 404, 416
Wellington, 88
Wesley Hall, 94
West and South Zone teams, 71
West End Hotel, 395
Western Cricket Association, 183
West Indian attack, 243
West Indies, 39, 59, 68, 71–73, 74–75, 101–2, 103, 113–14, 383
1976, 87–120
1983, 216–54
in 1979, 288
vs. Australia match, 177
defeat, 260–61
vs. North Zone match in Jalandhar, 171
rules, 261
script, 93–94
series, 170

team fitness, 221
tour in 1971, 56
West Yorkshire, 374–75
West Zone, 70
wilderness, 45–66
Willis, Bob, 103, 271
Wills Trophy matches, 183
Wilson, Harold, 42
Windies bowling attack, 90–91
wooden pavilion, 50
'Woolloongabba,' 127
Worcestershire, 362–63
World Championship, 312, 336, 341, 348
of 1985, 331
matches, 316–17
World Cup, 73, 152, 382, 397
1975, 176, 281
reception, 408
World Cup 1983, 255–84, 314
BCC commentator, 274
competition, 258, 260

customary team meeting, 275
dressing room, atmosphere in, 272
England at Old Trafford, 268
final, 273
game against Zimbabwe, 264–65
Indian domination, 267
lackadaisical approach, 256
preparation, 255, 257–59
schedule, 263–64
teams announcement, 257
track record, 259
West Indies team, 274
World Series Cricket, 128, 158, 170–71
Worrell, Frank, 88
Wright, Denis, 221

Zia-ul-Haq, 293, 401
Zimbabwe and Australia, 263

ABOUT THE AUTHORS

MOHINDER (JIMMY) AMARNATH (b.1950) is the son of the legendary cricketer Lala Amarnath. He played for the Indian national team from 1969 to 1989, scoring 4378 Test runs. Nine of his eleven Test centuries were scored overseas. He was Man of the Match in the semi-final and the final when India won the World Cup in 1983. He was named one of the *Wisden* Cricketers of the Year in 1984 and also received the Arjuna Award the same year.

RAJENDER AMARNATH is the youngest son of Lala Amarnath. A graduate from St. Stephen's College, he played first-class cricket in India and professional cricket in England. Later, he was a selector and coach for the Haryana state team. He is an author, commentator and cricket analyst.

HarperCollins *Publishers* India

At HarperCollins India, we believe in telling the best stories and finding the widest readership for our books in every format possible. We started publishing in 1992; a great deal has changed since then, but what has remained constant is the passion with which our authors write their books, the love with which readers receive them, and the sheer joy and excitement that we as publishers feel in being a part of the publishing process.

Over the years, we've had the pleasure of publishing some of the finest writing from the subcontinent and around the world, including several award-winning titles and some of the biggest bestsellers in India's publishing history. But nothing has meant more to us than the fact that millions of people have read the books we published, and that somewhere, a book of ours might have made a difference.

As we look to the future, we go back to that one word—a word which has been a driving force for us all these years.

Read.